D0321669

Social Identities

The concept of social identity occupies a central position in contemporary social psychology. *Social Identities: Motivational, Emotional and Cultural Influences* reports recent developments in the analysis of motivational and affective aspects of social identity processes. The book also examines the cross-cultural generality of social identity theory explanations of intergroup competitiveness, which have strongly influenced international research in this area. People's social identities and self-evaluation are thought to be largely derived from group memberships; it is presumed that people are motivated to attain positivity in these identities by favoring the ingroup in intergroup comparisons. An increasing stream of research is being devoted to extending the applicability of social identity concepts to intergroup relations and related fields.

The editors present here a collection of contributions from leading figures in social psychology which explore the state of the art in social identity theory. The most prominent motivational theories of identification are reported. Central themes concern:

- motivations that lead individuals to join a group and identify with it;
- the role emotions have in favoring (or hindering) intergroup relations;
- the effect of emotions on intergroup behavior;
- how people react to social identity threats.

Aiming to shed new light on important social problems like prejudice, bigotry, and intense conflicts around the world, this unique volume will be indispensable to students and researchers of social psychology, sociology, and cultural studies.

Rupert Brown received his PhD from the University of Bristol in 1979. Since then he has taught at the Universities of Kent and Sussex, where he has held Chairs in social psychology. His research interests include intergroup relations, prejudice and its reduction, and acculturation.

Dora Capozza has taught social psychology in different Italian universities and different faculties. Since 1981 she has been Full Professor of Social Psychology at the University of Padova. Her primary area of research is the study of social identity and intergroup relations.

Social Identities

Motivational, Emotional and
Cultural Influences

Edited by Rupert Brown and
Dora Capozza

Psychology Press
Taylor & Francis Group

HOVE AND NEW YORK

First published 2006 by Psychology Press
27 Church Road, Hove, East Sussex BN3 2FA

Simultaneously published in the USA and Canada
by Psychology Press
270 Madison Avenue, New York, NY 10016

Psychology Press is an imprint of the Taylor & Francis Group, an informa business

Copyright © 2006 Psychology Press

Cover design by Sandra Heath
Typeset in Times by Garfield Morgan, Mumbles, Swansea
Printed and bound in Great Britain by TJ International Ltd, Padstow,
Cornwall

British Library Cataloguing in Publication Data
A catalogue record for this book is available from the British Library

Library of Congress Cataloging-in-Publication Data
Social identities : motivational, emotional, cultural influences / [edited by]
  Rupert Brown and Dora Capozza.
      p. cm.
  ISBN 1-84169-549-1
  1. Group identity. I. Brown, Rupert, 1950– II. Capozza, Dora.
  HM753.S624 2006
  305.01–dc22
                                                              2005033061

ISBN13: 978-1-84169-549-5
ISBN10: 1-84169-549-1

Contents

Notes on contributors

Sabina Aharpour is a Senior Lecturer at Canterbury Christ Church University, UK. She completed her Ph.D. in 1999 at the University of Kent (UK) working on group diversity and functions of group identification. Her main research interests are in the area of intergroup relations, prejudice and stereotypes and the developments of social identity theory.

Nyla R. Branscombe is Professor of Psychology at the University of Kansas, with a primary emphasis on intergroup relations. Her research has considered the psychology of both disadvantaged and privileged social groups, with a focus on the types of threats to social identity that each experiences.

Marilynn B. Brewer is Professor of Psychology and Eminent Scholar in Social Psychology at the Ohio State University. Her primary area of research is the study of social identity and intergroup relations. In 2004 she was elected as a fellow of the American Academy of Arts and Sciences.

Rupert Brown received his Ph.D. from the University of Bristol (UK) in 1979. Since then he has taught at the University of Kent and Sussex (UK), where he has held Chairs in Social Psychology. His research interests include intergroup relations, prejudice and its reduction, and acculturation.

Mara R. Cadinu received from the University of Oregon her M.S. in Social Psychology in 1991, and her Ph.D. in 1996. She has been Reseacher at the University of Padova (Italy) from 1996 to 2003 and Associate Professor since 2004. Her current research interests are: self and stereotyping, personal and social identity, threat and stereotypes.

Ed Cairns is Professor of Psychology at the University of Ulster, Northern Ireland. His research interest is the psychological aspects of political violence in relation to the conflict in Northern Ireland. He is a fellow of the British Psychological Society and of the American Psychological Association (APA).

Linnda R. Caporael is Professor in the Department of Science and Technology Studies at Rensselaer Polytechnic Institute, Troy, New York. Her interests are in multi-level selection theory, the contributions of social psychology to a better understanding of the evolution of sociality (and vice versa), and socially situated cognition.

Dora Capozza is Professor of Group Psychology and Intergroup Conflict and Cooperation at the University of Padova, Italy. Her primary area of research is the study of social identity and intergroup relations.

Andrea Carnaghi received his Ph.D. in Psychological Science from the Catholic University of Louvain, Louvain-la-Neuve (Belgium). He is currently a postdoctoral fellow at the University of Padova (Italy). His work focuses on issues of language and cognition, social influence and stereotype change.

Emanuele Castano is Assistant Professor of Psychology at the New School for Social Research, New York. His research on social identification and group processes focuses on politically relevant identities, the dehumanization of outgroup, and the formation and impact of ideological beliefs.

John F. Dovidio (M.A., Ph.D. in Social Psychology from the University of Delaware) is currently Professor of Psychology at the University of Connecticut. His research interests are in stereotyping, prejudice, and discrimination; social power and nonverbal communication; altruism and helping.

Rossella Falvo received her Ph.D. from the University of Padova, Italy. She is currently Assistant Professor at the same institution, where she teaches Intra-group Processes. Her main research interests concern social identity processes and implicit measures of intergroup bias and identification.

Samuel L. Gaertner is Professor of Psychology at the University of Delaware. His research interests are intergroup relations. With John Dovidio, Samuel Gaertner has shared the SPSSI's Gordon Allport Intergroup Relations Prize in 1985 and 1998 and the Kurt Lewin Award in 2004.

Patricia Garcia-Prieto is a visiting postdoctoral scholar at the Stanford Graduate School of Business (CA). Her research interests include: the influence of social identity on emotions; the role of intergroup emotions in determining reactions to diversity management practices; identification and emotional processes in culturally diverse teams; intercultural emotional communication.

Roberto González, Ph.D. in Psychology from the University of Kent at Canterbury, UK, is currently Associate Professor in the Psychology Department of P. Universidad Católica de Chile. He works on intergroup contact, prejudice, discrimination and intergroup emotions in several settings in Chile and elsewhere.

Jake Harwood is Professor of Communication and Director of the Graduate Program in Gerontology at the University of Arizona. His research focuses on intergroup communication with a particular focus on age groups. His research draws on theories of social identity, intergroup behavior, and communication accommodation.

Miles Hewstone is Professor of Social Psychology and fellow of New College, Oxford University, UK. He has published widely on the topics of attribution theory, social cognition, stereotyping, and intergroup relations. His current research focuses on the reduction of intergroup conflict.

Michael A. Hogg is Professor of Social Psychology and an Australian Research Council Professorial Fellow at the University of Queensland. In 2006, he is joining the faculty, as Professor of Social Psychology at Claremont Graduate University in Los Angeles. Michael Hogg's research on group processes, intergroup relations, social identity, and self-conception is closely associated with the development of the social identity perspective.

Missy A. Houlette is Assistant Professor at the College of Mount St. Joseph in Cincinnati, Ohio. Her research combines her interest in intergroup relations and group decision making, examining how subgroup boundaries within groups affect information sharing and integration across subgroup lines. She has recently extended her research to include an examination of mechanisms that improve intergroup relations in community-based programs.

Jolanda Jetten is Professor of Social Psychology at the University of Exeter, UK. Her research is concerned with group processes and intergroup relations with a particular emphasis on peripheral and marginal group membership, deviance within groups, normative influence and conformity, discrimination and intergroup distinctiveness, coping with devalued group membership and stigmatized identities, identity change processes.

Kelly M. Johnson is currently Assistant Professor of Psychology at Dominican College in Orangeburg, New York. Her research interests concern the effects of personal control on intergroup anxiety and intergroup attitudes.

Karen M. Long has been Lecturer in Social Psychology at the University of Sussex (UK) since 1994. Her specific area of interest is the articulation of social and personal identities, and the relationship between these identities and intergroup behavior.

Anne Maass has been employed at the University of Kiel (Germany) and subsequently at Padova University (Italy). Her past and current research interests include: minority influence; eyewitness testimony; sexual harassment; prejudice, stereotyping, and intergroup relations; language and social cognition.

Diane M. Mackie is Professor of Psychology and Communication at the University of California, Santa Barbara. Her research examines the interplay of affective and cognitive processes in both intergroup relations and social influence.

Eric W. Mania is currently a graduate student in Social Psychology at the University of Delaware. His interests focus on understanding and improving intergroup relations.

Maria Paola Paladino is currently Assistant Professor at the Faculty of Sociology of the University of Trento, Italy. Her main research interests concern the process of infra-humanization in intergroup relations.

Stefania Paolini is a Lecturer of Social Psychology and Statistics at the University of Newcastle (Australia). Her research uses models of contact and cognitive models of social categorization to explore, in both controlled and naturalistic settings, "when" and "why" information about individual members of a social group affects judgements of the group as a whole.

Blake M. Riek is a doctoral student in Social Psychology at the University of Delaware. His research interests primarily involve identifying strategies to reduce intergroup biases. In particular, he is interested in examining the causes and consequences of intergroup threats and potential methods for reducing these threats.

Klaus R. Scherer holds the Chair for Emotion Psychology at the University of Geneva and directs the Geneva Emotion Research Group. His major research interest is the further theoretical development and empirical test of his component process model of emotion (CPM).

Eliot R. Smith is currently Professor in the Department of Psychology, Indiana University, Bloomington. His research interests include the role of emotions in prejudice and intergroup behavior, socially situated cognition, and multiagent models of social behavior.

Peter B. Smith is Emeritus Professor of Social Psychology at the University of Sussex (UK). His recent interests are focussed upon cross-cultural social and organizational psychology.

Russell Spears is Professor of Social Psychology at Cardiff University (UK) and the University of Amsterdam (Holland). His research interests are in social identity and intergroup relations (especially stereotyping and discrimination, the role of emotions and automatic processes in intergroup behavior), and social influence and power (especially as applied to computer-mediated communication).

Alberto Voci is Associate Professor of Social Psychology at the University of Padova, Italy. His research interests are prejudice reduction, perceptions of group variability, the antecedents of ingroup bias and, more broadly, the motivational and cognitive processes related to the dynamic between personal and social identity.

Vincent Y. Yzerbyt is Professor of Social Psychology at University of Louvain at Louvain-la-Neuve, Belgium. His research deals with stereotyping and intergroup relations, especially issues of stereotype formation and change, subjective essentialism and the use of stereotypes in the maintenance of social hierarchies.

Introduction

Chapter 1

Motivational, emotional, and cultural influences in social identity processes

Rupert Brown and Dora Capozza

Our aim in this chapter is to examine three sets of issues that were little analyzed in the original social identity theory (Tajfel & Turner, 1986): the nature of group identification, the impact of culture on self-conceptions, and intergroup emotions. Theories of ingroup identification will be reviewed, such as the optimal distinctiveness theory of Brewer (1991) and the model of subjective uncertainty reduction of Hogg and Abrams (1993; see also Hogg, 2000). We will then consider research on cultural differences with regard to the self-concept and the influence on behavior of self-criticism and self-enhancement motivations (Heine, 2001; Heine, Lehman, Markus, & Kitayama, 1999). Our aim is to analyze whether the relationship between need for self-esteem and intergroup differentiation, hypothesized by social identity theory and found in Western cultures, can also be valid for Eastern cultures. The subject of the final section will be intergroup emotions – the anxiety which is felt during early interactions with outgroup members; the empathy which may arise when knowledge of outgroup exemplars becomes more intimate; the anger, fear, and desire to hurt which are experienced when an attack injures members of the ingroup. We discuss how intergroup emotions can play a mediating role in many intergroup contexts, often controlling the positive effects of contact on intergroup representations and attitudes toward the ingroup and outgroup. Thus we hope to show how the recent motivational perspectives, an evaluation of the cultural generality or specificity of social identity processes, and the study of intergroup emotions have raised new problems and extended the range of group phenomena explained.

Motivations of identification

Social identity theory (Tajfel & Turner, 1986) was conceived to account for intergroup differentiation. According to this theory, people discriminate in favor of the ingroup, claim its prevalence in value-laden dimensions, and at times derogate the outgroup in order to enhance the value of their own belonging and social identity. The theory includes two basic concepts. One concerns the need for self-esteem: individuals wish to evaluate themselves and be evaluated positively (see, e.g., Leary, 1999; Leary & MacDonald, 2003). This need regards both the personal and the social self; that is, the groups an individual belongs to. The other concept is that the value of self and the value of the ingroup are defined through comparison: namely, the ingroup is positively evaluated if it is perceived as being superior to relevant outgroups on salient comparison dimensions.

People differentiate in favor of the ingroup in order to construct or protect its superiority; the positive ingroup attributes enhance social identity and satisfy the need for self-esteem. In the original social identity theory, the reasons for identification are not fully elaborated; it can, however, be deduced that the basic (motivational) determinant is the fact that belonging satisfies the need for self-esteem.

Self-esteem is, thus, the focal need in social identity processes. The influence of this need emerges from the findings of research. The relationship between discrimination and personal or collective self-esteem has been studied (Corollary 1 of the self-esteem hypothesis; Hogg & Abrams, 1990). As results from Rubin and Hewstone's (1998) narrative meta-analysis indicate, the number of studies which have supported this relationship strongly exceeds the number of studies which did not. Moreover, the majority of the experiments that failed to support the hypothesis analyzed the effects of discrimination on self-esteem measured as a stable personality trait ("global personal trait"), a distal component of self-esteem, rather remote from the collective state self-esteem construct envisaged by social identity theory.

The relationship between perception of threat to ingroup value and differentiation directed to the retrieval of self-esteem has also been studied (see Branscombe, Ellemers, Spears, & Doosje, 1999). The hypothesis of this relationship – a core construct in social identity theory – has been supported by numerous studies. It has been found that when the ingroup comes out as the loser in a task, or when it is perceived as being responsible for the outgroup unfavorable conditions, or is seen to be inferior on a salient dimension, its value is restored by derogating the outgroup or enhancing the importance of its positive attributes (Branscombe, 1998; Branscombe et al., 1999; Branscombe & Wann, 1994; Doosje, Ellemers, & Spears, 1995). The rediscovered value of the ingroup tends to increase collective self-esteem (Branscombe & Wann, 1994).

In the case of lower-status groups, in certain structural conditions, namely when intergroup boundaries are perceived as impermeable and own inferiority is perceived as legitimate and stable, ingroup value can be recovered through strategies of social creativity (Tajfel, 1981), as also shown by recent studies by Jetten and co-workers (Jetten, Schmitt, Branscombe, & McKimmie, 2005). The creativity strategies have the effect of enhancing identification. If inferiority is viewed as unstable, group identity may become politicized and willingness to collective action may increase (Simon & Klandermans, 2001). Jetten and co-workers (Chapter 5, this volume) also studied the identity enhancement strategies in minority groups that voluntarily break away from mainstream society.

The need to protect ingroup value can trigger acts of strong hostility. In work environments, for instance, males who see their superior status threatened by the other gender may react using an unusual expression of insult: sexual harassment in the sense of showing the female target some pornographic pictures (Maass & Cadinu, Chapter 6, this volume). However, the retrieval of ingroup worth, through outgroup derogation or ingroup enhancement, is found mainly in individuals who have a high ingroup identification (see also Cadinu & Cerchioni, 2001).

Concerning the hypothesized positive relationship between identification and ingroup bias (Hinkle & Brown, 1990), which may also be derived from social identity theory, while some research has supported it (e.g., Perreault & Bourhis, 1999), others have singled out some moderating variables. The relationship may be qualified, for instance, by individual difference traits, such as allocentric or idiocentric orientation (Triandis, 1995). In certain structural conditions (e.g., for large categories), the relationship appears to be valid for idiocentric but not for allocentric people (Aharpour & Brown, 2000; Capozza, Voci, & Licciardello, 2000).

Regarding the relationship between identification and self-esteem, as we have seen, identification moderates the link between perceived instability of the ingroup value and differentiation in its favor (Branscombe & Wann, 1994). The determining effects of collective self-esteem on identification appear to be confirmed by the few studies where they have been analyzed (e.g., Capozza, Falvo, & Carlotto, 2000; Maass & Cadinu, Chapter 6, this volume; Yuki, 2003).

*   If individuals need to evaluate positively their personal identity and their affiliations, further motivations are also important. Individuals need to be able to feel a measure of certainty in regard to their self-concept and the social and physical world, and appropriate attitudes to express in a given social context. Experiencing uncertainty can be aversive since one feels some lack of control over the events in one's social milieu. The importance of the need for order and structure in human thought is implicit in some psychosocial theories of the self, such as self-assessment theories (e.g., Sedikides & Skowronski, 2000), self-verification theory (Swann, Rentfrow, & Guinn, 2003), and individual differences approaches (e.g., Sorrentino & Roney, 2000). At a collective level, members of inferior groups at times adhere to ideologies which support the status quo in order to avoid the structural uncertainties that change implies (Jost, Burgess, & Mosso, 2001).

According to Hogg and Abrams (1993; see also Hogg, 2000, 2004, Chapter 2, this volume), one of the strategies individuals use to reduce uncertainty is to refer to relevant categorical memberships (subjective uncertainty reduction model). If in a given context an ingroup/outgroup distinction is salient, the individual perceives him/herself as included in the ingroup. Uncertainty is reduced because the ingroup prototypes are both descriptive and prescriptive: they absorb the attributes of the group and prescribe behaviors and attitudes. In the larger social context, one affiliation can become salient if it curbs temporarily important uncertainties. Therefore, in Hogg and Abrams' model, identification depends on the fact that the ingroup provides the individual with interpretations and meanings. Identification, in turn, elicits differentiation processes which serve to clarify the prototypes and enhance the value of the ingroup.

In an extensive research program, Hogg and co-workers have confirmed some hypotheses of this model (e.g., Grieve & Hogg, 1999; Hogg & Grieve, 1999). They found that uncertainty favors identification and fosters discriminatory choices in favor of the ingroup. Moreover, uncertainty influences the perceptions of homogeneity and leads to the preference for ingroups perceived as homogeneous (Jetten, Hogg, & Mullin, 2000). In one experiment, Reid and Hogg (2005) discovered that both the epistemic motivation and the need for self-esteem influenced identification. However, the epistemic motivation effect was found to be prevalent. In fact, it was only when uncertainty was weak that choices were driven by the need for self-esteem; that is, participants identified more with the higher-status ingroup.

From an evolutionary perspective, group life was the strategy which allowed the survival of the human species (Caporael, 1997). Accordingly, individuals are inherently inclined to live in collectives. They thus need to perceive themselves as included and assimilated, fearing that excessive singularity leads to exclusion and isolation. However, a further motivation is fundamental. Individuals also need to perceive themselves as distinctive: distinctiveness allows comparative evaluation and self-definition. The two needs are satisfied by belonging to groups that are clearly distinct from other groups or which adopt explicit rules of inclusion and exclusion. In optimal distinctiveness theory, identification – namely, self-definition in stereotypical terms, commitment toward the ingroup – depends on the extent to which belonging satisfies both these needs (Brewer, 1991, 2003; see also Brewer & Pickett, 1999; Brewer & Silver, 2000).

In studies performed to test this theory, it was found that instability in the satisfaction of one or the other of the two needs affects ingroup and outgroup perceptions. In fact, both when the need to feel assimilated and when the need to perceive oneself as distinct is salient the homogeneity evaluations of the two groups increase (Pickett & Brewer, 2001). When the need for distinctiveness is salient – that is, the outgroup is perceived as too similar to the ingroup – individuals whose affiliation is uncertain can be excluded from the ingroup, and its actual size is underestimated (Pickett, Silver, & Brewer, 2002). A strategy which high identifiers adopt to satisfy one or the other of the two needs is to accentuate own closeness to the ingroup prototypes (Pickett, Bonner, & Coleman, 2002). Assimilation to ingroup prototypes enhances the categorical contrast and, hence, ingroup distinctiveness. In one study (Brewer, Manzi, & Shaw, 1993), it was found that, when the need for distinctiveness is salient, people prefer to belong to minority rather than to majority groups regardless of the superior or inferior status of the minorities. Therefore, in choosing a particular group membership, satisfying the need for distinctiveness can prevail over satisfying the need for self-esteem.

People identify, therefore, with the ingroup which satisfies the need for self-esteem or with the ingroup which reduces salient uncertainties. People identify with the ingroup which satisfies the need to perceive themselves as assimilated but also clearly defined: these ingroups limit the boundaries of reciprocal altruism behaviors (for the evolutionary bases of optimal distinctiveness theory, see Brewer & Caporael, Chapter 7, this volume).

In an attempt to widen the heuristic power of social identity theory, Deaux (2000; see also Deaux, Reid, Mizrahi, & Cotting, 1999) has proposed a further explanation (the functional model of social identities). A basic construct in this model is that the different types of group present in society – wide social categories such as political and ethnical memberships, or face-to-face groups, such as family or work teams – can function in different ways. The principles of depersonalization, perception of self and others as category exemplars, and comparative definition of ingroup worth, hypothesized by social identity theory, may not be valid for all groups. Groups may also differ with respect to the functions they serve for their members. Deaux et al. and Aharpour and Brown (2002) discovered that identification can depend on satisfying the need for self-esteem (sports teams), the need to reduce salient uncertainties (religious groups), the need for cohesion (trade unionists) or the need to evaluate oneself positively through downward ingroup comparisons (group of students from own faculty). These different identity functions seem to elicit different processes. Discrimination and prejudice, for example, may be especially elicited by identifications stemming from the satisfaction of the need for self-esteem (for further motivational approaches, see Castano et al., Chapter 4, this volume; Vignoles, Chryssochoou, & Breakwell, 2000).

Research generated by the numerous models stemming from the fertile social identity theory has, without doubt, extended the field of group phenomena explained. As we have seen, the motivations which intervene in social identity processes are manifold, and behavioral consequences are different, when one of them prevails. When identification derives from the joint satisfaction of the need for distinctiveness and the need for inclusion, a perceived decrease in ingroup distinctiveness evokes differentiation processes which may also concern the negative attributes of the ingroup (Pickett & Brewer, 2001). The accentuation of one's own negative traits, which can be observed at times in real groups, serves to underline or protect one's own collective distinctiveness (see Mlicki & Ellemers, 1996).

Considering historical events, it is interesting how Hitler in *Mein Kampf* actively worked to construct the identity of the nascent National Socialist Party. Through many intergroup comparisons, Hitler differentiated the National Socialist Party from German bourgeois parties, from Marxism, from the Pan-Germanic and Christian Social Parties – the latter were influential political formations in Austria in the 1920s. The distinctive traits of own party were: young, confident, capable of winning over the masses, but also cynical, unscrupulous, anti-Semitic and racist. Adhesion to the party, a group with clear boundaries, could satisfy the needs for inclusion and distinctiveness, but also the need to reduce salient uncertainties, given the clarity of its prototypes: radical anti-Semitism, closeness to the masses, nationalism with explicit prominence of Germany (Capozza & Volpato, 2005).

When identification derives from the satisfaction of the need for self-enhancement and the need for distinctiveness, a perceived decrease in self-esteem *and* distinctiveness can produce intense differentiation processes. Hitler attempted to convince Germans of their failures and mistakes and the risk they were taking in losing their "racial purity." He attributed to Jews the responsibility for "contamination" ("they ape Aryans," "they bastardize Germans") and for German failures. The aim was to provoke not one but many motivations for differentiation, separation, and anti-Semitism (for an interpretation of anti-Semitism based on the incompatibility of material goals, see the stereotype content model by Fiske, Cuddy, Glick, & Xu, 2002).

The new models have widened the heuristic power of social identity theory. It is not difficult to predict that they will continue to stimulate new research pertaining to categorical inclusion and exclusion processes (optimal distinctiveness theory), social influence phenomena, and the singling out of identity types which most strongly foster intergroup discrimination and bias (functional model of social identities).

Social identity processes and cultural differences

Motivational models have shown how social identity can work in different ways depending on the needs that group belonging satisfies. Moreover, the functional model of social identities maintains that in society there are several types of groups: groups of different structure (e.g., large categories vs. face-to-face groups) and with different orientations (e.g., collectivistic vs. individualistic) can produce different processes and favor specific configurations of social identity (e.g., self-stereotyping vs. personalized self, included in a net of significant relationships; Yuki, 2003). The need to distinguish between types of groups and types of social identities is stressed by other investigators such as Lickel et al. (2000; social categories vs. dynamic groups) and Prentice, Miller, and Lightdale (1994; common identity vs. common bond groups).

A similar contribution may derive from comparing cultures; that is, from the analysis of the theory's adequacy when tested in Eastern Asian cultures. However, while models and studies concerning the self and individual motivations are numerous (Heine, 2001; Heine et al., 1999; Markus & Kitayama, 1991; Nisbett, Peng, Choi, & Norenzayan, 2001), empirical evidence regarding ingroup bias is scanty and incoherent (Smith & Long, Chapter 8, this volume). Moreover, the studies do not always refer to such central concepts of social identity theory as identification, collective self-esteem, and salience of personal or social identity (for exceptions see Kakimoto, 1995; Yuki, 2003, and the studies on regional and ethnic identity in Hong Kong, e.g., Hong et al., 2004). Without referring to such concepts it is difficult to establish the coherence of data with the theory. Nevertheless, the data can supply useful information for the generation of new theoretical constructs.

We begin with studies using the minimal group paradigm (Tajfel, Billig, Bundy, & Flament, 1971). It is interesting that some had the aim to contradict social identity theory; namely, the concept that in minimal groups ingroup bias derives from the need to enhance social identity. In one study conducted in Japan, student participants were examined in six groups of six (Karp, Jin, Yamagishi, & Shinotsuka, 1993). In each group, three participants were categorized as overestimators and three as underestimators. Of the six groups, three were assigned to the "multilateral" condition: a condition similar to the experiments on minimal groups. In this condition, each participant had to divide 500 yen between an anonymous member of the ingroup and an anonymous member of the outgroup. Participants knew that each player would receive an allocation of money both from a member of the ingroup and from a member of the outgroup; the final allocated quota would be the average of the two allocations. Once the task was concluded, each participant received the set quota.

In the "unilateral" condition (the other three groups), each participant was told that two of the six members (one overestimator and one under-estimator) had been randomly selected to complete the allocation task, while the other four were occupied in other activities. Each participant believed that he/she had been chosen as one of the two allocators. It was explained that, for completing the allocation task, he/she would be paid 300 yen. It was also stressed that one allocator would make a choice for one pair of the other participants (one overestimator and one underestimator), and the other allocator for the other pair. According to Karp et al. (1993), the unilateral condition allows two interpretations of ingroup bias occurring in minimal groups to be compared: either one favors ingroup members so that the ingroup obtains more and, therefore, is worth more – personal material interest does not influence the choices (social identity theory) – or one favors ingroupers because one thinks that they also favor us – personal material interest would be the determinant of ingroup bias. The behavior of allocators would be guided by the irrational belief in being able to control the choices of the other ingroup members through their own choices: by favoring ingroup members one is favored with the consequence of obtaining personal benefits (see also Rabbie, Schot, & Visser, 1989, and a response by Turner & Bourhis, 1996).

According to Karp et al. (1993), ingroup bias in the unilateral condition would support the explanation based on social identity, while absence of ingroup bias would support the hypothesis of personal interest. Results indicate that participants favored the ingroup in the multilateral condition, but were egalitarian in the unilateral condition. Thus, Karp et al. concluded that the main determinant of ingroup bias is an expectation that our favors are reciprocated, rather than the need to enhance the ingroup or to benefit a person who shares our identity. Karp et al. argued that these findings disconfirm social identity theory since they show that categorization is not a sufficient condition, and interdependence in resource acquisition is a necessary condition, of ingroup bias (these results have been replicated by Jin, Yamagishi, & Kiyonari, 1996).

However, the multilateral/unilateral paradigm does not allow a proper test of social identity theory. In the unilateral condition, the fact that the reward of the allocator is set (300 yen) promotes comparisons between oneself and the other ingroup members, thus making personal identity prominent. The absence of ingroup bias in this condition could therefore depend on the fact that social identity is not salient. Furthermore, even if social identity were salient, there would be interpretative problems. The allocator (e.g., an overestimator) who wishes to make a discriminatory choice in the unilateral condition could allocate 300 yen to the ingroup recipient and 200 yen to the outgroup recipient. However, this allocator could suppose that the other allocator (the underestimator) also makes the same choice; that is, he/she gives 300 yen to the ingroup and 200 to the outgroup recipient. The result of the two choices would be an excessive heterogeneity of resources inside the ingroup (300, 300, and 200 yen). The egalitarian strategy, in the unilateral condition, could have the function of attenuating such heterogeneity (for the need for ingroup homogeneity when social identity is salient, see e.g., Voci, 2000). Thus, processes determined by social and personal identity can explain the results of Karp et al. (1993) and Jin et al. (1996).

Moreover – still with reference to the experiments on minimal groups – it is difficult to explain in terms of personal advantage the preference for the strategy MD (maximum differentiation) in the matrices in which MD is opposed to MIP + MJP; that is, to the strategy of maximum ingroup profit (Tajfel et al., 1971).

Yamagishi and co-workers have tried to demonstrate the insufficiency of social identity theory by also considering cooperative behavior in the Prisoner Dilemma game (Jin & Yamagishi, 1997; Yamagishi & Kiyonari, 2000). The paradigm of minimal groups (in general, categorization was based on aesthetic preferences) was used in all of the studies, and participants made their choices by allocating one quota of money to their partner, once playing with a member of the ingroup and once with a member of the outgroup. According to social identity theory, the cooperative choice – that is, the choice which, if reciprocated, is advantageous for both players – should be more frequent in the ingroup than outgroup condition or, in any case, it should be that more money is allocated to the partner in the ingroup than outgroup condition.

Yamagishi and co-workers also predict greater cooperation in the ingroup condition. However, according to them, preference for the cooperative choice would not be mediated by the affiliation to a common identity; it would derive only from the expectation that one's own favor is reciprocated. To contradict the interpretation based on shared identity, Yamagishi and co-workers (Jin & Yamagishi, 1997; Yamagishi & Kiyonari, 2000) have developed some ingenious experimental paradigms. In one study, in addition to the ingroup/outgroup partner conditions – in which both players knew the respective memberships ("mutual knowledge") – Jin and Yamagishi used two other conditions defined as "unilateral knowledge". In these, the participant is informed that the partner, a member of the ingroup (unilateral ingroup) or a member of the outgroup (unilateral outgroup), knows his/her own membership but not that of the other player. Thus, the participant interacts with a member of the ingroup who does not know that the two players share the same affiliation, or with a member of the outgroup who does not know that the partner is a member of the other group.

Jin and Yamagishi (1997) hypothesized that in the mutual knowledge condition a higher reward should be allocated to the partner-member of the ingroup than to the partner-member of the outgroup. In contrast, choices should not differ between the two unilateral conditions, in which one knows that the partner is not informed of the membership of the other player. In fact, in this case, the participant does not expect cooperation either from the ingroup or from the outgroup member. In the case of the "ingroup conditions", moreover, more resources should be allocated in the mutual knowledge than in the unilateral knowledge condition since in the latter one does not expect the cooperative choice to be reciprocated.

According to Jin and Yamagishi (1997), on the basis of social identity theory there should be no difference between the two ingroup conditions since, in both, the participant is disposed to cooperation with the partner who shares the same identity. Results confirm the hypotheses derived from their model of reciprocity expectation. In fact, the level of cooperation was highest in the condition "ingroup/mutual knowledge" and did not differ between the other conditions. Specifically, these findings seem to contradict social identity theory. However, the fact of knowing that a partner does not know the fellow participant's group membership might generate an expectation of being perceived as a single individual – that is, it promotes the salience of personal identity. Social identity theory could thus explain the difference found between the conditions "mutual knowledge/ingroup" and "unilateral knowledge/ingroup" in terms of differential salience of social identity (see also Yamagishi & Kiyonari, 2000; corresponding results were found using social categories such as nationalities, instead of minimal groups, Yamagishi et al., 2005).

Thus, the studies made by Yamagishi and co-workers (e.g., Jin & Yamagishi, 1997; Karp et al., 1993) do not contradict social identity theory. As we will soon see, the tendency to minimize the importance of the social identity concept for explaining group behavior is also present in other investigators belonging to East Asian cultures (Yuki, 2003).

In relation to the expressions of ingroup favoritism, research findings appear inconsistent. Using the minimal group paradigm and tasks of resource allocation, Yamagishi and co-workers have found evidence of ingroup bias. In contrast, using the same paradigm and allocation measures, Wetherell (1982) discovered that Maori and Samoan children reliably used the cooperative strategy of maximum joint profit (New Zealand). Heine and Lehman (1997, Study 2) found significantly lower ingroup bias in Japanese rather than in Canadian participants – the groups in question were rival universities. In the case of the Japanese, Heine and Lehman also found that the higher-status group did not emphasize its superiority and that the group of lower status even stressed its inferiority. The value of one's own belonging did not seem to derive from the use of comparative strategies. Less ingroup favoritism was also found in cultures of Eastern Asia as compared to Western individualistic cultures by Bond and Hewstone (1988), Tinsley and Pillutla (1998), and Wade-Benzoni et al. (2002). And Chen and co-workers found that Chinese, but not American, students supported the losing minimal ingroup by derogating the outgroup (Chen, Brockner, & Chen, 2002; Chen, Brockner, & Katz, 1998). Finally, outgroup bias was revealed in Japanese students who compared their national ingroup with the Australian outgroup (Yamagishi et al., 2005) or evaluated patriotism in Japanese and Americans (Karasawa, 2003).

The inconsistency of such results, but above all the fact that ingroup bias seems less pronounced in East Asian cultures, has led Yuki (2003, p. 168) to argue that groups in such cultures have little inclination to compare with outgroups. In Hinkle and Brown's (1990) terms, their orientation could be considered as autonomous, not relational. That is, the value of the ingroup would not derive from the perception of its superiority vis à vis other groups, but from other considerations, such as better performance than in the past, or performance corresponding to ideal or absolute standards.

Smith and Long (Chapter 8, this volume) have also argued for such a hypothesis. The autonomous orientation determinants might be structural. In collectivistic Eastern cultures the structure of intergroup relations, perhaps by being relatively stable and clear-cut, would make the comparison with the lower- or higher-status outgroup less relevant, thus reducing competitiveness.

Autonomous orientation as assumed by Yuki (2003) and Smith and Long (Chapter 8, this volume) involves the following considerations. First of all, in East Asian cultures, rivalries between groups should be less determined by the need to enhance collective identity but could derive more from the divergence of material goals. Moreover, the fact that in these cultures the modal group has collectivistic values and non-relational orientation – that is, it functions differently from the modal group in Western cultures – supports the validity of the taxonomic extensions of social identity theory (Deaux et al., 1999; Hinkle & Brown, 1990; for distinctions regarding collectivistic groups, see Brewer & Roccas, 2001). The original social identity theory cannot explain such cultural differences. By incorporating such diversity, taxonomic theories comprise them in the explanation. Finally, the fact that ingroup value derives from intragroup evaluations (e.g., temporal comparisons) supports the validity of recent motivational theories of identification (e.g., Brewer, 1991; Hogg, 2000). In East Asian cultures, identification could depend on the satisfaction of the need to reduce salient uncertainties more than on the satisfaction of the need for self-esteem. Indeed, with respect to Western cultures, Eastern cultures seem to be less open to change (Schwartz, 1992; see also Hogg, Chapter 2, this volume), and uncertainty avoidance is high in Japan (Hofstede, 1980).

According to Yuki (2003), social identity theory also does not explain group behavior in Eastern Asian cultures because the group in these cultures is not a set of individuals perceiving one another on the basis of a shared categorization (Turner, 1987). Rather, it is a network of relationships in which individuals perceive themselves as being included. In such a network, individuals are aware of their singularity and the distinctiveness of their role. The prototypical group is family, conceptualized as a network organized in few cardinal relations. Larger groups, such as nation, would also be systems of roles, massive and complex. In this type of group, conceiving oneself in a depersonalized manner – as interchangeable exemplars of the same category – would not be functional since individuals must perceive their diversity in order to play their specific role. To explain this type of group, the traditional concept of social identity is irrelevant (Yuki, 2003) or only occasionally relevant (Yamagishi, 2003).

Finally, the lower ingroup bias found in Eastern Asian cultures could depend on the fact that, in such cultures, motivation to self-criticism prevails over motivation to self-enhancement. For example, in Rosenberg's

(1965) self-esteem scale, Japanese participants generally score lower than Canadian participants (Heine, Takata, & Lehman, 2000). In Japanese people the false uniqueness effect (Myers, 1987) – that is, the belief of being more competent than the average exemplar of a category to which one belongs – does not occur (Heine et al., 2000; Markus & Kitayama, 1991). Japanese examine information about themselves with more attention when it indicates their inferiority than when it indicates their superiority; the opposite result is found for Canadians (Heine et al., 2000). Among Japanese people the effect of compensatory self-enhancement (Baumeister & Jones, 1978), which is the tendency to compensate for one's own inferiority in some dimension by declaring one's own prevalence in others, does not occur (Heine, Kitayama, & Lehman, 2001).

It is possible that the motivation to self-criticism does not extend from personal to social self, given the attachment for the ingroup in Eastern cultures and the fact that the attitude of self-criticism has the function to improve the performance of one's personal role within the ingroup (for a different view, see Heine & Lehman, 1997). As has been said, lower ingroup bias or its inconsistency may depend on non-relational orientation which in turn may depend on the structural attributes of the social context.

Our final analysis concerns the studies on social identity performed in Eastern Asian countries which perceive reunification with China as possible (Taiwan) or have recently returned under the sovereignty of China (Hong Kong, in 1997). These studies make explicit reference to self-categorization theory (e.g., Hong et al., 2004; Li, 2003), optimal distinctiveness theory (e.g., Chiu & Hong, 1999), and the common ingroup identity model (Gaertner & Dovidio, 2000; see Hong et al., 2004).

In one study, Schack and Schack (2005) analyzed the representation of national, regional, and ethnic categories in students and employees in Hong Kong. Schack and Schack found that, two years after the handover, in cognitive representation a superordinate category was present (East Asians) including Hong Kongers, Mainland Chinese, and Japanese. The "values of Confucius", similar historical roots, and physical features were the common traits of the three groups. Within this cluster, however, participants operated clear distinctions. They differentiated Hong Kongers from Mainland Chinese, assigning to Hong Kongers the attributes of modernity and greater Westernization, and Hong Kongers from Japanese for the higher Westernization of Hong Kongers. These distinctions made regional identity *optimal* (Brewer, 1991), namely self-perception and self-presentation as Hong Kongers (or primarily Hong Kongers) rather than as Chinese (see Brewer, 1999a; and for the representations prior to the handover, Lam, Lau, Chiu, Hong, & Peng, 1999).

In the context of annexation, researchers tried to single out the conditions which could favor the formation, in the people of Hong Kong, of a common identity, inclusive of Hong Kongers and Mainland Chinese. In one study, carried out in Hong Kong shortly before the handover, Fu, Lee, Chiu, and Hong (1999) created two experimental conditions. In one condition student participants were given the task of writing an essay on the Japanese government's responsibility in the death of a Hong Kong patriot (David Chan, who died in 1996 during a demonstration in favor of Chinese – and not Japanese – possession of the Diaoyu Islands). In the other condition, they had to write an essay on the responsibility of the Beijing government. In the first condition, the context made salient the Chinese versus Japanese ethnic belonging; in it, both participants who defined themselves as "primarily Hong Konger" (the great majority) and those who defined themselves as "primarily Chinese" were not against the assimilation between Hong Kongers and Mainland Chinese (e.g., using Potunghua language in everyday communication). The condition "responsibility of the Chinese government" instead made salient the categorization Hong Kongers/Mainland Chinese, based on political and economic distinctions. In this condition, participants who identified themselves as "primarily Hong Konger" were less favorable to the assimilation compared with participants with primarily Chinese identity or the condition of Japanese responsibility. The frequent salience of common ethnic identity can make the relations between the two Chinese communities harmonious.

There are, however, conditions which can hinder cooperation with the Mainland Chinese. A critical factor is represented by the administrative actions on the part of Beijing authorities, who may not respect the need for distinctiveness of many Hong Kongers (see Brewer, 1999a). Another critical factor was singled out by Hong and co-workers (e.g., Hong et al., 2004). This group of researchers hypothesized and found two implicit theories which people use to explain the behavior of individuals and groups (Hong et al., 2003; Hong, Levy, & Chiu, 2001; Levy, Plaks, Hong, Chiu, & Dweck, 2001). One is entity theory. People who subscribe to this theory are convinced that human character is fixed. They believe, that is, that individuals are defined by static traits, which influence their behavior; the effect of situational factors is limited. Groups are conceived as sets of individuals sharing stable dispositional attributes (namely, essentialistic). The other theory is defined as incremental. People subscribing to it tend to believe that human character is malleable, and behavior is influenced by contextual factors. Group members are not ascribed with common attributes, but with common needs and goals which can change when changing the social context (e.g., intergroup). The distinction entity/incremental was assessed in different cultures, such as North America and Hong Kong (Chiu, Hong, & Dweck, 1997); it is not correlated with authoritarianism or conservatism and only weakly with cognitive elaboration styles, such as personal need for structure or attributional complexity (see Hong et al., 2004).

Hong and co-workers (2004) linked in an original way the two lay theories with self-categorization theory (Turner, 1987) and the common ingroup identity model (Gaertner & Dovidio, 2000); they proposed, in fact, that the entity/incremental variable moderates the effects of the self-categorization level – inclusive or exclusive of outgroup – on outgroup evaluations. With respect to the condition in which the two groups are perceived as separate, in the condition in which ingroup (e.g., Hong Kongers) and outgroup (Mainland Chinese) are perceived as included in a common ingroup (Chinese), the outgroup evaluation improves for incremental theorists, but not for entity theorists, who are inclined to view categorical attributes as static.

The moderation hypothesis was confirmed in two studies (Hong et al., 2004). In one, concerning the relationship between Hong Kongers and Mainland Chinese, the only participants (students in Hong Kong) who did not evaluate Mainland Chinese negatively were incremental theorists who defined themselves as "primarily Chinese". There was no difference between the other groups: entity theorists/primarily Chinese, entity theorists/ primarily Hong Konger, incremental theorists/primarily Hong Konger. In the second study, participants – Asian American students – showed less prejudice toward African Americans in the condition in which American identity was salient than in the condition in which Asian American identity was salient. However, this finding concerned only the "supporters" of malleability (both lay theory and salience of identity – American vs. Asian American – were experimentally manipulated).

Thus, the perception of a common affiliation may not be sufficient to promote positive evaluations of the outgroup. Beliefs regarding the non-malleability of human character can hinder the common identity effects. It is interesting how historical and contextual factors favored the identification of a result which may broaden Western theories of intergroup relations.

Studies on the relations between ethnic and national identity have also been carried out in Taiwan (e.g., Li, 2003) and Malaysia and Singapore (e.g., Liu, Lawrence, Ward, & Abraham, 2002).

Studying intergroup emotions and their effects

As is well known, Tajfel (1978b) defined social identity as "that part of an individual's self-concept that derives from his knowledge of his membership of a social group (or groups) together with the value and *emotional significance* attached to that membership" (p. 63, our emphasis). Given the prominence of the words "emotional significance" in that classic definition, it is remarkable how little attention affective processes have received in research inspired by social identity theory, at least until the last decade. A scrutiny of the early work that was concerned with developing, testing, and extending the theory reveals that the majority of it was concerned with explaining variations in different forms of intergroup differentiation in perceptions, judgments, and behavior (e.g., Abrams & Hogg, 1990; Brown, 1984a; Tajfel, 1978a, 1982; Turner & Giles, 1981). What is striking about this by now large social identity literature is how much of it is concerned with behavioral or cognitive phenomena that are affectively "cool" or neutral, and how little with the "warmer" emotional processes of liking, disliking, fearing, or admiring ingroups and outgroups. Whether as an independent or a dependent variable, affect was strangely neglected by social identity theory in the first twenty years of its existence.

Such an omission is surprising not just because Tajfel (1978b) clearly thought that emotions were important, as we saw above in his definition, but also because social identity processes are often invoked to explain phenomena such as prejudice and intergroup hostility, phenomena which most commentators would agree have a strong emotional component (Allport, 1954; Brown, 1995; Jones, 1997). And yet it was recognized early on in the genesis of social identity theory that liking (and disliking) outgroups was not usually strongly correlated with the conventional measures of ingroup bias and often seemed to be controlled by different variables (Brewer, 1979; Brown, 1984b; Turner, 1981). The following three examples may be considered. Brewer and Campbell (1976), in their large-scale study of interethnic attitudes in East Africa, found that the perceived cultural and linguistic similarity between the 30 ethnic groups they surveyed was predictive of the attraction that group members expressed toward other groups: similarity being linearly and positively related to attraction. On the other hand, indices of intergroup evaluation along various trait dimensions showed no such linear relationship with similarity, and factor analysis revealed the attraction measures to be orthogonal to the evaluation ones. In an experimental study of reactions to identity threat, Brown and Ross (1982) incorporated both affective measures (e.g., dislike of and annoyance toward the outgroup) and more conventional ingroup bias indices (e.g., evaluations of ingroup and outgroup on value dimensions). The former proved more consistently responsive to the threat variable and were largely uncorrelated with the evaluative bias measures. Struch and Schwartz (1989) found that group identification was implicated in predicting Israeli participants' aggressive intentions toward an ultra-orthodox religious outgroup – the effects of conflicting goal perceptions were more intense for high than for low identifiers. However, that measure of aggression was not at all correlated with the less affectively tinged measure of ingroup bias in group trait ratings. Moreover, the latter measure was only weakly – and paradoxically – *negatively* related to perceived conflict, and not at all to identification. All in all, then, it appears plain that evaluating one's group slightly more favorably than another (the standard indicator of ingroup bias) is not at all the same thing as actively derogating or disliking that other group. As Brewer (1999b) wisely observed, ingroup love should not be equated with outgroup hate (see also Brown & Zagefka, 2005).

Fortunately for students of intergroup relations, three developments subsequent to the publication of social identity theory have helped to place affective processes squarely back onto people's research agendas. The first was an article by Stephan and Stephan (1985) that identified anxiety as a causal ingredient in many intergroup encounters. Stephan and Stephan persuasively argued that, whether stemming from a perceived lack of familiarity with appropriate interactional norms or from a history of antagonism between the groups concerned, intergroup anxiety would be likely to have negative consequences for the quality of the subsequent intergroup behavior and attitudes. This prediction proved prescient. In several studies of intergroup contact, intergroup anxiety has repeatedly been found to lead to less favorable intergroup attitudes (e.g., Greenland & Brown, 1999; Islam & Hewstone, 1993; Wilder & Shapiro, 1989).

The resurgence of theoretical interest in the contact hypothesis in the 1980s (Gaertner, Mann, Murrell, & Dovidio, 1989; Hewstone & Brown, 1986; Miller & Brewer, 1984) proved to be a second stimulus for the study of intergroup emotions. Traditionally, contact studies have used a number of affectively laden measures to assess the efficacy of different kinds of contact: social distance, intergroup liking, intergroup forgiveness, and various measures of prejudice (Brown & Hewstone, 2005; Pettigrew, 1998). The fact that these theoretical elaborations of the contact hypothesis all drew on social identity theory principles, albeit to derive different implications, provided an important spur for social identity theory researchers to take affective processes more seriously. We return to the role of affect in contact shortly.

The third development was Smith's (1993) seminal chapter on intergroup emotions. Drawing simultaneously on appraisal theories of emotion (Frijda, 1986; Roseman, 1984; Scherer, 1988; see Garcia-Prieto & Scherer, Chapter 10, this volume) and self-categorization theory (Turner, 1987), Smith delineated various intergroup contexts that would be likely to be appraised by group members in particular ways, thus giving rise to certain emotions (e.g., fear, anger) and consequent action tendencies (e.g., avoidance, moving against). Two features of Smith's account are particularly significant. The first is that it is a genuinely intergroup theory, in the sense that it is the perception and appraisal of the intergroup situation by people whose group identities are salient that is proposed as the key causal factor in generating intergroup emotions. In other words, although individuals' own specific situations may or may not be likely to instigate an emotional response, because their group memberships are fully engaged, their appraisal of how the ingroup stands in relation to an outgroup becomes a determining factor. The second aspect of Smith's model is that it makes predictions about *specific* emotional reactions to situations rather than just diffused emotional states (e.g., anxiety). This gives it considerable potential as a theoretical and practical tool. Already, some of its central predictions have received empirical support (Devos, Silver, Mackie, & Smith, 2002; Mackie, Devos, & Smith, 2000; Smith & Mackie, Chapter 9, this volume), and its influence can be discerned in several recent publications and conferences (Dumont, Yzerbyt, Wigboldus, & Gordijn, 2003; Giner-Sorolla & Brown, 2004; Mackie & Smith, 2002).

Influential though Smith's (1993) model has undoubtedly been, it is obviously by no means the "last word" on intergroup emotions. A number of emotional responses remain to be incorporated into it. For example, the conditions under which positive intergroup emotions such as attraction, admiration, and sympathy might arise are not yet specified. Furthermore, there are other negative emotional responses that are not easily derivable from the model. One is "schadenfreude" – the pleasure gained from an outgroup's misfortunes – which may be a more common reaction from subordinate groups than was once supposed (Leach, Spears, Branscombe, & Doosje, 2003). It would also be of interest to determine the psychological links between these direct emotions felt or expressed toward outgroups and intergroup attitudes deriving *indirectly* from emotional attributions to ingroup and outgroup. Leyens and his colleagues have assembled an impressive set of arguments and evidence to show that a pervasive form of ingroup bias is that of a relative dehumanization of outgroups (e.g., Leyens et al., 2000; Leyens et al., 2001; Paladino et al., 2002). In their formulation, dehumanization is defined as the attribution of more uniquely human emotional attributes to the ingroup than to outgroup(s).

The above developments are concerned mainly with intergroup emotions as *dependent* variables, the outcome of certain intergroup situations or cognitive appraisals. It is also becoming apparent that there are emotions that can be *independent* variables in determining group members' subsequent intergroup attitudes and behavioral tendencies. One of these is collective guilt (Branscombe & Doosje, 2004; Doosje, Branscombe, Spears, & Manstead, 1998), which refers to the emotion experienced when one is reminded of the misdeeds of the ingroup toward an outgroup. Even though individual group members may have had no direct involvement with or responsibility for that illegitimate action – they may not even have been alive when it occurred – they may still feel guilt and seek to engage in compensatory behavior toward the outgroup (Doosje et al., 1998; Iyer, Leach, & Crosby, 2003; Swim & Miller, 1999). It is of particular interest to be able to identify the conditions which inhibit those reparatory intentions. One may be when the ingroup identity is threatened by the feelings of guilt (Doosje et al., 1998), perhaps because the countervailing emotion of collective shame is also present (Brown, González, Zagefka, Manzi, & Saiz, 2004).

Finally, it is worth recording that intergroup emotions are becoming increasingly implicated as mediator variables in controlling the effects of intergroup contact (Brown & Hewstone, 2005). Pettigrew and Tropp's

(2000) meta-analysis makes it clear that when Allport's (1954) criteria for optimal contact are satisfied, then the outcomes for prejudice reduction are especially beneficial. Brown and Hewstone conclude that the main mediators of those contact effects are affective in nature. They identify two variables in particular that seem to be influential: intergroup anxiety and empathy for the outgroup (see Paolini et al., Chapter 11, this volume). When contact takes place on an equal-status footing, involves cooperative activity, and is of a kind likely to generate friendships with outgroup members, then intergroup anxiety is reduced and empathy is increased. In turn, anxiety and empathy are related to prejudice reduction (negatively and positively respectively). These mediating processes still prevail when the contact takes place at an intergroup level (i.e., when the group memberships of the protagonists are salient), a condition which Hewstone and Brown (1986) had originally proposed as a prerequisite for the generalization of contact effects (González & Brown, Chapter 13, this volume). Note, too, that Gaertner and his colleagues (Chapter 12, this volume) also find that affective responses are mediators or moderators of the effects of contact in generating (or inhibiting) a sense of common ingroup identity.

Conclusion

In summary, then, we hope we have been able to show in this chapter that current research inspired by the social identity perspective has simultaneously challenged, enriched, and enlarged the core ideas in Tajfel and Turner's (1986) original formulation. As we saw above, the self-esteem construct, which has for some time been the subject of close empirical study and controversy, should no longer be regarded as the sole motivational factor underlying social identity processes. Thanks to several independent theoretical advances – most notably Hogg's (2000) uncertainty reduction model and Brewer's (1991) optimal distinctiveness theory – a better understanding is being reached of the range of identity motivations and their corresponding implications for intergroup relations (see Capozza et al., Chapter 3, this volume). Similarly, the emergence of cross-cultural analyses of intergroup behavior, while pointing to the potentially occidentocentric nature of much social identity thinking and research, has also contributed to the development of taxonomic models of groups and associated identity processes. A common theme of these models has been to argue for a less monolithic conception of the "group" than perhaps social identity theory had originally envisaged, and to hypothesize a more differentiated set of intergroup orientations than just the "search for positive distinctiveness". Finally, the recent upsurge of interest in the affective aspects of intergroup relations has provided many new insights into the conditions under which members of different groups come to hate (or love), avoid (or seek out), and despise (or admire) each other. In the chapters that follow, all these issues (and more) are re-examined in more detail than we have the space or ability to do here.

References

Abrams, D., & Hogg, M. A. (Eds.). (1990). *Social identity theory: Constructive and critical advances.* London: Harvester Wheatsheaf.

Aharpour, S., & Brown, R. (2000). *Group identification and ingroup bias: A meta-analysis testing the Hinkle and Brown model.* Unpublished manuscript, University of Kent at Canterbury, UK.

Aharpour, S., & Brown, R. (2002). Functions of group identification: An exploratory analysis. *Revue Internationale de Psychologie Sociale, 15,* 157–186.

Allport, G. W. (1954). *The nature of prejudice.* New York: Addison-Wesley.

Baumeister, R. F., & Jones, E. E. (1978). When self-presentation is constrained by the target's knowledge: Consistency and compensation. *Journal of Personality and Social Psychology, 36,* 608–618.

Bond, M. H., & Hewstone, M. (1988). Social identity theory and the perception of intergroup relations in Hong Kong. *International Journal of Intercultural Relations, 12,* 153–170.

Branscombe, N. R. (1998). Thinking about one's gender group's privileges or disadvantages: Consequences for well-being in women and men. *British Journal of Social Psychology, 37,* 167–184.

Branscombe, N. R. & Doosje, B. (2004). *Collective guilt: International perspectives.* Cambridge, UK: Cambridge University Press.

Branscombe, N. R., Ellemers, N., Spears, R., & Doosje, B. (1999). The context and content of social identity threat. In N. Ellemers, R. Spears, & B. Doosje (Eds.), *Social identity: Context, commitment, content* (pp. 35–58). Oxford, UK: Blackwell.

Branscombe, N. R., & Wann, D. L. (1994). Collective self-esteem consequences of outgroup derogation when a valued social identity is on trial. *European Journal of Social Psychology, 24,* 641–657.

Brewer, M. B. (1979). In-group bias in the minimal intergroup situation: A cognitive-motivational analysis. *Psychological Bulletin, 86,* 307–324.

Brewer, M. B. (1991). The social self: On being the same and different at the same time. *Personality and Social Psychology Bulletin, 17,* 475–482.

Brewer, M. B. (1999a). Multiple identities and identity transition: Implications for Hong Kong. *International Journal of Intercultural Relations, 23,* 187–197.

Brewer, M. B. (1999b). The psychology of prejudice: Ingroup love or outgroup hate? *Journal of Social Issues, 55,* 429–444.

Brewer, M. B. (2003). Optimal distinctiveness, social identity, and the self. In M. R. Leary & J. P. Tangney (Eds.), *Handbook of self and identity* (pp. 480–491). New York: Guilford Press.

Brewer, M. B., & Campbell, D. T. (1976). *Ethnocentrism and intergroup attitudes: East African evidence.* Oxford, UK: Sage.

Brewer, M. B., Manzi, J. M., & Shaw, J. S. (1993). Ingroup identification as a function of depersonalization, distinctiveness, and status. *Psychological Science, 4*, 88–92.

Brewer, M. B., & Pickett, C. L. (1999). Distinctiveness motives as a source of the social self. In T. R. Tyler, R. M. Kramer, & O. P. John (Eds.), *The psychology of the social self* (pp. 71–87). Mahwah, NJ: Lawrence Erlbaum Associates Inc.

Brewer, M. B., & Roccas, S. (2001). Individual values, social identity, and optimal distinctiveness. In C. Sedikides & M. B. Brewer (Eds.), *Individual self, relational self, collective self* (pp. 219–237). Philadelphia: Psychology Press.

Brewer, M. B., & Silver, M. D. (2000). Group distinctiveness, social identification, and collective mobilization. In S. Stryker, T. J. Owens, & R. W. White (Eds.), *Self, identity, and social movements* (pp. 153–171). Minneapolis, MN: University of Minnesota Press.

Brown, R. (1984a). Intergroup processes. *British Journal of Social Psychology, 23* [special issue].

Brown, R. (1984b). The role of similarity in intergroup relations. In H. Tajfel (Ed.), *The social dimension: European developments in social psychology* (pp. 603–623). Cambridge, UK: Cambridge University Press.

Brown, R. (1995). *Prejudice: Its social psychology.* Oxford, UK: Blackwell.

Brown, R., González, R., Zagefka, H., Manzi, J. M., & Saiz, J. L. (2004, June). *Collective guilt, shame and sympathy and their implications for reparation policies: A longitudinal study in Chile.* Paper presented at the annual meeting of the Society for the Psychological Study of Social Issues, Washington, DC.

Brown, R., & Hewstone, M. (2005). An integrative theory of intergroup contact. In M. P. Zanna (Ed.), *Advances in experimental social psychology* (Vol. 37, pp. 255–343). San Diego, CA: Academic Press.

Brown, R., & Ross, G. F. (1982). The battle for acceptance: An investigation into the dynamics of intergroup behaviour. In H. Tajfel (Ed.), *Social identity and intergroup relations* (pp. 155–178). Cambridge, UK: Cambridge University Press.

Brown, R., & Zagefka, H. (2005). Ingroup affiliations and prejudice. In J. F. Dovidio, P. Glick, & L. A. Rudman (Eds.), *On the nature of prejudice: Fifty years after Allport* (pp. 54–70). Oxford, UK: Blackwell.

Cadinu, M. R., & Cerchioni, M. (2001). Compensatory biases after ingroup threat: "Yeah, but we have a good personality." *European Journal of Social Psychology, 31*, 353–367.

Caporael, L. R. (1997). The evolution of truly social cognition: The core configurations model. *Personality and Social Psychology Review, 1*, 276–298.

Capozza, D., Falvo, R., & Carlotto, S. (2000). Verifica di teorie motivazionali dell'identificazione con il proprio gruppo tramite modelli di equazioni strutturali [Testing motivational theories of ingroup identification through structural equation models]. *Testing Psicometria Metodologia, 7*, 71–84.

Capozza, D., Voci, A., & Licciardello, O. (2000). Individualism, collectivism and social identity theory. In D. Capozza & R. Brown (Eds.), *Social identity processes: Trends in theory and research* (pp. 62–80). London: Sage.

Capozza, D., & Volpato, C. (2005). *Mein Kampf: Testing stereotype content models through the analysis of one case.* Unpublished manuscript, Universities of Padova and Milan, Italy.

Chen, Y. R., Brockner, J., & Chen, X. P. (2002). Individual-collective primacy and in-group favoritism: Enhancement and protection effects. *Journal of Experimental Social Psychology*, *38*, 482–491.

Chen, Y. R., Brockner, J., & Katz, T. (1998). Toward an explanation of cultural differences in in-group favoritism: The role of individual versus collective primacy. *Journal of Personality and Social Psychology*, *75*, 1490–1502.

Chiu, C., & Hong, Y. (1999). Social identification in a political transition: The role of implicit beliefs. *International Journal of Intercultural Relations*, *23*, 297–318.

Chiu, C., Hong, Y., & Dweck, C. S. (1997). Lay dispositionism and implicit theories of personality. *Journal of Personality and Social Psychology*, *73*, 19–30.

Deaux, K. (2000). Models, meanings and motivations. In D. Capozza & R. Brown (Eds.), *Social identity processes: Trends in theory and research* (pp. 1–14). London: Sage.

Deaux, K., Reid, A., Mizrahi, K., & Cotting, D. (1999). Connecting the person to the social: The functions of social identification. In T. R. Tyler, R. M. Kramer, & O. P. John (Eds.), *The psychology of the social self* (pp. 91–113). Mahwah, NJ: Lawrence Erlbaum Associates Inc.

Devos, T., Silver, L. A., Mackie, D. M., & Smith, E. R. (2002). Experiencing intergroup emotions. In D. M. Mackie & E. R. Smith (Eds.), *From prejudice to intergroup emotions: Differentiated reactions to social groups* (pp. 111–134). New York: Psychology Press.

Doosje, B., Branscombe, N. R., Spears, R., & Manstead, A. S. R. (1998). Guilty by association: When one's group has a negative history. *Journal of Personality and Social Psychology*, *75*, 872–886.

Doosje, B., Ellemers, N., & Spears, R. (1995). Perceived intragroup variability as a function of group status and identification. *Journal of Experimental Social Psychology*, *31*, 410–436.

Dumont, M., Yzerbyt, V. Y., Wigboldus, D., & Gordijn, E. H. (2003). Social categorization and fear reactions to the September 11th terrorist attacks. *Personality and Social Psychology Bulletin*, *29*, 1509–1520.

Fiske, S. T., Cuddy, A. J. C., Glick, P., & Xu, J. (2002). A model of (often mixed) stereotype content: Competence and warmth respectively follow from perceived status and competition. *Journal of Personality and Social Psychology*, *82*, 878–902.

Frijda, N. H. (1986). *The emotions*. Cambridge, UK: Cambridge University Press.

Fu, H., Lee, S., Chiu, C., & Hong, Y. (1999). Setting the frame of mind for social identity. *International Journal of Intercultural Relations*, *23*, 199–214.

Gaertner, S. L., & Dovidio, J. F. (2000). *Reducing intergroup bias: The common ingroup identity model*. Philadelphia: Psychology Press.

Gaertner, S. L., Mann, J. A., Murrell, A. J., & Dovidio, J. F. (1989). Reducing intergroup bias: The benefits of recategorization. *Journal of Personality and Social Psychology*, *57*, 239–249.

Giner-Sorolla, R., & Brown, R. (2004, September). *Intergroup emotions*. Paper presented at the European Science Foundation workshop, Canterbury, UK.

Greenland, K., & Brown, R. (1999). Categorization and intergroup anxiety in contact between British and Japanese nationals. *European Journal of Social Psychology*, *29*, 503–521.

Grieve, P. G., & Hogg, M. A. (1999). Subjective uncertainty and intergroup discrimination in the minimal group situation. *Personality and Social Psychology Bulletin, 25*, 926–940.

Heine, S. J. (2001). Self as cultural product: An examination of East Asian and North American selves. *Journal of Personality, 69*, 881–906.

Heine, S. J., Kitayama, S., & Lehman, D. R. (2001). Cultural differences in self-evaluation: Japanese readily accept negative self-relevant information. *Journal of Cross Cultural Psychology, 32*, 434–443.

Heine, S. J., & Lehman, D. R. (1997). The cultural construction of self-enhancement: An examination of group-serving biases. *Journal of Personality and Social Psychology, 72*, 1268–1283.

Heine, S. J., Lehman, D. R., Markus, H. R., & Kitayama, S. (1999). Is there a universal need for positive self-regard? *Psychological Review, 106*, 766–794.

Heine, S. J., Takata, T., & Lehman, D. R. (2000). Beyond self-presentation: Evidence for self-criticism among Japanese. *Personality and Social Psychology Bulletin, 26*, 71–78.

Hewstone, M., & Brown, R. (Eds.). (1986). *Contact and conflict in intergroup encounters*. Oxford, UK: Blackwell.

Hinkle, S., & Brown, R. (1990). Intergroup comparisons and social identity: Some links and lacunae. In D. Abrams & M. A. Hogg (Eds.), *Social identity theory: Constructive and critical advances* (pp. 48–70). London: Harvester Wheatsheaf.

Hofstede, G. (1980). *Culture's consequences: International differences in work-related values*. Beverly Hills, CA: Sage.

Hogg, M. A. (2000). Subjective uncertainty reduction through self-categorization: A motivational theory of social identity processes. In W. Stroebe & M. Hewstone (Eds.), *European review of social psychology* (Vol. 11, pp. 223–255). Chichester, UK: Wiley.

Hogg, M. A. (2004). Uncertainty and extremism: Identification with high entitativity groups under conditions of uncertainty. In V. Y. Yzerbyt, C. M. Judd, & O. Corneille (Eds.), *The psychology of group perception: Perceived variability, entitativity, and essentialism* (pp. 401–418). New York: Psychology Press.

Hogg, M. A., & Abrams, D. (1990). Social motivation, self-esteem and social identity. In D. Abrams & M. A. Hogg (Eds.), *Social identity theory: Constructive and critical advances* (pp. 28–47). London: Harvester Wheatsheaf.

Hogg, M. A., & Abrams, D. (1993). Towards a single-process uncertainty-reduction model of social motivation in groups. In M. A. Hogg & D. Abrams (Eds.), *Group motivation: Social psychological perspectives* (pp. 173–190). London: Harvester Wheatsheaf.

Hogg, M. A., & Grieve, P. G. (1999). Social identity theory and the crisis of confidence in social psychology: A commentary, and some research on uncertainty reduction. *Asian Journal of Social Psychology, 2*, 79–93.

Hong, Y., Chan, G., Chiu, C., Wong, R. Y. M., Hansen, I. G., Lee, S., et al. (2003). How are social identities linked to self-conception and intergroup orientation? The moderating effect of implicit theories. *Journal of Personality and Social Psychology, 85*, 1147–1160.

Hong, Y., Coleman, J. M., Chan, G., Wong, R. Y. M., Chiu, C., Hansen, I. G., et al. (2004). Predicting intergroup bias: The interactive effects of implicit theory and social identity. *Personality and Social Psychology Bulletin, 30*, 1035–1047.

Hong, Y., Levy, S. R., & Chiu, C. (2001). The contribution of the lay theories approach to the study of groups. *Personality and Social Psychology Review, 5*, 98–106.

Islam, M. R., & Hewstone, M. (1993). Dimensions of contact as predictors of intergroup anxiety, perceived out-group variability, and out-group attitude: An integrative model. *Personality and Social Psychology Bulletin, 19*, 700–710.

Iyer, A., Leach, C. W., & Crosby, F. J. (2003). White guilt and racial compensation: The benefits and limits of self-focus. *Personality and Social Psychology Bulletin, 29*, 117–129.

Jetten, J., Hogg, M. A., & Mullin, B.-A. (2000). In-group variability and motivation to reduce subjective uncertainty. *Group Dynamics, 4*, 184–198.

Jetten, J., Schmitt, M. T., Branscombe, N. R., & McKimmie, B. M. (2005). Suppressing the negative effect of devaluation on group identification: The role of intergroup differentiation and intragroup respect. *Journal of Experimental Social Psychology, 41*, 208–215.

Jin, N., & Yamagishi, T. (1997). Group heuristics in social dilemmas [in Japanese with English summary]. *Japanese Journal of Social Psychology, 12*, 190–198.

Jin, N., Yamagishi, T., & Kiyonari, T. (1996). Bilateral dependency and the minimal group paradigm [in Japanese with English summary]. *Japanese Journal of Psychology, 67*, 77–85.

Jones, J. M. (1997). *Prejudice and racism* (2nd ed.). New York: McGraw-Hill.

Jost, J. T., Burgess, D., & Mosso, C. O. (2001). Conflicts of legitimation among self, group, and system: The integrative potential of system justification theory. In J. T. Jost & B. Major (Eds.), *The psychology of legitimacy: Emerging perspectives on ideology, justice, and intergroup relations* (pp. 363–388). New York: Cambridge University Press.

Kakimoto, T. (1995). Effects of social categorization and a personal trait on the evaluation of others [in Japanese with English summary]. *Japanese Journal of Social Psychology, 11*, 94–104.

Karasawa, M. (2003). Projecting group liking and ethnocentrism on ingroup members: False consensus effect of attitude strength. *Asian Journal of Social Psychology, 6*, 103–116.

Karp, D., Jin, N., Yamagishi, T., & Shinotsuka, H. (1993). Raising the minimum in the minimal group paradigm. *Japanese Journal of Experimental Social Psychology, 32*, 231–240.

Lam, S., Lau, I. Y., Chiu, C., Hong, Y., & Peng, S. (1999). Differential emphases on modernity and Confucian values in social categorization: The case of Hong Kong adolescents in political transition. *International Journal of Intercultural Relations, 23*, 237–256.

Leach, C. W., Spears, R., Branscombe, N. R., & Doosje, B. (2003). Malicious pleasure: Schadenfreude at the suffering of another group. *Journal of Personality and Social Psychology, 84*, 932–943.

Leary, M. R. (1999). The social and psychological importance of self-esteem. In R. M. Kowalski & M. R. Leary (Eds.), *The social psychology of emotional and behavioral problems: Interfaces of social and clinical psychology* (pp. 197–221). Washington, DC: American Psychological Association.

Leary, M. R., & MacDonald, G. (2003). Individual differences in self-esteem: A review and theoretical integration. In M. R. Leary & J. P. Tangney (Eds.), *Handbook of self and identity* (pp. 401–418). New York: Guilford Press.

Levy, S. R., Plaks, J. E., Hong, Y., Chiu, C., & Dweck, C. S. (2001). Static versus dynamic theories and the perception of groups: Different routes to different destinations. *Personality and Social Psychology Review, 5,* 156–168.

Leyens, J.-Ph., Paladino, P. M., Rodriguez, R., Vaes, J., Demoulin, S., Rodriguez, A., et al. (2000). The emotional side of prejudice: The attribution of secondary emotions to ingroups and outgroups. *Personality and Social Psychology Review, 4,* 186–197.

Leyens, J. Ph., Rodriguez, A., Rodriguez, R., Gaunt, R., Paladino, M. P., Vaes, J., et al. (2001). Psychological essentialism and the differential attribution of uniquely human emotions to ingroups and outgroups. *European Journal of Social Psychology, 31,* 395–411.

Li, M. (2003). Basis of ethnic identification in Taiwan. *Asian Journal of Social Psychology, 6,* 229–237.

Lickel, B., Hamilton, D. L., Wieczorkowska, G., Lewis, A., Sherman, S. J., & Uhles, A. N. (2000). Varieties of groups and the perception of group entitativity. *Journal of Personality and Social Psychology, 78,* 223–246.

Liu, J. H., Lawrence, B., Ward, C., & Abraham, S. (2002). Social representations of history in Malaysia and Singapore: On the relationship between national and ethnic identity. *Asian Journal of Social Psychology, 5,* 3–20.

Mackie, D. M., Devos, T., & Smith, E. R. (2000). Intergroup emotions: Explaining offensive action tendencies in an intergroup context. *Journal of Personality and Social Psychology, 79,* 602–616.

Mackie, D. M., & Smith, E. R. (Eds.). (2002). *From prejudice to intergroup emotions: Differentiated reactions to social groups.* New York: Psychology Press.

Markus, H. R., & Kitayama, S. (1991). Culture and the self: Implications for cognition, emotion, and motivation. *Psychological Review, 98,* 224–253.

Miller, N., & Brewer, M. B. (Eds.). (1984). *Groups in contact: The psychology of desegregation.* Orlando, FL: Academic Press.

Mlicki, P. P., & Ellemers, N. (1996). Being different or being better? National stereotypes and identifications of Polish and Dutch students. *European Journal of Social Psychology, 26,* 97–114.

Myers, D. (1987). *Social psychology* (2nd ed.). New York: McGraw-Hill.

Nisbett, R. E., Peng, K., Choi, I., & Norenzayan, A. (2001). Culture and systems of thought: Holistic and analytic cognition. *Psychological Review, 108,* 291–310.

Paladino, M. P., Leyens, J.-Ph., Rodriguez, R., Rodriguez, A., Gaunt, R., & Demoulin, S. (2002). Differential association of uniquely and non uniquely human emotions with the ingroup and the outgroup. *Group Processes and Intergroup Relations, 5,* 105–117.

Perreault, S., & Bourhis, R. Y. (1999). Ethnocentrism, social identification, and discrimination. *Personality and Social Psychology Bulletin, 25,* 92–103.

Pettigrew, T. F. (1998). Intergroup contact theory. *Annual Review of Psychology, 49,* 65–85.

Pettigrew, T. F., & Tropp, L. R. (2000). Does intergroup contact reduce prejudice? Recent meta-analytic findings. In S. Oskamp (Ed.), *Reducing prejudice and discrimination* (pp. 93–114). Mahwah, NJ: Lawrence Erlbaum Associates Inc.

Pickett, C. L., Bonner, B. L., & Coleman, J. M. (2002). Motivated self-stereotyping: Heightened assimilation and differentiation needs result in increased levels of positive and negative self-stereotyping. *Journal of Personality and Social Psychology*, *82*, 543–562.

Pickett, C. L., & Brewer, M. B. (2001). Assimilation and differentiation needs as motivational determinants of perceived in-group and out-group homogeneity. *Journal of Experimental Social Psychology*, *37*, 341–348.

Pickett, C. L., Silver, M. D., & Brewer, M. B. (2002). The impact of assimilation and differentiation needs on perceived group importance and judgments of ingroup size. *Personality and Social Psychology Bulletin*, *28*, 546–558.

Prentice, D. A., Miller, D. T., & Lightdale, J. R. (1994). Asymmetries in attachments to groups and to their members: Distinguishing between common-identity and common-bond groups. *Personality and Social Psychology Bulletin*, *20*, 484–493.

Rabbie, J. M., Schot, J. C., & Visser, L. (1989). Social identity theory: A conceptual and empirical critique from the perspective of a behavioural interaction model. *European Journal of Social Psychology*, *19*, 171–202.

Reid, S. A., & Hogg, M. A. (2005). Uncertainty reduction, self-enhancement, and ingroup identification. *Personality and Social Psychology Bulletin*, *31*, 804–817.

Roseman, I. J. (1984). Cognitive determinants of emotion: A structural theory. In P. Shaver (Ed.), *Review of personality and social psychology* (Vol. 5, pp. 11–36). Beverly Hills, CA: Sage.

Rosenberg, M. (1965). *Society and the adolescent self-image*. Princeton, NJ: Princeton University Press.

Rubin, M., & Hewstone, M. (1998). Social identity theory's self-esteem hypothesis: A review and some suggestions for clarification. *Personality and Social Psychology Review*, *2*, 40–62.

Schack, T., & Schack, E. (2005). In- and outgroup representation in a dynamic society: Hong Kong after 1997. *Asian Journal of Social Psychology*, *8*, 123–137.

Scherer, K. R. (1988). Criteria for emotion-antecedent appraisal: A review. In V. Hamilton, G. H. Bower, & N. H. Frijda (Eds.), *Cognitive perspectives on emotion and motivation* (Vol. 4, pp. 89–126). New York: Kluwer.

Schwartz, S. H. (1992). Universals in the content and structure of values: Theoretical advances and empirical tests in 20 countries. In M. P. Zanna (Ed.), *Advances in experimental social psychology* (Vol. 25, pp. 1–65). San Diego, CA: Academic Press.

Sedikides, C., & Skowronski, J. J. (2000). On the evolutionary functions of the symbolic self: The emergence of self-evaluation motives. In A. Tesser, R. B. Felson, & J. Suls (Eds.), *Psychological perspectives on self and identity* (pp. 91–117). Washington, DC: American Psychological Association.

Simon, B., & Klandermans, B. (2001). Politicized collective identity: A social psychological analysis. *American Psychologist*, *56*, 319–331.

Smith, E. R. (1993). Social identity and social emotions: Toward new conceptualizations of prejudice. In D. M. Mackie & D. L. Hamilton (Eds.), *Affect, cognition, and stereotyping: Interactive processes in group perception* (pp. 297–315). San Diego, CA: Academic Press.

Sorrentino, R. M., & Roney, C. J. R. (2000). *The uncertain mind: Individual differences in facing the unknown*. Philadelphia: Psychology Press.

Stephan, W. G., & Stephan, C. W. (1985). Intergroup anxiety. *Journal of Social Issues, 41*, 157–175.

Struch, N., & Schwartz, S. H. (1989). Intergroup aggression: Its predictors and distinctness from in-group bias. *Journal of Personality and Social Psychology, 56*, 364–373.

Swann, W. B. Jr., Rentfrow, P. J., & Guinn, J. S. (2003). Self-verification: The search for coherence. In M. R. Leary & J. P. Tangney (Eds.), *Handbook of self and identity* (pp. 367–383). New York: Guilford Press.

Swim, J. K., & Miller, D. L. (1999). White guilt: Its antecedents and consequences for attitudes toward affirmative action. *Personality and Social Psychology Bulletin, 25*, 500–514.

Tajfel, H. (Ed.). (1978a). *Differentiation between social groups: Studies in the social psychology of intergroup relations.* London: Academic Press.

Tajfel, H. (1978b). Social categorization, social identity and social comparison. In H. Tajfel (Ed.), *Differentiation between social groups: Studies in the social psychology of intergroup relations* (pp. 61–76). London: Academic Press.

Tajfel, H. (1981). *Human groups and social categories.* Cambridge, UK: Cambridge University Press.

Tajfel, H. (Ed.). (1982). *Social identity and intergroup relations.* Cambridge, UK: Cambridge University Press.

Tajfel, H., Billig, M. G., Bundy, R. P., & Flament, C. (1971). Social categorization and intergroup behaviour. *European Journal of Social Psychology, 1*, 149–178.

Tajfel, H., & Turner, J. C. (1986). The social identity theory of intergroup behavior. In S. Worchel & W. G. Austin (Eds.), *Psychology of intergroup relations* (pp. 7–24). Chicago: Nelson-Hall.

Tinsley, C. H., & Pillutla, M. M. (1998). Negotiating in the United States and Hong Kong. *Journal of International Business Studies, 29*, 711–727.

Triandis, H. C. (1995). *Individualism and collectivism.* Boulder, CO: Westview Press.

Turner, J. C. (1981). The experimental social psychology of intergroup behaviour. In J. C. Turner & H. Giles (Eds.), *Intergroup behaviour* (pp. 66–101). Oxford, UK: Blackwell.

Turner, J. C. (1987). A self-categorization theory. In J. C. Turner, M. A. Hogg, P. J. Oakes, S. D. Reicher, & M. S. Wetherell (Eds.), *Rediscovering the social group: A self-categorization theory* (pp. 42–67). Oxford, UK: Blackwell.

Turner, J. C., & Bourhis, R. Y. (1996). Social identity, interdependence and the social group: A reply to Rabbie et al. In W. P. Robinson (Ed.), *Social groups and identities: Developing the legacy of Henri Tajfel* (pp. 25–63). Oxford, UK: Butterworth-Heinemann.

Turner, J. C., & Giles, H. (Eds.). (1981). *Intergroup behaviour.* Oxford, UK: Blackwell.

Vignoles, V. L., Chryssochoou, X., & Breakwell, G. M. (2000). The distinctiveness principle: Identity, meaning, and the bounds of cultural relativity. *Personality and Social Psychology Review, 4*, 337–354.

Voci, A. (2000). Perceived group variability and the salience of personal and social identity. In W. Stroebe & M. Hewstone (Eds.), *European review of social psychology* (Vol. 11, pp. 177–221). Chichester, UK: Wiley.

Wade-Benzoni, K. A., Okumura, T., Brett, J. M., Moore, D. A., Tenbrunsel, A. E., & Bazerman, M. H. (2002). Cognitions and behavior in asymmetric social dilemmas: A comparison of two cultures. *Journal of Applied Psychology, 87,* 87–95.

Wetherell, M. S. (1982). Cross-cultural studies of minimal groups: Implications for the social identity theory of intergroup relations. In H. Tajfel (Ed.), *Social identity and intergroup relations* (pp. 207–240). Cambridge, UK: Cambridge University Press.

Wilder, D. A., & Shapiro, P. (1989). Role of competition-induced anxiety in limiting the beneficial impact of positive behavior by an out-group member. *Journal of Personality and Social Psychology, 56,* 60–69.

Yamagishi, T. (2003, January). *The group heuristic: A psychological mechanism that creates a self-sustaining system of generalized exchanges.* Paper presented at the workshop on "The co-evolution of institutions and behavior", Santa Fe Institute.

Yamagishi, T., & Kiyonari, T. (2000). The group as the container of generalized reciprocity. *Social Psychology Quarterly, 63,* 116–132.

Yamagishi, T., Makimura, Y., Foddy, M., Matsuda, M., Kiyonari, T., & Platow, M. J. (2005). Comparisons of Australians and Japanese on group-based cooperation. *Asian Journal of Social Psychology, 8,* 173–190.

Yuki, M. (2003). Intergroup comparison versus intragroup relationships: A cross-cultural examination of social identity theory in North American and East Asian cultural contexts. *Social Psychology Quarterly, 66,* 166–183.

Part I

Motivation, identification, and intergroup relations

Chapter 2

Self-conceptual uncertainty and the lure of belonging

Michael A. Hogg

The social identity approach in social psychology has rested on the assumption that social identity processes are motivated by intergroup competition for status that reflects relatively positively on the social identity of ingroup members. Collective self-enhancement underpins intergroup behavior and social identification.

In this chapter I describe the role played in social identity processes by another motivation, uncertainty reduction. The point I wish to make is that people strive to reduce uncertainty about where they are located in their social field – what sort of person they are, how they should behave, how others will perceive them, and how they should relate to and interact with others. This is a fundamental motive that articulates with a desire also to feel good about oneself. I propose that the process of social identification (identifying with and belonging to a group) is a powerful force for uncertainty reduction.

After giving some background on the social identity perspective, in particular the role of self-enhancement motivation, I describe the uncertainty reduction hypothesis in the context of a discussion of social categorization, prototypicality and entitativity. I touch on extremism, and explore the motivational relationship between self-enhancement and uncertainty reduction in the social identity approach. I close with a short section on culture, self-construal, and the uncertainty-identification relationship. This is primarily a conceptual chapter so, although I do report new research mainly from my own lab, the coverage is not detailed.

Social identity and group life

Tajfel first defined social identity as ". . . the individual's knowledge that he belongs to certain social groups together with some emotional and value significance to him of this group membership" (Tajfel, 1972, p. 292). For Tajfel, the concept of social identity tied the conceptual knot between his work on social categorization (Tajfel, 1970, 1972), cognitive aspects of prejudice (Tajfel, 1969), intergroup relations (Tajfel, 1975), and social comparison between groups (Turner, 1975). This integration produced the social identity theory of intergroup relations (Tajfel & Turner, 1979), and the later social identity theory of the group, self-categorization theory (Turner, Hogg, Oakes, Reicher, & Wetherell, 1987).

This social identity approach theorizes how cognitive, social interactive, and societal processes and structures interact to produce group and intergroup phenomena (for integrative overviews see Abrams & Hogg, 2001; Hogg, 2001c, 2003; Hogg & Abrams, 1988; Hogg, Abrams, Otten, & Hinkle, 2004). The approach theorizes a wide range of group phenomena, including stereotyping, leadership, deviance, collective behavior, language, norms, social influence, attitudes, and behavior, and small group and organizational processes.

From status to self-esteem, and back again

The key feature of intergroup relations is that groups struggle to preserve or promote their status and prestige relative to other groups with which they have to, or choose to, compare themselves. This process, which is shaped by beliefs about the nature of intergroup relations and the effectiveness of various courses of action, is a reflection of competition for positive intergroup distinctiveness and thus for evaluatively positive social identity (Tajfel & Turner, 1979). Social identity based intergroup comparisons strive to maximize intergroup differences in ways that favor the ingroup (Hogg, 2000a; Turner, 1975).

Groups and their members pursue positive social identity because, all things being equal, people like to feel positive about themselves – they like to hold themselves in relatively high esteem (e.g., Sedikides & Strube, 1997), and in group contexts social identity is the aspect of self that is salient. At the individual level self-enhancement motivates social identity processes (Tajfel, 1972; Turner, 1975). Turner, in particular, linked this to an underlying motivation for self-esteem: "those aspects of an individual's self-concept, and hence self-esteem, which are anchored in his social category memberships can be referred to as his perceived social identity" (Turner, 1978, p. 105). He considered the "need for positive self-esteem" (Turner, 1982, p. 33) to be a fundamental human motivation which, under heightened social identity salience, is satisfied by relatively positive evaluation of one's own group. He stated: "I do assume that there is a need for positive self-esteem, not as an axiom, but on the basis of extensive research (into, for example, social comparison, cognitive dissonance, interpersonal attraction, self-presentation, defensive attribution, and so on)" (Turner, 1981, p. 133).

The motivational role of self-esteem was formalized by Abrams and Hogg (1988) who argued that if self-esteem motivated social identity processes, then low self-esteem should promote group identification and group identification should raise self-esteem. Research has found some evidence for identification raising self-esteem, but much less evidence for low self-esteem motivating social identification (see Rubin & Hewstone, 1998). One of the key problems with the self-esteem hypothesis is that of level of explanation – in invoking *self*-esteem, what level of self are we talking about? From a social identity point of view *personal* self-esteem would not be expected to play any role in social identity processes, however collective self-esteem would – a point exploited by Crocker and Luhtanen (1990; Luhtanen & Crocker, 1992).

Probably the safest conclusion to be drawn from research on self-esteem and social identity is that although self-enhancement is a powerful social motive, in group contexts it is only collective self-esteem, in other words the positivity of social identity, that is motivationally relevant. In many respects we may not need to invoke self-esteem at all to explain group behavior. We can simply argue that people strive to identify with groups that are positively distinctive – and this of course returns us to the original social identity theory of intergroup relations decribed by Tajfel (1972, 1975) and by Tajfel and Turner (1979).

Self-enhancement and social connectedness

Self-enhancement clearly plays a motivational role in social identity processes, however it is at the level of *collective* self that this motivation operates. This explains why groups struggle in all sorts of creative ways to be better than one another, and probably why, within groups, members compete to be seen as central members of valued groups. However, this does not really answer the question of what motivates people to belong to groups in the first place. Why does social identity exist, and why is it so important to human beings?

One answer to this question is provided by the sociometer hypothesis (Baumeister & Leary, 1995; Leary, Tambor, Terdal, & Downs, 1995). People do not pursue self-esteem, rather they strive to be socially connected to other people. People are fundamentally social because they depend on others for their survival and for the survival of the species, and so the establishment and maintenance of social connections makes one feel good – self-esteem is "merely" an indicator of how well socially connected one feels. This analysis does not distinguish among different types of social connections (e.g., interpersonal vs. group), and so in that sense does not actually answer the question of why *social* identity is so important.

Social categorization and uncertainty reduction

A different answer to the question of why social identity exists in the first place is that people have a basic need to reduce uncertainty about the social world and their place within it, and that this need is satisfied by social categorization. Uncertainty reduction may work in conjunction with collective self-enhancement to motivate social identity processes and configure social identity phenomena – uncertainty reduction may be a fundamental social identity motivation (Hogg, 2000b, 2001b, 2004; Hogg & Mullin, 1999).

The idea that social identity is motivated by uncertainty reduction pivots on the key role that social categorization plays in group life – without social categories there would, of course, be no social identities. We can now ask the question, what motivates social categorization – what does social categorization buy us?

Categories and prototypes

From a social identity perspective, social categories are cognitively represented as prototypes (Turner et al., 1987; also see Hogg, 2001c) – fuzzy sets of attributes that capture a family resemblance among members of one group and differentiate that group from relevant other groups (e.g., Cantor & Mischel, 1979). An individual member is unlikely to embody all prototypical attributes, although some members will embody the prototype better than others and thus be more prototypical. Prototypes capture similarities within groups and differences between groups, and thus they narrow attentional focus onto a limited set of human attributes (perceptions, attitudes, feelings, behaviors) that serve this function. Prototypes, and thus categories, replace boundless diversity and perceptual possibility with a bounded reality.

Prototypes obey the meta-contrast principle – they maximize the ratio of differences between ingroup and outgroup members to differences among ingroup members. They make groups more distinctive, and endow them with entitativity – the property of a group, resting on clear boundaries, internal homogeneity, clear internal structure, and common fate, which makes a group appear "groupy" (e.g., Hamilton & Sherman, 1996; Lickel et al., 2000). Because of meta-contrast, the group prototype is usually not the central tendency of a group but is displaced from the mean in a direction away from the relevant outgroup – prototypes are generally polarized and are therefore often more ideal than real.

People carry prototypes in their head (for example one's prototype of "students"), but they can be modified by comparative context – for example students in comparison to high-school kids vs. students in comparison to bankers. Prototypes can also be constructed in situ – for example if you rounded a corner and stumbled upon a group of Martians you would need to develop a prototype there and then.

Categorization and depersonalization

Social perception and subjective social reality are structured, to a significant extent, by categories – instead of a limitless variety of unique individuals there is a much smaller number of social categories. The act of categorizing someone assigns the relevant prototype to that person. Instead of seeing a unique person we see a prototype – a process of depersonalization. The act of categorizing oneself has exactly the same effect on self-perception – we embody the contextually relevant ingroup prototype. The prototype governs perception, affect, and behavior – it describes, and more importantly prescribes, how we think, feel, and behave.

Social categorization-based depersonalization reduces uncertainty in multiple ways –resting on the descriptive and prescriptive properties of the relevant ingroup and outgroup prototype. Social categorization tells us what someone thinks and feels, how someone will behave, and how they will treat us. Self-categorization provides us with an identity that regulates our interaction with others as ingroup or outgroup members – it tells us what to expect of ourselves and others, and thus renders the social world and our place within it relatively predictable. Uncertainty is reduced.

The nature of group life means that prototypes tend to be shared – for example, members of group-A are likely to agree on their prototype of group-A and their prototype of a rival group-B. In this sense social stereotypes and group norms are shared prototypes. Because prototypes are shared, depersonalization provides consensual support, from one's ingroup, for one's identity, perceptions, feelings, and behaviors. Consensual validation is another, powerful, way in which social categorization and group identification reduce uncertainty.

Uncertainty and identification in minimal group settings

The idea that uncertainty reduction is a motivation for social categorization generates the simple prediction that people will contextually identify with a given group more strongly (or at all) if they are uncertain. A number of minimal group studies support this prediction – people identified with minimal groups and engaged in ingroup favoritism and intergroup discrimination only when they were categorized under uncertainty (e.g., Grieve & Hogg, 1999) – for an overview of this program of research see Hogg (2000b) and Hogg and Mullin (1999). In these studies uncertainty was manipulated in a variety of ways. For example, participants described what they thought was happening in ambiguous or unambiguous pictures, or they estimated the number of objects displayed in pictures in which there were very few objects or so many objects that they could only make a wild guess. Other studies in the series showed that uncertainty was a stronger motivation for identification if participants were uncertain about something they felt was important and self-relevant, and if the prototypical properties of the available social category were relevant to the focus of uncertainty.

Uncertainty and entitativity

Identification reduces uncertainty because social categorization makes salient ingroup and outgroup prototypes that structure social interaction and prescribe thought, feeling, and action. This prompts the question of what kinds of prototypes, groups, and identities are most effective at reducing uncertainty. The answer is quite straightforward (Hogg, 2004) – relatively simple prototypes that are unambiguous, prescriptive, consensual, and enduring.

Extreme uncertainty and totalist groups

Taken to an extreme, the sorts of groups with which these prototypes are associated are highly distinctive – they have high entitativity (e.g., Yzerbyt, Castano, Leyens, & Paladino, 2000) and impermeable membership boundaries (e.g., Yzerbyt, Leyens, & Bellour, 1995). They are ones with orthodox belief systems and negative outgroup stereotypes. They are intolerant of people who are different from themselves and, in particular, intolerant and punitive of ingroup dissenters, critics, and deviants (Hogg, 2005). They are also often relatively authoritarian and hierarchically structured with a powerful leader or leadership clique (Hogg, 2001a; Hogg & van Knippenberg, 2003), or a powerful integrating idea or ideology. Such groups work hard to insulate their belief systems and their identities (their prototypes) from ideological attack from outside (or inside) that might raise uncertainty. Within these groups, members work particularly hard to be central and to appear highly prototypical – they themselves are, therefore, conformist and may act like zealots.

This analysis links uncertainty reduction to extremism and totalism (cf. Baron, Crawley, & Paulina, 2003; Staub, 1989). This outcome is most likely when uncertainty is chronic and extreme – for example, where there are economic and social disasters or a history of intergroup threat and hostility, or where people experience serious identity crises due perhaps to relocation, redundancy, adolescence, or family and relationship crises. More usually, uncertainty, particularly self-conceptual uncertainty, simply motivates people to construct a sense of self that reduces uncertainty about their social location. Such identities and groups may be distinctive and relatively high in entitativity, but they are certainly not totalist. Totalism is an extreme response to extreme uncertainty.

Buffers against totalism

The development and maintenance of extremist identities are buffered by a variety of factors. People generally have a number of personal and social identities that contribute to an overall sense of self-conceptual certainty, so no single group or personal identity saturates the self-concept (cults, some families, and being "in love" may be exceptions). Orthodoxy is hard work to maintain, and in the long run requires a formidable edifice of implicit and explicit rules and sanctions. The prototype needs to be policed for ideological purity and to defend against revisionism, dissent, and deviance. Likewise, hierarchy and authoritarian leadership are difficult to maintain because they rest on the exercise of power, with all the infrastructure that requires. Ultimately, highly orthodox groups with hierarchical leadership are not always the most effective types of group – they are prone to group-think and tend to inhibit innovation and creativity (e.g., Nemeth & Staw, 1989; Stasser, Stewart, & Wittenbaum, 1995; Tindale, Kameda, & Hinsz, 2003). Such groups may not be positioned to respond effectively to social change, and may, paradoxically, disintegrate rather easily.

High-entitativity orthodox groups generally call for almost complete subjugation of individual self to collective self, and so, drawing on Brewer's (1991) theory of optimal distinctiveness, they oversatisfy people's need for inclusion/sameness. There will, therefore, be some motivation among members to strive for a degree of distinctiveness/uniqueness within or outside the group, in order to attain a state of optimal distinctiveness.

Finally, uncertainty reduction is a continuous process in which life presents us with uncertainties to resolve. Although (self-conceptual) uncertainty is aversive and people try to minimize it, overwhelming and enduring social certainty may be stultifying. People (and groups) may seek small social uncertainties to resolve – one might talk of "uncertainty management" or even "optimal uncertainty". However, unless the social context remains absolutely static, uncertainty is a reality of the dynamic nature of everyday life – of meeting new people in new contexts, of sudden changes in intergroup relations or intragroup composition and structure, and so forth. The pursuit of uncertainty reduction does not deliver a static world that is devoid of diversity, a world of maximized entropy – rather it reduces subjective uncertainty to an acceptable level that allows one to act adaptively. In this respect, uncertainty reduction operates within the parameters of the "cognitive miser" or "cognitive tactician" models of social cognition.

Studies of uncertainty and identification with high entitativity groups

In Australia at the end of the 1990s an ultra-conservative political party, called *One Nation*, emerged. It had the properties of extremist right-wing parties that are xenophobic, orthodox, racist, nationalistic, anti-immigration, and anti-intellectual (see Rapley, 1998). It was also a high-entitativity group, with a clear and simple prototype. Hogg and Reid (1998) administered a questionnaire to about 200 university students at a large urban and a smaller regional university in south-east Queensland. We asked respondents questions about their feelings of uncertainty about their own economic, employment, and interpersonal future, and about the economic and cultural future of Australia. We also focused on self-conceptual uncertainty. Since Australian university students typically did not endorse *One Nation*, we framed questions about identification with *One Nation* rather carefully – focusing on endorsement of *One Nation*'s ideology and world-view rather than on identifying with *One Nation* itself. Regression analyses revealed, as predicted, that increasing subjective uncertainty was associated with increasing endorsement of *One Nation*'s world-view.

A second piece of research capitalized on the fact that students arriving at university for the first time can experience uncertainty, including uncertainty about how they will fit in and what sort of identity they will have. They can also join university clubs and societies that vary in terms of entitativity and prototype clarity. We conducted two questionnaire studies (Hogg & Sussman, 1999), one with new psychology students at the University of Queensland and the other with new students at Princeton University – in each case we had about 200 respondents. At the start of the semester we measured demographic and background variables, as well as the focal variables of (a) self-conceptual uncertainty, (b) intention to join clubs and societies, and (c) perception of how distinctive they felt the clubs they were intending to join were relative to other clubs (a measure of entitativity). Using hierarchical multiple regression to control for demographic and background variables, we found, for both samples, a positive association between uncertainty and the intention to join clubs, to join more clubs, and to join clubs that were distinctive.

With the Princeton sample we administered a follow-up questionnaire near the end of the academic year to re-measure uncertainty and to measure respondents' identification with clubs and societies they had joined. We found that uncertainty at time-one predicted identification with clubs at time-two, and that at time-two identification was associated with a reduction of uncertainty from time-one. In line with the uncertainty reduction hypothesis, these studies suggest that the more self-conceptually uncertain people are, the more they want to join groups, in particular high-entitativity groups with clear prototypes, and the more strongly they identify with these groups, the greater the reduction in uncertainty.

Finally, D. Sherman, Hogg, and Maitner (2004) conducted a questionnaire study of 68 striking grocery store employees in Santa Barbara in December 2003, near the end of a five-month strike over pay and conditions. We measured (a) uncertainty about the future, (b) identification with the striking grocery store employees, (c) perceptions of ingroup groupness, and (d) perceptions of intergroup attitude polarization between the strikers and the non-union labor that had been brought in by the stores to replace them. Groupness and polarization were combined into a single scale that captured entitativity. In a regression format we found that uncertainty predicted identification and entitativity, and identification predicted entitativity. The uncertainty–entitativity relationship was fully mediated by identification. With increasing uncertainty about the future, strikers identified more strongly with their group and accentuated the perceived entitativity and distinctiveness of their group.

Uncertainty reduction and self-enhancement

Uncertainty reduction plays a motivational role in social identification – begging the question of how uncertainty reduction and self-enhancement are related. Because social categorization lies at the heart of social identification, and because social categorization so decisively reduces uncertainty, uncertainty reduction may be the most basic motivation for social identification. However, self-evaluation also plays a critical role because people would rather belong to positively distinctive groups.

One question that can be asked is whether studies of uncertainty and identification are actually studies of self-enhancement motivation. Feeling uncertain may cause one to have lower self-esteem, particularly when uncertainty is manipulated via task difficulty, and so identification may be motivated by self-enhancement not uncertainty reduction. Of course, finding something difficult does not necessarily make one feel less positive about oneself.

Hogg and Svensson (2006) conducted two experiments to address this concern. The first experiment was a $2 \times 2 \times 2$ computer-mediated minimal group style study in which state self-esteem was measured immediately after judgmental uncertainty was manipulated via a difficult or easy task. Participants ($N = 168$) then had, or did not have, the opportunity to self-affirm prior to indicating their identification with a more or less self-definitionally relevant social group. In the second experiment participants ($N = 101$) were in face-to-face interactive groups. Judgmental uncertainty and self-affirmation only were manipulated (2×2), and self-esteem was not measured. As predicted, across the two experiments participants identified more strongly under high than low uncertainty, particularly with a highly self-relevant group. The effect was not influenced by self-affirmation or by self-esteem. In Experiment 1, when state self-esteem was partialed out uncertainty still motivated identification, and in both experiments uncertain participants who had self-affirmed still identified. The clear conclusion is that uncertainty motivates identification, quite independently of any self-enhancement motivation.

So, how are the two motivations related? Perhaps they interact? Reid and Hogg (2005) conducted two experiments ($N = 64$ and 210) in which uncertainty and group status (thus self-enhancement concerns) were orthogonally manipulated. They found that where uncertainty was high, participants identified with the group irrespective of its status – behavior was motivated only by uncertainty reduction. When uncertainty was low, they were driven by self-enhancement concerns and only identified with the high-status group. Another way to read this is that participants were, under conditions of elevated subjective uncertainty, prepared to identify with a low-status, non-self-enhancing group. This finding fits nicely with what we know about real intergroup relations. In many cases subordinate groups do not rise up to challenge the status quo, but engage in system justification (e.g., Jost & Kramer, 2002) or hierarchy legitimizing (e.g., Sidanius, Levin, Federico, & Pratto, 2001) tactics that maintain their subordinate status and identity. From an uncertainty reduction perspective we can argue that sometimes the prospect of uncertainty posed by challenging the system can be so aversive that people would rather be certain of their place in the world than risk improving their status.

Another key question, to do with what conditions provoke uncertainty reduction or self-enhancement motivation, can be answered in terms of identity threat (e.g., Hogg, 2005; Hogg, Fielding, & Darley, 2005; Hogg & Hornsey, in press). Where intergroup comparisons, wider societal perceptions, or prospects for action threaten group status or the valence of one's social identity, then self-enhancement is the primary motive that governs social identity processes. Where the distinctiveness or entitativity of one's group, or the clarity of what the group represents, the integrity of its prototype, is threatened, then uncertainty reduction is the primary motivation that guides behavior. Of course in many real contexts both threats co-occur.

Uncertainty reduction and self-enhancement may also provide the motivational framework for social identity salience. Self-categorization theory specifies the interaction of "accessibility" and "fit" as the principle governing social identity salience (Turner et al., 1987). A social categorization becomes psychologically salient to the extent that the categorization is chronically accessible in memory and perceptually accessible in the situation, and the categorization fits relevant similarities and differences among people (structural fit) and makes sense of people's behavior (normative fit). At first sight there is no motivational component to this analysis, and indeed the apparent absence of a motivational emphasis in self-categorization theory has led some people to argue that self-categorization theory and social identity theory are two entirely different theories (e.g., S. J. Sherman, Hamilton, & Lewis, 1999). However, if one adopts a motivated tactician model of social cognition (e.g., Taylor, 1998) then the problem is resolved – self-enhancement and uncertainty reduction motivations guide category retrieval (accessibility) and judgments of category fit, and thus impact which categorizations and what forms of particular categorizations become psychologically salient.

Culture and identification under uncertainty

The motivation to reduce uncertainty is a general human motive. Its strength varies as a function of contextual factors, such as group entitativity threat, socioeconomic crises, social change, and so forth. There are also individual differences in the extent to which people seek out or avoid uncertainty (e.g., Kruglanski & Webster, 1996; Sorrentino & Roney, 2000).

There may also be cultural differences in avoidance of uncertainty. For example, one of Hofstede's (1980) four dimensions to differentiate cultures was uncertainty avoidance. Western cultures (e.g., Denmark) are low on uncertainty avoidance, whereas Eastern cultures (e.g., Japan) are high on uncertainty avoidance. Related to uncertainty avoidance, Schwartz (1992) reported that Eastern cultures are less open to change. Overall, relative to Western cultures, Eastern cultures are not only more uncertainty avoidant and less open to change, but they are also more collectivist (e.g., Hofstede, 1980) and they are associated with a more interdependent self-concept (e.g., Markus & Kitayama, 1991) and a more relational self-concept (e.g., Brewer & Gardner, 1996; Yuki, 2003) – for a critical review see Oyserman, Coon, and Kemmelmeier (2002). There appears to be an association between a stronger desire to reduce or avoid uncertainty and self-conception in more collectivist, interdependent, or relational terms. This is consistent with the uncertainty reduction hypothesis – where the need to reduce uncertainty is elevated, people identify more strongly with groups, particularly high-entitativity groups.

Hogg and Alit (2004) conducted a preliminary study to test the hypothesis that uncertainty-based identification with high-entitativity groups would be accentuated among people with a stronger inclination towards collectivist/interdependent/relational self-construal. Participants were 115 Indonesian tertiary students from the island of Bali, and 105 Australian tertiary students from the city of Brisbane ($N = 220$). They completed a pencil-and-paper role-playing exercise in which we first measured independent–interdependent self-construal (median split produced "independents" and "interdependents"), had them perform a difficult or easy perception task (a standard uncertainty manipulation), and then had them role-play being in a high- or low-entitativity discussion group (entitativity manipulation). The key dependent measure was a multi-item scale measuring identification with the group. The three-way interaction was significant, $F(1, 212) = 4.97$, $p < .05$. Under high uncertainty, participants identified more strongly with a high- than a low-entitativity group, and the effect was stronger for interdependent, $F(1, 212) = 10.39$, $p < .001$, than independent participants, $F(1, 212) = 5.43$, $p < .05$.

Closing comments

Social identity processes are driven by two basic motivations – self-enhancement and uncertainty reduction. Self-enhancement underpins competition for evaluatively positive social identity. Uncertainty reduction underpins social categorization and the pursuit of entitativity and intergroup distinctiveness. Social contextual factors and individual life experiences influence which motives are stronger in which contexts and how strong the motives are, and therefore the sorts of group or interpersonal behaviors people engage in.

This chapter focuses on uncertainty reduction. Uncertainty reduction is a basic human motive, because uncertainty is a poor basis for adaptive action (being unsure about whether to cuddle or flee from a Rottweiler foaming at the mouth would not be adaptive). Uncertainty can be reduced in many ways (for example, I can read a book to find something out), however the most basic uncertainty about one's self-concept and one's transactions with other human beings is most effectively managed by social identity.

Social categorization of self and others depersonalizes perception, thought, feeling, and behavior to conform to the relevant ingroup or outgroup prototype. Prototypes define who you and others are, how you should interact with and treat others, how they will interact with and treat you. The most effective prototypes are ones that are simple, unambiguous, clearly prescriptive, and consensual. Typically, prototypes with these properties define membership in distinctive high-entitativity groups – in extreme cases such groups will be orthodox, insular, intolerant of outgroups and of ingroup dissent, and authoritarian, with strong leaders and a pronounced hierarchical structure. However, such totalism may be unstable – the last resort for people under extreme uncertainty.

Self-conceptual uncertainty can, of course, be resolved via interpersonal relationships that define personal identity – if one never encountered strangers this would probably be enough. However, in a world where one is continually interacting with strangers one needs to rely on social categorization to generate prototypes that structure expectations and configure action. Social identity assumes a greater role than personal identity.

Uncertainty reduction provides an explanation for why, in general, social structures remain stable and social change is more the exception than the rule. Uncertainty is a powerful inhibitor of risk taking and social change, even where one's own group has relatively low status and one needs to go to great lengths to derive a positive sense of self from it. However, self-enhancement and uncertainty reduction interact to govern when and how groups justify the status quo or strive to change it. In addition, uncertainty reduction is not an end state but a process. People (and groups) seek small uncertainties to resolve, including self-conceptual uncertainty – uncertainty is exciting and motivating, and there are individual, cultural, and developmental differences in tolerance for uncertainty.

In conclusion, uncertainty reduction completes the motivational platform for social identity processes by making explicit the motivation for the social categorization process that underpins collective self-conception and group and intergroup phenomena. Uncertainty reduction and self-enhancement provide the motivational frame for social categorization and prototype-based depersonalization, and for the general form and context-specific content of group processes and intergroup relations.

Author note

The writing of this chapter, and my own research reported in the chapter, were made possible by grant support from the Australian Research Council (ARC). The chapter was written while I was spending a sabbatical year as a Visiting Professor in the Department of Psychology at the University of California, Santa Barbara.

References

Abrams, D., & Hogg, M. A. (1988). Comments on the motivational status of self-esteem in social identity and intergroup discrimination. *European Journal of Social Psychology, 18,* 317–334.

Abrams, D., & Hogg, M. A. (2001). Collective identity: Group membership and self-conception. In M. A. Hogg & R. S. Tindale (Eds.), *Blackwell handbook of social psychology: Group processes* (pp. 425–460). Oxford, UK: Blackwell.

Baron, R. S., Crawley, K., & Paulina, D. (2003). Aberrations of power: Leadership in totalist groups. In D. van Knippenberg & M. A. Hogg (Eds.), *Leadership and power: Identity processes in groups and organizations* (pp. 169–183). London: Sage.

Baumeister, R. F., & Leary, M. R. (1995). The need to belong: Desire for interpersonal attachments as a fundamental human motivation. *Psychological Bulletin, 117,* 497–529.

Brewer, M. B. (1991). The social self: On being the same and different at the same time. *Personality and Social Psychology Bulletin, 17,* 475–482.

Brewer, M. B., & Gardner, W. L. (1996). Who is this "We"? Levels of collective identity and self representations. *Journal of Personality and Social Psychology, 71,* 83–93.

Cantor, N., & Mischel, W. (1979). Prototypes in person perception. In L. Berkowitz (Ed.), *Advances in experimental social psychology* (Vol. 12, pp. 3–52). San Diego, CA: Academic Press.

Crocker, J., & Luhtanen, R. (1990). Collective self-esteem and ingroup bias. *Journal of Personality and Social Psychology, 58,* 60–67.

Grieve, P. G., & Hogg, M. A. (1999). Subjective uncertainty and intergroup discrimination in the minimal group situation. *Personality and Social Psychology Bulletin, 25*, 926–940.

Hamilton, D. L., & Sherman, S. J. (1996). Perceiving persons and groups. *Psychological Review, 103*, 336–355.

Hofstede, G. (1980). *Culture's consequences: International differences in work-related values.* Beverly Hills, CA: Sage.

Hogg, M. A. (2000a). Social identity and social comparison. In J. Suls & L. Wheeler (Eds.), *Handbook of social comparison: Theory and research* (pp. 401–421). New York: Kluwer/Plenum.

Hogg, M. A. (2000b). Subjective uncertainty reduction through self-categorization: A motivational theory of social identity processes and group phenomena. In W. Stroebe & M. Hewstone (Eds.), *European review of social psychology* (Vol. 11, 223–255). Chichester, UK: Wiley.

Hogg, M. A. (2001a). From prototypicality to power: A social identity analysis of leadership. In S. R. Thye, E. J. Lawler, M. W. Macy, & H. A. Walker (Eds.), *Advances in group processes* (Vol. 18, pp. 1–30). Oxford, UK: Elsevier Science.

Hogg, M. A. (2001b). Self-categorization and subjective uncertainty resolution: Cognitive and motivational facets of social identity and group membership. In J. P. Forgas, K. D. Williams, & L. Wheeler (Eds.), *The social mind: Cognitive and motivational aspects of interpersonal behavior* (pp. 323–349). New York: Cambridge University Press.

Hogg, M. A. (2001c). Social categorization, depersonalization, and group behavior. In M. A. Hogg & R. S. Tindale (Eds.), *Blackwell handbook of social psychology: Group processes* (pp. 56–85). Oxford, UK: Blackwell.

Hogg, M. A. (2003). Social identity. In M. R. Leary & J. P. Tangney (Eds.), *Handbook of self and identity* (pp. 462–479). New York: Guilford Press.

Hogg, M. A. (2004). Uncertainty and extremism: Identification with high entitativity groups under conditions of uncertainty. In V. Y. Yzerbyt, C. M. Judd, & O. Corneille (Eds.), *The psychology of group perception: Perceived variability, entitativity, and essentialism* (pp. 401–418). New York: Psychology Press.

Hogg. M. A. (2005). All animals are equal but some animals are more equal than others: Social identity and marginal membership. In K. D. Williams, J. P. Forgas, & W. von Hippel (Eds.), *The social outcast: Ostracism, social exclusion, rejection, and bullying.* New York: Psychology Press.

Hogg, M. A., & Abrams, D. (1988). *Social identifications: A social psychology of intergroup relations and group processes.* London: Routledge.

Hogg, M. A., Abrams, D., Otten, S., & Hinkle, S. (2004). The social identity perspective: Intergroup relations, self-conception, and small groups. *Small Group Research, 35*, 246–276.

Hogg, M. A., & Alit, L. (2004). *Identification under uncertainty: Moderation by entitativity and self-construal preference.* Unpublished manuscript, University of Queensland, Australia.

Hogg, M. A., Fielding, K. S., & Darley, J. (2005). Fringe dwellers: Processes of deviance and marginalization in groups. In D. Abrams, M. A. Hogg, & J. Marques (Eds.), *Social psychology of inclusion and exclusion* (pp. 191–210). Philadelphia: Psychology Press.

Hogg, M. A., & Hornsey, M. J. (in press). Self-concept threat and multiple categorization within groups. In R. J. Crisp & M. Hewstone (Eds.), *Multiple social categorization: Processes, models, and applications.* New York: Psychology Press.

Hogg, M. A., & Mullin, B.-A. (1999). Joining groups to reduce uncertainty: Subjective uncertainty reduction and group identification. In D. Abrams & M. A. Hogg (Eds.), *Social identity and social cognition* (pp. 249–279). Oxford, UK: Blackwell.

Hogg, M. A., & Reid, S. A. (1998). *Uncertainty, social identification and extremism in Australia.* Unpublished manuscript, University of Queensland, Australia.

Hogg, M. A., & Sussman, K. (1999). *Uncertainty, entitativity, and group identification: Studies of student affiliation with campus clubs and societies.* Unpublished manuscript, University of Queensland, Australia.

Hogg, M. A., & Svensson, A. (2006). *Uncertainty reduction, self-esteem and group identification.* Manuscript submitted for publication.

Hogg, M. A., & van Knippenberg, D. (2003). Social identity and leadership processes in groups. In M. P. Zanna (Ed.), *Advances in experimental social psychology* (Vol. 35, pp. 1–52). San Diego, CA: Academic Press.

Jost, J. T., & Kramer, R. M. (2002). The system justification motive in intergroup relations. In D. M. Mackie & E. R. Smith (Eds.), *From prejudice to intergroup emotions: Differentiated reactions to social groups* (pp. 227–245). New York: Psychology Press.

Kruglanski, A. W., & Webster, D. M. (1996). Motivated closing of the mind: "Seizing" and "freezing". *Psychological Review, 103,* 263–283.

Leary, M. R., Tambor, E. S., Terdal, S. K., & Downs, D. L. (1995). Self-esteem as an interpersonal monitor: The sociometer hypothesis. *Journal of Personality and Social Psychology, 68,* 518–530.

Lickel, B., Hamilton, D. L., Wieczorkowska, G., Lewis, A., Sherman, S. J., & Uhles, A. N. (2000). Varieties of groups and the perception of group entitativity. *Journal of Personality and Social Psychology, 78,* 223–246.

Luhtanen, R., & Crocker, J. (1992). A collective self-esteem scale: Self-evaluation of one's social identity. *Personality and Social Psychology Bulletin, 18,* 302–318.

Markus, H. R., & Kitayama, S. (1991). Culture and the self: Implications for cognition, emotion, and motivation. *Psychological Review, 98,* 224–253.

Nemeth, C. J., & Staw, B. M. (1989). The tradeoffs of social control and innovation in groups and organizations. In L. Berkowitz (Ed.), *Advances in experimental social psychology* (Vol. 22, pp. 175–210). San Diego, CA: Academic Press.

Oyserman, D., Coon, H. M., & Kemmelmeier, M. (2002). Rethinking individualism and collectivism: Evaluation of theoretical assumptions and meta-analyses. *Psychological Bulletin, 128,* 3–72.

Rapley, M. (1998). "Just an ordinary Australian": Self-categorization and the discursive construction of facticity in "new racist" political rhetoric. *British Journal of Social Psychology, 37,* 325–344.

Reid, S. A., & Hogg, M. A. (2005). Uncertainty reduction, self-enhancement and ingroup identification. *Personality and Social Psychology Bulletin, 31,* 804–817.

Rubin, M., & Hewstone, M. (1998). Social identity theory's self-esteem hypothesis: A review and some suggestions for clarification. *Personality and Social Psychology Review, 2,* 40–62.

Schwartz, S. H. (1992). Universals in the content and structure of values: Theoretical advances and empirical tests in 20 countries. In M. P. Zanna (Ed.), *Advances in experimental social psychology* (Vol. 25, pp. 1–65). San Diego, CA: Academic Press.

Sedikides, C., & Strube, M. J. (1997). Self-evaluation: To thine own self be good, to thine own self be sure, to thine own self be true, and to thine own self be better. In M. P. Zanna (Ed.), *Advances in experimental social psychology* (Vol. 29, pp. 209–269). San Diego, CA: Academic Press.

Sherman, D., Hogg, M. A., & Maitner, A. T. (2004). *Uncertainty, identification and accentuation: A study of striking grocery store employees.* Unpublished manuscript, University of California, Santa Barbara.

Sherman, S. J., Hamilton, D. L., & Lewis, A. (1999). Perceived entitativity and the social identity value of group memberships. In D. Abrams & M. A. Hogg (Eds.), *Social identity and social cognition* (pp. 80–110). Oxford, UK: Blackwell.

Sidanius, J., Levin, S., Federico, C. M., & Pratto, F. (2001). Legitimizing ideologies: The social dominance approach. In J. T. Jost & B. Major (Eds.), *The psychology of legitimacy: Emerging perspectives on ideology, justice, and intergroup relations* (pp. 307–331). New York: Cambridge University Press.

Sorrentino, R. M., & Roney, C. J. R. (2000). *The uncertain mind: Individual differences in facing the unknown.* Philadelphia: Psychology Press.

Stasser, G., Stewart, D. D., & Wittenbaum, G. M. (1995). Expert roles and information exchange during discussion: The importance of knowing who knows what. *Journal of Experimental Social Psychology, 31,* 244–265.

Staub, E. (1989). *The roots of evil: The origins of genocide and other group violence.* New York: Cambridge University Press.

Tajfel, H. (1969). Cognitive aspects of prejudice. *Journal of Social Issues, 25,* 79–97.

Tajfel, H. (1970). Experiments in intergroup discrimination. *Scientific American, 223,* 96–102.

Tajfel, H. (1972). Social categorization. English manuscript of "La catégorisation sociale". In S. Moscovici (Ed.), *Introduction à la psychologie sociale* (Vol. 1, pp. 272–302). Paris: Larousse.

Tajfel, H. (1975). The exit of social mobility and the voice of social change: Notes on the social psychology of intergroup relations. *Social Science Information, 14,* 101–118.

Tajfel, H., & Turner, J. C. (1979). An integrative theory of intergroup conflict. In W. G. Austin & S. Worchel (Eds.), *The social psychology of intergroup relations* (pp. 33–47). Monterey, CA: Brooks/Cole.

Taylor, S. E. (1998). The social being in social psychology. In D. T. Gilbert, S. T. Fiske, & G. Lindzey (Eds.), *The handbook of social psychology* (4th ed., Vol. 1, pp. 58–95). New York: McGraw-Hill.

Tindale, R. S., Kameda, T., & Hinsz, V. B. (2003). Group decision-making. In M. A. Hogg & J. Cooper (Eds.), *The Sage handbook of social psychology* (pp. 381–403). London: Sage.

Turner, J. C. (1975). Social comparison and social identity: Some prospects for intergroup behaviour. *European Journal of Social Psychology, 5,* 5–34.

Turner, J. C. (1978). Social categorization and social discrimination in the minimal group paradigm. In H. Tajfel (Ed.), *Differentiation between social groups: Studies in the social psychology of intergroup relations* (pp. 101–140). London: Academic Press.

Turner, J. C. (1981). Redefining the social group: A reply to the commentaries. *Cahiers de Psychologie Cognitive*, *1*, 131–138.

Turner, J. C. (1982). Towards a cognitive redefinition of the social group. In H. Tajfel (Ed.), *Social identity and intergroup relations* (pp. 15–40). Cambridge, UK: Cambridge University Press.

Turner, J. C., Hogg, M. A., Oakes, P. J., Reicher, S. D., & Wetherell, M. S. (1987). *Rediscovering the social group: A self-categorization theory*. Oxford, UK: Blackwell.

Yuki, M. (2003). Intergroup comparison versus intragroup relationships: A cross-cultural examination of social identity theory in North American and East Asian cultural contexts. *Social Psychology Quarterly*, *66*, 166–183.

Yzerbyt, V. Y., Castano, E., Leyens, J.-Ph., & Paladino, M. P. (2000). The primacy of the ingroup: The interplay of entitativity and identification. In W. Stroebe & M. Hewstone (Eds.), *European review of social psychology* (Vol. 11, 257–275). Chichester, UK: Wiley.

Yzerbyt, V. Y., Leyens, J.-Ph., & Bellour, F. (1995). The ingroup overexclusion effect: Identity concerns in decisions about group membership. *European Journal of Social Psychology*, *25*, 1–16.

Chapter 3

A comparison of motivational theories of identification

Dora Capozza, Rupert Brown, Sabina Aharpour, and Rossella Falvo

Introduction

As should be clear from most of the chapters of this book, what has characterized what we may broadly describe as the "social identity tradition" in intergroup relations has been its depiction of intergroup phenomena as being determined by some powerful social psychological *motives*. In other words, people are "driven" to manifest various intergroup biases, emotions, and behaviors by a presumed lack in certain key needs. This perspective can be contrasted with other approaches – again, rather loosely, we might subsume them under the label "socio-cognitive" – in which the hypothesized causal factors are the operation of some relatively autonomous, sometimes automatic, cognitive processes (e.g., Fiske & Taylor, 1991). Of course, such a simplistic polarization does grave injustice to many theories that have attempted to bridge this divide, some of which are well represented in recent publications (e.g., Abrams & Hogg, 1999; Sedikides & Brewer, 2001). Nevertheless, it is safe to say that the last decade or so has seen a resurgence of motivational approaches. Inspired by social identity theory (Tajfel, 1981; Tajfel & Turner, 1979), in which group (and self) enhancement is posited as the primary motivation, we have seen optimal distinctiveness theory, in which countervailing needs for distinctiveness and inclusion are proposed (Brewer, 1991), uncertainty reduction theory, in which a desire for clarity and meaning is seen as the primary driver of group members' behavior (Hogg, 2000), and functional models in which several functions are suggested as underlying identification and intergroup processes (see Deaux, Reid, Mizrahi, & Cotting, 1999). Our aim in this chapter is to examine the predictive power of some of these motivational accounts in three empirical studies.

In the first study, a cross-sectional survey, a model was tested where each of the three motivations – self-enhancement, uncertainty reduction, need for inclusion and distinctiveness – independently influence ingroup identification; structural equation models were used. Studies 2 and 3 are relevant to the functional model of social identities (Deaux et al., 1999; see also Aharpour & Brown, 2002). In Study 2, an experiment performed on a natural group, identity functions were manipulated while holding constant group membership. Our goal was to ascertain if emphasizing one class of functions or another (e.g., materialistic vs. socio-emotional) would affect the relationship between identification and ingroup bias. In Study 3, which was longitudinal, we analyzed whether identity functions change over a group life-span. The idea is that different functions may underpin group affiliations, functions – and social identity processes – being responsive to the situational constraints and demands.

Social identity theory

According to social identity theory, individuals need to belong to groups which enhance or do not diminish their self-esteem. The more a group satisfies the need for self-esteem, the stronger self-definition is in terms of the prototypical attributes of the group, the more positively one's own group membership is evaluated, and the more intense are the positive emotions linked to that membership. From social identity theory, moreover, the prediction is derived that the more central the ingroup is to the self-concept (strength of identification), the more one should differentiate in its favor on evaluative dimensions or resource allocation tasks (e.g., Brown, 2000; for minimal groups see the results by Perreault & Bourhis, 1999). However, a correlation between identification and differentiation in favor of the ingroup is not always found (Hinkle & Brown, 1990). The effect of identification may be curbed by contextual factors such as the norms or prototypes of the ingroup which, in resource allocation tasks, may prescribe fairness (Spears, Doosje, & Ellemers, 1999); the effect can also be constrained by socio-structural variables, such as a perception of ingroup superiority as legitimate and stable (Bettencourt, Dorr, Charlton, & Hume, 2001) which, on dimensions not linked to status, can restrain ingroup bias. Also, individual difference variables such as allocentric or idiocentric orientation (Triandis, 1995) may have a moderating effect on the relationship between identification and ingroup bias. In certain structural conditions (e.g., for broad social categories), the relationship is valid for idiocentrics but not for allocentrics (Aharpour & Brown, 2000; Capozza, Voci, & Licciardello, 2000).

Subjective uncertainty reduction model

Another theory which is stimulating much research interest is the subjective uncertainty reduction model of Hogg and Abrams (1993; Hogg, 2000; Hogg & Mullin, 1999; see Chapter 2, this volume). According to this model, people need to feel certain about their self-concept, perceptions, attitudes, and behaviors, and the world around them. To experience uncertainty is aversive since one feels some lack of control over the events in one's social milieu. Thus, uncertainty motivates behaviors aimed at its reduction. The importance of the need for order and structure in human thought is implicit in several psychosocial theories of the self, such as self-assessment theories (e.g., Sedikides & Strube, 1995), Swann's self-verification theory (1990), self-affirmation theory (Steele, Spencer, & Lynch, 1993), and the individual difference approach of Sorrentino, Hodson, and Huber (2001). At a collective level, high uncertainty regarding one's social identity can be a motivation for identification with extremist parties or totalitarian groups (Billig, 1991; Capozza & Volpato, 2005; Hogg, 2000).

According to Hogg (2000), one of the ways in which people decrease uncertainty is to refer to a relevant categorical belonging. If, in a given context, an ingroup/outgroup distinction is cognitively salient (Turner, 1987), the individual classifies him/herself as a member of that ingroup. Uncertainty is reduced because the context is perceived as less complex and more meaningful, and because the ingroup prototypes, to which an individual assimilates him/herself, have a descriptive and prescriptive meaning. They summarize the attributes of the ingroup and prescribe attitudes and behaviors. Thus, the more people identify, the more they perceive themselves and behave in terms of the prototypical attributes of the ingroup, the more they evaluate positively and feel attraction toward their fellow ingroup members and, ultimately, the more uncertainty is reduced. According to Hogg, this need to reduce uncertainty is more fundamental than the need for self-esteem.

The main hypotheses from this subjective uncertainty reduction model have been tested in a series of experiments mainly performed with minimal groups. As hypothesized, it has been found that when people experience uncertainty, compared to when they do not, they identify with a relevant ingroup; that is, the need to reduce uncertainty motivates self-perception in categorical terms and, as a consequence, activates differentiation processes which can also have the effect of enhancing self-esteem (Grieve & Hogg, 1999; Hogg & Grieve, 1999; Jetten, Hogg, & Mullin, 2000; Mullin & Hogg, 1999; see also Hogg, Chapter 2, this volume).

Optimal distinctiveness theory

Another motivational theory of identification is Brewer's optimal distinctiveness theory (Brewer, 1991; Brewer & Pickett, 1999; Brewer & Roccas, 2001). According to Brewer, two fundamental needs are present in individuals. One is the need for assimilation and inclusion, since excessive singularity can lead to exclusion and isolation. The other is the need for differentiation and distinctiveness; it is necessary to perceive oneself as different in order to have a basis for comparative appraisal and self-definition. There are groups which satisfy both the need for inclusion and the need for differentiation because they are clearly distinct from other groups. These are "optimal" identities and it is predicted that levels of identification will be highest in such groups. Identification, in turn, determines behaviors of loyalty, the attribution of positive traits to the ingroup and also, if a specific outgroup is present (i.e., the outgroup is not the generic "not us"), attitudes of ingroup bias.

The hypotheses of this theory have been tested in experiments mainly performed with naturally occurring groups. Consistent with the tenets of the theory, it was found that, when the need for distinctiveness is salient, people prefer to belong to minority rather than to majority groups, given the more defined boundaries of minority groups; this effect is not moderated by the superior or inferior status of the minority (Brewer, Manzi, & Shaw, 1993). Moreover, it was found that both when the need to perceive oneself as distinct and when the need to perceive oneself as assimilated is salient, the perception of ingroup and outgroup homogeneity increases. The accentuation of the intercategorical contrast satisfies the need for distinctiveness, and the accentuation of the perceived ingroup homogeneity satisfies the need to feel definitely included (Pickett & Brewer, 2001). Finally, a particularly interesting issue is the search for a balance between personal needs and ingroup attributes. In fact, when the need for assimilation is salient people overestimate the real size of their ingroup, while they underestimate that size when the need for differentiation is salient (Pickett, Silver, & Brewer, 2002). A strategy which high identifiers use to satisfy one or the other of the two needs is to enhance one's own closeness to the ingroup prototype (self-stereotyping process; Pickett, Bonner, & Coleman, 2002).

The relationships posited by these various models are shown in Figure 3.1.

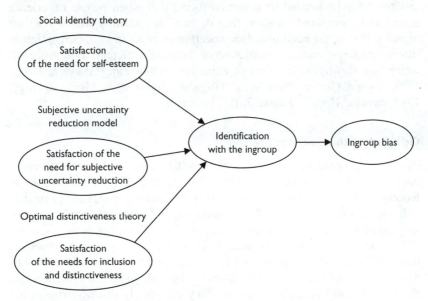

Figure 3.1 Motivational antecedents and effects of ingroup identification.

Functional model of social identities

Consistent with these trends to broaden the scope of social identity theory, Deaux et al. (1999) and Aharpour and Brown (2002) have proposed that group memberships can serve a variety of identity functions, in addition to the enhancement motive specified by social identity theory. This line of work was instigated by the observations of Deaux, Reid, Mizrahi, and Ethier (1995) and Lickel et al. (2000) that the array of common social categories tend to be grouped together psychologically in quite different ways by "observers" and "members" alike. For example, small face-to-face groups like families are distinguished from more task-oriented work-groups and large-scale ethnic or national categories. This suggests that these various group memberships might carry with them different meanings for their members. This idea was confirmed by Deaux et al. (1999) and Aharpour and Brown when they explored the range of identity functions that people reported their group memberships as serving – for example, "self-insight", "reciprocal help", "social interaction", "intragroup comparisons", in addition to intergroup comparisons and collective self-esteem. Moreover, the extent to which these identity functions were privileged seemed to vary across different types of groups. For instance, sports teams tended to emphasize intergroup comparisons, collective esteem, and social interaction, while religious groups placed more stress on self-insight, ingroup cohesion, and collective esteem (Deaux et al., 1999). Aharpour and Brown found that such between-group differences were associated with variations in patterns of correlation between functions, identification, and intergroup attitudes: for instance, British trade unionists and Japanese students showed a robust correlation between identification and negative intergroup attitudes, while that relationship was completely absent among British football supporters. Although much remains to be understood about the precise significance of these variations in identity functions, it does seem likely that they are implicated in different manifestations of intergroup bias.

In the following sections we report the three studies that have attempted to investigate these different models of identity processes.

Study 1

The aim of this study was to determine which were the main motivational ingredients of identification: self-esteem, uncertainty reduction, or optimal distinctiveness. The intergroup context was the relationship between Northern Italians and Southern Italians. These two groups are perceived by their members as similar in size but Northerners are consensually recognized as having superior socio-economic status (Capozza et al., 2000).

Method

Participants and procedure

Participants were 505 university students ($N = 232$, for Northerners; $N = 273$, for Southerners), mean age 22.15, and predominantly female (81% in the Northern and 98% in the Southern samples). Respondents were classified as Northern or Southern when they were born and lived in the north or south, with parents born and living in the north or south.

Measures

Self-esteem   To assess the extent to which belonging satisfies the need for self-esteem, three items were used, for example: "Being Northern (Southern) allows people to have a positive self-image." For all the measures, responses were elicited on a seven-step scale.

Subjective uncertainty reduction   Three items indicated uncertainty concerning the physical and social world (work and politics), such as: "Being Northern (Southern) means having clear norms as regards the world of work." Three items indicated uncertainties pertaining to values and rules to follow in interpersonal relationships, such as: "The Northern (Southern) environment shows what are the important values to follow."

Optimal distinctiveness   This variable was measured by three items: "In the north (south) there are many occasions in which you feel similar to other Northerners (Southerners) and, at the same time, definitely different from people who are not Northern (Southern)"; "In the north (south) there are many occasions in which you feel similar to other Northerners (Southerners)"; "In the north (south) there are many occasions in which you feel definitely different from people who are not Northern (Southern)."

Identification   A 20-item scale was used which measures the identity components of self-stereotyping, awareness of belonging, and the evaluative and emotional components. Applied to various ingroups – ethnic, national, regional – the scale has shown convergent and discriminant validity; for each component, the reliability of the respective items was always satisfactory. The items were partly taken from the most widely used identification scales (e.g., Brown, Condor, Mathews, Wade, & Williams, 1986; Ellemers, Kortekaas, & Ouwerkerk, 1999). Seven items elicited self-stereotyping, for example: "I have the typical qualities of Northerners (Southerners)." Five items measured awareness of belonging, such as: "In the course of a day, it often crosses my mind that I am a Northerner (Southerner)." Four items elicited the evaluative component (e.g., "I evaluate the fact of being a

Northerner [Southerner] positively"). Four items, afterwards reduced to three for reliability reasons, measured the emotional component, such as: "I feel attachment toward other Northerners (Southerners)." The items of this component mean attraction for the fellow ingroup members.

Ingroup bias   To measure ingroup bias, semantic differential was applied. Twenty-five scales were used and two concepts, *Northerner* and *Southerner*. The scales represent the evaluation, potency, and activity factors, but they do not describe the stereotypical attributes of the two groups (Capozza et al., 2000). Ingroup bias was measured by subtracting, for each scale, the outgroup from the ingroup score and calculating the mean of the 25 algebraic differences (evaluative differentiation) – the higher the positive score, the stronger ingroup bias. Resource allocation matrices were also used. These measured the strength of the discriminatory strategies: MD and MD + MIP (see, e.g., Bourhis, Sachdev, & Gagnon, 1994).

Data analyses

The following method was used. The effect of the three needs on identification was tested simultaneously through multiple regression, which allows the impact of each motivation to be ascertained while controlling for the impact of the others. This control is necessary given the link which may exist between the satisfaction of the three needs. A more articulated model than the one appearing in Figure 3.1 was therefore tested by expressing concepts and relations into a structural equation model (LISREL 8; Jöreskog & Sörbom, 1996). The factor structure of the identification scale and the convergent and discriminant validity of measures were ascertained by using confirmatory factor analysis (CFA). The extension of the model of Figure 3.1 was verified by means of regression with latent variables. The goodness-of-fit of the models was evaluated with the chi-square test, the Comparative Fit Index (CFI), and the Standardized Root Mean Squared Residual (SRMR). Satisfactory fits are obtained when χ^2 is nonsignificant, CFI is greater or equal to .95, and SRMR is less or equal to .08 (see Hu & Bentler, 1999). Alternative models were compared with chi-square difference tests for nested models, and with the other fit indices for non-nested models.

Results

Measurement models

The reliability of measures (Cronbach's alpha) was always sufficient (all > .60, most ≥ .70). To test the multifaceted structure of the identification scale, a confirmatory factor analysis model was employed. The CFA model contained four latent and eight observed variables (see the identity components in Figures 3.2 and 3.3). For each component, items were averaged to form two indicators for latent variable (Bagozzi & Heatherton, 1994). The model revealed a reasonable fit in both the Northern and Southern sample. In fact, although chi-squared was significant, Northern sample: $\chi^2(14) = 36.12$, $p \cong .001$; Southern sample: $\chi^2(14) = 41.19$, $p \cong .0002$, the other two indices pointed to a good fit (Northern sample: SRMR = .028, CFI = .98; Southern sample: SRMR = .043, CFI = .97). In both samples the four-factor CFA model explained the data better than the one-factor or the three-factor model, where the two indicators of the self-stereotyping component and the two indicators of the awareness of belonging component measured a unitary cognitive component – for the three-factor structure: $\chi^2(17) = 164.00$, $p \cong .00$, SRMR = .076, CFI = .89, in the Northern group; $\chi^2(17) = 124.63$, $p \cong .00$, SRMR = .076, CFI = .86, in the Southern group.

To ascertain the convergent and discriminant validity of measures, a CFA model with nine latent and 17 observed variables was tested (see Figures 3.2 and 3.3 for the definition of factors and their relations to the measures). Two aggregates of items were used as indicators for each construct, for both motivations and identity components. Evaluative differentiation was measured by a single indicator; however error variance was not fixed to zero, but estimated on the basis of reliability (Jöreskog & Sörbom, 1996, p. 196).[1] In both samples, the model showed a good fit. Chi-squares were significant, $\chi^2(84) = 144.42$, $p \cong .00$: Northern sample; $\chi^2(84) = 152.74$, $p \cong .00$: Southern sample, but the other indices pointed to a good fit as a practical matter (SRMRs < .05, CFIs ≥ .95). Concerning validity, convergent validity emerged from the fact that measures were loaded only on the respective factor, while discriminant validity emerged from the fact that latent variables showed correlations less than 1.00 ($p < .05$). The same results were obtained when ingroup bias was measured by the discriminatory strategies. Measures, therefore, allow us to differentiate among the hypothesized constructs: the four motivations, identity components, and indices of ingroup bias.

The effects of motivations: Testing the theories

To verify the heuristic power of the three motivational theories, a regression model was tested in which motivations influence all the identity components, and the identity components, in turn, influence ingroup bias (LISREL 8, Jöreskog & Sörbom, 1996).

Northern group   The regression model fitted satisfactorily overall, $\chi^2(88) = 145.78$, $p \cong .0001$, SRMR = .030, CFI = .98 (Figure 3.2). Factor loadings were uniformly high and error variances were low to moderate in value.

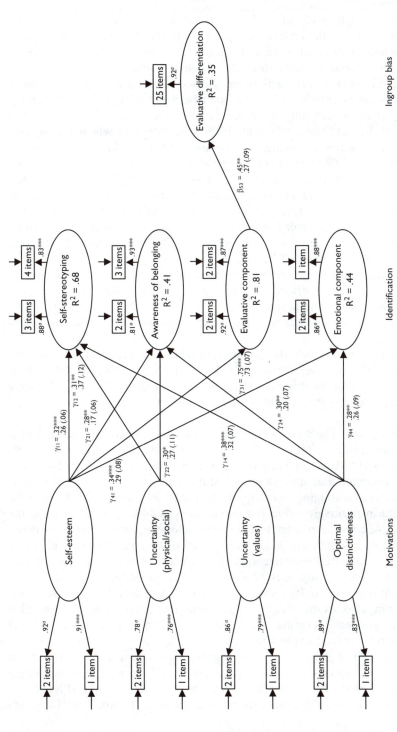

Figure 3.2 Motivational antecedents and effects of ingroup identification, Northern sample ($N = 232$). The completely standardized solution is presented; only the significant γs and βs are reported. For γs and βs, the number above is the standardized coefficient, the number below is the unstandardized coefficient (standard errors in parentheses). Parameter estimates for correlations among latent variables are omitted for simplicity. a = fixed parameter. * $p < .05$. ** $p < .01$. *** $p < .001$.

Relatively high levels of explained variance occurred for identity components and a moderate level of explained variance resulted for the measure of ingroup bias (evaluative differentiation). Next, looking at the paths (Figures 3.2 and 3.3 only show the significant structural parameters), we can see how the need for self-esteem affected all the identity features, and to the greatest extent the evaluative one (the γ regarding this component is higher than γs regarding the other components, $ps < .001$). The effect of optimal distinctiveness was also strong: the extent to which the ingroup makes people feel assimilated and distinct influenced three components of identity (the difference between the three γs is nonsignificant, $ps > .10$). Finally, the reduction of uncertainties concerning the physical and political world and the world of work equally influenced the two facets of the cognitive component (the two γs are not significantly different, $p > .10$). Hence, while each theory stresses the influence of a specific motivation, actually, all motivations influence social identity. Among the identity components only the value of belonging influences ingroup bias (Figure 3.2).

Chi-square difference tests were used to determine the significance of direct paths from motivations to evaluative differentiation. No direct path turned out to be significant, $\Delta s_{\chi^2(1)} \leq 0.70$, $ps > .10$. Motivations, therefore, did not produce direct effects, either positive or negative, on evaluative ingroup bias.

The model in which the outcome-variable was the mean of MD and MD + MIP fitted well overall, $\chi^2(88) = 146.48$, $p \cong .00$, SRMR $= .032$, CFI $= .98$. Also in this case, the only component of identity influencing ingroup bias was the evaluative one ($\beta = .48$, $p < .01$).

Southern group   The regression model also fitted satisfactorily overall for the Southern group, $\chi^2(88) = 159.37$, $p \cong .00$, SRMR $= .045$, CFI $= .95$ (Figure 3.3).[2] Moderate amounts of explained variance occurred for evaluative differentiation and identity features (the least explained feature is awareness of belonging). Looking at the paths, we can see that the need for self-esteem positively influenced two identity components, albeit more the evaluative component than awareness of belonging (the difference between the two γs is significant, $p < .01$). Optimal distinctiveness also had strong effects: it enhanced self-stereotyping, awareness of belonging, and attachment to the ingroup members (emotional component); the difference between the γs is nonsignificant, $ps > .50$. In contrast, the extent to which belonging satisfies the need to reduce subjective uncertainties did not elicit significant effects. Identification (evaluative and emotional components), in turn, gave rise to ingroup bias.

Direct effects of motivations on ingroup bias were also not found in the Southern group, $\Delta s_{\chi^2(1)} \leq 1.71$, $ps > .10$. Finally, using the multi-sample procedure (LISREL 8), findings from the Northern sample (Figure 3.2) were compared to those from the Southern sample (Figure 3.3). If only the

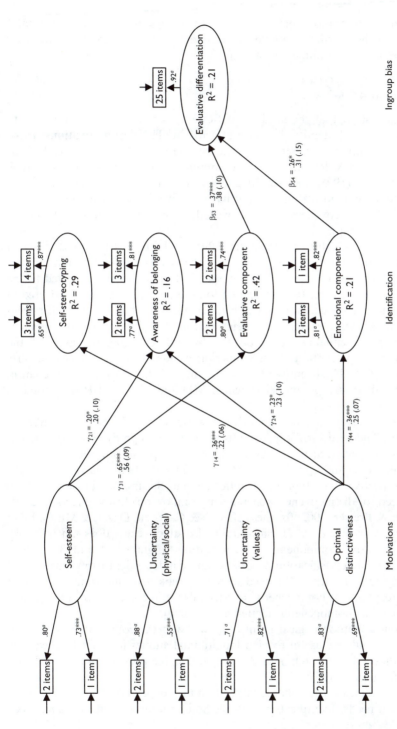

Figure 3.3 Motivational antecedents and effects of ingroup identification, Southern sample ($N = 268$). The completely standardized solution is presented; only the significant γs and βs are reported. For γs and βs, the number above is the standardized coefficient, the number below is the unstandardized coefficient (standard errors in parentheses). Parameter estimates for correlations among latent variables are omitted for simplicity. a = fixed parameter. * $p < .05$. *** $p < .001$.

significant regression coefficients in both models are considered, no parameter in the Northern sample was different from the respective parameter in the Southern sample ($ps > .10$).[3]

Discussion

Findings show that the need for self-esteem is not the only motivation to influence social identity; it is also affected by the other motivations. However, in contrast to what is assumed by Brewer (1991; Brewer & Pickett, 1999; Brewer & Roccas, 2001), for optimal distinctiveness, and by Hogg and Abrams (1993; see also Hogg, 2000), for the need to reduce uncertainties, these two motivations do not have a prevailing effect on identification (optimal distinctiveness prevails over the other motivations only in the Southern group).

Therefore, all three motivations influence the processes linked to social identity and, thus, intra- and intergroup behaviors. Differentiation in favor of the ingroup, as hypothesized by social identity theory, is related to the need for self-esteem. It is interesting to note the causal chain discovered in three models: the extent to which belonging satisfies the need for self-esteem influences – and is the only determinant of – its evaluation; value of belonging is enhanced or protected by differentiating in favor of the ingroup, the perception of one's superiority ends the process since it satisfies the need for self-esteem (see Figures 3.2 and 3.3; this path is also present in the Northern sample model in which MD and MD + MIP were used as measures of ingroup bias).

The effects of the various motivations can also be found in a number of studies. The need for distinctiveness gives rise to cognitive effects: it accentuates the perceived homogeneity of the ingroup and outgroup (Pickett & Brewer, 2001) and increases the extent to which the two groups are assigned the respective stereotypical attributes (Jetten, Spears, & Manstead, 2001); the need for distinctiveness generates ingroup overexclusion effects (Pickett, Silver, & Brewer, 2002; for these effects see Capozza, Dazzi, & Minto, 1996; Leyens & Yzerbyt, 1992). Since optimal distinctiveness does not influence the evaluative component of identification (Figures 3.2 and 3.3), these cognitive and classification processes can be independent from those aimed at enhancing identity. The need to reduce subjective uncertainty is related to perceptions of homogeneity, in particular to the preference for ingroups perceived as homogeneous (Jetten et al., 2000).

From a methodological point of view, given the correlational paradigm used, it would be useful to plan longitudinal studies in order to check the hypothesized causal relations discovered and the possible presence of reciprocal causality effects.

Our findings suggest that identification may depend on the satisfaction of different needs. Identification with the Southern ingroup, for instance, does not depend on satisfying the need to reduce subjective uncertainties, and depends less, compared to the Northern group, on satisfying the need for self-esteem. In the functional approach to social identities (Deaux et al., 1999), it is suggested that there may be a number of functions served by group membership (perhaps as many as seven), and not all these functions may be associated with the manifestation of ingroup bias. Which motive assumes pre-eminence in any situation may depend on both the nature of the group and contextual variables, as we now discuss.

Study 2

Aharpour and Brown (2002) found that different classes of identity functions seem to be differentially endorsed by different groups. Among trade unionists, for example, there seemed to be some emphasis on materialistic functions like reciprocal help (to obtain benefits for members of the group) while Japanese students appeared more motivated by socio-emotional identity functions (to get to know themselves and others better). These variations were observed with extant groups and could have arisen for many reasons and over some time. What was not possible to ascertain in the Aharpour and Brown study was how stable these functional differences between the groups were or how sensitive they might have been to contextual variation. Both stability and flexibility are plausible a priori. One might argue that because many of our important social identities (e.g., occupational, ethnic) are used on a regular and similar basis over many years, one could expect that their functional significance would become internalized and hence rather stable over time and situations. On the other hand, as several theorists have argued (e.g., Allport, 1954; Brewer, 1991; Tajfel & Turner, 1979), identities are contextually labile. In this experiment we sought to manipulate identity functions while holding constant group membership. Our goal was to ascertain if emphasizing one class of identity functions or another (materialistic vs. socio-emotional) would affect the relationship between identification and bias.

Method

Participants and procedure

Participants were 97 psychology students. They were provided with a bogus newspaper extract allegedly reporting on the characteristics of the new generation of psychology students according to BPS (British Psychological Society) data. After carefully reading this extract, students were then asked to give their opinions on a series of policy issues related to their department with the view of increasing their involvement with the management of the department. In fact, the newspaper article served as an experimental manipulation.

Half of the participants were given a version describing psychology as a "passport to success" and stating that psychology students are the ones who, thanks to the skills acquired during their degree, are the most sought-after in the job market. This was intended to make the materialistic function of group identification particularly salient. The remaining half of the participants instead read a newspaper article describing psychology as a "passport to serenity" and psychology students as having excellent social skills and being very good at judging themselves and others, thereby making the socio-emotional function of group identification more salient.

Measures

The dependent measures included, first of all, identification with the group of psychology students, a variant of the scale devised by Brown et al. (1986) comprising six items (e.g., "It is important to me to be a psychology student"). A semantic differential then measured ingroup favoritism by using 10 bipolar scales (including evaluation, potency, and activity factors) to judge the concepts *Psychology Student* and *Accountancy Student*. Scores were computed by averaging the 10 differences between points given to psychology and accountancy students on each scale so that a more positive value represented higher levels of ingroup bias. Manipulation checks then measured the materialistic or socio-emotional function of group identification served by the group, using five items, such as: "Being part of this group I benefit from some material rewards that wouldn't be available to me otherwise" or "Being part of this group I can understand myself better and learn more about the way I personally interact with other people."

Results

Manipulation checks revealed that manipulation was effective. The key question was whether the experimental condition would affect the relationship between identification and intergroup attitude. In fact it did. In the materialistic function condition, group identification was significantly correlated with the semantic differential measure of ingroup bias ($r = .56$, $p < .001$). On the other hand, in the socio-emotional condition the same correlation was not significant ($r = .20$, $p < .20$). These results therefore confirm that the specific functions of a group identification have consequences for the relation between that identification and intergroup attitude. Moreover, they seem to suggest that functions of group identification are not so fixed that they cannot respond to the demands of particular (experimental) situations.

Study 3

Identity functions may also change over the life-span of the group. More-land and Levine's (1989) well-known model of group socialization suggests that there is a continuous process of accommodation and assimilation between the group's and the group members' needs. According to this view, a newcomer might explore a potential group to see which of his/her needs can be satisfied by the group, while the group would accept newcomers only if they satisfy the group's needs. At the full socialization stage both group and members reach an equilibrium in terms of needs and goals. If we transfer these concepts to our model, we can hypothesize that both the group and its individual members have a core set of needs that require satisfaction, and of functions that one can serve for the other. Therefore, we can expect each group to be able to serve only a specific and distinctive set of identification functions, and also for group members to show change in some functions but not others as they become more socialized in a group.

This hypothesis was tested in a longitudinal study following a group of addicts in recovery in a residential center. The specific recovery center chosen for this study had particularly interesting and relevant charac-teristics in so far as the philosophy embraced by the staff follows the "twelve step methodology" adopted in the Alcoholics Anonymous groups (Alcoholics Anonymous, 1952). Clients at the center are therefore presented with the idea that addiction is a permanent disease and is likely to affect them permanently, and they are encouraged to accept this social identity as a first step toward their recovery. Moreover, the center's clinical staff believes in the view that all forms of addiction are psychologically similar. The concept of cross-addiction is used to explain that alcoholism, drugs use, eating disorders, compulsive help, etc. are just different ways in which the same addictive tendency manifests itself. The aims and goals of the therapy group are therefore very clear and, as such, the group offered a unique opportunity to observe the extent to which newcomers assimilate with the group's needs and the functions of identification offered by it.

Method

Participants and procedure

Clients in treatment spend a period of time ranging from three to six weeks at the center, during which they participate in at least two group therapy sessions a day, plus specific personal treatment. They can start and leave the treatment at the center at any time although leaves are assessed by the clinical staff. As part of their program, clients are asked to answer to a series of standardized measures in the format of a questionnaire in the first week they join the center. It is in the context of this testing session that the study was introduced to participants. The second administration of the questionnaire containing measures relevant for the study took place after two or three weeks depending on the total period of treatment of each client. Forty clients participated in the study.

Measures

Group identification was measured using the same six-item scale adapted from Brown et al. (1986) used in Study 2. This was assessed with regard to two groups: that of "addicts" intended as a broad superordinate category, and that of "my therapy group" that better defines participants once they joined the center. In the subsequent pages of the questionnaire functions of group identification with the therapy group were measured using Aharpour and Brown's (2002) 24-item scale measuring the following six functions or factors of group identification: reciprocal help (e.g., "In this group we do what we can to help each other"), collectivism (e.g., "In this group we work together very well"), self-insight and confidence (e.g., "Other members of this group help me to understand myself better"), material benefits (e.g., "I get so many material rewards in this group that it is worth staying"), intergroup comparison (e.g., "To judge this group it is not necessary to make comparisons with other groups"), and intragroup comparison (e.g., "Some others in this group are doing worse than I am"). For all items of this measure a seven-step *agreement/disagreement* scale was used.

Results

Means and standard deviations for measures of group identification at Time 1 and 2 are shown in Table 3.1. Inspection of these means reveals some interesting patterns. Participants tend to identify more with the "therapy group" than with the "addicts group" at both times. However, the level of identification with the "addicts group" increases over time, while identification with the "therapy group" remains constant. This can be interpreted

Table 3.1 Means and standard deviations for measures of group identification with the "addicts group" and "therapy group" at Time 1 and Time 2

	Time			
	Time 1		Time 2	
Identification	M	SD	M	SD
Addicts group	3.89_a	1.12	4.34_b	0.84
Therapy group	5.56_c	0.96	5.66_c	0.87

Means, in the same row or column, with a different subscript differ significantly, $p < .05$.

as part of the clients' way of dealing with their stigmatized identity – that is, to accept being part of a therapy group from the outset, but to initially deny the concept of addiction. It is at Time 2 that members show an increased identification with the group of "addicts", a sign of a process of acceptance of their membership to the group as part of their recovery.

As far as changes in functions of identification were concerned, participants showed a significant change between Time 1 and Time 2 in three of the functions considered, that is reciprocal help, self-insight, and intergroup comparison ($p < .05$) (see Figure 3.4). But while group members report a higher endorsement for two functions of identification that can be considered central to the philosophy of the group (reciprocal help and self-insight) they decrease their belief in intergroup comparisons, an aspect which is little emphasized by the addiction center. Endorsement of the other functions remains more or less unchanged between Time 1 and Time 2.

Discussion

From Studies 2 and 3 three simple points can be made. First, they underline the findings from Deaux et al. (1999) and Aharpour and Brown (2002) that groups differ markedly in the functions they may serve for their members. To the range of groups studied in that earlier research, we can now add "therapy group". The profile of means shown in Figure 3.4 – clearly different from that observed in those earlier studies – reminds us again of

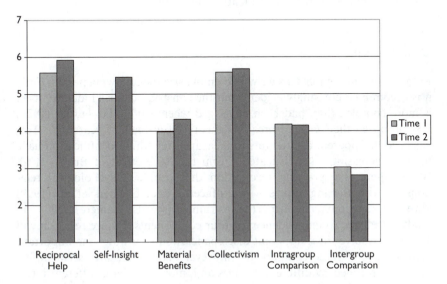

Figure 3.4 Mean values of identification functions with the therapy group at Time 1 and Time 2.

the psychological heterogeneity of groups that people belong to. The second conclusion concerns the apparent flexibility of these group-specific functions. As we saw in Study 2 as a consequence of an artificially induced experimental manipulation, and now here in Study 3 as a consequence of the temporal progress of group socialization to a therapy group, social identity functions are far from static entities. In other words, while different kinds of groups may vary in the extent to which they will tend to serve some functions rather than others, situational contingencies can bring about changes in these functional priorities for groups and group members. In Study 3 we examined only changes in group members' perceptions but, from Moreland and Levine's (1989) group socialization model, we might speculate that group (or institutional) norms might also change in accommodation to the changes among the group members. Third, there is a methodological lesson to be learned. In these studies we have successfully used laboratory and longitudinal designs, both with real groups. Although both studies were quite limited in their scope – and in that sense should be regarded as preliminary investigations – they are still quite rare in the research corpus on identity functions, which hitherto has relied mainly on cross-sectional survey designs with their attendant difficulties of causal interpretability. What might be a particularly interesting next step would be to *combine* these methodologies, to exploit the control afforded by experimentation with the possibility of tracking temporal change in identities that longitudinal work uniquely allows. Studies of small friendship or family groupings might be an interesting avenue to explore since these are still under-represented in the social identity literature.

Conclusions

In these concluding remarks we would emphasize the following points. First, it is becoming increasingly evident that the construct of social identity itself is more complex than had been envisaged when Tajfel and Turner (1979) first proposed their ground-breaking theory more than 25 years ago. This has become apparent as attempts to measure strength of identification have become increasingly sophisticated. From the early effort of Brown et al. (1986), there is a growing recognition that people's psychological relationship with the ingroup is a multi-faceted one. Ellemers et al. (1999) have offered a convincing tripartite instrument (see also Cameron, 2004); in Study 1 we have found evidence for four components. Future research will doubtless resolve these apparent discrepancies but, for now, one important message is that these components (however many there are) seem differentially controlled by different motives and, moreover, have different intergroup outcomes. While we only had one intergroup outcome measure (differentiation), which seems mainly controlled by the evaluation feature, we venture to suggest that other intergroup indicators (e.g., stereotyping, perceptions of homogeneity, hostility) may well be linked to the other components.

Second, we believe these studies provide promising support for the various theoretical models we outlined earlier in the chapter. The classical social identity model found support in the associations between self-esteem and identification observed in Study 1. So, too, did the optimal distinctiveness and uncertainty reduction theories, although it seems that the role of these motives is somewhat context dependent since their relative importance differed between the Northern and Southern Italian samples. And the idea that different identity functions underpin people's group affiliations also found support in Studies 2 and 3. Furthermore, such studies also revealed that these functions seem to be responsive to situational demands and constraints. This provides a useful corrective to what might otherwise have seemed a rather static conception in the first models of identity functions (Aharpour & Brown, 2002; Deaux et al., 1999).

The final "take home" message is again to stress the importance of group diversity (Deaux et al., 1995; Lickel et al., 2000). The Northern and Southern Italian groups in Study 1 showed a different pattern of relationships between underlying identity motives and identification; the therapy group in Study 3 could be distinguished from other groups in which identity functions have been studied (Aharpour & Brown, 2002; Deaux et al., 1999). Although incorporating this heterogeneity in a systematic way into our theories of social identity will undoubtedly not be easy (for an important recent contribution, see Ashmore, Deaux, & McLaughlin-Volpe, 2004), and somewhat goes against social psychology's disciplinary preference for simple nomothetic theoretical models, a proper understanding of the role of social identity in intergroup relations will not be achieved until we do so.

Notes

1 The same procedure was followed for the model in which ingroup bias was measured by the two discriminatory strategies: MD and MD + MIP.
2 All the models concerning the Southern sample were tested with $N = 268$; in fact, for five respondents the measures of one or more indicators were not available.
3 In the Southern group the only component of social identity to influence the use of the discriminatory strategies was awareness of belonging ($\beta = .24$, $p < .05$).

References

Abrams, D., & Hogg, M. A. (Eds.). (1999). *Social identity and social cognition.* Oxford, UK: Blackwell.
Aharpour, S., & Brown, R. (2000). *Group identification and ingroup bias: A meta-analysis testing the Hinkle and Brown model.* Unpublished manuscript, University of Kent at Canterbury, UK.

Aharpour, S., & Brown, R. (2002). Functions of group identification: An exploratory analysis. *Revue Internationale de Psychologie Sociale, 15,* 157–186.

Alcoholics Anonymous (1952). *Twelve steps and twelve traditions.* New York: Alcoholics Anonymous World.

Allport, G. W. (1954). *The nature of prejudice.* New York: Addison-Wesley.

Ashmore, R. D., Deaux, K., & McLaughlin-Volpe, T. (2004). An organizing framework for collective identity: Articulation and significance of multidimensionality. *Psychological Bulletin, 130,* 80–114.

Bagozzi, R. P., & Heatherton, T. F. (1994). A general approach to representing multifaceted personality constructs: Application to state self-esteem. *Structural Equation Modeling, 1,* 35–67.

Bettencourt, B. A., Dorr, N., Charlton, K., & Hume, D. L. (2001). Status differences and in-group bias: A meta-analytic examination of the effects of status stability, status legitimacy, and group permeability. *Psychological Bulletin, 127,* 520–542.

Billig, M. G. (1991). *Ideology and opinions.* London: Sage.

Bourhis, R. Y., Sachdev, I., & Gagnon, A. (1994). Intergroup research with the Tajfel matrices: Methodological notes. In M. P. Zanna & J. M. Olson (Eds.), *The psychology of prejudice: The Ontario symposium* (Vol. 7, pp. 209–232). Hillsdale, NJ: Lawrence Erlbaum Associates Inc.

Brewer, M. B. (1991). The social self: On being the same and different at the same time. *Personality and Social Psychology Bulletin, 17,* 475–482.

Brewer, M. B., Manzi, J. M., & Shaw, J. S. (1993). In-group identification as a function of depersonalization, distinctiveness, and status. *Psychological Science, 4,* 88–92.

Brewer, M. B., & Pickett, C. L. (1999). Distinctiveness motives as a source of the social self. In T. R. Tyler, R. M. Kramer, & O. P. John (Eds.), *The psychology of the social self* (pp. 71–87). Mahwah, NJ: Lawrence Erlbaum Associates Inc.

Brewer, M. B., & Roccas, S. (2001). Individual values, social identity, and optimal distinctiveness. In C. Sedikides & M. B. Brewer (Eds.), *Individual self, relational self, collective self* (pp. 219–237). Philadelphia: Psychology Press.

Brown, R. (2000). Social identity theory: Past achievements, current problems and future challenges. *European Journal of Social Psychology, 30,* 745–778.

Brown, R., Condor, S., Mathews, A., Wade, G., & Williams, J. A. (1986). Explaining intergroup differentiation in an industrial organization. *Journal of Occupational Psychology, 59,* 273–286.

Cameron, J. E. (2004). A three-factor model of social identity. *Self and Identity, 3,* 239–262.

Capozza, D., Dazzi, C., & Minto, B. (1996). Ingroup overexclusion: A confirmation of the effect. *International Review of Social Psychology, 9,* 7–18.

Capozza, D., Voci, A., & Licciardello, O. (2000). Individualism, collectivism and social identity theory. In D. Capozza & R. Brown (Eds.), *Social identity processes: Trends in theory and research* (pp. 62–80). London: Sage.

Capozza, D., & Volpato, C. (2005). *Mein Kampf: Testing stereotype content models through the analysis of one case.* Unpublished manuscript, Universities of Padova and Milan, Italy.

Deaux, K., Reid, A., Mizrahi, K., & Cotting, D. (1999). Connecting the person to the social: The functions of social identification. In T. R. Tyler, R. M. Kramer, &

O. P. John (Eds.), *The psychology of the social self* (pp. 91–113). Mahwah, NJ: Lawrence Erlbaum Associates Inc.

Deaux, K., Reid, A., Mizrahi, K., & Ethier, K. A. (1995). Parameters of social identity. *Journal of Personality and Social Psychology, 68,* 280–291.

Ellemers, N., Kortekaas, P., & Ouwerkerk, J. W. (1999). Self-categorisation, commitment to the group and group self-esteem as related but distinct aspects of social identity. *European Journal of Social Psychology, 29,* 371–389.

Fiske, S. T., & Taylor, S. E. (1991). *Social cognition* (2nd ed.). New York: McGraw-Hill.

Grieve, P. G., & Hogg, M. A. (1999). Subjective uncertainty and intergroup discrimination in the minimal group situation. *Personality and Social Psychology Bulletin, 25,* 926–940.

Hinkle, S., & Brown, R. (1990). Intergroup comparisons and social identity: Some links and lacunae. In D. Abrams & M. A. Hogg (Eds.), *Social identity theory: Constructive and critical advances* (pp. 48–70). London: Harvester Wheatsheaf.

Hogg, M. A. (2000). Subjective uncertainty reduction through self-categorization: A motivational theory of social identity processes. In W. Stroebe & M. Hewstone (Eds.), *European review of social psychology* (Vol. 11, pp. 223–255). Chichester, UK: Wiley.

Hogg, M. A., & Abrams, D. (1993). Towards a single-process uncertainty-reduction model of social motivation in groups. In M. A. Hogg & D. Abrams (Eds.), *Group motivation: Social psychological perspectives* (pp. 173–190). London: Harvester Wheatsheaf.

Hogg, M. A., & Grieve, P. G. (1999). Social identity theory and the crisis of confidence in social psychology: A commentary, and some research on uncertainty reduction. *Asian Journal of Social Psychology, 2,* 79–93.

Hogg, M. A., & Mullin, B.-A. (1999). Joining groups to reduce uncertainty: Subjective uncertainty reduction and group identification. In D. Abrams & M. A. Hogg (Eds.), *Social identity and social cognition* (pp. 249–279). Oxford, UK: Blackwell.

Hu, L.-T., & Bentler, P. M. (1999). Cutoff criteria for fit indexes in covariance structure analysis: Conventional criteria versus new alternatives. *Structural Equation Modeling, 6,* 1–55.

Jetten, J., Hogg, M. A., & Mullin, B.-A. (2000). In-group variability and motivation to reduce subjective uncertainty. *Group Dynamics, 4,* 184–198.

Jetten, J., Spears, R., & Manstead, A. S. R. (2001). Similarity as a source of differentiation: The role of group identification. *European Journal of Social Psychology, 31,* 621–640.

Jöreskog, K. G., & Sörbom, D. (1996). *LISREL 8 user's reference guide.* Chicago: Scientific Software International.

Leyens, J.-Ph., & Yzerbyt, V. Y. (1992). The ingroup overexclusion effect: Impact of valence and confirmation on stereotypical information search. *European Journal of Social Psychology, 22,* 549–569.

Lickel, B., Hamilton, D. L., Wieczorkowska, G., Lewis, A., Sherman, S. J., & Uhles, A. N. (2000). Varieties of groups and the perception of group entitativity. *Journal of Personality and Social Psychology, 78,* 223–246.

Moreland, R. L., & Levine, J. M. (1989). Newcomers and oldtimers in small groups. In P. B. Paulus (Ed.), *Psychology of group influence* (2nd ed., pp. 143–186). Hillsdale, NJ: Lawrence Erlbaum Associates Inc.

Mullin, B.-A., & Hogg, M. A. (1999). Motivations for group membership: The role of subjective importance and uncertainty reduction. *Basic and Applied Social Psychology, 21,* 91–102.

Perreault, S., & Bourhis, R. Y. (1999). Ethnocentrism, social identification, and discrimination. *Personality and Social Psychology Bulletin, 25,* 92–103.

Pickett, C. L., Bonner, B. L., & Coleman, J. M. (2002). Motivated self-stereotyping: Heightened assimilation and differentiation needs result in increased levels of positive and negative self-stereotyping. *Journal of Personality and Social Psychology, 82,* 543–562.

Pickett, C. L., & Brewer, M. B. (2001). Assimilation and differentiation needs as motivational determinants of perceived in-group and out-group homogeneity. *Journal of Experimental Social Psychology, 37,* 341–348.

Pickett, C. L., Silver, M. D., & Brewer, M. B. (2002). The impact of assimilation and differentiation needs on perceived group importance and judgments of ingroup size. *Personality and Social Psychology Bulletin, 28,* 546–558.

Sedikides, C., & Brewer, M. B. (Eds.). (2001). *Individual self, relational self, collective self.* Philadelphia: Psychology Press.

Sedikides, C., & Strube, M. J. (1995). The multiply motivated self. *Personality and Social Psychology Bulletin, 21,* 1330–1335.

Sorrentino, R. M., Hodson, G., & Huber, G. L. (2001). Uncertainty orientation and the social mind: Individual differences in the interpersonal context. In J. P. Forgas, K. D. Williams, & L. Wheeler (Eds.), *The social mind: Cognitive and motivational aspects of interpersonal behavior* (pp. 199–227). New York: Cambridge University Press.

Spears, R., Doosje, B., & Ellemers, N. (1999). Commitment and the context of social perception. In N. Ellemers, R. Spears, & B. Doosje (Eds.), *Social identity: Context, commitment, content* (pp. 59–83). Oxford, UK: Blackwell.

Steele, C. M., Spencer, S. J., & Lynch, M. (1993). Self-image resilience and dissonance: The role of affirmational resources. *Journal of Personality and Social Psychology, 64,* 885–896.

Swann, W. B. Jr. (1990). To be adored or to be known? The interplay of self-enhancement and self-verification. In E. T. Higgins & R. M. Sorrentino (Eds.), *Handbook of motivation and cognition: Foundations of social behavior* (Vol. 2, pp. 408–448). New York: Guilford Press.

Tajfel, H. (1981). *Human groups and social categories.* Cambridge, UK: Cambridge University Press.

Tajfel, H., & Turner, J. C. (1979). An integrative theory of intergroup conflict. In W. G. Austin & S. Worchel (Eds.), *The social psychology of intergroup relations* (pp. 33–47). Monterey, CA: Brooks/Cole.

Triandis, H. C. (1995). *Individualism and collectivism.* Boulder, CO: Westview Press.

Turner, J. C. (1987). A self-categorization theory. In J. C. Turner, M. A. Hogg, P. J. Oakes, S. D. Reicher, & M. S. Wetherell (Eds.), *Rediscovering the social group: A self-categorization theory* (pp. 42–67). Oxford, UK: Blackwell.

Chapter 4

Extending the self in space and time: Social identification and existential concerns

Emanuele Castano, Vincent Y. Yzerbyt, Maria Paola Paladino, and Andrea Carnaghi

The concept of social identity is most influential in modern social psychological theory. A distinctive outcome of the European tradition, it has helped the discipline in one of its most important challenges, namely in modeling the relationship between the individual and the social group.

The concept originated in Tajfel's (1981) early research on intergroup relations and it thus comes as no surprise that empirical work stemming from social identity theory has focused on the consequences of social identification and self-categorization (Turner, Hogg, Oakes, Reicher, & Wetherell, 1987), especially in terms of intergroup behavior. Interestingly, however, we know comparatively little when it comes to understanding the determinants of social identification (see Brewer & Harasty, 1996; Stevens & Fiske, 1995). It is on this issue that we focus in the present chapter. Specifically, we propose a perspective on the motives for social identification and argue that social identities may serve, among other needs, the fundamental need of human beings to transcend their mortal fate.

Personal and social identity

Lay people and social psychologists alike would hardly question the assumption that "in the beginning there was the individual". With a standard configuration comprising two legs, two arms, a connecting part in the middle, and a protuberance that we call the head on top, we humans are very easy to identify. Walk down the street and you can count many of us, potentially talk to each of us, and identify idiosyncrasies and similarities between us. And if this was not enough, there is the fact that we do seem to act as single entities most of the time. We are individual units and we are aware of this (this self-awareness turns out to have important consequences on our behavior, as we discuss below).

Yet, if we ponder our emotional and cognitive reactions to a host of small and large events that happen in our daily lives, the idea that we are individual, separate entities begins to crumble. We surely feel joy or anger when we are praised or insulted, but we do so as well when it is our beloved partner who is honored or criticized, or when our national soccer team scores a goal or suffers a humiliating defeat (Mackie & Smith, 2002; E. R. Smith, 1993; Yzerbyt, Dumont, Gordijn, & Wigboldus, 2002).

These findings are of course consistent with social psychological theory which suggests that our sense of identity extends well beyond our own individuality. The very concept of *social identity* refers precisely to the fact that individuals can see themselves as group members and that the shift from personal to social identity leads to a radical change in the perception of the social world and in the norms that guide behavior (Reicher, 1987; Turner et al., 1987). Furthermore, empirical evidence indicates that individuals include important others (Aron, Aron, & Smollan, 1992) as well as their own ingroup in the cognitive representation of their self (Coats, Smith, Claypool, & Banner, 2000). In other words, individuals show a remarkable ability and readiness to extend their sense of self to incorporate others and to see themselves as members of social groups. But why do people identify with social groups?

Brewer's (1991; Brewer & Caporael, Chapter 7, this volume) optimal distinctiveness theory and Hogg and Abrams' (1993; Abrams & Hogg, 1988; Hogg, Chapter 2, this volume) uncertainty reduction model provide two interesting and complementary perspectives on the motives for social identification. In our work, however, we propose that identification with social groups may satisfy yet another need of human beings, arguably a more fundamental one. We propose that social identities provide individuals with a sense of transcendence that is necessary for their psychological equanimity, which is continuously threatened by the awareness of the inevitability of their own death.

Surviving (the awareness of) death

Among the many scholars who addressed the issue of death and examined how human beings cope with the awareness of its inevitability, cultural anthropologist Ernst Becker (1971, 1973) is recognized as one of the most influential. The basic tenet of his general theory of human social behavior revolves around the fact that, with the development of a sophisticated intellect, humans developed self-awareness and with it the awareness of the inevitability of death. This awareness clearly does not come without its costs. In fact, it has the potential to create a paralyzing terror. Fortunately, thanks to their sophisticated intellectual abilities, humans developed cultural conceptions of reality. These conceptions are thought to buffer the anxiety derived from the awareness of the inevitability of death. In other words, the "problem" and the "solution" evolved concurrently.

Intriguing as they are, Becker's (1971, 1973) ideas would probably not have made it into modern social psychological theory, were it not for the work of social psychologists Jeff Greenberg, Tom Pyszczynski, and Sheldon

Solomon. These scholars took on the challenge of testing Becker's intriguing propositions empirically. They also developed them further, into what is now known as terror management theory (Greenberg, Pyszczynski, & Solomon, 1986). According to this theory, the "faith in a culturally derived worldview that imbues reality with order, stability, meaning, and permanence", coupled with the "belief that one is a significant contributor to this meaningful reality" are the two psychological mechanisms that allow humans to maintain psychological equanimity in the face of death (Pyszczynski, Solomon, & Greenberg, 2003, pp. 16–17).

According to the terror management theory, seeing oneself as a "meaningful contributor" corresponds to having positive self-esteem. Support for the theory comes from research demonstrating the existence of a negative correlation between self-esteem and anxiety (for a review, see Solomon, Greenberg, & Pyszczynski, 1991) as well as from work showing that people whose self-esteem has been raised respond to threats with lower levels of anxiety (Greenberg, Solomon, Pyszczynski, & Rosenblatt, 1992, Study 2) and also engage in less vulnerability denial (Greenberg, Pyszczynski, Solomon, & Pinel, 1993).

The greatest impact of the terror management theory comes from the research it triggered regarding the link between cultural worldviews and the salience of death thoughts. Terror management theorists reasoned that "if a psychological structure provides protection against the potential terror engendered by knowledge of mortality, then, reminders of mortality should increase the need to maintain that structure" (Greenberg, Solomon, & Pyszczynski, 1997, p. 78). This postulate has been empirically tested in a series of *mortality salience* experiments, in which participants are randomly assigned to an experimental condition in which the idea of death is made salient – for instance by asking them to write a paragraph about their own death – or to a control condition – in which they are asked, say, to write a paragraph about watching television. In endless studies, compared to participants in the control condition, mortality salience participants have been found to value behaviors consistent with their cultural worldview more and to more strongly denigrate individuals who behave contrary to such views (for reviews, see Greenberg et al., 1997; Solomon et al., 1991).

Because people's cultural worldviews are elaborated and maintained within a social group, one can conjecture that the well-documented tendency to enhance the image of the ingroup would be more pronounced when death is salient. Consistent with this hypothesis, Greenberg et al. (1990, Experiment 1) found that, when mortality was made salient, Christian participants viewed Christian targets more positively and Jewish targets more negatively. They also rated Christian targets more positively on a series of traits. In an even more stringent test of this idea, Harmon-Jones, Greenberg, Solomon, and Simon (1996) found that when personal death was made salient, participants in a minimal group paradigm displayed greater levels of ingroup bias compared to participants whose death had not been made salient.

The transcendental value of social identity

As is apparent from the above section, the hypothesis that social identity can serve an existential function is indebted to terror management theory. Our perspective differs, however, on one important count. Terror management theory argues that social identity serves an anxiety-buffer role because of its possible relations with self-esteem and because it is the repository of cultural worldviews (see Greenberg et al., 1990). In contrast, we propose that social identity can serve as a buffer for the anxiety because it allows for an extension of the self in space and time. Thanks to this possibility, individuals manage to escape the limitation *par excellence* of their humanity, namely being mortal.

To better appreciate the difference between the terror management theory conception and our own perspective on this issue, it helps to focus on the characteristics of social identity and more precisely on the difference between *social* and *personal* identity. Personal identity is that portion of identity that directly concerns the individual self. Clearly, personal identity is related to our body, which is finite. Our body not only limits us spatially, but it is the ultimate reminder of our limited time (see Goldenberg, Pyszczynski, Greenberg, & Solomon, 2000). With good exercise, a high-quality diet, and a generous dose of luck, an individual can hope to stick around for some 80 years. Due to these limitations, the various experiences that we see associated with our selves are bound to disappear. In other words, our individuality, with its host of private experiences and unique features, will unmistakably come to an end.

The groups with which we may identify do not face the same constraints. Their fate is not linked to a particular human body, and therefore not subject to the decay to which all humans, individually, are. Groups extend spatially well beyond the limits of the individual members and tend to outlive them; members can very often come and go without necessarily threatening the existence of the group. Also, the group is a much more abstract entity than the individuals, and as such is likely to survive for much longer, or at least to be perceived as doing so. This is especially the case for large social entities like ethnic groups, nations, or even ideological categories, which seem to have been constructed with the precise intent to appear immortal (e.g., Anderson, 1991; A. D. Smith, 1995).

If, as we argue, social identity provides a buffer against anxiety, the more chronically it is activated – that is to say, the more central it is to one's sense of self – the less one should be concerned with the idea of one's own demise. We found support for this conjecture in a historical analysis of the consequences of the conquest of Alexander the Great – around 330 BC.

In what is referred to as the pre-Hellenistic era, entities like the tribe or the polis, i.e., the city, were central to a person's understanding of his or her own identity. Such centrality should not be understood simply as an attachment of the individual to his or her group. Rather, it should be thought of as a deeper communion of the self and the community, so much so that the former could be understood only within the latter. Such a primacy of collective identities meant, according to Ulansey, that the problem of individual death was not at the forefront of individuals' psyche: "the fact that the collective would continue after one's personal death was experienced unconsciously as reducing the stress that the knowledge of human mortality might otherwise produce" (Ulansey, 2000, p. 216).

Things changed, however, as a result of Alexander's conquests. The collective identities were lost when the small communities in which they were grounded lost their autonomy in the new Hellenistic imperial order, and as a consequence of an enhancement in communication and transportation that accompanied it. These societal changes are thought to have been so important in modifying individuals' self-perception that they can be summarized by the sentence that "with Alexander begins *man as an individual*" (Tarn, 1968, p. 79). And with the individual as such, the problem of individual death becomes more salient. To say it with terror management theory, the "new individual" had lost what perhaps constituted his foremost anxiety-buffer mechanism.

What we learn from the analyses of this case study in the history of human civilization is that the extent to which different cultural systems and societal arrangements have stressed individual autonomy *versus* connection seems to be related to the way death was, and needed to be, understood. Specifically, death seems to be a great problem when one's identity is highly individualized, and less so when it is highly collective. This conclusion is consistent with our perspective on the role of social identity in dealing with existential concerns.

The loss of corporate identity brings individual mortality to the foreground. Is the reverse true? Does making mortality salient increase the importance of social identity? We believe that this is indeed the case. If social identity is a vehicle for transcendence, then it is reasonable to expect that when people are reminded of their mortality they will attach greater importance to membership in social groups. This can take the form of stronger identification and stronger defenses of the symbolic existence of the ingroup and of its integrity. It is also reasonable to expect that ingroups will be reified to a greater extent, since this process leads to the perception of the group as an entity having real existence, or, as put by Campbell (1958), as high in entitativity. These straightforward hypotheses were tested across a series of experiments in which individuals were asked to think of their own death or were subliminally primed with death-related words. We assessed the effects of these manipulations on the variables outlined above.

It is to the presentation of the results emerging from this research program that we now turn.

Testing the existential value of social identification

A preliminary test of our hypothesis was carried out in a study conducted in Italy and Belgium. The very simple design consisted of priming half of the participants with death, by asking them to write a short paragraph describing the emotions that the thought of their death aroused in them (cf. Greenberg et al., 1990). The other half were asked to engage in a parallel writing task – they were asked to write a short paragraph describing the emotions that arise in them when reading a book. Subsequently, all participants were asked to complete the who-am-I? task, and we counted the social identities that were listed (male/female; Belgian/Italian; student; etc.). Consistent with expectations, participants in the mortality-salient condition listed a greater number of social identities than those in the control condition (Castano & Sacchi, 1999).

A second study allowed for a more elaborate test of our hypothesis (Castano, Yzerbyt, Paladino, & Sacchi, 2002). Participants were either asked to write about their death (mortality-salient condition) or to write about reading a book (control condition). After a brief delay, in what was presented to them as the second, unrelated, part of the study, participants in both conditions filled out another questionnaire which included measures of ingroup entitativity (e.g., "Italians have many characteristics in common", "Italians have a sense of common fate", "Italy has real existence as a group"; Castano, Yzerbyt, & Bourguignon, 1999), ingroup identification (e.g., "I identify with Italians", "Being Italian has nothing to do with my identity"), and ingroup bias. The latter consisted of ratings of Italians and Germans (the outgroup) on 10 traits (e.g., gourmet, warm, hard-working).

The pattern of results was highly consistent with our hypothesis. Compared to the control participants, the mortality participants, all Italian students, identified more strongly with Italy, perceived Italy as more entitative, and judged Italians, but not Germans, more positively. Further analyses yielded evidence for the mediating role of entitativity and identification on the impact of the manipulation on ingroup bias, a result that nicely complements previous findings on the impact of mortality salience on ingroup bias (Harmon-Jones et al., 1996) and of entitativity on ingroup bias (Gaertner & Schopler, 1998).

Shifting from common-identity to common-bond groups (Prentice, Miller, & Lightdale, 1994), a third experiment was conducted, on a sample of Belgian undergraduates at the Catholic University of Louvain at Louvain-la-Neuve (Yzerbyt, Castano, & Vermeulen, 1999). After a manipulation of mortality salience of the kind described above, participants were presented with a series of circles that represented the participant himself/

herself and his/her friends. Six different diagrams were proposed, in which the circles could vary in the extent to which they overlapped with each other, going from no overlap at all to an important overlap (cf. Aron et al., 1992). The higher the overlap, the higher the perceived entitativity of the group (see Gaertner & Schopler, 1998). In line with expectations, we observed a higher perception of entitativity of the group of friends in the mortality-salient condition, suggesting that the effect of mortality salience on the tendency of individuals to cling to the ingroup applies to common-bond groups as well.

The findings reviewed above illustrate the fact that when individuals contemplate their own demise, they cling to the ingroup more strongly than when they have not been thinking of their death. However, the origins of the precise psychological mechanism through which such an effect is produced need further consideration.

Research stemming from terror management theory has shown that when mortality is salient, individuals engage in two kinds of behaviors (see Pyszczynski, Greenberg, & Solomon, 1999). They utilize *proximal* strategies that supposedly would delay death, like adopting a good diet or engaging in physical exercise. They also engage in the cultural worldview defenses we described above, which because of their bearing no rational relation with death are called *distal*. After all, one is unlikely to prolong one's life by fining prostitutes more harshly (cf. Rosenblatt, Greenberg, Solomon, Pyszczynski, & Lyon, 1989). We therefore asked ourselves, what is the precise nature of the mechanisms that we observed in our studies on social identification? Specifically, are mortality-salient participants thinking that they are better off identifying with their countries or another entity because they realize that as single individuals their existence is threatened, or are they largely unaware of the processes that occur when death thoughts are salient? To answer this question, we conducted two studies, in which the death manipulation was subliminal (Castano, 2004) and indirect measures of the extent to which individuals cling to their ingroup were used (Castano, 2004; Yzerbyt, Carnaghi, & Castano, 2003).

A first study relied on a categorization paradigm, in which participants are asked to classify individual targets as members of the ingroup or the outgroup. Research using this paradigm has shown that group members are reluctant to include ambiguous targets in the ranks of the ingroup, and that this tendency results in what has been referred to as the "ingroup over-exclusion effect" (Leyens & Yzerbyt, 1992; Yzerbyt, Leyens, & Bellour, 1995). This effect has been interpreted as stemming from the motivational concerns of individuals to protect the ingroup from the erroneous inclusion of outgroup members. This interpretation is supported by evidence that the level of ingroup identification moderates the magnitude of overexclusion. Castano, Yzerbyt, Bourguignon, and Seron (2002) asked Northern Italian participants to classify pictures as Northern Italians or Southern Italians and found that highly identified Northern Italians classified a greater number of pictures in the Southern Italian category. In contrast, Northern Italians who did not identify strongly with their ingroup did not show any tendency to overexclude from the ingroup. The degree of ingroup over-exclusion can thus be considered a good measure of the importance attached to the ingroup by the participants. Moreover, it has the distinct advantage of being fairly indirect. It was thus used in one experiment in which we attempted to provide further evidence that mortality salience would increase the importance attached to the ingroup.

A series of pictures of male students were first pre-tested among Scottish students at the University of St. Andrews, Scotland, so as to be able to classify them into various levels of "Scottishness" or "ingroupness". Pic-tures at level 1 tended to be classified as English, pictures at level 5 tended to be classified as Scottish, and the remaining levels consisted of inter-mediate pictures. This material was then used in an experiment in which half of a sample of Scottish students was primed subliminally with the word "death", while the other half was primed subliminally with the word "field". Subsequently, they completed an ingroup–outgroup categorization task which required classifying the pre-tested pictures as either Scottish (the ingroup) or English (the outgroup).

The subliminal priming paradigm is not only a well-known technique within social cognition in general (Bargh & Pietromonaco, 1982) and stereotyping research in particular (Devine, 1989; Lepore & Brown, 1997), it has been successfully used by Arndt and colleagues (Arndt, Allen, & Greenberg, 2001; Arndt, Greenberg, Pyszczynski, & Solomon, 1997) to replicate the classic terror management theory findings. In line with other studies showing that aversive events do not produce effects parallel to mortality salience, subliminally priming the word "death" but not other negative words such as "pain" has been found to produce typical mortality-salience effects. Indeed, only those participants who had been confronted with subliminal presentations of the word "death" were later found to be more positively disposed toward people or ideas that support their world-view and self-esteem, and more negatively toward people or ideas that threaten these two psychological entities (Arndt et al., 1997, Study 2). This pattern strongly suggests that it is not just the negativity of the primes that is at stake but indeed the fact that people are automatically activating the notion of their own death.

Building on previous overexclusion findings, we anticipated that parti-cipants in the death-prime condition would show a stronger degree of ingroup overexclusion, particularly at lower levels of ingroupness; that is, for target pictures that the pretest indicated were likely to be categorized as English (i.e., outgroup members). The reverse pattern was expected to emerge for targets that very much looked like ingroup members. This was precisely the pattern that was observed. While at lower levels of ingroupness, death-prime participants classified more pictures than control participants as outgroup members, the opposite trend was observed at higher levels of ingroupness (Castano, 2004).

In addition to the categorization decisions, the latency for categorization was also recorded. The findings on this additional variable showed that while the control condition revealed no relationship between the type of target to be classified and the categorization latency, most interesting linear and quadratic trends emerged in the mortality-salient condition. Closer inspection of the data suggests that mortality-salient participants took longer to classify pictures when these looked like ingroup members. Moreover, they took longer to classify more ambiguous pictures. This result is entirely consistent with the hypothesis that ingroup–outgroup categorization indeed becomes a more important task under mortality-salient conditions.

The relevance of the results from a study using the ingroup overexclusion paradigm is twofold. First, since subliminal primes were used, the observed difference clearly stems from the operation of some unconscious processes rather than from the deliberate thinking of individuals engaged in resolving the problem of their own demise. Second, the fact that the pattern emerged on indirect measures of "ingroup clinging", also suggests that participants may not be as much aware that they are boosting their representation of the ingroup as they are when explicit ingroup evaluation measures are used.

Support for the hypothesis that clinging to the ingroup is a spontaneous reaction to the confrontation with death-related stimuli is not restricted to this study, in which we relied on the ingroup overexclusion paradigm. Another study conducted among psychology students at the Catholic University of Louvain at Louvain-la-Neuve yielded highly convergent results (Yzerbyt et al., 2003).

In this study, we hypothesized that individuals perceive a greater overlap between themselves and the ingroup when they find themselves confronted with the idea of their finitude. Concretely, participants first rated the extent to which a series of traits were characteristic of themselves and then, depending on the experimental condition, were instructed to write a paragraph about their own death (mortality-salient condition) or about their leaving their parental home in order to start living on their own (control condition). Subsequently, participants were asked to rate the ingroup (the group of psychologists) on the same traits that they had used to rate the self. Both lists of traits comprised a series of filler traits along with six traits that pretest work had revealed were stereotypical of psychologists. There were three positive traits (empathic, understanding, sensitive) and three negative traits (disorganized, messy, disordered). In order to make participants' task somewhat less obvious, the order of the presentation of the traits differed between the self and group.[1]

The critical dependent variable was the degree of overlap between the self and the ingroup ratings, which was measured by means of a d-square score.

This score provides a measure of the similarity between two profiles (in the present context, the self and the ingroup) while taking into account the distance between the ratings given to the traits. We computed one d-score for the positive traits and one for the negative traits to obtain two indices of self–group similarity. Analyses on these scores revealed that the self–ingroup overlap was much higher in the mortality-salience condition than in the control condition. However, this was the case only for the negative traits. The absence of effects of the manipulation on the positive traits was most likely due to a ceiling effect. Indeed, the self–ingroup overlap on positive traits was very high in both conditions.

These data yield further evidence for the claim that stronger attachment to the ingroup in a mortality-salience compared to a control condition, can be observed on indicators that are not easily controllable by participants. Moreover, because the enhanced self–ingroup overlap occurred on negative traits, the present findings suggest that this phenomenon is not driven by self-serving considerations.

Conclusion

In this chapter we proposed that social identification with entities that are broader and longer lasting than the individual self has a unique value for humans: it allows escape from the *unbearable finitude of being*. By shifting from a personal, finite identity to a social, abstract, and more encompassing identity, human beings may experience a different level of existence which is not threatened by the biological fate that they know, as individuals, they cannot escape.

If our conjecture holds some value, then the loss of social identity may entail an enhanced anxiety about individual death. Conversely, making the idea of death more salient should increase the importance of social membership and the associated identification. In support of the former corollary, we have noted scholars' observations on how the loss of corporate identity following the conquest of Alexander the Great brought to the foreground the issue of individual death and transcendence, in a way that was unknown to the pre-Hellenistic societies (Ulansey, 2000).

The results of a series of experimental studies yield evidence for the second corollary. After being reminded of their mortality or being subliminally primed with death, individuals listed a greater number social identities in the who-am-I? task and perceived their group of friends as more bounded. We also found that Italian participants perceived themselves as more Italian and saw Italy as more of a real entity. Finally, we observed that Scottish participants displayed a greater concern for Scotland and even that psychology students perceived a greater overlap between their individual features and those characterizing the members of their ingroup.

These findings are consistent with our conjecture, as well as with terror management theory, which played a fundamental role in shaping our thinking about this issue. Indeed, terror management theory suggests that "symbolic immortality is provided through identification with entities larger and longer-lasting than the self" (Greenberg et al., 1997, p. 65). Social identification, however, is conceptualized in terror management theory as a means toward an end, which remains one's consensual validation (Greenberg et al., 1990). Consistent with this view, research stemming from terror management theory has examined whether the possibility of deriving positive self-esteem from social groups affects social (de)identification processes under mortality-salience conditions, and found support for this rationale (Arndt, Greenberg, Schimel, Pyszczynski, & Solomon, 2002; Dechesne, Greenberg, Arndt, & Schimel, 2000; Dechesne, Janssen, & van Knippenberg, 2000).

As pointed out above, we adopted a somewhat different perspective with respect to the role of social identification in the management of existential concerns. Indeed, we argued that social identification could be an end in itself: it is through the very fact of extending the self in space and time, and thus through their provision of a different level of existence, that groups become a vehicle for transcendence (Castano, Yzerbyt, Paladino, & Sacchi, 2002b). By arguing this position we are by no means suggesting that social identification does not provide self-esteem and/or that it cannot boost one's cultural worldview. Social identity may serve as an anxiety-buffer mechanism in several different ways, and we see our own proposition as complementary to, rather than as in contrast to, the two mechanisms proposed by terror management theory. (The interested reader will find elsewhere an elaboration of the relationship between our perspective and the self-esteem interpretation of the role of social identification; see Castano, Yzerbyt, & Paladino, 2004).

Are all social identities born equal?

In our empirical work, we have used a variety of social groups as repositories of social identities: from national and professional groups to small, relational groups like a group of friends. Are the social identities derived from these groups equivalent? Common sense and research findings alike tell us that this is unlikely to be the case. For one thing, the former type of groups (e.g., national, professional) are large social categories where contact among all or even most group members, as members, is rare and certainly not a defining feature. The latter kind of groups, like a group of friends or family, are relational, common-bond groups. These groups clearly provide different kinds of "WEs" (Brewer & Gardner, 1996). Social identities derived from these different kinds of groups can thus vary in the ways in which they alleviate existential concerns. Small, interacting groups may alleviate them because they provide individuals with a sense of intimacy and this may be a powerful buffer for the anxiety deriving from contemplating one's demise (cf. Wisman & Koole, 2003; this is perhaps a proximal rather than distal defense). Other mechanisms, like cultural worldview defense and the attachment to more abstract social identities based on membership in large social categories, may be more *distal*, activated automatically and without individuals' awareness. Given the wealth of research on this theme, we are optimistic that these questions will soon be answered.

In the beginning there was the individual. Or was there?

Similar to other contributions to this volume (e.g., Brewer & Caporael, Chapter 7; Hogg, Chapter 2), the perspective presented here focuses on a fundamental need of the human being as an *individual*. Given the physical properties of human beings, it may seem artificial to see individuals as anything other than single individual entities. As elegantly put by Geertz (1979), "The Western conception of the person as a bounded, unique, more or less integrated motivational and cognitive universe . . ., however incorrigible it may seem to us, [is] a rather peculiar idea within the context of the world's cultures" (p. 229; quoted in Semin & Rubini, 1990, p. 465). In fact, other, non-Western cultures seem to have a conception of the person which varies greatly from ours. Most notably, so-called interdependent cultures have been shown to see human beings as much more interconnected with their environment and other human beings (e.g., Menon, Morris, Chiu, & Hong, 1999; Miller, 1984).

The issue, of course, is not who is getting it right. Reality is defined by the cultural experience and it therefore becomes an issue of beliefs rather than one of truth. However, a careful examination of these cultural differences, especially with respect to the conception of human identity, is of interest. It reminds us that other conceptualizations are possible, and indeed, as we described in the introduction to this chapter, have existed. Acknowledgement of these different "worlds" allows consideration that perhaps, in the beginning, there was not the individual, or at least not the individual as we know it. Such a point can be more clearly understood in light of the model of human evolution proposed by Caporael (1997). According to Caporael, sociality is a constitutive part rather than a consequence of individually evolved beings. It would thus be misleading to consider human cognitive functioning as well as human needs (and perhaps even human drives) as stemming exclusively from the individual, at least the individual seen as a biological, separate entity. Human needs most likely emerged thanks to, or have been shaped by, the evolutionary history of humanity. And this is far more *groupal* than it is individual (see Brewer & Caporael, Chapter 7, this volume).

From this perspective, social identification processes may not be considered exclusively as a strategy available to individuals to, say, boost their self-esteem but rather as a constituent part of their being. Similarly, social identification with groups may not have been "invented" by full-fledged human beings when they were first confronted with the annoying realization of the inevitability of their death. Rather, the cognitive complexity that allows for self-awareness and for the awareness of the inevitability of one's demise may have emerged together, in synergy, with the capacity for collective self-definitions which extend each human being's physical and psychological boundaries. Life in groups and the social identification processes that are constituents of such a strategy may have played a critical role in the emergence of human cognitive complexity, as much as it serves the management of one of its most inconvenient consequences.

Acknowledgement

We would like to thank Dora Capozza and Rupert Brown for their helpful comments on an earlier draft of this chapter.

Note

1 As can be seen, this paradigm builds on earlier work on social projection (Krueger & Clement, 1994) with the important exception that ratings made about the ingroup now replace ratings made about people in general (see also Arndt et al., 2002; Simon et al., 1997). Note also that we are confronted here with the way people relate to a real group. Because there is no way to prevent people from spontaneously self-projecting to the ingroup if they were to fill in the ratings for the ingroup first and only then indicate the extent to which the various traits were self-descriptive, we needed to restrict ourselves to the opposite order in the measures. Moreover, our goal was not to disentangle people's tendency to project the self to the group *versus* to introject the group into the self, but rather to have a valid index of self–group overlap.

References

Abrams, D., & Hogg, M. A. (1988). Comments on the motivational status of self-esteem in social identity and intergroup discrimination. *European Journal of Social Psychology, 18*, 317–334.

Anderson, B. (1991). *Imagined communities: Reflections on the origin and spread of nationalism* (2nd ed.). London: Verso.

Arndt, J., Allen, J. J. B., & Greenberg, J. (2001). Traces of terror: Subliminal death primes and facial electromyographic indices of affect. *Motivation and Emotion, 25*, 253–277.

Arndt, J., Greenberg, J., Pyszczynski, T., & Solomon, S. (1997). Subliminal exposure to death-related stimuli increases defense of the cultural worldview. *Psychological Science, 8*, 379–385.

Arndt, J., Greenberg, J., Schimel, J., Pyszczynski, T., & Solomon, S. (2002). To belong or not to belong, that is the question: Terror management and identification with gender and ethnicity. *Journal of Personality and Social Psychology*, *83*, 26–43.

Aron, A., Aron, E. N., & Smollan, D. (1992). Inclusion of other in the self scale and the structure of interpersonal closeness. *Journal of Personality and Social Psychology*, *63*, 596–612.

Bargh, J. A., & Pietromonaco, P. (1982). Automatic information processing and social perception: The influence of trait information presented outside of conscious awareness on impression formation. *Journal of Personality and Social Psychology*, *43*, 437–449.

Becker, E. (1971). *The birth and death of meaning: An interdisciplinary perspective on the problem of man*. New York: Free Press.

Becker, E. (1973). *The denial of death*. New York: Free Press.

Brewer, M. B. (1991). The social self: On being the same and different at the same time. *Personality and Social Psychology Bulletin*, *17*, 475–482.

Brewer, M. B., & Gardner, W. L. (1996). Who is this "We"? Levels of collective identity and self representations. *Journal of Personality and Social Psychology*, *71*, 83–93.

Brewer, M. B., & Harasty, A. S. (1996). Seeing groups as entities: The role of perceiver motivation. In R. M. Sorrentino & E. T. Higgins (Eds.), *Handbook of motivation and cognition: The interpersonal context* (Vol. 3, pp. 347–370). New York: Guilford Press.

Campbell, D. T. (1958). Common fate, similarity, and other indices of the status of aggregates of person as social entities. *Behavioural Science*, *3*, 14–25.

Caporael, L. R. (1997). The evolution of truly social cognition: The core configurations model. *Personality and Social Psychology Review*, *4*, 276–298.

Castano, E. (2004). In case of death, cling to the ingroup. *European Journal of Social Psychology*, *34*, 375–384.

Castano, E., & Sacchi, S. (1999). *The effect of mortality salience on self-definition*. Unpublished raw data.

Castano, E., Yzerbyt, V. Y., & Bourguignon, D. (1999). *Measuring entitativity*. Unpublished manuscript, Catholic University of Louvain, Belgium.

Castano, E., Yzerbyt, V. Y., Bourguignon, D., & Seron, E. (2002). Who may enter? The impact of ingroup identification on in-group/out-group categorization. *Journal of Experimental Social Psychology*, *38*, 315–322.

Castano, E., Yzerbyt, V. Y., & Paladino, M. P. (2004). Transcending oneself through social identification. In S. L. Koole, T. Pyszczynski, & J. Greenberg (Eds.), *Handbook of experimental existential psychology* (pp. 305–321). New York: Guilford Press.

Castano, E., Yzerbyt, V. Y., Paladino, M. P., & Sacchi, S. (2002). I belong, therefore, I exist: Ingroup identification, ingroup entitativity, and ingroup bias. *Personality and Social Psychology Bulletin*, *28*, 135–143.

Coats, S., Smith, E. R., Claypool, H. M., & Banner, M. J. (2000). Overlapping mental representations of self and in-group: Reaction time evidence and its relationship with explicit measures of group identification. *Journal of Experimental Social Psychology*, *36*, 304–315.

Dechesne, M., Greenberg, J., Arndt, J., & Schimel, J. (2000). Terror management and the vicissitudes of sports fan affiliation: The effects of mortality salience on optimism and fan identification. *European Journal of Social Psychology, 30,* 813–835.

Dechesne, M., Janssen, J., & van Knippenberg, A. (2000). Derogation and distancing as terror management strategies: The moderating role of need for closure and permeability of group boundaries. *Journal of Personality and Social Psychology, 79,* 923–932.

Devine, P. G. (1989). Stereotypes and prejudice: Their automatic and controlled components. *Journal of Personality and Social Psychology, 56,* 5–18.

Gaertner, L., & Schopler, J. (1998). Perceived ingroup entitativity and intergroup bias: An interconnection of self and others. *European Journal of Social Psychology, 28,* 963–980.

Geertz, C. (1979). From the native's point of view. On the nature of anthropological understanding. In P. Rabinow & W. M. Sullivan (Eds.), *Interpretive social science.* Berkeley, CA: University of California Press.

Goldenberg, J. L., Pyszczynski, T., Greenberg, J., & Solomon, S. (2000). Fleeing the body: A terror management perspective on the problem of human corporeality. *Personality and Social Psychology Review, 4,* 200–218.

Greenberg, J., Pyszczynski, T., & Solomon, S. (1986). The causes and consequences of the need for self-esteem: A terror management theory. In R. F. Baumeister (Ed.), *Public self and private self* (pp. 189–212). New York: Springer-Verlag.

Greenberg, J., Pyszczynski, T., Solomon, S., & Pinel, E. (1993). Effects of self-esteem on vulnerability-denying defensive distortions: Further evidence of an anxiety-buffering function of self-esteem. *Journal of Experimental Social Psychology, 29,* 229–251.

Greenberg, J., Pyszczynski, T., Solomon, S., Rosenblatt, A., Veeder, M., Kirkland, S., et al. (1990). Evidence for terror management theory II: The effects of mortality salience on reactions to those who threaten or bolster the cultural worldview. *Journal of Personality and Social Psychology, 58,* 308–318.

Greenberg, J., Solomon, S., & Pyszczynski, T. (1997). Terror management theory of self-esteem and cultural worldviews: Empirical assessments and conceptual refinements. In M. P. Zanna (Ed.), *Advances in experimental social psychology* (Vol. 29, pp. 61–139). San Diego, CA: Academic Press.

Greenberg, J., Solomon, S., Pyszczynski, T., & Rosenblatt, A. (1992). Why do people need self-esteem? Converging evidence that self-esteem serves an anxiety-buffering function. *Journal of Personality and Social Psychology, 63,* 913–922.

Harmon-Jones, E., Greenberg, S., Solomon, S., & Simon, L. (1996). The effects of mortality salience on intergroup bias between minimal groups. *European Journal of Social Psychology, 26,* 677–681.

Hogg, M. A., & Abrams, D. (1993). Towards a single-process uncertainty-reduction model of social motivation in groups. In M. A. Hogg & D. Abrams (Eds.), *Group motivation: Social psychological perspectives* (pp. 173–190). London: Harvester Wheatsheaf.

Krueger, J., & Clement, R. W. (1994). The truly false consensus effect: An ineradicable and egocentric bias in social perception. *Journal of Personality and Social Psychology, 67,* 596–610.

Lepore, L., & Brown, R. (1997). Category and stereotype activation: Is prejudice inevitable? *Journal of Personality and Social Psychology, 72,* 257–287.

Leyens, J.-Ph., & Yzerbyt, V. Y. (1992). The ingroup overexclusion effect: Impact of valence and confirmation on stereotypical information search. *European Journal of Social Psychology, 22,* 549–569.

Mackie, D. M., & Smith, E. R. (Eds.). (2002). *From prejudice to intergroup emotions: Differentiated reactions to social groups.* New York: Psychology Press.

Menon, T., Morris, M. W., Chiu, C., & Hong, Y. (1999). Culture and the construal of agency: Attribution to individual versus group dispositions. *Journal of Personality and Social Psychology, 76,* 701–717.

Miller, J. G. (1984). Culture and the development of everyday social explanation. *Journal of Personality and Social Psychology, 46,* 961–978.

Prentice, D. A., Miller, D. T., & Lightdale, J. R. (1994). Asymmetries in attachments to groups and to their members: Distinguishing between common-identity and common-bond groups. *Personality and Social Psychology Bulletin, 20,* 484–493.

Pyszczynski, T., Greenberg, J., & Solomon, S. (1999). A dual-process model of defense against conscious and unconscious death-related thoughts: An extension of terror management theory. *Psychological Review, 106,* 835–845.

Pyszczynski, T., Solomon, S., & Greenberg, J. (2003). *In the wake of 9/11: The psychology of terror.* Washington, DC: American Psychological Association.

Reicher, S. D. (1987). Crowd behavior as social action. In J. C. Turner, M. A. Hogg, P. J. Oakes, S. D. Reicher, & M. S. Wetherell (Eds.), *Rediscovering the social group: A self-categorization theory* (pp. 171–202). Oxford, UK: Blackwell.

Rosenblatt, A., Greenberg, J., Solomon, S., Pyszczynski, T., & Lyon, D. (1989). Evidence for terror management theory I: The effects of mortality salience on reactions to those who violate or uphold cultural values. *Journal of Personality and Social Psychology, 57,* 681–690.

Semin, G. R., & Rubini, M. (1990). Unfolding the concept of person by verbal abuse. *European Journal of Social Psychology, 20,* 463–474.

Simon, L., Greenberg, J., Arndt, J., Pyszczynski, T., Clement, R., & Solomon, S. (1997). Perceived consensus, uniqueness, and terror management: Compensatory responses to threats to inclusion and distinctiveness following mortality salience. *Personality and Social Psychology Bulletin, 23,* 1055–1065.

Smith, A. D. (1995). *Nations and nationalism in a global era.* Cambridge, MA: Polity Press.

Smith, E. R. (1993). Social identity and social emotions: Toward new conceptualizations of prejudice. In D. M. Mackie & D. L. Hamilton (Eds.), *Affect, cognition, and stereotyping: Interactive processes in group perception* (pp. 297–315). San Diego, CA: Academic Press.

Solomon, S., Greenberg, J., & Pyszczynski, T. (1991). Terror management theory of self-esteem. In C. R. Snyder & D. R. Forsyth (Eds.), *Handbook of social and clinical psychology: The health perspective* (Vol. 162, pp. 21–40). Elmsford, NY: Pergamon Press.

Stevens, L. E., & Fiske, S. T. (1995). Motivation and cognition in social life: A social survival perspective. *Social Cognition, 13,* 189–214.

Tajfel, H. (1981). *Human groups and social categories.* Cambridge, UK: Cambridge University Press.

Tarn, W. W. (1968). *Hellenistic civilization*. Cleveland, OH: Meridian Books.

Turner, J. C., Hogg, M. A., Oakes, P. J., Reicher, S. D., & Wetherell, M. S. (1987). *Rediscovering the social group: A self-categorization theory*. Oxford, UK: Blackwell.

Ulansey, D. (2000). Cultural transition and spiritual transformation: From Alexander the Great to cyberspace. In T. Singer (Ed.), *The vision thing: Myth, politics, and psyche in the world* (pp. 213–231). New York: Routledge.

Wisman, A., & Koole, S. L. (2003). Hiding in the crowd: Can mortality salience promote affiliation with others who oppose one's worldviews? *Journal of Personality and Social Psychology, 84*, 511–526.

Yzerbyt, V. Y., Carnaghi, A., & Castano, E. (2003). *The impact of mortality salience on self–ingroup overlapping*. Unpublished manuscript, Catholic University of Louvain, Belgium.

Yzerbyt, V. Y., Castano, E., & Vermeulen, J. (1999). *The impact of mortality salience on ingroup entitativity*. Unpublished raw data.

Yzerbyt, V. Y., Dumont, M., Gordijn, E. H., & Wigboldus, D. (2002). Intergroup emotions and self-categorization: The impact of perspective-taking on reactions to victims of harmful behavior. In D. M. Mackie & E. R. Smith (Eds.), *From prejudice to intergroup emotions: Differentiated reactions to social groups* (pp. 67–88). New York: Psychology Press.

Yzerbyt, V. Y., Leyens, J.-Ph., & Bellour, F. (1995). The ingroup overexclusion effect: Identity concerns in decisions about group membership. *European Journal of Social Psychology, 25*, 1–16.

Chapter 5

Living on the edge: Dynamics of intragroup and intergroup rejection experiences

Jolanda Jetten, Nyla R. Branscombe, and Russell Spears

Introduction

Rejection is a painful experience. Considerable research has shown that people are negatively affected by exclusion because their intrinsic need for belongingness is violated (Baumeister & Leary, 1995; Tajfel & Turner, 1979). Those who are excluded are prone to feelings of alienation, depression, low self-esteem, anxiety, and loneliness, and they are more likely to engage in self-defeating behavior (Baumeister & Tice, 1990; Cozzarelli & Karafa, 1998; Rosenberg, 1979; Twenge, Cantanese, & Baumeister, 2002). While no one disputes the harmful and painful effects that rejection can lead to, what is unresolved is how those who are rejected react to their treatment. We know that following rejection some individuals distance themselves from the group, criticize and potentially even damage it, and some even betray the group that rejects them (e.g., Lewin, 1948; Schuetz, 1944; Twenge, Baumeister, Tice, & Stucke, 2001). On the other hand, those who are rejected may also maintain their loyalty and aspire to meet the norms or standards of the group even more strenuously (e.g., Breakwell, 1979; Noel, Wann, & Branscombe, 1995; Tajfel, 1978). Similarly, at the group level, groups that are marginalized in society or are rejected by other social groups may seek ways of gaining greater acceptance, or they can turn against and reject those who marginalize their group.

The aim of the present chapter is to bring together the scattered and diverse literature on intragroup and intergroup rejection, and examine the factors that determine the responses of those who are marginalized by such rejection. We argue that in order to understand the nature of the pain that rejection evokes and how people cope with it, we have to consider the source of the rejection and the response options available to different targets of rejection. We first consider research that has varied the source of the rejection – whether it is from other ingroup members, or stems from an outgroup or the society as a whole. We then examine differences in the stability of the categorization – whether rejection is stable and unlikely to change over time or unstable and open to recategorization.

A framework of reactions to peripheral states: Source of rejection and category stability

We argue that the perceived source of the rejection determines whether intragroup processes or intergroup processes drive responses to exclusion. Intragroup processes dominate when the ingroup rejects one of its members, while intergroup processes come into play when an outgroup rejects or devalues the ingroup as a whole. Although the literature on intragroup rejection and rejection or devaluation of the ingroup as a whole has developed rather separately, one of our starting assumptions is that there are important parallels and similarities in people's responses to these different types of rejection. For instance, rejection based on one's social category and intragroup rejection can affect both group identification and other indicators of group loyalty (Branscombe, Schmitt, & Harvey, 1999; Branscombe, Spears, Ellemers, & Doosje, 2002; Jetten, Branscombe, Schmitt, & Spears, 2001), evaluations of other ingroup members (Schmitt & Branscombe, 2001), and personal and group-based self-esteem (Branscombe et al., 1999; Jetten, Branscombe, & Spears, 2002; Schmitt, Spears, & Branscombe, 2003).

We argue that a second important factor for understanding responses to rejection is the stability of the peripheral categorization. For some group members, as well as some groups, rejection will be relatively stable, unchangeable, and not under the individual's own control (e.g., blacks, females). However, for others, the peripheral experience may revolve around ways of changing or eliminating the peripheral label. In other words, such individuals or groups do not assume that their peripheral state is fixed and pre-determined. As a consequence, their behavior is directed toward alleviating, in one way or the other, the peripheral status. For instance, some group members that are currently rejected by fellow ingroup members may recognize the temporary nature of the exclusion. They may realize that depending on their own behavior within the group, their position may improve or deteriorate even further in the future. Likewise, some groups may expect their group's position to change and they are driven by the awareness that the group's actions are crucial in determining the degree of acceptance by those that reject the group (i.e. cognitive alternatives, Tajfel, 1978).[1]

In sum, we argue that individuals or groups can be peripheral for different reasons and one has to understand the basis of the marginal status to predict responses to being excluded. We identified two dimensions that fundamentally affect the experience of being rejected – source of the rejection and stability of the peripheral condition. Four rather distinct types of rejection are suggested by combining these two dimensions. As illustrated in Figure 5.1, deviants, those in transition, classic minorities, and rebels can be distinguished based on these two dimensions. Each of these peripheral states will be discussed in turn, and we outline how the source of rejection and stability of the peripheral categorization affects the

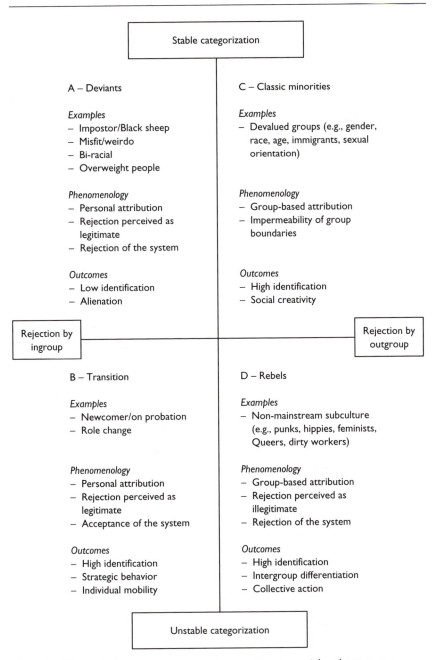

Figure 5.1 Schematic framework representing reactions to peripheral states as a function of source of rejection and stability of rejection.

phenomenology of these types of reactions to peripheral experiences. Finally, we consider how reactions to peripheral states differ in the way they respond to and cope with their plight.

Deviants

The first category of peripherals we identify are those who are rejected by the ingroup, and their categorization as peripheral is stable and unlikely to change. Examples of deviants are black sheep whose performance reflects badly on the group and for this reason they are rejected by other ingroup members (Marques, Abrams, Paez, & Martinez-Taboada, 1998; Marques, Yzerbyt & Leyens, 1988; see also the subjective group dynamics model; Marques et al., 1998; Marques, Abrams, & Serodio, 2001). Impostors, such as vegetarians who are caught eating meat, also face rejection because they violate central group norms and damage what the group stands for (see Hornsey & Jetten, 2003). We found that these rejected group members may even face more hostility from other ingroup members (vegetarians) than from outgroup members (non-vegetarians). For instance, vegetarians showed more negative affect in response to a meat-eating vegetarian than in response to an authentic vegetarian, whereas non-vegetarians did not (Experiment 1). In addition, we found in follow-up studies that commitment to the vegetarian group moderated the reaction to an impostor. While highly identified vegetarians reported the target to be most likeable, their liking for the target plummeted after finding out the target ate meat, bringing them on a par with evaluations by non-vegetarians and moderately identified vegetarians. Highly identified vegetarians were also more likely than non-vegetarians (Experiment 2) and moderately identified vegetarians (Experiment 3) to perceive that the meat-eating vegetarian was doing damage to the group.

Perceptions of deviance can also stem from a group member not matching the attitudes, behaviors, or culture of the group as a whole (Cozzarelli & Karafa, 1998). Such misfits often perceive their excluded state as stable and may not perceive that it is possible for them to gain greater acceptance. Note that deviants can also be those who are rejected by more than one ingroup or by both ingroup and outgroup. As an example of the former, in the case of bisexuals, the fact that they fit neither the heterosexual nor the homosexual category implies that they may face exclusion from both groups. Overweight people are another example of those who are rejected not only by outgroups (non-overweight people), but also by other ingroup members (other overweight people; see Crandall, 2000).

Given the stability of the deviants' peripheral condition, and that the rejection stems from others who share their group membership, a rather bleak picture emerges for such deviants' emotional well-being. Those who face rejection without any hope of future inclusion report more negative emotions than those who know that acceptance by other group members may be gained in the future (Jetten et al., 2001). Negative consequences are also likely because the target of rejection may make a personal attribution for the rejection and may even perceive the rejection as legitimate – either because their performance is not good enough, because they can not live up to the group's standards, or because they do not fit central group attributes.

Deviants may cope with rejection in a number of ways. First, group members may try to counteract the negative consequences of the threat by disidentifying with the ingroup, withdrawing from the group, and by emphasizing individuality or by stressing personal self-esteem (see Jetten et al., 2001; Williams, 2001). Second, when peripheral group members do not expect to be accepted by the ingroup in the future, and when characteristics that are deemed unacceptable by the ingroup are concealable, group members may try to hide their true identity and become impostors (see Hornsey & Jetten, 2003). In this way, the negative consequences and rejection may be avoided as long as group members pass as prototypical members of the group.

Transition

Our second category of responses to peripheral states – *transitions* – captures forms of rejection due to exclusion by the ingroup under conditions of instability. In such cases, the marginal status experienced by the individual is likely to be perceived as changeable. This form of exclusion is typically associated with situations where individuals have just joined the group and are still in the process of gaining acceptance by other group members (Brown, 1988; Levine & Moreland, 1994; Moreland, 1985). These newcomers have to assimilate to the group and change some of their behaviors to become more similar to full or more senior group members. It is also possible that group members are peripheral because it is their own choice to be excluded from groups in general (e.g., to be a loner), or because they anticipate leaving the group because of expected changes in roles and they do not invest in the group any further (e.g., those who are close to retirement).

We predict that the way these peripheral group members respond to exclusion by the group depends on their expectations about their future in that group. For instance, if one expects to become more prototypical in the future, group behavior might be determined by showing others that one is a "good" group member in order to speed up the acceptance process (Noel et al., 1995). There is some evidence that group members are motivated to present the self as group influenced when they feel junior in the group but not when they feel their intragroup status is moderate or high (Jetten, Hornsey, & Adarves-Yorno, 2006). We conducted a series of studies in contexts where responses were relatively public (i.e., responding over e-mail and data made available to third parties). In one of our studies, we made participants' identity as undergraduate psychology students salient and we then manipulated perceptions of status within the group psychology *students* (Jetten et al., 2006, Experiment 4). We either informed these psychology students that their responses would be compared to responses of professional psychologists (making salient participants' junior position within the broader *psychologists* group) or that their responses would be compared to college students who take psychology as a subject (making salient participants' senior position within the group psychologists). We then asked participants to rate conformity of the self in relation to other psychology students. We found that participants perceived themselves as more conformist in these public response settings than other psychology students when they felt junior in the group than when they felt more senior. These findings link in well with other research showing that those in transition typically accept the norms and values of the groups to which they are peripheral and they are often anxious and confused about future acceptance in the group (Moreland, 1985; Schuetz, 1944; Van Maanen, 1977). However, when an individual is marginal within a group because there is an expectation of exiting the group or because it is the individual's choice to not be included, few negative effects are likely because the group has lost its importance for the individual (Levine & Moreland, 1994).

Because of the instability of the peripheral position, those in transition are often attuned to the demands of the group and they are expected to be willing to make personal sacrifices for the group. High identification and expressing group loyalty can not only help to buffer against the negative affective consequences of being marginal, but can also be a way to demonstrate good group member behavior.[2] While such expressions of group loyalty may be genuine and reflect true concern for the group, they can also be strategic in the sense that they are aimed at gaining greater acceptance in the group (see Jetten et al., 2001; Jetten, Hornsey, Spears, Haslam, & Cowell, 2006; Noel et al., 1995). Importantly though, possibilities afforded by the social context moderate these peripherals' expressions of loyalty.

There is evidence for the important role of expectations concerning the likelihood that one's current peripheral position might change in the future (Jetten, Branscombe, Spears, & McKimmie, 2003). In two studies, peripheral group members learned that their acceptance by other group members would improve in the future or that they could expect rejection by other group members. It was found on various indices of group loyalty (ingroup homogeneity, motivation to work for the group, and evaluation of a motivated group member) that peripheral group members were less loyal to the group when they anticipated future rejection. In contrast, those who expected future acceptance were more loyal (more motivated to work for the group). These results were obtained only for low identifiers and appear to reflect strategic behavior on the part of those who are not very committed to the group. Those peripheral group members who were highly identified with the group remained loyal regardless of whether they expected future rejection or future acceptance.

Other research also suggests the importance of future expectations concerning intragroup position and that anticipating a change can represent a powerful identity threat for peripheral group members. In two studies by Jetten et al. (2002), the mere anticipation of becoming more prototypical or remaining at the same peripheral position affected collective and personal self-esteem. Both studies revealed that those who were peripheral within a valued group had higher collective self-esteem when they anticipated becoming more prototypical in the future compared to when they expected to become even more peripheral. It was also found that personal self-esteem was higher for those whose identity was presently insecure and who expected to become even more peripheral to the group than when a more prototypical position was anticipated. This shows, in line with self-affirmation theory (Steele, 1988; Steele & Liu, 1983), that when group members expect there is no chance they will gain greater acceptance in the group in the future, they cope with the expectation of maintaining their peripheral status by stressing their personal identity.

Recent research provides further evidence for the strategic nature of peripheral members' loyalty expressions and that they make use of the opportunities afforded by the social context (Jetten et al., 2006). Whereas prototypical group members were prepared to express commitment regardless of the social context, expressing commitment to the group was conditional for peripherals. They were found to assess the costs and benefits of doing so. They considered whether their performance was being monitored, whether or not the group was under threat, whether the audience was high or low status, and whether their expressions of commitment were going to upset or appeal to other group members.

Classic minorities

The upper right quadrant of Figure 5.1 involves rejection by an outgroup or by society in general and it encompasses a number of devalued groups that we term *classic minorities*. Groups that typically fall into this quadrant have been the subject of much research. Indeed, they are the groups that typically come to mind when thinking of excluded groups (e.g., women, gays, the elderly, immigrants, ethnic minorities). Research examining the perspective of excluded groups has accelerated over the last two decades, and our knowledge of the excluded group's perspective has dramatically increased (for reviews see Crocker & Major, 1989; Schmitt & Branscombe, 2002; Swim & Stangor, 1998).

Theorizing from social identity theory principles regarding the role of socio-structural variables in low status groups' response to inequality informs us about the phenomenology of classic minorities (Tajfel & Turner,

1979). For classic minorities, group membership is typically perceived as stable, and ability to change the excluded state is perceived to be unlikely either because there are limited possibilities for upward mobility or because group boundaries are impermeable. When group boundaries are perceived to be impermeable, exclusion on the basis of group membership is likely to enhance perceptions of "we" versus "them" which fuels group-based attributions for rejection. The path to collective responses to exclusion is paved by a combination of impermeable group boundaries and the perception that status inequality is illegitimate (Ellemers, van Knippenberg, & Wilke, 1990; Wright, Taylor, & Moghaddam, 1990).

Similar to our observation that stable intragroup rejection negatively affects individual group members, there is an abundance of evidence among a range of devalued groups that recognizing rejection and discrimination relates negatively to psychological well-being (see Branscombe et al., 1999; Klonoff & Landrine, 1999; Schmitt, Branscombe, Kobrynowicz, & Owen, 2002). However, there is also evidence that rejected groups have coping mechanisms at their disposal. It has been demonstrated in a number of studies that when the devalued group status is perceived as illegitimate, the more devalued group members perceive rejection and discrimination as pervasive, the more these group members will identify with their devalued group (Branscombe et al., 1999; Dion & Earn, 1975; Schmitt, Spears, & Branscombe, 2003; Simon et al., 1998). Such increased identification in response to perceived discrimination has clear psychological benefits that at least partially counteract the negative effects of perceived discrimination on well-being. Support for rejection-identification has been found in a number of social groups, including African-Americans (Branscombe et al., 1999), people with body piercings (Jetten et al., 2001), women (Schmitt et al., 2002; Schmitt, Branscombe, & Postmes, 2003) and international students (Schmitt, Spears, & Branscombe, 2003). Interestingly, in line with the rejection-identification model, Schmitt et al. (2002) found that women partially cope with discrimination by increasing their identification with other women, but no such pattern was observed for men facing discrimination against their gender group. For men, perceptions of discrimination were not correlated with well-being or identification with other men. These differences were attributed to the status differences in society between women and men, with perceptions of discrimination not having the same harmful effects for traditionally privileged groups (i.e., men) as they do for devalued groups (i.e., women). It was also observed by Schmitt, Spears, and Branscombe (2003) that those who face discrimination (international students) do not identify more with just any group they are member of (e.g., home country) but that they identify more with the group that is facing discrimination (international students).

When group boundaries are impermeable and status relations are secure (i.e., legitimate and stable), collective attempts to change the social structure are unlikely. Group members may instead engage in social creativity strategies that do not involve direct attempts to change the social structure (Lemaine, 1974; Tajfel & Turner, 1979). These social creativity strategies protect well-being by diverting attention away from the unfavourable intergroup comparison, changing the connotation of the comparison dimension, or allowing for a positive evaluation of the group along another dimension. There is also recent evidence that devalued groups use social creativity strategies to cope with rejection and protect group identification (Jetten, Schmitt, Branscombe, & McKimmie, 2005). Specifically, in this study, we manipulated threat to the value of the group by presenting participants with either positive or negative feedback concerning how their residential state (Queensland in Australia) was viewed by other states in Australia. We found that group members who face a threat to the value of their group identity engaged in social creativity strategies and countered such threats by emphasizing the distinctiveness of their state from other states and the respect they receive from fellow Queenslanders. In addition, we found that intergroup differentiation and intragroup respect were in turn positively related to group identification. Further mediational analyses showed that while threats to the ingroup's value can have a direct negative effect on ingroup identification, social creativity responses to value threat (emphasising intergroup differences and intragroup respect) can mediate a positive effect on ingroup identification, thereby suppressing the direct negative effect of such threats.

Rebels

The fourth and final quadrant encompasses those groups that are rejected by an outgroup, but for whom the rejection is likely to be unstable. Exclusion can be unstable because the source of rejection itself is controllable (e.g., those with body piercings), voluntary (e.g., self-defining as feminist), or even, to some extent, sought out (e.g., punks, hippies). Indeed, rejection may become the "raison d'être" for these groups and an important part of the identity of the subculture as a whole. Rebels may take pride in being different from mainstream society, and exclusion from it rather than inclusion may be actively sought out (Jetten & Branscombe, in press).

We argue that this quadrant represents the most collective response to being rejected. It brings together groups that consist of individuals who reject the system and decided to challenge and confront those rejecting their group (e.g., feminist). While the identity of rebels is often highly politicized and aimed at actively challenging the status quo, there are some important exceptions to this. Some groups that are marginalized develop strong subcultures and, precisely because members of such groups can resort to these subgroups, they may isolate the subgroup further from those that reject them. For instance, so-called "dirty workers" (employees with jobs that are physically, morally, or socially tainted such as garbage collectors and prison guards; Ashforth & Kreiner, 1999), who have difficulty constructing a positive sense of self within the mainstream, have been found to identify strongly with their subgroup and to set themselves apart from the broader organization.

While these ideas can be directly derived from classic social identity theory reasoning (see Tajfel & Turner, 1979), we argue that these types of rejected groups have been studied less often. Furthermore, the psychological consequences of being excluded also differ for these groups compared to those groups who face stable exclusion. For instance, groups such as people with body piercings that are in control of their marginal status within society (i.e., they can remove their piercings to avoid discrimination) are not as negatively affected by perceptions of discrimination (Jetten et al., 2001) as those for whom discrimination is both unavoidable and stable. This finding is consistent with recent research showing that perceiving discrimination impacts more negatively on the elderly, for whom group membership is irreversible and unchangeable, than for the young who will be leaving their devalued group very rapidly (Garstka, Schmitt, Branscombe, & Hummert, 2004).

Even though individual mobility may be a viable option for rebels, they may nevertheless decide to turn to their group membership as a means of coping with group-based rejection. We have repeatedly found that the psychological costs of group membership (i.e., pervasiveness of discrimination) are likely to be responded to by group members stressing their commitment and loyalty to the group. Furthermore, intergroup distinctions are not downplayed but are sought out. We found among people with body piercings that the more they faced discrimination by the mainstream, the more they emphasized differences between their own group and the mainstream (see Jetten et al., 2001).

Moving from one peripheral state to another

The four quadrants identified in Figure 5.1 should not be seen as a typology of different types of peripherals. Indeed, while there are many differences between the psychological states for those who find themselves in each quadrant, as should be evident from our analysis, there are also important similarities in the way these groups or individuals respond to being excluded. Another reason why we avoid labelling our framework a typology is that we assume that the peripheral states in each of the quadrants are not fixed and that movement between them is possible. Changes across time, as well as changes in the socio-structural context itself, may affect the phenomenology of being excluded and the way that rejection is coped with. The rejected individual or group is not a passive entity. People can also drive structural changes and they can decide to make use of some possibilities that are afforded by the social context and not others.

The question that arises then is what peripheral states can change or are most likely to do so, and what are the underlying causes and reasons for such change? We propose that change will mainly occur when rejection shifts from being stable to unstable, allowing for recategorization of the peripheral state. Specifically, we predict that instability of the social context may encourage deviants and classic minorities to follow individualistic recategorization (through individual mobility) or more collective routes (e.g., by recategorizing with others who face similar forms of rejection). We discuss these processes in more detail below.

Recategorization by deviants

Those who face stable rejection by other ingroup members need to develop an awareness that rejection is changeable and unstable before recategorization of the peripheral state is likely to occur. The trigger for a change in perceptions of stability may be that individual mobility and exit options become more salient or because there is increased awareness that there are other ingroup members who face similar forms of rejection. That is, deviants may recategorize by attempting to physically leave the group that rejects them and seek out other groups that are more accepting, or they may recategorize by forming subgroups with similar-minded others. Both strategies are aimed at protecting the self from the negative consequences of rejection.

The main motivation for joining together with others who are also rejected is that group identification can be an important source of coping with stressful challenges to one's identity and is an important way of restoring a damaged sense of belonging (Branscombe et al., 1999; Haslam, 2004; Miller & Kaiser, 2001). This transition of the nature of the peripheral state implies that one no longer deals with rejection as an individual, allowing group-level coping mechanisms to be employed (see Jetten et al., 2005; Underwood, 2000).

Recategorizing as a subgroup to cope with rejection is not such an easy strategy for all deviants. For instance, it has been found that overweight people do not identify and support other overweight people and it is therefore unlikely that they will recategorize as a subgroup (Crandall, 2000). Stigmas that are concealable are particularly unlikely to have this effect, and impostors who seek to hide their condition will be unlikely to form a group because the nature of their peripheral status is by definition concealed.

Recategorization by classic minorities

In line with social identity theory (Tajfel & Turner, 1979), we propose that responses by classic minorities to their marginal status can vary from individual mobility to social competition strategies. It has been proposed that individual exit strategies are usually tried before collective responses to rejection are selected as ways to escape rejection when group boundaries are permeable and legitimate (see Ellemers, 1993; Ellemers et al., 1990; see also Tajfel & Turner, 1979). Those who successfully leave their rejected group and gain entry into a more accepted group are likely to start off as peripherals on probation (i.e., in transition) and may attain greater acceptance over time by showing group loyalty. However, individual mobility attempts are not without risks, and they may incur costs if they turn out to be unsuccessful (see Branscombe & Ellemers, 1998). In the case of failed individual mobility, deviants may be negatively affected because they face exclusion not only from the group they would like to join but also from the ingroup they attempted to leave behind. Postmes and Branscombe (2002) demonstrated that well-being among African-Americans was most negatively affected when exclusion implied the loss of social support from other ingroup members.

A collective response to rejection becomes more likely when classic minorities perceive that group relations are not as stable as they used to be, and when exclusion is perceived to be increasingly illegitimate (Tajfel & Turner, 1979). Classic minorities turn into rebels when they begin to make use of the change possibilities afforded by the social context. In this case, group identity becomes politicized and willingness to engage in collective action increases (Simon & Klandermans, 2001).

While we predict that changes in the stability of the peripheral state may open up recategorization opportunities for those at the stable end of the continuum, at the unstable end of the spectrum, historical and socio-structural conditions may also affect the peripheral experience. For instance, we predict that changes in the pervasiveness of rejection may affect whether groups that originated as rebels cease to exist. It is for example conceivable that once greater status equality between males and females is achieved, there will be less room for a feminist movement. In the case of body markers, one consequence of the increasing popularity of specific body markers over time (e.g., ear lobe piercings) is that as they become more common and acceptable by mainstream society, those who decide to mark themselves in this particular way are no longer targets of discrimination. Indeed, it is even possible that certain body modifications become normative over time and that those who do not conform to these new norms and adopt the identity markers may face exclusion or rejection.

Final comments

In an attempt to link the scattered literature on different sources of exclusion, we examined and mapped out different peripheral states. We started this enterprise by identifying two dimensions that we see as crucial for differentiating between peripheral states. We distinguished intragroup rejection as a result of exclusion by the ingroup, from intergroup rejection where the source of the rejection is an outgroup or society at large. We also differentiated between stable and unstable classes of rejection. Combining the source of rejection dimension with the stability of the peripheral condition dimension resulted in the following types of peripheral states: (a) individuals who face stable rejection by other ingroup members (deviants), (b) individuals who face ingroup rejection that is unstable and may change in the future (transitions), (c) stable exclusion of groups by other groups (classic minorities), and (d) unstable exclusion of groups by other groups (rebels).

While the two central dimensions and the four peripheral states that we identified are by no means the only meaningful dimensions or possible classifications, this analysis provided a helpful framework for thinking about the experience of being peripheral. It showed the different but also, often surprisingly, similar phenomenology of the rejected, as well as the ways in which those who are excluded cope with their marginal position. Our analysis showed that specific coping strategies were not confined to specific quadrants and that different strategies or outcomes were expected for more than one peripheral state. For instance, we predict high identification following rejection not only when the ingroup is rejected by the outgroup (classic minorities and rebels), but also when individual group members face unstable rejection by the ingroup (transitions). Importantly though, identification serves a different function in different quadrants. Classic minorities identify more following rejection because identification protects against the negative effects of discrimination (Branscombe et al., 1999; Schmitt & Branscombe, 2002). Rebels, in contrast, show high identification because it helps to mobilize for the collective struggle (Reicher & Hopkins, 1996; Simon & Klandermans, 2001). For those in transition, however, high group identification and group loyalty when it occurs may serve a strategic function, aimed at speeding up the acceptance process and showing other ingroup members that one is a worthy member of the group (Jetten et al., 2002; Noel et al., 1995).

The distinction between unstable and stable rejection allowed us to examine peripheral states in a more dynamic way. It pointed to the possibility that the nature of the peripheral state can change when sociostructural changes allow for recategorization. We propose that, over time, stable rejection can become unstable and that opportunities afforded by a new social order provide leeway for deviants to explore different ways to cope. In an unstable social context, peripherals can either make use of individual mobility strategies (recategorizing at the individual level) or recategorize into subgroups, either aimed at changing the status quo (rebels) or at benefiting from social support offered by similar others. In short, we propose that examining peripheral states in a more dynamic way, taking into account changes over time and changes in socio-structural conditions (e.g., unequal status relations becoming more or less legitimate), allows for a better understanding of how people experience and change peripheral states.

We suggest that future research examining rejection and exclusion should take account of the similarities and differences among various peripheral states that can flow from ingroup or outgroup rejection and its stability. Such attempts will help to develop a more dynamic and integrated picture of the peripheral experience.

Acknowledgements

This research was supported by an ESRC grant (R000223981) awarded to the first author. We would like to thank Alex Haslam for his helpful suggestions on an earlier draft of this chapter.

Notes

1 Our dimension relating to stability of categorization should not be confused with stability of status relations. The latter type of stability is commonly examined in research on factors affecting responses by low-status groups to status inequality (Tajfel & Turner, 1979). Stability of categorization is different in that it is concerned with possibilities to recategorize offered by the social context. Another reason to differentiate between the two is that stability of status relations has been used exclusively in the context of intergroup relations in past research while we also consider the possibility of stability of categorization within groups in this chapter.
2 We focus in our analysis on those in transition almost exclusively in terms of those who are motivated to gain greater acceptance in the group and not on those who are in transition because they would like to leave the group behind. We acknowledge that the phenomenology and coping strategies for those who are exiting the group are rather different than for newcomers to the group. For instance, we predict that those who plan to leave the group will not be highly identified with the group and they are less likely to engage in strategic group behavior.

References

Ashforth, B. E., & Kreiner, G. (1999). "How can you do it?": Dirty work and the dilemma of identity. *Academy of Management Review, 24*, 413–434.
Baumeister, R. F., & Leary, M. R. (1995). The need to belong: Desire for interpersonal attachments as a fundamental human motivation. *Psychological Bulletin, 117*, 497–529.
Baumeister, R. F., & Tice, D. M. (1990). Anxiety and social exclusion. *Journal of Social and Clinical Psychology, 9*, 165–195.
Branscombe, N. R., & Ellemers, N. (1998). Coping with group-based discrimination: Individualistic versus group-level strategies. In J. K. Swim & C. Stangor

(Eds.), *Prejudice: The target's perspective* (pp. 243–266). New York: Academic Press.

Branscombe, N. R., Schmitt, M. T., & Harvey, R. D. (1999). Perceiving pervasive discrimination among African-Americans: Implications for group identification and well-being. *Journal of Personality and Social Psychology, 77*, 135–149.

Branscombe, N. R., Spears, R., Ellemers, N., & Doosje, B. (2002). Intragroup and intergroup evaluation effects on group behavior. *Personality and Social Psychology Bulletin, 28*, 744–753.

Breakwell, G. M. (1979). Illegitimate group membership and inter-group differentiation. *British Journal of Social and Clinical Psychology, 18*, 141–149.

Brown, R. (1988). *Group processes: Dynamics within and between groups*. Oxford, UK: Blackwell.

Cozzarelli, C., & Karafa, J. A. (1998). Cultural estrangement and terror management theory. *Personality and Social Psychology Bulletin, 24*, 253–267.

Crandall, C. S. (2000). Ideology and lay theories of stigma: The justification of stigmatisation. In T. F. Heatherton, R. E. Kleck, M. R. Hebl, & J. G. Hull (Eds.), *The social psychology of stigma* (pp. 126–150). New York: Guilford Press.

Crocker, J., & Major, B. (1989). Social stigma and self-esteem: The self-protective properties of stigma. *Psychological Review, 96*, 608–630.

Dion, K. L., & Earn, B. M. (1975). The phenomenology of being a target of prejudice. *Journal of Personality and Social Psychology, 32*, 944–950.

Ellemers, N. (1993). The influence of socio-structural variables on identity enhancement strategies. In W. Stroebe & M. Hewstone (Eds.), *European review of social psychology* (Vol. 4, pp. 27–57). Chichester, UK: Wiley.

Ellemers, N., van Knippenberg, A., & Wilke, H. (1990). The influence of permeability of group boundaries and stability of group status on strategies of individual mobility and social change. *British Journal of Social Psychology, 29*, 233–246.

Garstka, T. A., Schmitt, M. T., Branscombe, N. R., & Hummert, M. L. (2004). How young and older adults differ in their responses to perceived age discrimination. *Psychology and Aging, 19*, 326–335.

Haslam, S. A. (2004). *Psychology in organizations: The social identity approach* (2nd ed.). London: Sage.

Hornsey, M. J., & Jetten, J. (2003). Not being what you claim to be: Impostors as sources of group threat. *European Journal of Social Psychology, 33*, 639–657.

Jetten, J., & Branscombe, N. R. (in press). Seeking minority group memberships: Responses to discrimination when group membership us self-selected. To appear in F. Butera and J. Levine (Eds.), *Coping with minority status: Responses to exclusion and inclusion*. New York: Cambridge.

Jetten, J., Branscombe, N. R., Schmitt, M. T., & Spears, R. (2001). Rebels with a cause: Group identification as a response to perceived discrimination from the mainstream. *Personality and Social Psychology Bulletin, 27*, 1204–1213.

Jetten, J., Branscombe, N. R., & Spears, R. (2002). On being peripheral: Effects of identity insecurity on personal and collective self-esteem. *European Journal of Social Psychology, 32*, 105–123.

Jetten, J., Branscombe, N. R., Spears, R., & McKimmie, B. M. (2003). Predicting the paths of peripherals: The interaction of identification and future possibilities. *Personality and Social Psychology Bulletin, 29*, 130–140.

Jetten, J., Hornsey, M. J., & Adarves-Yorno, I. (2006). When group members admit to being conformist: The role of relative intragroup status in conformity self-reports. *Personality and Social Psychology Bulleting, 32*, 162–175.

Jetten, J., Hornsey, M. J., Spears, R., Haslam, S. A., & Cowell, E. (2004). *Keeping up appearances: The conditional nature of peripheral group members' loyalty expressions and actions.* Manuscript submitted for publication.

Jetten, J., Schmitt, M. T., Branscombe, N. R., & McKimmie, B. M. (2005). Suppressing the negative effect of devaluation on group identification: The role of intergroup differentiation and intragroup respect. *Journal of Experimental Social Psychology, 41*, 208–215.

Klonoff, E. A., & Landrine, H. (1999). Cross-validation of the schedule of racist events. *Journal of Black Psychology, 25*, 231–254.

Lemaine, G. (1974). Social differentiation and social originality. *European Journal of Social Psychology, 4*, 17–52.

Levine, J. M., & Moreland, R. L. (1994). Group socialization: Theory and research. In W. Stroebe & M. Hewstone (Eds.), *European review of social psychology* (Vol. 5, pp. 305–336). Chichester, UK: Wiley.

Lewin, K. (1948). *Resolving social conflicts.* New York: Harper.

Marques, J., Abrams, D., Paez, D., & Martinez-Taboada, C. (1998). The role of categorization and in-group norms in judgments of groups and their members. *Journal of Personality and Social Psychology, 75*, 976–988.

Marques, J., Abrams, D., & Serodio, R. G. (2001). Being better by being right: Subjective group dynamics and derogation of ingroup deviants when generic norms are undermined. *Journal of Personality and Social Psychology, 81*, 436–447.

Marques, J., Yzerbyt, V. Y., & Leyens, J.-Ph. (1988). The "black sheep effect": Extremity of judgments towards ingroup members as a function of group identification. *European Journal of Social Psychology, 18*, 1–16.

Miller, C. T., & Kaiser, C. R. (2001). A theoretical perspective on coping with stigma. *Journal of Social Issues, 57*, 73–92.

Moreland, R. L. (1985). Social categorization and the assimilation of "new" group members. *Journal of Personality and Social Psychology, 48*, 1173–1190.

Noel, J. G., Wann, D. L., & Branscombe, N. R. (1995). Peripheral ingroup membership status and public negativity toward outgroups. *Journal of Personality and Social Psychology, 68*, 127–137.

Postmes, T., & Branscombe, N. R. (2002). Influence of long-term racial environmental composition on subjective well-being in African Americans. *Journal of Personality and Social Psychology, 83*, 735–751.

Reicher, S., & Hopkins, N. (1996). Self-category constructions in political rhetoric: An analysis of Thatcher's and Kinnock's speeches concerning the British miners' strike (1984–1985). *European Journal of Social Psychology, 26*, 353–371.

Rosenberg, M. (1979). *Conceiving the self.* New York: Basic Books.

Schmitt, M. T., & Branscombe, N. R. (2001). The good, the bad, and the manly: Threats to one's prototypicality and evaluations of fellow in-group members. *Journal of Experimental Social Psychology, 37*, 510–517.

Schmitt, M. T., & Branscombe, N. R. (2002). The meaning and consequences of perceived discrimination in disadvantaged and privileged social groups. In

W. Stroebe & M. Hewstone (Eds.), *European review of social psychology* (Vol. 12, pp. 167–199). Chichester, UK: Wiley.

Schmitt, M. T., Branscombe, N. R., Kobrynowicz, D., & Owen, S. (2002). Perceiving discrimination against one's gender group has different implications for well-being in women and men. *Personality and Social Psychology Bulletin, 28,* 197–210.

Schmitt, M. T., Branscombe, N. R., & Postmes, T. (2003). Women's emotional responses to the pervasiveness of gender discrimination. *European Journal of Social Psychology, 33,* 297–312.

Schmitt, M. T., Spears, R., & Branscombe, N. R. (2003). Constructing a minority group identity out of shared rejection: The case of international students. *European Journal of Social Psychology, 33,* 1–12.

Schuetz, A. (1944). The stranger: An essay in social psychology. *American Journal of Sociology, 49,* 499–507.

Simon, B., & Klandermans, B. (2001). Politicized collective identity: A social psychological analysis. *American Psychologist, 56,* 319–331.

Simon, B., Loewy, M., Sturmer, S., Weber, U., Freytag, P., Habig, C., et al. (1998). Collective identification and social movement participation. *Journal of Personality and Social Psychology, 74,* 646–658.

Steele, C. M. (1988). The psychology of self-affirmation: Sustaining the integrity of the self. In L. Berkowitz (Ed.), *Advances in experimental social psychology* (Vol. 21, pp. 261–302). San Diego, CA: Academic Press.

Steele, C. M., & Liu, T. J. (1983). Dissonance processes as self-affirmation. *Journal of Personality and Social Psychology, 45,* 5–19.

Swim, J. K., & Stangor, C. (Eds.). (1998). *Prejudice: The target's perspective.* New York: Academic Press.

Tajfel, H. (1978). *The social psychology of minorities.* London: Minority Rights Group.

Tajfel, H., & Turner, J. C. (1979). An integrative theory of intergroup conflict. In W. G. Austin & S. Worchel (Eds.), *The social psychology of intergroup relations* (pp. 33–47). Monterey, CA: Brooks/Cole.

Twenge, J. M., Baumeister, R. F., Tice, D. M., & Stucke, T. S. (2001). If you can't join them, beat them: Effects of social exclusion on aggressive behavior. *Journal of Personality and Social Psychology, 81,* 1058–1069.

Twenge, J. M., Cantanese, K. R., & Baumeister, R. F. (2002). Social exclusion causes self-defeating behavior. *Journal of Personality and Social Psychology, 83,* 606–615.

Underwood, P. W. (2000). Social support: The promise and reality. In B. H. Rice (Ed.), *Handbook of stress, coping and health* (pp. 367–391). Newbury Park, CA: Sage.

Van Maanen, J. (1977). Experiencing organization: Notes on the meaning of careers and socialization. In J. Van Maanen (Ed.), *Organizational careers: Some new perspectives* (pp. 15–45). New York: Wiley.

Williams, K. D. (2001). *Ostracism: The power of silence.* New York: Guilford Press.

Wright, S. C., Taylor, D. M., & Moghaddam, F. M. (1990). Responding to membership in a disadvantaged group: From acceptance to collective protest. *Journal of Personality and Social Psychology, 58,* 994–1003.

Chapter 6

Protecting a threatened identity through sexual harassment: A social identity interpretation

Anne Maass and Mara R. Cadinu

Introduction

One of the most robust findings in the recent social identity literature is that people whose social identity is threatened or questioned tend to engage in identity-defensive behaviors, including the discrimination against outgroup members. According to Branscombe, Ellemers, Spears, and Doosje (1999), people may experience different kinds of ingroup threat all of which are likely to play a causal role in ingroup favoritism and outgroup discrimination. For example, people may experience a *threat to group value* referring to any situation in which the value of the ingroup is undermined – such as by information suggesting that one's own group performs less well or is morally inferior to a relevant outgroup. One way to re-establish the value of the ingroup is to derogate a relevant outgroup (Cadinu & Reggiori, 2002). Alternatively, people may be exposed to so-called *acceptance* or *prototypicality threat* that challenges their status as a good or as a prototypical group member. For instance, men whose masculinity is questioned may find this information highly threatening, especially if they are strongly identified with their gender group (Schmitt & Branscombe, 2001). Yet another kind of threat identified by Branscombe et al. challenges the *distinctiveness* of the ingroup compared to an outgroup.[1] Because people strive for meaningful and distinct social identities, any kind of information suggesting that ingroup and outgroup are indistinguishable will be perceived as threatening. Often, people may prefer a negative differentiation of the ingroup from the outgroup to no differentiation at all (Mlicki & Ellemers, 1996). Thus, group members may experience a wide range of social identity threat. Although people may respond very differently to different forms of threat, there is *one* reaction that has been observed for all of the above forms of identity threat, namely outgroup derogation. Outgroup derogation in response to identity-threatening experiences appears to be common to different forms of threat and is predominantly shown by those individuals who are highly committed to their group.

Most of the research on identity threat has employed classical measures used in social identity research: reward allocation, trait attribution, and verbal hostility toward or devaluation of outgroup. What we want to argue here is that social identity theory can reasonably be extended to social behaviors not generally investigated in this field. In our specific case we believe that sexual harassment constitutes a form of outgroup derogation that has strong social implications for the victim and for the society at large, and that this behavior can be understood in the light of social identity theory. In other words, we will try to link two research areas that have traditionally developed in complete independence (social identity and sexual harassment research), but that can greatly profit from cross-fertilization. In this chapter we will first provide some background information on the definition and pervasiveness of sexual harassment. We will then report on a research project in which we have investigated the role of different forms of identity threat in sexual harassment. Subsequently, we will advance the hypothesis that sexual harassment may also serve ingroup bonding. Finally, we will close the chapter by indicating some tentative strategies of reducing harassment, among which is the introduction of social norms discouraging harassment.

Sexual harassment

Sexual harassment is a widespread phenomenon in practically all countries in which women have entered the job market (Gruber, Smith, & Kauppinen-Toropainen, 1996). Although sexual harassment is counter-normative in most countries and illegal in some, the cumulative probability of becoming a victim of sexual harassment is surprisingly high. A large proportion of working women experience harassment in some form at least once during their lifetime, with risks being particularly high at hiring and at promotion. The negative consequences of harassment for both victim and organization are well documented in the literature (Baker, Terpstra, & Larntz, 1990; Morrow, McElroy, & Phillips, 1994; Rubinstein, 1987; Schneider, Swan, & Fitzgerald, 1997). Victims of harassment have been shown to suffer a wide range of physical and psychological symptoms, including distress, depression, and decreased job satisfaction. Sexual harassment also causes a number of negative consequences for the organization, including high absenteeism rates and decreased productivity.

There has been considerable debate about how to define sexual harassment and how to distinguish it from "normative" sexual advances. Most researchers and legal practitioners now agree that the behavior, in order to be defined as "harassment," has to be considered unwelcome by the victim and/or be considered inappropriate and offensive according to what is now called the "reasonable woman standard" (Wiener & Hurt, 2000). The different definitions offered by the Equal Employment Opportunity

Commission (1980) in the United States, by the Rubinstein (1987) report in Europe, and by most researchers in the field, all converge in that they define sexual harassment as verbal or physical behavior of a sexual nature that is unwelcomed by the victim, that tends to interfere with the recipient's work, and that tends to create a hostile work environment.

The second aspect on which there is agreement is that the severity of the phenomenon varies greatly. In line with Fitzgerald's three-fold classification (see Fitzgerald & Hesson-McInnis, 1989; Fitzgerald et al., 1988), sexual harassment may range from relatively benign episodes of *gender harassment* (e.g., telling sexist jokes or exposing pornographic material at the work place) over *unwanted sexual attention* (e.g., touching or making explicit sexual remarks), all the way up to *sexual coercion* (including sexual black-mail or physical attacks). In our own research, we focus mainly on the most benign, but also most common, form: gender harassment or misogyny.

Misogyny poses a particular puzzle as it is not aiming at sexual satisfaction. Whereas other forms of sexual harassment may, at least in part, be explained with the fact that the perpetrator is searching for some form of sexual satisfaction, this is not true for gender harassment. Behaviors such as the diffusion of pornographic material and sexual epithets or the telling of sexual jokes are not made with the intent to obtain sex but to offend women. The question then arises of what motivation is driving gender harassment and what kind of satisfaction the perpetrator might get out of it. In our opinion, a reasonable answer to these questions can be found in social identity work.

According to social identity theory, outgroup derogation often derives from the desire to enhance or protect the status of one's own group with respect to a relevant outgroup (Abrams & Hogg, 1990; Brewer, 1979; Hinkle & Brown, 1990; Tajfel & Turner, 1986). Especially those whose social identity is insecure or has been threatened temporarily may try to restore the threatened identity through outgroup derogation (Branscombe et al., 1999). This may be exactly the situation of males who have enjoyed a privileged status in society and who have had exclusive access to many professions, including high-level careers, but who suddenly find themselves competing with women entering the job market. It would not be surprising if these women were perceived as highly threatening, especially when they possess better credentials and a higher educational level than the men already employed in the organization. From a social identity perspective, we may then expect these men to defend their privileged status as males and to re-establish differences in favor of their gender group. Sexual harassment may offer one possible strategy to protect or restore the male's threatened gender identity. In line with this interpretation, survey studies have often shown a particularly high incidence of harassment in professions that were traditionally reserved for men (military or police; see Fitzgerald, Magley, Drasgow, & Waldo, 1999; see also Gruber, 1998; Levorato & Savani, 2000;

Rosenberg, Perlstadt, & Phillips, 1993). If this account is correct, then gender harassment should be interpreted as a generalized reaction against females (as a category) in situations where the male's gender identity is threatened, rather than as a pathological reaction of a single male toward a specific female. We have investigated this interpretation in a research project in which we exposed males to different kinds of identity threat and provided them with the opportunity to sexually harass female interaction partners. Unlike the majority of sexual harassment research that tends to be correlational, we have developed an experimental paradigm that allows us to investigate causal relations between identity threat and harassment.

The computer harassment paradigm

The aim of the computer harassment paradigm is to simulate a prototypical form of gender harassment, namely the display of pornographic material, without actually exposing female participants or collaborators to sexual harassment (see Pryor, 1987; Pryor, Hesson-McInnis, Hitlan, Olson, & Hahn, 2001; Pryor, La Vite, & Stoller, 1993). The exposure of female co-workers (or chatline users) to pornographic material has frequently been observed in field studies and is considered a prototypical form of gender harassment (Dekker & Barling, 1998; Pryor & Whalen, 1997).

Modeled after this type of harassment, we have developed a paradigm in which the male participant is led to believe that he is interacting with a female participant via computer. Under the disguise of a "free association" or "visual memory" experiment, participants are exchanging images, chosen from different computer files, with the (fictitious) female participant in another laboratory. Importantly, one file, labeled *porno*, contains porno-graphic material. The main dependent variables are whether (and how often) the participant would send pornographic material and the degree to which these images are offensive. Across experiments, we varied the pres-ence (or absence) of a collaborator who instigated the participant to send pornographic material, the type of identity threat to which males were exposed prior to the computer exchange, and a number of additional variables that will be explained further on.

The role of social identity threat in sexual harassment

Using this paradigm we have investigated the effects of four types of social identity threat on sexual harassment. First, *feminist threat* consisted in the exposure of males to a feminist woman challenging not the value of males as a category per se, but the legitimacy of their status advantage in society. Second, under *value threat*, the competence of males compared to females was challenged in a specific performance domain. Third, *distinctiveness threat* consisted in letting participants know that men are becoming increasingly similar to females, whereas the fourth type of threat, *proto-typicality threat*, made them believe that they are personally lacking masculinity.

Feminist threat

In our first experiment (Dall'Ara & Maass, 1999), male Italian students, together with a male collaborator pretending to be another participant, interacted via computer with two female students. The participant's task was to send a series of images to one of the women, choosing them from 10 different computer files that were clearly labeled (*nature, art, animals,* etc.), each containing a series of images. Half of the files were red, half blue, and participants were asked to use only the red files since the blue files were supposedly reserved for a later phase of the experiment. One of the blue ("forbidden") files was labeled *"porno"* and contained four pornographic images. The collaborator consistently encouraged the participant to send the pornographic images contained in one of the "forbidden" folders. We wanted to test whether our participants would indeed send the forbidden porno images and how many persuasion attempts would be required. Our main interest was to investigate whether harassment would vary as a function of the woman's gender role attitude (traditional vs. feminist).[2]

During an initial getting-acquainted phase, the participant's female interaction partner presented herself either as holding rather old-fashioned ideas about her future role in society (traditional victim) or as a career woman holding egalitarian values supportive of equal rights (feminist victim). We expected that feminist women challenging the legitimacy of the male's status advantage at work would induce greater harassment than traditional women.

The main result emerging from this study (see Figure 6.1) was indeed that feminist women were harassed more frequently than their traditional counterparts, presumably because they pose a threat as they challenge the status advantage of males. Along the same line, when the woman expressed feminist views, fewer persuasion attempts from the harassing role model were needed to convince participants to send pornographic material.

We also investigated the moderating role of a number of individual difference variables, among which sexist attitudes (*Ambivalent Sexism Inventory*, Glick & Fiske, 1996), gender identity (the Private and Importance subscales of Luhtanen & Crocker's, 1992, *Collective Self Esteem Scale* applied to gender), and a modified version of Pryor's (1987) *Likelihood to Sexually Harass* (LSH) *Scale*. This latter scale, measuring people's proclivity for sexual exploitation, is widely used in sexual harassment research and has proven to be an excellent predictor of harassment (cf. Pryor, Giedd, & Williams, 1995; Pryor & Whalen, 1997). The inclusion of these variables was important in light of Pryor's (Pryor et al., 1993; Pryor &

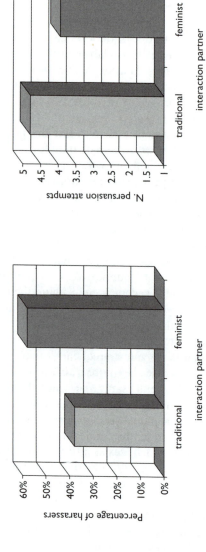

Figure 6.1 Percentage of harassers (left side) and mean number of persuasion attempts necessary to convince participants to harass (right side) as a function of traditional versus feminist victim condition. (From Dall'Ara & Maass, 1999.) Reprinted with kind permission of Springer Science and Business Media.

Whalen, 1997) person × situation model stressing the interactive role of personality and context variables. According to Pryor's reasoning, sexual harassment is unlikely to occur unless there is a specific constellation of personality (e.g., high LSH) *and* situational variables (e.g., permissive norms, threat to ingroup) conducive to such behavior (Pryor, 1987; Pryor et al., 1993; Pryor & Stoller, 1994).

In line with this idea, results show that not all men harass when confronted with a feminist woman. When the female interaction partner expressed feminist gender-role attitudes, confederates encountered little difficulty in convincing those participants who have a high propensity to harass (high LSH), who hold sexist attitudes, who identify strongly with their male category. In contrast, low LSH, low sexism, and less identified males were less likely to harass regardless of whether or not they had been exposed to feminist threat. In other words, it is a specific subgroup of men who react to feminist women in harassing ways.

In a subsequent study (Maass, Cadinu, Guarnieri, & Grasselli, 2003, Experiment 1) we investigated the role of feminist threat in a simplified version of the computer harassment paradigm, in which the confederate was substituted by a virtual co-participant in an intra-laboratory chat-line. Both the real and the virtual participant interacted with the same woman and, during the exchange, the harassing role model sent increasingly offensive images to the woman while encouraging the male participant to do likewise.[3] Importantly, the woman receiving the pornographic images consistently stated that she disapproved of these images and felt offended by them.

In this study, we also refined the dependent measure; rather than investigating the sheer number of pornographic images sent to the female interaction partner, we weighted the images for the degree to which they were offensive.[4] The main question was whether participants would follow the example of the harassing role model despite the woman's protest, and if such treatment was mainly reserved to the feminist. As can be seen in Figure 6.2 (left side), participants were much more likely to harass a feminist than a traditional woman. In this experiment, we also assessed the intention to engage in quid-pro-quo harassment or sexual blackmail in hypothetical future situations, this time using four scenarios from Pryor's (1987) LSH Scale as dependent variable (rather than as predictor variable). As can be seen on the right side of Figure 6.2, participants who interacted with the feminist woman reported a greater intention to engage in quid-pro-quo harassment than those interacting with a traditional woman. Thus, men interacting with a feminist not only engaged in more harassing behaviors toward this particular woman by exposing her to pornographic material, but they also expressed a greater willingness to sexually exploit other women in hypothetical hiring situations in which they imagined having power over female job applicants.

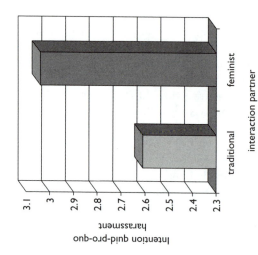
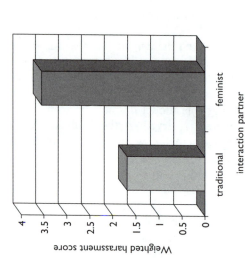

Figure 6.2 Weighted harassment score (left) and intention to engage in quid-pro-quo harassment (right) as a function of traditional versus feminist victim condition. (From Maass et al., 2003, Experiment 1.)

We also investigated the moderating function of two personality variables, namely gender identity and social dominance orientation. In line with previous research (see Branscombe & Wann, 1994; Cadinu & Cerchioni, 2001), we found social identity threat to be effective to the extent that individuals actually identify with the social group to which they belong. The more participants identified with their gender group, the more they tended to react to feminist threat in a harassing manner. A similar argument was made for social dominance orientation. People with a high social dominance orientation hold strong beliefs in the legitimacy of hierarchical group structures and have a desire to dominate *as a group* over other groups (Pratto, Sidanius, Stallworth, & Malle, 1994). We therefore expected socially dominant men to feel particularly provoked by feminist views that question the legitimacy of the existing power differential between men and women, and to show a marked tendency to sexually harass feminist women. In support of this idea, we found that socially dominant men not only tended to harass more than others, but they also showed a specific tendency to react in a highly harassing manner when challenged by a feminist woman.

Together, the findings of these two studies (Dall'Ara & Maass, 1999; Maass et al., 2003, Experiment 1) suggest that feminist women are at higher risk for sexual harassment, a finding already observed in correlational field studies (Salvadori, 1997). However, previous survey findings were open to multiple interpretations: feminists may indeed be harassed more frequently, but alternatively they may be more sensitive to the issue and hence report more episodes of harassment, or else they may have turned into feminists as a function of having been harassed. In other words, within correlational designs, it is impossible to disambiguate the causal relation between holding feminist views and the likelihood of becoming victims of harassment. In contrast, the experimental evidence from our studies provides unequivocal evidence that women with egalitarian views are indeed more likely to be harassed, presumably because they are considered a threat to the males' dominant position.

The other important result emerging from these studies is that only certain men react to feminist threat in a harassing manner, namely those with sexist attitudes, those highly identified with their gender, those with a high propensity towards harassment, and those with strong beliefs in a hierarchical social structure.

Threat to group value

In the same experiment (Maass et al., 2003, Experiment 1), we also investigated a different kind of threat called *threat to group value* by Branscombe et al. (1999). Any information that undermines the ingroup's value, competence, moral qualities, and the like can be perceived as threatening and may elicit a tendency to restore the relative status of the ingroup through

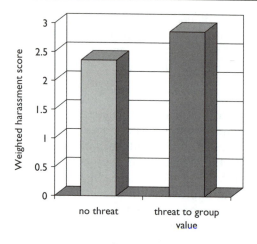

Figure 6.3 Weighted harassment score as a function of threat versus no threat to group value. (From Maass et al., 2003, Experiment 1.)

outgroup derogation. Extending this reasoning to sexual harassment, one may suspect that men may harass women when they are confronted with information that challenges the value of their gender group. In order to test this possibility, we manipulated threat to group value by providing (or not providing) category-based performance information, claiming that women generally outperformed men in the domain that was relevant to the experimental cover story (visual memory). Contrary to predictions, we found only a modest (nonsignificant) increase of harassment under threat to group value (see Figure 6.3). The small magnitude of this effect may not surprise if one considers that our manipulation was very bland.

We subsequently replicated this experiment with a somewhat more powerful manipulation (Maass, Cadinu, & Giusta, 2002). In this case, the study was described as an experiment investigating creativity in which participants had to exchange images and find an appropriate title for each image. In the threat condition, participants learned that women have generally shown much greater fantasy and creativity in this type of task and that such creativity is highly predictive of success in life. Our findings show a reliable increase in the percentage of men engaging in harassing behaviors in the threat compared to the no-threat condition, together with a nonsignificant increase in offensiveness of the pornographic material sent.

Apparently, threat to group value tends to increase the likelihood of sexual harassment, but the magnitude of this effect is relatively small. Note, however, that threat to the male gender group, as operationalized in these two studies, was relatively benign as it referred to a domain that is generally not central to the definition of being male (visual memory or creativity).

Moreover, the threat came from the experimenter rather than from the potential victim of harassment. Stronger manipulations of threat to ingroup values may well produce more robust effects on harassment.

Distinctiveness and prototypicality threat

In a subsequent experiment (Maass et al., 2003, Experiment 2), we investigated two additional types of social identity threat that were directed at the defining feature of being male: masculinity. *Distinctiveness threat* refers to situations in which the differentiation of ingroup versus outgroup is challenged (Branscombe et al., 1999). In the first condition (*distinctiveness threat*), participants were told that male students at their university were becoming increasingly feminine, as evidenced by a graph representing the scores allegedly obtained by male and female students on the Bem Sex Role Inventory (Bem, 1981) during the past 11 years. The graph showed a rather stable line for females, whereas the males' scores, that years back used to be clearly in the masculine range, were now becoming increasingly similar to the women's scores. Extrapolating from the graph, it was easy to predict that, in a few years time, the difference between males and females would disappear altogether. The experimenter commented on the graph, stating that "men were becoming less and less macho".

In the second condition (*prototypicality threat*), the participant's personal membership was questioned, as he was told that he was a rather atypical male (see Schmitt & Branscombe, 2001, for a similar manipulation). After having taken the Bem Sex Role Inventory, participants received fictitious test results from the experimenter that placed them into the feminine range, thereby assigning them a peripheral status within their gender group. In this case it was the personal rather than the group-based masculinity that was questioned. The third condition consisted of a no-threat control condition. Note that the male collaborator was entirely omitted from the design in all three conditions in order to see whether male students would harass women even in the absence of a harassing role model.

We expected males in both the prototypicality and the distinctiveness threat condition to harass their female interaction partner sexually in an attempt to restore their threatened masculinity. In a sense, sexual harassment is an "ideal" form of outgroup derogation as it offends the relevant outgroup while proving the male's own masculinity. We expected harassing reactions to be particularly strong for those participants whose personal masculinity was at stake. Although both types of threat are relevant to the male's gender identity, being told that one personally lacks masculinity may be even more threatening to a young man than the knowledge that males in general are becoming less masculine.

A look at Figure 6.4 confirms these predictions. Compared to control participants, those whose personal masculinity had been questioned showed

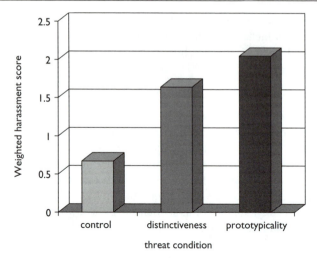

Figure 6.4 Weighted harassment score as a function of no threat versus
distinctiveness threat versus prototypicality threat. (From Maass et al.,
2003, Experiment 2.)

a sharp increase in harassment. An intermediate level of gender harassment
was found when the distinctiveness of males had been challenged at the
group level. Again, gender identification was predictive of harassment in
interaction with threat. It was mostly the highly identified males that
reacted to prototypicality threat, and to a lesser extent to distinctiveness
threat, by harassing their interaction partners sexually.

Together, these studies provide a rather coherent picture in line with our
social identity interpretation. First, it emerges very clearly that men tend to
harass women when their social identity is threatened, and they do so
regardless of whether or not they are under the influence of a harassing role
model. This is true across a wide range of threat manipulations challenging
different facets of social identity (personal vs. group level threat), concerning
different domains (status advantage, performance, masculinity), and coming
from different sources (the potential victim or the experimenter). At the
same time, the magnitude of harassment varies across threat manipulations,
suggesting that some types of threat are perceived as more threatening. As
manipulated in the present studies, the most powerful forms of threat
appeared to be the feminist threat that challenges the legitimacy of the males'
status advantage and the prototypicality threat that challenges the individual's personal level of masculinity. Reliable, though slightly smaller,
increases in harassment were observed under distinctiveness threat. Threat
to group value was least effective in inducing harassment, presumably
because the domain that was the target of the manipulation was not a
defining feature of gender. All other forms of threat were found to play a
causal role in harassment, confirming the idea that identity protection is an

important force driving gender harassment. If our interpretation is correct, then sexual harassment has a precise function, namely to protect a hurt gender identity.

A second general conclusion that can be drawn from these studies is that personality and situational variables interact in a predictable fashion. In line with Pryor et al.'s (1993) person × situation model, we found that some males react very strongly to social identity threat whereas others seem practically immune to any kind of threat. Not only are individual difference variables such as gender identity, sexist attitudes, social dominance, and LSH predictive of harassment in and of themselves, but they interact reliably with threat. All of the interindividual difference variables considered here become highly predictive of harassment only in situations in which the male's identity is threatened (with correlations in the $r = .7$ to .8 range). This confirms Pryor's idea that sexual harassment, a counter-normative behavior in most societies, is unlikely to occur unless personal predisposition and "favorable" context variables coincide. From a social identity perspective it is not surprising that social status threat will mainly affect those who are highly identified with their own group (see Branscombe et al., 1999), a finding that emerged across all of our studies. Interestingly, feminist threat provoked the strongest reaction in males with highly sexist attitudes and in those with a strong social dominance orientation. This latter finding is quite in line with social dominance theory, considering that feminist thought challenges what is at the very heart of the dominance philosophy, namely the legitimacy of status differentials. Together, our results not only shed light on the interplay between individual characteristics and situated social identity threat, but also help identify those sub-populations of males that are at risk of becoming harassers. It is these high-risk males that prevention programs should pay particular attention to.

Is sexual harassment an efficient strategy to protect one's social identity?

Our social identity interpretation assumes that males harass females as a way of protecting a threatened gender identity. If harassment has a self-protective function, the question arises of whether it is actually an efficient strategy. In other words, does sexual harassment achieve the aim it is designed for? In two of our studies (Maass et al., 2003, Experiment 1 and Experiment 2), we have investigated this question by assessing gender identity both before and after the computer exchange. We expected that males who harassed women by sending at least one pornographic image would report a more positive gender identity following the computer interaction, whereas non-harassers should maintain a stable identity. As evident in Figure 6.5, this prediction was borne out. Our participants felt more positively about being male after they had harassed their female interaction

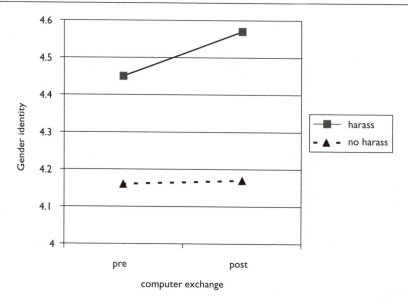

Figure 6.5 Pre- and post-experimental gender identity as a function of sending versus not sending pornographic images. (From Maass et al., 2003, Experiment 1.) Reprinted with the kind permission of the APA.

partner, whereas their non-harassing counterparts shown no variation in gender identity. Thus, sexual harassment not only aims at preserving or restoring a threatened gender identity but it also seems to serve this purpose quite successfully.

Ingroup bonding through sexual harassment

Besides serving identity-protective functions of the individual, sexual harassment may also serve as a way to reaffirm the harasser's gender identity in front of other ingroup members. In other words, it provides a means for constructing a public image of the self that is consistent with the group's goals and expectancies (see self-categorization theory, Turner, Hogg, Oakes, Reicher, & Wetherell, 1987) and that ultimately serves to establish or strengthen ingroup bonds. Indeed, men often show harassing behaviors in the presence of other harassing men (see Dall'Ara & Maass, 1999; Pryor et al., 1995). Pryor and Whalen (1997) have argued that contagious harassment, rather than being merely a function of imitation, reflects an attempt to reinforce ties with and to construct a masculine reputation in front of other males. If this account is correct, then the simple co-presence of other males may be sufficient to trigger harassing behaviors.

We have investigated this possibility in a study in which male students engaged in a computer interaction with a (virtual) female interaction partner either by themselves or together with a same-sex friend (Maass et al., 2002). The participants' task was to send images chosen from six clearly labelled files (including a *porno* file) to a female interaction partner who then had to select the most creative title for each image. Participants were either assigned to a no-threat control condition or to a *threat to group value* condition in which they were told that women, being more creative, generally performed much better on this task.

The main question was whether our participants would harass more in dyads than individually and whether this tendency would be more pronounced under threat. As can be seen in Figure 6.6, both the number of harassers and the offensiveness of the pornographic images were considerably higher when men were acting in dyads (rather than individually) reaching a peak when their social identity had been threatened *and* they were acting jointly.

Thus, dyads not only were more likely to harass but their greater propensity to harass was particularly pronounced under threat (although the interaction fell short of significance). This confirms our suspicion that harassment may in part be functional to gain (or restore) prestige in front of other males. It is interesting to note that harassing behaviors were particularly likely in presence of strong friendship ties. Indeed, the strength of the friendship ties within the dyad predicted harassment quite accurately ($r = .45$).

This suggests that sexual harassment may not only serve to defend the privileged status of males by derogating females (reflecting a need for differentiation), but it may also function as an intragroup ingratiation strategy (reflecting a need for assimilation; see the optimal distinctiveness hypothesis described in Brewer, 1991). We suspect that the tendency to harass in the presence of other males will be even more pronounced when the individual's prototypicality (rather than group value) is threatened. We suspect that men who have an insecure status as males will be particularly motivated to present themselves as highly masculine in front of other ingroup members, and what better way could there be than to harass women? This issue, as well as the exact processes underlying harassment in dyads, remains to be explored by future research.

How to prevent harassment?

Harassment is widespread and very costly, both in terms of the psychological and physical costs for the victim and in terms of the economic costs for organizations. Our research project suggests that harassment is, in part, driven by an attempt to protect a threatened male identity. From a practical viewpoint, it is therefore important to understand how harassment can be prevented or at least discouraged. We believe that there are different potential strategies each of which has specific advantages and limits.

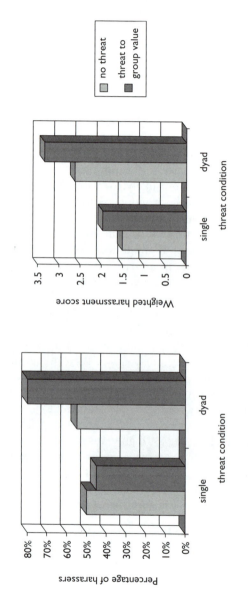

Figure 6.6 Percentage of harassers (left) and weighted harassment score (right) as a function of single versus dyad and threat versus no threat condition. (From Maass et al., 2002.)

First, if harassment is a reaction to gender-related identity threat, then any strategy that reduces the power of categorization along gender lines may be effective. It may be possible to modify those contextual aspects of work or educational settings that are sources of gender categorization and identity threat, and that may ultimately be conducive to sexual harassment. The social identity literature offers a wide range of such strategies, including individuation or decategorization, superordinate categorization, cross-categorization, and the creation of interdependence (for a comparative overview of possible strategies, see Brown, 2000), although their effectiveness in preventing sexual harassment remains to be tested.

A second way to prevent males from feeling threatened is to define male identity in less stereotypical terms (including less traditional masculine traits and more counterstereotypical traits). In this case, men would feel less threatened when told that they possess nontraditional traits (prototypicality threat) or when exposed to a woman claiming equal rights (legitimacy threat). In other words, rather than healing a hurt identity, it may be more efficient to *prevent* damage to male pride by changing the perception of what is typically masculine. Much of what is now seen as a threat to the male's gender identity could be perceived as compatible with the male self-image. By changing the content of the male's gender identity, one could prevent males from feeling threatened in the first place, while at the same time allowing them to maintain a positive sense of identification with the male ingroup. The obvious disadvantage of this strategy is that it would most likely reduce the differentiation between males and females thereby possibly constituting a distinctiveness threat.

Third, if gender identity threat cannot be prevented, there may be alternative and less damaging ways to deal with such threat. Depending on the type of threat, it may be possible to restore or maintain a positive and distinct gender identity or to reaffirm one's status as a prototypical male without necessarily engaging in sexual degradation of women. One strategy to discourage harassment that is highly cited in the sexual harassment literature, and that is contained in most policy statements (see the Rubinstein report, 1987), regards the creation of organizational norms that sanction harassment. Normative changes are the backbone of practically all harassment prevention programs currently in use although the effectiveness of this strategy has rarely been investigated systematically.

Lovison (1998–99) has explored this strategy experimentally using the computer harassment paradigm. At the beginning of the experiment, male students were left waiting in front of a computer whose screen saver was varied so as to introduce either a permissive norm, a restrictive norm, or no norm at all. In the *permissive norm condition*, two highly sexist cartoons were displayed, suggesting that such material was normatively acceptable in the laboratory.[5] In the *restrictive* norm condition, an "*ethics code of psychological research*" was exposed on the screen reminding both experimenters and participants of their duties. The experimenters' duties corresponded closely to those defined by the Italian Psychological Association (informed consent, privacy, etc.) whereas the participants were asked to behave in a correct way and "*not to offend, through words or images, the dignity of other participants.*" In the control condition, a plain screen was used.

As can be seen in Figure 6.7, the norm manipulation had the desired effect, but only on those participants who tend to regulate their behavior to meet the demands of situational norms and are aware of the impression they make on others. Only high self-monitors (Snyder, 1974, 1979) and those with high public self-consciousness (Fenigstein, Scheier, & Buss, 1975) harassed less in the ethics code than in the permissive norm condition, with the control condition occupying an intermediate position. Unexpectedly, this tendency was reversed for low self-monitors and men with low public self-awareness, a finding that remains a mystery at this point.

If supported by future research, this would suggest that interventions based on normative strategies may produce the desired results only in certain populations, while they may have little impact on those who pay no attention to the normative context or who are unlikely to modify their behaviors so as to meet the expectations of others. Although we currently have no comparative data on the efficiency of different harassment prevention strategies, it may be easier to prevent social identity threats from occurring than to intervene once males feel threatened. This important question is awaiting future investigation.

Concluding remarks

Our research project suggests that it may be useful to interpret misogyny or gender harassment in the frame of social identity (and social dominance) theory and to link these research areas more explicitly than has been done in the past (see Pryor & Whalen, 1997, for a similar argument). We believe that *both* research areas can profit from such cross-fertilization. On one side, principles derived from social identity theory are of great utility to sexual harassment research as they shed light on the motivation driving sexual harassment, and as they may ultimately help to develop theoretically guided intervention programs. As a case in point, the one finding emerging very clearly and consistently from our research program is that harassment fulfills an ingroup protective or enhancing function in situations in which the males' gender identity is threatened. This may explain why gender harassment, a form of harassment that is not aiming at sex, is such a widespread and persistent phenomenon across different cultural contexts.

On the other side, social identity theory itself may derive some advantages from the extension to sexual harassment. First of all, our research shows that the predictions of social identity theory can profitably be applied to areas that do not traditionally fall into the realm of the theory. If

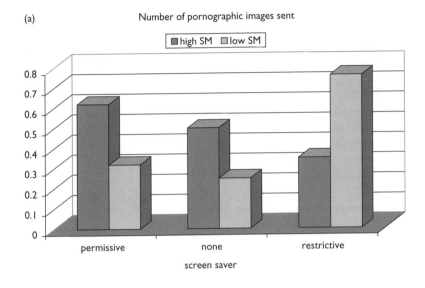

(a) Number of pornographic images sent

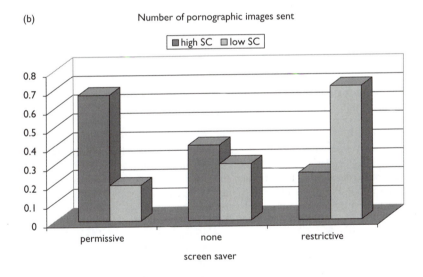

(b) Number of pornographic images sent

Figure 6.7 (a) The effect of the norm manipulation (restrictive norm vs. no norm vs. permissive norm) on high versus low self-monitors. (From Lovison, 1998–1999.) (b) The effect of the norm manipulation (restrictive norm vs. no norm vs. permissive norm) on participants with high versus low public self consciousness. (From Lovison, 1998–1999.)

nothing else, this demonstrates the generality of its principles. This should encourage researchers to abandon the narrow focus on old-and-tried measures and to venture into new areas of application. A second general implication derives from the consistent interaction between situational and individual difference variables that has emerged in our research and that is well established in the sexual harassment literature (see Pryor, 1992). Although social identity theorists have shown increasing interest in the moderating role of individual difference variables (in particular, ingroup identification), the extent to which outgroup discrimination derives from specific *constellations* of personal and situational factors remains to be explored.

Acknowledgements

This research was funded by a Start-up Research Grant on "Sexual Harassment at the University" granted by the University of Padova. We want to thank the other members of the research team, Franca Agnoli, Luciano Arcuri, Chiara Levorato, and Massimo Santinello, for their valuable help during the different stages of this project.

Notes

1 A fourth type of threat identified by Branscombe et al. (1999) is category threat referring to situations in which people are categorized against their will. This kind of threat is not relevant to the current research and is unlikely to induce outgroup derogation.

2 In addition, we varied the salience of gender by stressing either the interpersonal (use of first names) or the intergroup dimension of the interaction (consistent reference to "males" versus "females"). In line with social identity reasoning, harassment was reliably higher when the situation was construed as an intergroup (rather than interindividual) setting, but this was reliable only for those males that had a high proclivity to sexually harass women.

3 In this experiment, the file containing the "porno" images was again clearly labelled as such but did not belong to a "forbidden" set of folders.

4 In a pretest, all pornographic images had been rated by an independent sample of students for the degree to which they were offensive to women. The weighted harassment scores was calculated by weighting each image sent by the participant for its degree of offensiveness based on these pre-test scores. For example, if a hypothetical participant sent two images, one moderately offensive (rated 2.6 in pretest) and one highly offensive (4.4 on the pretest), the total weighted harassment score for this participant would be the sum of the two values (score of 7.0).

5 For instance, one portrayed an office in the Physics Department in which the older, overweight professor had placed the file drawers unusually low on the floor so as to get a good look at his mini-skirted secretary every time she bent over to pick up a folder.

References

Abrams, D., & Hogg, M. A. (Eds.). (1990). *Social identity theory: Constructive and critical advances*. London: Harvester Wheatsheaf.

Baker, D. D., Terpstra, D. E., & Larntz, K. (1990). The influence of individual characteristics and severity of harassing behavior on reactions to sexual harassment. *Sex Roles, 22*, 305–325.

Bem, S. L. (1981). *Bem Sex Role Inventory: Professional manual*. Palo Alto, CA: Consulting Psychologists Press.

Branscombe, N. R., Ellemers, N., Spears, R., & Doosje, B. (1999). The context and content of social identity threat. In N. Ellemers, R. Spears, & B. Doosje (Eds.), *Social identity: Context, commitment, content* (pp. 35–58). Oxford, UK: Blackwell.

Branscombe, N. R., & Wann, D. L. (1994). Collective self-esteem consequences of outgroup derogation when a valued social identity is on trial. *European Journal of Social Psychology, 24*, 641–657.

Brewer, M. B. (1979). In-group bias in the minimal intergroup situation: A cognitive-motivational analysis. *Psychological Bulletin, 86*, 307–324.

Brewer, M. B. (1991). The social self: On being the same and different at the same time. *Personality and Social Psychology Bulletin, 17*, 475–482.

Brown, R. (2000). *Group processes*. Oxford, UK: Blackwell.

Cadinu, M. R., & Cerchioni, M. (2001). Compensatory biases after ingroup threat: "Yeah, but we have a good personality". *European Journal of Social Psychology, 31*, 353–367.

Cadinu, M. R., & Reggiori, C. (2002). Discrimination of a low-status outgroup: The role of ingroup threat. *European Journal of Social Psychology, 32*, 501–515.

Dall'Ara, E., & Maass, A. (1999). Studying sexual harassment in the laboratory: Are egalitarian women at higher risk? *Sex Roles, 41*, 681–704.

Dekker, I., & Barling, J. (1998). Personal and organizational predictors of workplace sexual harassment of women by men. *Journal of Occupational Health Psychology, 3*, 7–18.

Equal Employment Opportunity Commission (1980). *Guidelines on discrimination because of sex*. 29 CFR Part 1604. Federal Register 45:210, USA.

Fenigstein, A., Scheier, M. F., & Buss, A. H. (1975). Public and private self-consciousness: Assessment and theory. *Journal of Consulting and Clinical Psychology, 43*, 522–527.

Fitzgerald, L. F. & Hesson-McInnis, M. S. (1989). The dimensions of sexual harassment: A structural analysis. *Journal of Vocational Behavior, 35*, 309–326.

Fitzgerald, L. F., Magley, V. J., Drasgow, F., & Waldo, C. R. (1999). Measuring sexual harassment in the military: The sexual experiences questionnaire (SEQ-DoD). *Military Psychology, 11*, 243–263.

Fitzgerald, L. F., Shullman, S. L., Bailey, N., Richards, M., Swecker, J., Gold, Y., et al. (1988). The incidence and dimensions of sexual harassment in academia and the workplace. *Journal of Vocational Behavior, 32*, 152–175.

Glick, P., & Fiske, S. T. (1996). The ambivalent sexism inventory: Differentiating hostile and benevolent sexism. *Journal of Personality and Social Psychology, 70*, 491–512.

Gruber, J. E. (1998). The impact of male work environments and organizational policies on women's experiences of sexual harassment. *Gender and Society, 12*, 301–320.

Gruber, J. E., Smith, M., & Kauppinen-Toropainen, K. (1996). Sexual harassment types and severity: Linking research and policy. In M. S. Stockdale (Ed.), *Sexual harassment in the workplace: Perspectives, frontiers, and response strategies* (pp. 151–173). Thousand Oaks, CA: Sage.

Hinkle, S., & Brown, R. (1990). Intergroup comparisons and social identity: Some links and lacunae. In D. Abrams & M. A. Hogg (Eds.), *Social identity theory: Constructive and critical advances* (pp. 48–70). London: Harvester Wheatsheaf.

Levorato, M. C., & Savani, N. (2000). La propensione alla molestia sessuale: Un'indagine su studenti universitari [The propensity for sexual harassment: A study of university students]. *Bollettino di Psicologia Applicata, 232*, 49–59.

Lovison, R. (1998–99). *Molestia sessuale e norme sociali [Sexual harassment and social norms]*. Unpublished laurea thesis, University of Padova, Italy.

Luhtanen, R., & Crocker, J. (1992). A collective self-esteem scale: Self-evaluation of one's social identity. *Personality and Social Psychology Bulletin, 18*, 302–318.

Maass, A., Cadinu, M. R., & Giusta, V. (2002). *When men act together: Sexual harassment in dyads*. Unpublished manuscript, University of Padova, Italy.

Maass, A., Cadinu, M. R., Guarnieri, G., & Grasselli, A. (2003). Sexual harassment under social identity threat: The computer harassment paradigm. *Journal of Personality and Social Psychology, 85*, 853–870.

Mlicki, P. P., & Ellemers, N. (1996). Being different or being better? National stereotypes and identifications of Polish and Dutch students. *European Journal of Social Psychology, 26*, 97–114.

Morrow, P. C., McElroy, J. C., & Phillips, C. M. (1994). Sexual harassment behaviors and work related perceptions and attitudes. *Journal of Vocational Behavior, 45*, 295–309.

Pratto, F., Sidanius, J., Stallworth, L. M., & Malle, B. F. (1994). Social dominance orientation: A personality variable predicting social and political attitudes. *Journal of Personality and Social Psychology, 67*, 741–763.

Pryor, J. B. (1987). Sexual harassment proclivities in men. *Sex Roles, 17*, 269–290.

Pryor, J. B. (1992). The social psychology of sexual harassment: Person and situation factors which give rise to sexual harassment. In Northwest Women's Law Center, *Sex and power issues in the workplace: An interdisciplinary approach to understanding, preventing, and resolving harassment* (pp. 89–105). Seattle, WA: Northwest Women's Law Center.

Pryor, J. B., Giedd, J. L., & Williams, K. B. (1995). A social psychological model for predicting sexual harassment. *Journal of Social Issues, 51*, 69–84.

Pryor, J. B., Hesson-McInnis, M. S., Hitlan, R. T., Olson, M., & Hahn, E. J. (2001). *Antecedents of gender harassment: Analysis of person and situation factors*. Unpublished manuscript.

Pryor, J. B., La Vite, C. M., & Stoller, L. M. (1993). A social psychological analysis of sexual harassment: The person/situation interaction. *Journal of Vocational Behavior, 42*, 68–83.

Pryor, J. B., & Stoller, L. M. (1994). Sexual cognition processes in men high in the likelihood to sexually harass. *Personality and Social Psychology Bulletin, 20*, 163–169.

Pryor, J. B., & Whalen, N. J. (1997). A typology of sexual harassment: Characteristics of harassers and the social circumstances under which sexual harassment occurs. In W. T. O'Donohue (Ed.), *Sexual harassment: Theory, research and treatment* (pp. 129–151). Needham Heights, MA: Allyn & Bacon.

Rosenberg, J., Perlstadt, H., & Phillips, W. R. (1993). Now that we are here: Discrimination, disparagement and harassment at work and the experience of women lawyers. *Gender and Society*, 7, 415–433.

Rubinstein, M. (1987). *The dignity of women at work: Report on the problem of sexual harassment in the member states of the European Community*. Brussels: European Commission.

Salvadori, S. (1997). *Molestie sessuali nei luoghi di lavoro: Fattori normativi e disposizionali* [*Sexual harassment at work: Normative and dispositional factors*]. Unpublished laurea thesis, University of Padova, Italy.

Schmitt, M. T., & Branscombe, N. R. (2001). The good, the bad, and the manly: Threats to one's prototypicality and evaluations of fellow ingroup members. *Journal of Experimental Social Psychology*, 37, 510–517.

Schneider, K. T., Swan, S., & Fitzgerald, L. F. (1997). Job-related and psychological effects of sexual harassment in the workplace: Empirical evidence from two organizations. *Journal of Applied Psychology*, 82, 401–415.

Snyder, M. (1974). Self-monitoring of expressive behaviour. *Journal of Personality and Social Psychology*, 30, 526–537.

Snyder, M. (1979). Self-monitoring processes. In L. Berkowitz (Ed.), *Advances in experimental social psychology* (Vol. 12, pp. 85–128). San Diego, CA: Academic Press.

Tajfel, H., & Turner, J. C. (1986). The social identity theory of intergroup behavior. In S. Worchel & W. G. Austin (Eds.), *Psychology of intergroup relations* (pp. 7–24). Chicago: Nelson-Hall.

Turner, J. C., Hogg, M. A., Oakes, P. J., Reicher, S. D., & Wetherell, M. S. (1987). *Rediscovering the social group: A self-categorization theory*. Oxford, UK: Blackwell.

Wiener, R. L., & Hurt, L. E. (2000). How do people evaluate social sexual conduct at work? A psycholegal model. *Journal of Applied Psychology*, 85, 75–85.

Part II

Cultural and evolutionary aspects of ingroup identification

Chapter 7

Social identity motives in evolutionary perspective

Marilynn B. Brewer and Linnda R. Caporael

The aim of this chapter is to suggest an evolutionary model that can accommodate research on self and social identity. Drawing on recent developments in evolutionary biology and on considerations of morphology and ecology, we hypothesize that human social groups consist of a small number of evolutionarily significant core configurations, and that uniquely human cognitive and motivational systems are adapted to these configurations. This model is then applied to a specific theory of the motivations underlying social identity at the individual, relational, and collective levels of analysis.

Evolution and core configurations

Multilevel evolutionary theory

Most behavioral scientists today accept the basic premise that human beings are adapted for group living. Even a cursory review of the physical endowments of our species – weak, hairless, extended infancy – makes it clear that we are not suited for survival as lone individuals, or even as small family units. Many of the evolved characteristics that have permitted humans to adapt to a wide range of physical environments, such as omnivorousness and tool making, create dependence on collective knowledge and cooperative information sharing. As a consequence, human beings are characterized by *obligatory interdependence* (Caporael & Brewer, 1995), and our evolutionary history is a story of co-evolution of genetic endowment, social structure, and culture (Boyd & Richerson, 1985; Caporael, 2001; Fiske, 2000; Janicki & Krebs, 1998; Li, 2003).

Recent developments in evolutionary psychology (e.g., Crawford & Krebs, 1998; Simpson & Kenrick, 1997) have raised awareness of the evolutionary roots of human social behavior, but much of the theorizing that has been promulgated under this rubric has been criticized for relying on a narrow, gene-based view of biological evolution (see, e.g., Scher &

Rauscher, 2003). We have argued that psychological theory will be better served by reference to more modern multilevel, hierarchical models of evolution that recognize that natural selection operates at multiple levels of organization – from DNA molecules to cells to organisms to groups and regional ecosystems (Caporael & Brewer, 1995, 2000).

Stimulated by the publication of Leo Buss's influential book *The evolution of individuality* (1987), biological evolution theory has moved beyond the gene-centered notion of natural selection to multilevel selection theory (Brandon, 1990; Maynard Smith & Szathmáry, 1995; Sober & Wilson, 1998). Proponents of multilevel evolutionary theory recognize that evolutionary processes operate over multiple levels of hierarchical organ-ization – macromolecules, genes, cells, organisms and even groups (Buss, 1987; Maynard Smith & Szathmáry, 1995; Wilson & Sober, 1994). Entities at one level of the biological hierarchy are the environment for entities at another. In effect, hierarchical models of evolution recognize that the concept of "fit" must be conceptualized in terms of embedded structures. Genes, as one level of organization, must fit the environment of their cellular machinery; cells must fit the environment of the individual organ-ism; and individual organisms must fit the next higher level of organization within which they function. Accordingly, the cellular machinery that signals and responds to gene action is the environment for genes, and, closer to the topic of this chapter, the group is the environment for individuals.

This view of adaptation and natural selection provides a new perspective on the concept of group selection as a factor in human evolution (Caporael & Brewer, 1991). With coordinated group living as the primary survival strategy of the species, the social group, in effect, provided a buffer between the individual organism and the exigencies of the physical environment. As a consequence, then, the physical environment exercises only indirect selective force on human adaptation, while the requirements of social living constitute the immediate selective environment.

Given the morphology and ecology of evolving hominids, the interface between hominids and their habitat must have been a group process. Finding food, defense from predation, moving across a landscape – these matters of coping with the physical habitat – are largely group processes. Over time, if exploiting a habitat is more successful as a collective group process than as an individual process, then not only would more successful groups persist, but so also would individuals better adapted to group living. The result would be a shift to face-to-face groups as the selective context for uniquely human mental systems. The result of selection *in* groups would be the evolution of perceptual, affective, and cognitive processes that support the development and maintenance of membership in groups (Caporael, Dawes, Orbell, & van de Kragt, 1989). Without a group, the probability of reproduction and survival to reproductive age is lowered for humans.

Table 7.1 Core configurations of social groups

Configuration	Prototypic group size	Modal tasks
Dyad	2	Sex; parent–child interaction
Work/family group	5	Foraging; hunting; working on a common task
Deme (band)	30	Workgroup coordination; migration; sharing knowledge
Macrodeme (macroband)	300	Seasonal gatherings; exchange of persons, resources, and information

Adapted from Caporael, 1997.

The core configuration model

Based on a consideration of tasks necessary for survival and reproduction and on research on group size, Caporael (1997) suggested that the topography of the selective environment for humans consists of four configurations – dyad, work/family group, deme (or band), and macrodeme (or macroband). A core configuration is the *joint* function of group size and activity. Configurations provide a context for tasks or activities that are specific to that level of organization. That is, each group configuration affords functional possibilities and coordination problems not existent at any other level. Table 7.1 lists the configurations, along with an approximate group size and examples of modal tasks for the configuration.

The names of core configurations are not intended to represent roles, but rather kinds of interaction. For example, a dyad is an interaction between two entitites, one of which can be non-human (e.g., an animal or even a machine). A work/family group need not point to work or families; it is merely a label for small-group interactions oriented toward a common task. For example, the size of a group that can go to dinner in a restaurant and still function as a single interacting unit is four to six individuals; maintaining casual conversation among eight people is hard. The tasks listed in the table are characteristic of hunter-gatherer groups, but as the restaurant example suggests, these have analogues in present-day life. The relevance of tasks (from an evolutionary perspective) for a configuration is not the activity per se, but rather the set of social cognitive processes – afforded by the core configuration – that enable the activity.

Dyads afford the evolution and development of coordinated body movements such as those used in facial imitation in the mother–infant dyad, interactional synchrony, and human sexual attraction (Perper, 1985), or the entrainment that occurs when two people walk together. Dyads are the most ancient of configurations, minimally necessary for all forms of internal fertilization (although mechanisms across species will vary). Among humans (and perhaps primates more generally), dyads are probably evolutionarily significant not so much because new capacities appear, but because this configuration functions in (and is influenced by) the initial social organization and entrainment of biological clocks, rhythmicity, and temporal patterning (Jones, 1976; Jones & Boltz, 1989; McGrath & Kelly, 1986).

The *work/family group* affords possibilities for distributed cognition; this means that cognitive tasks such as perception, classification, inference, and contextually cued responses are distributed over group members, particularly when the group is confronted with ambiguous or anomalous data from the habitat (a modern example would be control-tower personnel at airports). The work/family group is also a primary site for the transmission of culture between generations, especially for learning subsistence modes in hunter-gatherer cultures. Vygotsky (1978) coined the phrase "zone of proximal development" to describe how children participate with adults in activities slightly beyond the young learner's competence. This zone is a dynamic cognitive region of heightened responsiveness to the tools, skills, and practices in a culture, in which children must learn to participate fully as adults (Rogoff, 1990).

The *deme* (or as anthropologists say, the band) affords a shared construction of reality or "common knowledge", as well as skills, practices, and rituals. (We use the term deme, from the Greek *demos*, in its original sense of a neighborhood unit rather than the biological sense of breeding population.) The deme or band is the basic economic unit, the first configuration that can be self-sustaining for survival and child rearing (but not reproduction). The deme is the staging ground for domestic life, including work/family group coordination, and for cooperative alliances, which are the basis for fissioning when the community exceeds resources or is fractured by conflict. The deme is also a locus for articulated social identity, "we-groupness" (Sumner, 1906), communicated in terms of stories and songs.

Among hunter-gatherer groups, related bands met seasonally as *macrobands* for the exchange of marriage partners, gifts, and information, and the performance of rituals and playing of competitive games. Macrobands are generally related by common-origin stories and history, customs, ritual, and most enduringly, language. They complete the cycle of biological and social reproduction. A Monte Carlo simulation of paleodemographics by Wobst (1974, cited by Hassan, 1981) indicates that about 175–475 people, or seven to nineteen 25-person bands are needed to maintain genetic viability by providing mates for members reaching sexual maturity in a population. Macrobands are also historically transitional. They tended to be seasonal in the evolutionary past because of limitations of resources, but as agriculture took root, settled macrodemes simply became settlements. Macrobands are rare in the modern world, but there are analogous forms of group structures, which we can call *macrodemes*. For example, scientific conferences are often seasonal meetings where information and young people are exchanged, and where the standardization and stabilization of distinctive terminology and the reaffirmation of group identity occurs.

There are a few general points to be made about the core configuration model. First, core configurations repeatedly assemble, in evolutionary time, in ontogeny, and in daily life. As infants develop, their increasing scope of interaction increases demands for reciprocity, skills, memory, social judgment, and so on. Second, the core configurations differ in their generative entrenchment. Dyads are deeply entrenched; change in their proper functions should predict poor developmental outcomes. In contrast, macrodemes are shallowly entrenched and are relatively easy to change. Third, humans have dramatically altered their lifestyles over the past ten millenia, and especially in the last 300 years. Clearly the functions that evolve and develop in core configurations are capable of being extended, combined, and used in new domains. For example, a heart surgery team combines microcoordination and distributed cognition. Technology can also provide bridges between the functions of configurations. A group of 500 people given an order to march on a football field are likely to clump and straggle, but if a rousing marching song is broadcast, they can hardly avoid keeping time. Some institutions have been particularly successful in exploiting core configurations, the military being a prime example.

Core configurations and social identity

Some social psychologists have turned to evolutionary theory to better ground psychological theorizing. For example, Sedikides and Skowronski (1997) proposed that the self evolved from social processes in the past, and Baumeister and Leary (1995) argued that the need to belong evolved in response to social processes. The core configuration model extends these efforts. If group living is the human mind's natural environment, we should expect corresponding psychological adaptations that respond to structural features of groups and tasks. We suggest that the psychological glue maintaining core configurations is shifts in social identity. Core configurations, which are concretely situated in life activities, and social identity, which is psychological, have nested hierarchical structures that appear to fit each other. Social identity is automatic, labile, based on perception and categorization, and can result from various conditions including group size, task characteristics, shared fate or outcomes, and salient group boundaries (Brewer, 1991; Turner, Hogg, Oakes, Reicher, & Wetherell, 1987). Social identity also plays an important role in the distribution of resources, self-evaluation, and expectations for behavior.

Levels of social identity

If social identity plays a central role in core configurations, then there should be evidence of "group selves" that correspond to different levels of core configuration and are connected with knowledge sharing, as in distributed cognition or shared reality (Hardin & Higgins, 1996). Some research suggests that "dyadic selves" exist as cognitive representations and in the coordination of bodily motion. Self–other confusions in close relationships can be detected by lags in reaction time latencies. Research participants have longer latencies for judging whether traits are different between themselves and their spouse as compared to whether the traits are similar for both (Aron, Aron, Tudor, & Nelson, 1991). Participants in the same study also had more difficulty recalling nouns about themselves versus their mothers compared to recall for nouns about themselves versus a stranger. Other research suggests that couples in long-term relationships share a transactive memory – a system for encoding, storing, and retrieving information – and even impromptu couples perform significantly better than chance on experimental memory tasks (Wegner, 1986; Wegner, Erber, & Raymond, 1991). Interactional synchrony between strangers may also significantly enhance recall (Newbern, Dansereau, & Pitre, 1994) and is also a necessary feature in the early stages of interpersonal attraction in courtship and a common feature of interaction between married couples (Perper, 1985).

Group selves also occur at higher levels of organization. An experiment on work teams (Liang, Moreland, & Argote, 1995) demonstrated that groups trained together (to assemble radios) outperformed groups composed of individuals trained separately to do the same task. The researchers found that group training enhanced not only recall about assembly procedures, but also specialization for remembering distinct aspects of the assembly procedure and trust in one another's knowledge about the task. Such research indicates that distributed cognition is not simply having the same bits of information.

Hutchins (1996) also studied teams, but in the real-life situation of navigating a large naval ship into port. Establishing the fix cycle, or position of the ship, recurs every two to three minutes. Hutchins found that no single individual is "in charge" of the performance; rather the performance emerges interactively as individuals coordinate their activities with the people "adjacent" to them, in the sense of input–output of information.

Core configurations, repeatedly assembled generation-to-generation and throughout the lifespan, could provide a sufficient framework for understanding the evolution of social cognition and human coordination through the level of macroband. However, human beings are capable of coordination on scales far beyond the level of macrobands. Modern humans may live in cities with populations numbering in the millions. They may identify with others as parts of huge nation states. At yet higher levels of social identity, depersonalized collective selves (e.g., based on gender, or national or ethnic identity) would be an extension of the self/social identity system, with origins in macrodeme organization.

In part, modern society is less an aggregate of self-interested individuals than it is a mosaic of multiple overlapping, sometimes nested, usually cross-cutting, demic structures and parts of structures, ceaselessly under negotiation across various group boundaries, and yet somehow still coherent enough to merit the term "society". Society is a coordination system that has no proper evolutionary history; it must operate with social cognitive processes evolved for core configurations, and the relevant processes must be "reweaveable" for higher-level coordination. Although specific skills and practices are concretely situated in face-to-face groups, the psychological correlates of grouping, most especially social identity from the demic and macrodemic levels, may be extended to more abstract, superordinate groups: "la raza", "American", or "workers". The more labile the regrouping along collective dimensions the greater the fluidity of a society. The capacity for ingroup loyalty that evolved in the context of demes may be evoked, for example, by an evening television broadcast, and extended, with swelling heart and deep pride, to an organization, a nation, or a social movement. Depersonalized collective identity is engaged by the categorization aspects of identification, in contrast to the relational identities that emerge from interpersonal interactions over time.

Motives for social identification: Optimal distinctiveness theory

The idea that human beings evolved for group living does not imply non-contingent altruism or self-sacrifice. Human beings are clearly vested with self-interest, but this view of evolutionary history contends that self-interest is naturally mitigated by identification with groups. From an evolutionary perspective, we should expect that individual, relational, and collective identities are semi-autonomous regulatory systems that hold each other in check (Brewer, 1991; Kurzban & Leary, 2001). Just as prices in a free market system are regulated by the independent forces of supply and demand, so unbridled individual self-interest is held in check by the demands of interdependence, but at the same time sociality is constrained by the demands of individual survival and reproduction.

In most cases, individual self-interest and group interests coincide, so that cooperation and interdependence serve group goals and satisfy individual needs at the same time. If I desire the benefits of winning in a team sport competition, for instance, then cooperating with my fellow team members is clearly the best way for all of us to meet our individual and collective goals. But individual goals and collective interests do not always coincide so perfectly. If my individual interests are enhanced by being the one member of my team who scores the most points, but my team's chances of winning depend on my providing other team members with the opportunity to score, working for my personal goal and achieving the group goal are not completely compatible.

Since individual self-interest and collective interests do not always coincide, the necessities of group living require coordination not only between individuals but within individuals, to meet competing demands from different levels of organization. Human social life can be characterized as a perpetual juggling act – maintaining the integrity of individual identity, interpersonal relationships, and collective interests simultaneously. Humans are not driven either by unmitigated individual selfishness or by non-contingent altruism, but instead show the capacity for variable motivation and behavior patterns contingent on the state of the environment.

The necessity for meeting demands of existence at the individual, inter-personal, and collective levels of organization suggests that human social life is regulated not by single social motives but by the complex effects of multiple, competing motivational systems. The model of optimal distinc-tiveness (Brewer, 1991) provides one illustration of how such competing motivational systems might work. The model posits that humans are characterized by two opposing needs that govern the relationship between the self-concept and membership in social groups. The first is a need for assimilation and inclusion, a desire for belonging that motivates immersion in social groups. The second is a need for differentiation from others that operates in opposition to the need for immersion. As group membership becomes more and more inclusive, the need for inclusion is satisfied but the need for differentiation is activated; conversely, as inclusiveness decreases, the differentiation need is reduced but the need for assimilation is activated. These competing drives ensure that interests at one level are not consistently sacrificed to interests at the other. According to the model, the two opposing motives produce an emergent characteristic – the capacity for social identi-fication with distinctive groups that satisfy both needs simultaneously.

Optimal distinctiveness theory was in part the product of an exercise in thinking about downward causation from the group to the individual level of analysis. The advantage of extending social interdependence and cooperation to an ever wider circle of conspecifics comes from the ability to exploit resources across an expanded territory and buffer the effects of temporary depletions or scarcities in any one local environment. But expansion comes at the cost of increased demands on obligatory sharing, and regulation of reciprocal cooperation and free-riding. Both the carrying capacity of physical resources and the capacity for distribution of resources, aid, and information inevitably constrain the potential size of cooperating social networks. Thus, effective social groups cannot be either too small or too large. To function, social collectives must be restricted to some optimal size – sufficiently large and inclusive to realize the advantages of extended cooperation, but sufficiently exclusive to avoid the disadvantages of spread-ing social interdependence too thin.

Based on this analysis of one structural requirement for group survival, Brewer (1991) hypothesized that the conflicting benefits and costs

associated with expanding group size would have shaped social motivational systems at the individual level. If humans are adapted to live in
groups and depend on group effectiveness for survival, then our motivational systems should be tuned to the requirements of group effectiveness.
We should be uncomfortable depending on groups that are too small to
provide the benefits of shared resources, but also uncomfortable if group
resources are distributed too widely. A unidirectional drive for inclusion
would not have been adaptive without a counteracting drive for differentiation and exclusion. Opposing motives hold each other in check, with
the result that human beings are not comfortable either in isolation or in
huge collectives. These social motives at the individual level create a propensity for adhering to social groups that are both bounded and distinctive.
As a consequence, groups that are optimal in size are those that will elicit
the greatest levels of member loyalty, conformity, and cooperation, and the
fit between individual psychology and group structure is ensured.

The importance of collective social identities and the underlying social
motives postulated by optimal distinctiveness theory is evidenced by
empirical demonstrations of efforts to achieve or restore group identification when these needs are deprived. Results of experimental studies have
shown that activation of the need for assimilation or the need for differentiation increases the importance of distinctive group memberships
(Pickett, Silver, & Brewer, 2002), that threat to inclusion enhances self-
stereotyping on group-characteristic traits (Brewer & Pickett, 1999; Pickett,
Bonner, & Coleman, 2002), and that threat to group distinctiveness motivates overexclusion (Pickett, 1999) and intergroup differentiation (Jetten,
Spears, & Manstead, 1998; Roccas & Schwartz, 1993).

The importance of the collective self is particularly evident when efforts to
achieve or restore optimal group identities involve some cost to personal
self-interest. This is supported by research indicating that individuals often
identify strongly with stigmatized groups (e.g., Crocker, Luhtanen, Blaine,
& Broadnax, 1994; Simon, Glassner-Bayerl, & Stratenwerth, 1991), that
identification with distinctive groups leads to assimilation to the ingroup
even when it entails loss of personal self-esteem (Brewer & Weber, 1994);
that activation of the need for differentiation increases the value of distinctive low-status minority ingroups over high-status majority ingroups
(Brewer, Manzi, & Shaw, 1993; Leonardelli, 1998); and that threats to
inclusion or distinctiveness increase self-stereotyping even on negatively
evaluated group characteristics (Branscombe & Ellemers, 1998; Pickett,
Bonner, & Coleman, 2002).

Optimal distinctiveness and levels of social identity

Consistent with the core configuration model, Brewer and Gardner (1996)
postulated that the *individual, relational, and collective* levels of self define

Table 7.2 Opposing drives and levels of self-representation

	Motivational pole	
Level of self	Separation	Assimilation
Individual	uniqueness	similarity
Relational	autonomy	intimacy/interdependence
Collective	differentiation	inclusion/belonging

From Brewer and Roccas (2001, p. 223).

three distinct self-representations with different structural properties, bases of self-evaluation, and motivational concerns (see also E. S. Kashima & Hardie, 2000). The theory of optimal distinctiveness is originally a theory of collective social identity. More specifically, it is a model of the motivational underpinnings of group identification, where a group is defined as a large collective unit, or entity, that transcends individual-level identities. However, elaborating on the optimal distinctiveness theory of social identity, Brewer and Gardner also suggested that a fundamental tension between needs for assimilation and differentiation of the self from others plays itself out at each level of self-representation.

According to the theory, optimality at the collective level is regulated by the counterpressures of need for inclusion (assimilation with others in a larger collective unit) and the need for differentiation (separation from others). Analogous opposing needs for separateness and assimilation may also operate at the levels of individual and relational selves to determine optimal identities at those levels as well.

As depicted in Table 7.2, at the collective level the conflict is between belonging and inclusion on the one hand, and separation and distinctiveness on the other. At the interpersonal (relational) level the tension is represented by conflicts between the need for autonomy and the need for interdependence and intimacy with specific others. Finally, at the individual level the needs are expressed in the opposition between the desire for similarity on the one hand and the need for uniqueness on the other (Snyder & Fromkin, 1980). (The distinction between inclusion–differentiation on the one hand and similarity–uniqueness on the other is subtle but important. Similarity refers to the *degree* or extent of overlap between one's own characteristics – attributes, attitudes, etc. – and those of another individual or a group prototype. Inclusion refers to the *number* of others with whom one shares a collective bond, which may be based on a single shared characteristic.) At each level, the person must achieve some optimal balance between these conflicting motives for defining self in relation to others.

Although the three levels of self-representation are hypothesized to be distinct self-systems, it is reasonable to assume that the way needs for identity and esteem are met at one level will have some influence on the activation of parallel motives at other levels. More specifically, we propose here that cultural values and group norms that emphasize either separation or assimilation at each level have carry-over effects at other levels. For instance, if the needs for autonomy and intimacy are optimized by relatively high levels of intimacy (relative to autonomy) at the interpersonal level, there may be a particularly strong activation of the need for uniqueness (difference relative to similarity) at the individual level. Similarly, the relative emphasis on autonomy and uniqueness versus interdependence and similarity at the individual and interpersonal levels may influence the relative activation of the needs for inclusion and differentiation at the collective level.

Cultural values and social identity motives

Drawing on the potential interrelationships among opposing needs at different levels of social identity, Brewer and Roccas (2001) speculated that cultural values regarding the relative importance placed on independence and autonomy versus interdependence and similarity are among the important factors that determine the pattern of activation of the needs for inclusion and differentiation. These differences in values and self-construals are, in turn, associated with cultural differences along the dimension of *individualism–collectivism* (Hofstede, 1980; Triandis, 1995).

Although individualism and collectivism are complex, multidimensional constructs, the primary distinction between them is the relative priority given to individual autonomy, self-expression, and achievement on the one side versus obligations, mutual cooperation, and concern for others on the other. Consistent with Brewer and Gardner's (1996) comparison between relational social identities and collective social identities, we make a further distinction between two types of collectivism.

One form of collectivism (relational collectivism) stresses interpersonal relationships, mutual cooperation, dependence, and concern for specific persons within a closely interconnected social network. Relational collectivism is associated with the degree of felt obligation and responsibility to one's family, close friends, and immediate community. The second form of collectivism (group-based collectivism) stresses dependence on and obligation to a group as a whole, valuing obedience to group norms and authority and subordinating individual interests to those of the collective. Collectivist values are not directed to fellow group members as individuals but to the group as a whole. (See Y. Kashima et al., 1995, and Kim, 1994, for a similar distinction between relational and collective forms of collectivism.)

Individualism and relational and group-based collectivism can refer to characteristics of individuals, of groups, and of societies or cultures (Deaux & Reid, 2000). The shared socialization practices that characterize a culture give precedence to either individualistic or collectivist social values, but variations in socialization experiences give rise to individual differences in degree of individualism–collectivism even within a culture. Within and between cultures, different types of groups have norms and expectations that may vary in the importance placed on individualistic, relational, or group-based collectivist values. Some groups are defined by the interpersonal bonds among group members (Prentice, Miller, & Lightdale, 1994), some are defined by collective goals and ideologies that demand a strong sense of duty, obedience, and concern for group interests, and some are defined by shared interests with norms that encourage individual responsibility and self-expression.

With their emphasis on obligation, mutual interdependence, and responsibility to ingroup others, relational and group collectivist values imply that social identification with groups is a high-investment commitment. The benefits of group inclusion are high in that groups provide security and guaranteed mutual aid. But the costs of inclusion are commensurate with the benefits in terms of obligations and duties to fellow group members that demand time and resources on a non-negotiable basis. Under such a system of values, both the benefits and latent costs of group membership are related to the size and exclusivity of the collective. When intragroup obligations are strong and underwritten by group norms and sanctions, the benefits of group inclusion can be met within a relatively small, exclusive social unit. (To put it more formally, as the probability of receiving help and support from a fellow group member approaches 1.00, fewer group members are needed to ensure that help will be available when needed.) By the same token, when obligations to fellow group members (or the group as a whole) are strong, it becomes especially important to limit the scope of obligation to those who are clearly a part of the same system of reciprocal aid and mutual obligation (Takagi, 1996; Yamagishi & Kiyonari, 2000).

With relational values, the primary constraints are the size–task features of the group's activities or the number of persons that can be accommodated within one's ingroup network before the costs of interdependence and obligation become too high. Thus, relational values should be associated with strong social identification with relatively small social groups and with high sensitivity to changes that would increase ingroup size. Group-based collectivist values, on the other hand, should be less sensitive to variation in group size. Since group collectivists are obligated to the welfare of the group as a whole, rather than to individual group members, the implications of increases in group size are somewhat different than for relational collectivists. Although the number of persons involved affects the volume of group interest, it is also the case that the more individuals working in support of a common group, the less the burden on any one individual. Thus, group size per se should be less important than concern about the impermeability of group boundaries. Group-based collectivist values, then, should be associated with high concern for any threat to the clarity and stability of ingroup–outgroup distinctions.

One non-intuitive outcome of thinking about optimal distinctiveness at different levels of self-representation is the idea that members of highly individualistic societies, such as the United States, will also tend to be relatively collectivistic. At first glance, it may appear that individualistic values are incompatible with the very notion of collective social selves. To the contrary, we believe that individualism has very direct effects on the need for inclusion in larger social units. Members of individualistic groups and societies are dependent on each other just as members of collectivist groups are. The difference is in how this interdependence is negotiated and reflected in shared values. Individualism gives greater weight to personal interests and preferences in resolving potentially conflicting demands of individual achievement and the welfare of others. In such a value system, obligations to groups and fellow group members are not absolute or highly reliable. Thus, the potential benefits of ingroup inclusion are diffused and probabilistic, and individuals need to be part of larger and more inclusive social units in order to reap the benefits of security and mutual aid associated with group membership. Consistent with the ideas presented by Simon and Kampmeier (2001), we argue that individual autonomy and collective identity (especially identification with large, majority groups) are quite compatible.

Some evidence for our proposal that individualism and group-based collectivism may coincide comes from a recent meta-analysis of cross-national studies of individualism and collectivism (Oyserman, Coon, & Kemmelmeier, 2002). Results indicate that Americans (who rate themselves high on measures of individualism) also score relatively high on certain aspects of collectivism, particularly belonging to ingroups. That individualistic Americans are also high in need for belonging to groups, and enjoy being a part of groups, is consistent with our idea that individual autonomy values are associated with high needs for inclusion and assimilation. Further evidence comes from research on gender differences in relational and collective interdependence. Across societies, males generally score higher on individualism than do females, whereas females consistently score higher on relational or interdependent self-construal (Cross & Madson, 1997; Y. Kashima et al., 1995). Not surprisingly, then, women focus more on relational aspects of the social world than do men (Gabriel & Gardner, 1999) and base their attachment to groups on their relational bonds with other group members (Seeley, Gardner, Pennington, & Gabriel, 2003). By contrast, however, men show a higher focus on *collective* aspects of social experience and show greater attachment to groups based on shared identity (Gabriel & Gardner, 1999; Seeley et al., 2003). These gender differences are consistent with our hypothesis that individualism and group-based collectivism are mutually compatible and, perhaps, complementary.

Conclusion

The evolutionary perspective represented in the core configuration model suggests not only that humans are a social species but that we are bioculturally adapted to function in multiple group contexts with different forms of interdependence and coordination. Corresponding to the structural demands and functions of interacting in dyads, work groups, demes, and macrodemes, humans have developed different self-regulatory systems that correspond to different levels of the biological hierarchy, and monitor and maintain individual survival, interpersonal relationships, and group belonging respectively. Within each system there is a need to achieve equilibrium between assimilation to and separation from others. Cultural values (as well as individual differences) influence the relative strength of assimilation and separation motives at each level of social identity, but no single motive can be pursued to the exclusion of others. Psychologically, humans are on a dynamic and ongoing quest for balance between levels of organization and levels of social identity. This is a far cry from the old view of evolution that sees human on a march of progress to perfect adaptation. It is also much closer to a view of evolutionary psychology that can contribute to a better understanding of social psychology.

References

Aron, A., Aron, E. N., Tudor, M., & Nelson, G. (1991). Close relationship as including other in the self. *Journal of Personality and Social Psychology, 60,* 241–253.

Baumeister, R. F., & Leary, M. R. (1995). The need to belong: Desire for interpersonal attachments as a fundamental human motivation. *Psychological Bulletin, 117,* 497–529.

Boyd, R., & Richerson, P. J. (1985). *Culture and the evolutionary process.* Chicago: University of Chicago Press.

Brandon, R. N. (1990). *Adaptation and environment.* Princeton, NJ: Princeton University Press.

Branscombe, N. R., & Ellemers, N. (1998). Coping with group-based discrimination: Individualistic versus group-level strategies. In J. K. Swim & C. Stangor (Eds.), *Prejudice: The target's perspective* (pp. 243–266). New York: Academic Press.

Brewer, M. B. (1991). The social self: On being the same and different at the same time. *Personality and Social Psychology Bulletin, 17,* 475–482.

Brewer, M. B., & Gardner, W. L. (1996). Who is this "We"? Levels of collective identity and self representations. *Journal of Personality and Social Psychology, 71,* 83–93.

Brewer, M. B., Manzi, J. M., & Shaw, J. S. (1993). In-group identification as a function of depersonalization, distinctiveness, and status. *Psychological Science, 4,* 88–92.

Brewer, M. B., & Pickett, C. L. (1999). Distinctiveness motives as a source of the social self. In T. R. Tyler, R. M. Kramer, & O. P. John (Eds.), *The psychology of the social self* (pp. 71–87). Mahwah, NJ: Lawrence Erlbaum Associates Inc.

Brewer, M. B., & Roccas, S. (2001). Individual values, social identity, and optimal distinctiveness. In C. Sedikides & M. B. Brewer (Eds.), *Individual self, relational self, collective self* (pp. 219–237). Philadelphia: Psychology Press.

Brewer, M. B., & Weber, J. G. (1994). Self-evaluation effects of interpersonal versus intergroup social comparison. *Journal of Personality and Social Psychology, 66,* 268–275.

Buss, L. W. (1987). *The evolution of individuality.* Princeton, NJ: Princeton University Press.

Caporael, L. R. (1997). The evolution of truly social cognition: The core configurations model. *Personality and Social Psychology Review, 1,* 276–298.

Caporael, L. R. (2001). Evolutionary psychology: Toward a unifying theory and a hybrid science. *Annual Review of Psychology, 52,* 607–628.

Caporael, L. R., & Brewer, M. B. (1991). Reviving evolutionary psychology: Biology meets society. *Journal of Social Issues, 47,* 187–195.

Caporael, L. R., & Brewer, M. B. (1995). Hierarchical evolutionary theory: There is an alternative, and it's not creationism. *Psychological Inquiry, 6,* 31–34.

Caporael, L. R., & Brewer, M. B. (2000). Metatheories, evolution, and psychology: Once more with feeling. *Psychological Inquiry, 11,* 23–26.

Caporael, L. R., Dawes, R. M., Orbell, J. M., & van de Kragt, A. J. (1989). Selfishness examined: Cooperation in the absence of egoistic incentives. *Behavioral and Brain Sciences, 12,* 683–739.

Crawford, C. B., & Krebs, D. L. (Eds.). (1998). *Handbook of evolutionary psychology: Ideas, issues, and applications.* Mahwah, NJ: Lawrence Erlbaum Associates Inc.

Crocker, J., Luhtanen, R., Blaine, B., & Broadnax, S. (1994). Collective self-esteem and psychological well-being among White, Black, and Asian college students. *Personality and Social Psychology Bulletin, 20,* 503–513.

Cross, S. E., & Madson, L. (1997). Models of the self: Self-construals and gender. *Psychological Bulletin, 122,* 5–37.

Deaux, K., & Reid, A. (2000). Contemplating collectivism. In S. Stryker, T. J. Owens, & R. W. White (Eds.), *Self, identity, and social movements* (pp. 172–190). Minneapolis, MN: University of Minnesota Press.

Fiske, A. P. (2000). Complementarity theory: Why human social capacities evolved to require cultural complements. *Personality and Social Psychology Review, 4,* 76–94.

Gabriel, S., & Gardner, W. L. (1999). Are there "his" and "hers" types of interdependence? The implications of gender differences in collective versus relational interdependence for affect, behavior, and cognition. *Journal of Personality and Social Psychology, 77,* 642–655.

Hardin, C., & Higgins, E. T. (1996). Shared reality: How social verification makes the subjective objective. In R. M. Sorrentino & E. T. Higgins (Eds.), *Handbook of motivation and cognition: The interpersonal context* (Vol. 3, pp. 28–84). New York: Guilford Press.

Hassan, F. A. (1981). *Demographic archaeology.* New York: Academic Press.

Hofstede, G. (1980). *Culture's consequences: International differences in work-related values.* Beverly Hills, CA: Sage.

Hutchins, E. (1996). *Cognition in the wild*. Cambridge, MA: MIT Press.

Janicki, M., & Krebs, D. L. (1998). Evolutionary approaches to culture. In C. B. Crawford & D. L. Krebs (Eds.), *Handbook of evolutionary psychology: Ideas, issues, and applications* (pp. 163–207). Mahwah, NJ: Lawrence Erlbaum Associates Inc.

Jetten, J., Spears, R., & Manstead, A. S. R. (1998). Intergroup similarity and group variability: The effects of group distinctiveness on the expression of ingroup bias. *Journal of Personality and Social Psychology, 74*, 1481–1492.

Jones, M. R. (1976). Time, our lost dimension: Toward a new theory of perception, attention and memory. *Psychological Review, 83*, 323–355.

Jones, M. R., & Boltz, M. (1989). Dynamic attending and responses to time. *Psychological Review, 96*, 459–491.

Kashima, E. S., & Hardie, E. A. (2000). The development and validation of the relational, individual, and collective self-aspects (RIC) Scale. *Asian Journal of Social Psychology, 3*, 19–48.

Kashima, Y., Yamaguchi, S., Kim, U., Choi, S. C., Gelfand, M. J., & Yuki, M. (1995). Culture, gender, and self: A perspective from individualism-collectivism research. *Journal of Personality and Social Psychology, 69*, 925–937.

Kim, U. (1994). Individualism and collectivism: Conceptual clarification and elaboration. In U. Kim, H. C. Triandis, Ç. Kagitçibasi, S. C. Choi, & G. Yoon (Eds.), *Individualism and collectivism: Theory, method, and applications* (pp. 19–40). Thousand Oaks, CA: Sage.

Kurzban, R., & Leary, M. R. (2001). Evolutionary origins of stigmatization: The functions of social exclusion. *Psychological Bulletin, 127*, 187–208.

Leonardelli, G. (1998). *The motivational underpinnings of social discrimination: A test of the self-esteem hypothesis*. Unpublished master's thesis, Ohio State University, USA.

Li, S. C. (2003). Biocultural orchestration of developmental plasticity across levels: The interplay of biology and culture in shaping the mind and behavior across the life span. *Psychological Bulletin, 129*, 171–194.

Liang, D. W., Moreland, R., & Argote, L. (1995). Group versus individual training and group performance: The mediating factor of transactive memory. *Personality and Social Psychology Bulletin, 21*, 384–393.

Maynard Smith, J., & Szathmáry, E. (1995). *The major transitions in evolution*. New York: Freeman.

McGrath, J. E., & Kelly, J. R. (1986). *Time and human interaction: Toward a social psychology of time*. New York: Guilford Press.

Newbern, D., Dansereau, D. F., & Pitre, U. (1994, June–July). *Ratings of synchrony in cooperative interaction predict cognitive performance*. Paper presented at the Annual Convention of the American Psychological Society, Washington, DC.

Oyserman, D., Coon, H. M., & Kemmelmeier, M. (2002). Rethinking individualism and collectivism: Evaluation of theoretical assumptions and meta-analyses. *Psychological Bulletin, 128*, 3–72.

Perper, T. (1985). *Sex signals: The biology of love*. Philadelphia: ISI Press.

Pickett, C. L. (1999). *The role of assimilation and differentiation needs in the perception and categorization of ingroup and outgroup members*. Unpublished dissertation, Ohio State University, USA.

Pickett, C. L., Bonner, B. L., & Coleman, J. M. (2002). Motivated self-stereotyping:

Heightened assimilation and differentiation needs result in increased levels of positive and negative self-stereotyping. *Journal of Personality and Social Psychology, 82*, 543–562.

Pickett, C. L., Silver, M. D., & Brewer, M. B. (2002). The impact of assimilation and differentiation needs on perceived group importance and judgments of ingroup size. *Personality and Social Psychology Bulletin, 28*, 546–558.

Prentice, D. A., Miller, D. T., & Lightdale, J. R. (1994). Asymmetries in attachments to groups and to their members: Distinguishing between common-identity and common-bond groups. *Personality and Social Psychology Bulletin, 20*, 484–493.

Roccas, S., & Schwartz, S. H. (1993). Effects of intergroup similarity on intergroup relations. *European Journal of Social Psychology, 23*, 581–595.

Rogoff, B. (1990). *Apprenticeship in thinking: Cognitive development in social context*. New York: Oxford University Press.

Scher, S. J., & Rauscher, F. (Eds.). (2003). *Evolutionary psychology: Alternative approaches*. Boston: Kluwer.

Sedikides, C., & Skowronski, J. J. (1997). The symbolic self in evolutionary context. *Personality and Social Psychology Review, 1*, 80–102.

Seeley, E. A., Gardner, W. L., Pennington, G., & Gabriel, S. (2003). Circle of friends or members of a group? Sex differences in relational and collective attachment to groups. *Group Process and Intergroup Relations, 6*, 251–263.

Simon, B., Glassner-Bayerl, B., & Stratenwerth, I. (1991). Stereotyping and self-stereotyping in a natural intergroup context: The case of heterosexual and homosexual men. *Social Psychology Quarterly, 54*, 252–266.

Simon, B., & Kampmeier, C. (2001). Revisiting the individual self: Toward a social psychological theory of the individual self and the collective self. In C. Sedikides & M. B. Brewer (Eds.), *Individual self, relational self, collective self* (pp. 199–218). Philadelphia: Psychology Press.

Simpson, J. A., & Kenrick, D. T. (Eds.). (1997). *Evolutionary social psychology*. Mahwah, NJ: Lawrence Erlbaum Associates Inc.

Snyder, C. R., & Fromkin, H. L. (1980). *Uniqueness: The human pursuit of difference*. New York: Plenum Press.

Sober, E., & Wilson, D. S. (1998). *Unto others: The evolution and psychology of unselfish behavior*. Cambridge, MA: Harvard University Press.

Sumner, W. (1906). *Folkways*. New York: Ginn.

Takagi, E., (1996). The generalized exchange perspective on the evolution of altruism. In W. Liebrand & D. Messick (Eds.), *Frontiers in social dilemmas research* (pp. 311–336). Berlin: Springer-Verlag.

Triandis, H. C. (1995). *Individualism and collectivism*. Boulder, CO: Westview Press.

Turner, J. C., Hogg, M. A., Oakes, P. J., Reicher, S. D., & Wetherell, M. S. (1987). *Rediscovering the social group: A self-categorization theory*. Oxford, UK: Blackwell.

Vygotsky, L. S. (1978). *Mind in society*. Cambridge, MA: Harvard University Press.

Wegner, D. M. (1986). Transactive memory: A contemporary analysis of the group mind. In B. Mullen & G. R. Goethals (Eds.), *Theories of group behavior* (pp. 185–208). New York: Springer-Verlag.

Wegner, D. M., Erber, R., & Raymond, P. (1991). Transactive memory in close relationships. *Journal of Personality and Social Psychology, 61*, 923–929.

Wilson, D. S., & Sober, E. (1994). Re-introducing group selection to the human behavioral sciences. *Behavioral and Brain Sciences*, 17, 585–654.

Yamagishi, T., & Kiyonari, T. (2000). The group as the container of generalized reciprocity. *Social Psychology Quarterly*, *63*, 116–132.

Chapter 8

Social identity theory in cross-cultural perspective

Peter B. Smith and Karen M. Long

The development of research in social psychology over the past century can be seen as a continuing struggle between two perspectives. On the one hand there lies the priority that must be given to social context if we are to understand social behaviors. On the other hand there lies the ambition of social psychologists to follow scientific method. If one is to be a good scientist, one must either strip away the extraneous aspects of the process one wishes to study, or else find ways of holding them constant. From the point in history when Wilhelm Wundt published his numerous volumes of *Völkerpsychologie* to the present day, social context has from time to time been cast aside, only for others later to find it necessary to reinstall it within our theorizing.

   This chapter will not attempt to follow this sequence of action and reaction through the last century. It will take as its point of departure the celebrated chapter by Tajfel (1972), which lamented the manner in which these authors saw the North American social psychology of the time progressing toward a characterization of persons as no more than pro- cessors of social cognitions. Tajfel's (1981) concurrent formulation of social identity theory sought to restore group membership to a central role in our thinking about social behavior. Our intention here is to address a series of questions touching on the way in which social identity theory and its various reformulations became for a while a "European" theory, and then to consider possible convergences or conflicts with the recent perspectives of cross-cultural psychology. Tajfel's concerns were certainly focused on the impact of real-world group affiliations on the turbulent European history through which he had lived. It is ironic that his theory was nonetheless given its initial prominence through his development of the minimal group research paradigm. The original Bristol group of researchers has by now dispersed to the corners of the earth, but the early development of the theory was clearly a European enterprise. Why did Europeans find par- ticular value in this formulation? Some answers to this question must be pragmatic ones. The concurrent creation of the *European Journal of Social Psychology* and of the European Association of Experimental Social

Psychology ensured more widespread dispersal of these ideas on this side of the Atlantic than in North America. The point of interest here, however, is whether there is something about the culture of European nations that provided more fertile ground for more contextualized theories of social psychology. Hofstede's (1980) survey found European nations less individualistic than the USA, but it would be perilous to expect that extrapolation from such nation-level characterizations would give us a good basis for understanding the actions of a few dozen European social psychologists. A more likely explanation can be formulated in terms of social identity theory itself. Faced with a predominantly North American social psychology, European social psychologists were able to define a more coherent identity for themselves by identifying with distinctively European theories such as those of Tajfel, Moscovici and others (Hogg, 2001).

Thirty years on, social identity theory has been extensively reformulated, and no longer has such a sharply distinguished regional basis, as illustrated by the contributors to this book. Nonetheless, one attribute of Tajfel and collaborators' (see Tajfel, Billig, Bundy, & Flament, 1971) initial approach remains salient: the great majority of social identity studies continue to be based on laboratory experiments. The social and cultural contexts within which most studies are done have been excluded, except in so far as they can actually be manipulated experimentally. We discuss three ways in which greater attention to context may help the field to move forward. First, we consider the prevailing cultural attributes of the contexts in which social identity studies have been and are being done. This leads us next to consider cultural variations in the nature of social identity. Finally, we debate the extent to which culture can be conceptualized as a series of constantly recurring primes.

Locating social identity studies

The great majority of studies derived from social identity theory have been conducted within a single country. The country in question has of course not always been the same one, but one country per study has been the norm. Published reports of these studies typically contain no discussion of whether the results obtained were influenced by the particular cultural orientations of the respondents who had been sampled. A meta-analysis by Mullen, Brown, and Smith (1992) compared 137 ingroup bias effects obtained in studies from Western Europe and the USA. The magnitude of effects obtained was more dependent on variations in design than on differing locations.

One set of studies in which greater attention has been given to cultural context is provided by research focused on national identity (Cinnirella, 1997; Mlicki & Ellemers, 1996; Mummendey, Klink, & Brown, 2001; Poppe & Linssen, 1999; Rutland & Cinnirella, 2000), and on relations between regional (Ros, Huici, & Gomez, 2000) or minority identity (Verkuyten & Nekuee, 1999) and national identity. However, the concern in these studies has not been to identify culture-specific determinants of effects, but rather to test whether the local effects found are compatible with more generalized formulations of social identity theories.

A second, rather larger group of studies comprises those in which explicit comparisons have been made between social identity effects found within two or more samples drawn from different cultural groups. It is not always easy to determine whether studies attributable to this second group are or are not to be thought of as social identity studies. For instance, cross-cultural comparisons of the division of rewards between ingroup and outgroup members are certainly focused on ingroup bias, but researchers within this tradition have rarely derived their hypotheses from social identity theory. We shall draw on selected studies from this latter group because they enable us to test for potential convergences between the interests of social identity theorists and of cross-cultural researchers.

The earliest cross-cultural test of social identity theory was also one of the few that used the original minimal group paradigm in a non-Western context. Wetherell's (1982) study compared the responses of 8-year-old children in New Zealand of Pakeha (white), Maori, and Samoan origin. Pakeha results replicated the findings of Tajfel et al. (1971), but the Maoris and especially the Samoans favored maximizing joint reward. Wetherell discussed several possible reasons for this apparently anomalous result. Her non-Pakeha respondents may have misunderstood the instructions, or else they may have been guided by local cultural norms that favor the giving of gifts, or they may have seen their main priority as relieving the Pakeha experimenter of as much reward as possible. We shall never know. What is clear, however, is that similar effects can still be found. For instance, Wade-Benzoni et al. (2002) compared the performance of US and Japanese students in a complex simulation, in which various parties were concerned with the harvesting of shark populations in the sea. US participants favored their own group, whereas Japanese students made much more equal distributions between the various groups involved. Similarly, in a buyer–seller simulation, Tinsley and Pillutla (1998) found that US student negotiators favored their own group more than did Chinese. Graham, Mintu, and Rodgers (1994) have shown in a series of simulation studies that negotiators from Western nations are much more competitive, whereas those from Pacific Asian nations are more inclined toward problem-solving approaches.

Simple descriptions of possible cultural differences in ingroup bias do not advance the field. What is required is a theoretical formulation that can predict where such differences will or will not occur. Cross-cultural psychologists have taken the position over the past two decades that this can best be achieved by identifying dimensions of variation in the values espoused in different parts of the world (Smith & Schwartz, 1997). The most influential perspective has been that of Hofstede (1980) and particularly his identification of individualism and collectivism as key predictors of cultural variance. While many different definitions of cultural collectivism have by now been formulated, the crucial aspect of the concept from the present perspective is that collectivists are seen as favoring ingroups over outgroups to a greater extent than are individualists. Since collectivist values are espoused by more people in Pacific Asian nations than in the USA and Europe, the results obtained by Wetherell (1982), Wade-Benzoni et al. (2002), and others might appear hard to explain. In order to fit the data to the theory, we need to postulate that Pacific Asian respondents in these studies felt that they were allocating resources within the ingroup, not to an outgroup.

The resolution of these difficulties lies in studies that include direct measurement of the key variables, namely collectivist values and in- or outgroup status of the parties within an experiment. Leung and Bond (1984) provided a first step in this direction. They asked US and Chinese students to decide how grades for a course should be allocated. When grades were to be allocated among friends, the Chinese made more equal allocations. However, when grades were to be allocated among strangers, the Chinese made allocations that were even more unequal than those made by the Americans. A further study by Hui, Triandis, and Yee (1991) used a similar design comparing US and Chinese students, but they included a measure of collectivist values as well. It was found that differentiation between in- and outgroup allocations was greatest for those who endorsed collectivist values. When the effects of collectivism were partialled out, the differences between in- and outgroup allocations were no longer significant. Tinsley and Pillutla (1998) also collected a values measure from their student respondents. Greater US competitiveness was consistent with their more individualistic values. These studies included no direct check on whether respondents did perceive friends or fellow students as ingroup members and strangers as outgroup members, but they certainly strengthen the case for exploring links between collectivist values and social identity effects.

The emphasis that cross-cultural psychologists have placed on the importance of distinguishing between ingroups and outgroups in the context of collectivist cultures has an importance consequence for our examination of the cross-cultural literature. Few studies have obtained any precise indication of whether participants perceived those with whom they were dealing as ingroup or outgroup members. Consequently, we should expect to find some studies that do show contrasts between east and west, and could speculate that participants in these assumed they were dealing with an outgroup. We should also expect to find some studies detecting no such effects, and could speculate that in these, participants assumed that they were dealing with an ingroup. We have considered some that did find differences. Others did not. For instance, Lind, Tyler, and Huo (1997) found that the same three factors could explain satisfactory resolution of self-reported real-life conflicts of students from the USA, Germany, Hong Kong, and Japan. The success factors were recognition of status differences, neutrality, and trust in benevolence of the other party.

Two of the studies that come closest to resolving these ambiguities are by Chen, Brockner, and Katz (1998) and Chen, Brockner, and Chen (2002). In the first of these studies, students in the USA and China were arbitrarily assigned to minimal groups. They were then led to believe that their group had performed either well or poorly on a task, and that they personally had performed well or poorly. The point of interest lies in how participants responded to the information that they had performed well when their own group had not. US respondents reacted by rating their ingroup lower than was found in other conditions of the experiment. Chinese respondents reacted by rating the outgroup lower than was found in other experimental conditions. In other words, US respondents dissociated themselves from their ingroup, whereas the Chinese acted to sustain their ingroup. These effects were found to be mediated by a measure of individualism–collectivism. The second study was similar, but here participants were also given feedback about the performance of the outgroup. Where the outgroup did well and the ingroup did not, collectivists were found to sustain ingroup favoritism to a greater extent.

Derlega, Cukur, Kuang, and Forsyth (2002) also obtained support for hypotheses derived directly from social identity theory. They asked US and a heterogeneous set of non-US students to rate various ways in which they might handle interpersonal, intergroup, and international conflicts and to complete the Singelis (1994) self-construal scales. Each respondent made ratings for only one type of conflict. Interdependent self-construal (which is assumed to equate to collectivism) predicted greater acceptance of the other's view for interpersonal conflicts, but greater use of threats for the conflicts with outgroups. Those with high interdependence also reported greater negative affect in relation to the outgroup conflicts. Derlega et al. suggest that this could be because those who are high on interdependence will identify more strongly with their ingroups. However, their study had no measure of identification.

Collectivism and bias

The cross-national studies thus suggest that ingroup bias is dependent on an interaction between collectivist values and the types of group that are involved. Within the literature focused on single-nation social identity studies, a rather similar proposition has been advanced by Hinkle and Brown (1990). These authors examined 143 published correlations between measures of identification and ingroup bias, most of them collected in field settings. Given the wide variability that they observed in these results, they proposed that identification would lead to ingroup bias only where groups have goals that are collective and which involve comparison with other groups. The cross-cultural perspective and that of Hinkle and Brown differ in three ways, none of which is likely to prove insuperable. First, the cross-cultural studies focus on the magnitude of bias, whereas Hinkle and Brown consider the correlation between identification and bias. Second, the cross-cultural studies treat the values of individual respondents as the basis for explanation, whereas Hinkle and Brown focus on the goals of different types of groups. Finally, cross-culturalists focus on contrast between responses to one's ingroup and outgroups, whereas Hinkle and Brown make comparisons between responses of members of groups that have different types of goals.

In order to marry these two perspectives, we need only to make a series of plausible assumptions about the persons sampled in prior studies from collectivist cultures. First, we must assume that their identification with group membership is high. Second, we must assume that groups with members endorsing collectivist values will also have collective goals. Finally, we must assume that the outgroups specified in cross-cultural studies are those with which social comparison is relevant. None of these assumptions could be tested without further investigation. However, if they are tenable, then the finding that members of collectivist cultures reject outgroups even more strongly than do those from individualist cultures can be considered as support for the Hinkle–Brown hypothesis.

This attempt to link the Hinkle–Brown hypothesis to the cross-cultural data has a further interesting consequence that takes us to the heart of one of the debates that have occurred among social identity theorists. Hinkle and Brown (1990) argue that the degree of identification determines the amount of ingroup bias. Social categorization theorists favor the view that self-categorization as a group member is a sufficient condition for the occurrence of bias. Within the relatively individualistic nations within which social identity theory has mostly found favor, it is likely that identification with a variety of group memberships is a relatively volatile process. Within individualistic cultures one has an abundance of alternate potential identities, and choices between them could vary in degree and over time. Within collectivist cultures, one's attachment to core sources of identity is much less fluid. Identifications and self-categorizations will fluctuate much less and even when they do, one's group affiliations are less negotiable. Abrams, Ando, and Hinkle (1998) found that social norms were a strong predictor of turnover intentions over and above identification with the organization among employees in Japan, but not in Britain. Thus we might expect that the differentiations proposed by Hinkle and Brown would prove less necessary when tested in collectivist cultures.

Two such tests have been reported thus far. Torres and Brown (1996) asked students in UK and Brazil to characterize different types of group in which they were involved. Consistent with Hinkle and Brown (1990), they found that identification predicted ingroup bias only in the groups that were characterized as collectivist and as relational, i.e., which involved comparison with other groups. These were religious groups. Capozza, Voci, and Licciardello (2000) tested the Hinkle–Brown predictions in northern and southern Italy. However, rather than asking respondents to characterize different types of groups, they obtained measures of the collectivist and relational values of their respondents. Their results did not support Hinkle–Brown, but it is unclear whether this was due to the use of novel and untested value measures rather than characterizations of types of group.

It is thus too soon to evaluate the degree to which there is a direct convergence between the Hinkle–Brown model and cross-cultural studies, and whether either approach could benefit from the other. One important step forward will be to incorporate measures of identification in future studies. There are further issues that require discussion concerning the conceptualization and measurement of collectivism, which we address in the next section.

Individual- and culture-level collectivism

Much of the enthusiasm for using collectivism as an explanatory variable in cross-cultural research stems from Hofstede's (1980) pioneering project. However, Hofstede has always maintained that the dimensions of culture that he identified are applicable only to culture-level analyses, a view he has recently reiterated (Hofstede, 2001). If we simply take culture-level concepts and apply them to individual-level analyses, we risk measurement invalidity and conclusions based on the ecological fallacy. Some scrutiny is therefore required of the plethora of individual-level measures now in use. The great majority of individual measures that have been created thus far are intended to refer to individualism–collectivism, rather than to any of Hofstede's other dimensions of cultural variance. The formulation of these measures has been influenced by Hofstede's conceptualization of collectivism and by Markus and Kitayama's (1991) delineation of the contrast between independence and interdependence. Among the most widely used have been various versions of the INDCOL index (Triandis, McCusker, & Hui, 1990), the self-construal scales of Singelis (1994) and measures of vertical and horizontal individualism–collectivism (Singelis, Triandis, Bhawuk, & Gelfand, 1995). The growth in popularity of these scales may lie in their apparent applicability to the study of contrasts between US and Pacific Asian samples.

The point of interest here is to consider the extent to which the individual-level measures actually do reflect Hofstede's (1980) culture-level definition. Hofstede defined collectivist cultures as those in which the employees in his sample emphasized goals that were dependent on the organization rather than those that emphasized individual autonomy. He contrasted this with the distinction between masculine cultures in which employees endorsed egocentric goals and feminine cultures in which employees were concerned to have good relations with those around them. He thus characterized individualism–collectivism in terms of *category membership*, and masculinity–femininity in terms of *preference for different types of relationship*, regardless of category membership. The individual-level measures do not always reflect this contrast. Many items within these scales refer to aspects of relationship quality and the need to maintain harmony. Although these scales have been shown to achieve at least modest reliability, some items could equally well reflect cultural femininity as collectivism. Thus, there is potential confusion as to whether some published results that have been interpreted in terms of Pacific Asian respondents' interdependent self-construals may actually be reflections of cultural femininity rather than collectivism.

Very few studies have provided individual-level measures that reflected both of Hofstede's dimensions. Y. Kashima et al. (1995) obtained responses to collectivism and relatedness scales from students in Australia, the USA, Hawaii, and Japan. They found mean scores for Japan to be low on relatedness but high on collectivism. Uleman, Rhee, Bardoliwalla, Semin, and Toyama (2000) obtained ratings for various types of emotional closeness to family, relations, and relatives from Japanese, European, and Asian American, Dutch, and Turkish students. Closeness means were consistently lowest for Japan, again supporting Hofstede's delineation of Japan as a masculine culture. These findings underline the need for cross-culturalists to distinguish their measures of self-reported relatedness and collectivism.

Self and social identity

In recent years, rather similar issues have been under discussion among social identity theorists. Two issues of particular relevance to our discussion are the moderating role of identification (or commitment) in social identity processes, and the decoupling of the link between intergroup differentiation and self-esteem enhancement or maintenance.

A considerable body of research, particularly from the Netherlands, has clearly demonstrated the moderating role of identification on social identity processes (e.g., Ellemers, Spears, & Doosje, 1997; Spears, Doosje, & Ellemers, 1997). On this basis, we know that there is a difference in behavior of high and low identifiers, yet this variable is not often incorporated into cross-cultural research. It is often assumed that identification will be higher in collectivistic cultures. For example, in the study by Chen et al. (1998) described earlier, US respondents demonstrated behavior suggesting individual mobility (disassociation from an ingroup when personal performance was superior). In contrast, Chinese participants adopted the more collective strategy of social competition that is typical of high identifiers, namely intergroup differentiation, achieved in this case through outgroup derogation. Although we might expect individuals in collective cultures to identify with their groups more highly than individuals in individualistic cultures, there is still likely to be considerable inter-individual variation in identification within a particular social group, and intra-individual variation in the strength of identifications with different social groups to which the person belongs. It would seem to be important to take measures of identification and to test for moderating effects in any cross-cultural tests of social identity theory.

In the previous section, we argued that a theoretical formulation of when cultural differences in ingroup bias would and would not occur is required. Building on their earlier work, Ellemers, Spears, and Doosje (2002) have recently proposed a model which stresses the overwhelming importance of social context and of level of commitment (strength of ties to the group, i.e., identification) in determining whether or not individuals will be primarily motivated by social or personal identity concerns, and furthermore, what kind of cognitive, affective, and behavioral consequences are likely to follow. They pay particular attention to whether the social context is experienced as threatening (either at individual or group level) or not, and how responses to such threats depend on level of group commitment. Their review brings together a wealth of recent work which demonstrates that there is a considerable variety of behavioral responses to social situations other than intergroup differentiation. Although they do not address cross-cultural applications directly, the social situations they describe may well arise more frequently in certain cultural contexts.

Of particular relevance to our discussion are, first, situations where individuals identify strongly with a group, and the value of the group is under threat. Behavior is most likely to follow conventional social identity theory predictions in this situation. Collective esteem will be threatened, so intergroup differentiation and group affirmation are likely to ensue.

In the absence of threat, highly committed individuals are argued to be more concerned with identity expression, and maintaining group distinctiveness. If distinctiveness is satisfactory, then there will be no need to further emphasize it through intergroup differentiation, and committed members will be more concerned with expressing their identity in other ways, for example through enacting behaviors that adhere to group norms (e.g., Jetten, Postmes, & McAuliffe, 2002). "When group identity is not threatened, it is not clear that differentiation should function to enhance self-esteem, especially if group distinctiveness is satisfied" (Ellemers et al.,

2002, p. 170). Thus, identity expression motivation would result in strong adherence to ingroup norms. This situation may be particularly common in collectivistic cultures, where individuals' social affiliations are highly valued (by themselves and others), social categories are a well-established aspect of life, and relatively stable. Ellemers et al. even suggest that the motivation for distinctiveness can be stronger than the need for ingroup enhancement, resulting in the acceptance of negative characteristics as definitive of the ingroup.

In contexts where social identities are not clearly recognized, and their importance is not acknowledged, individuals who are committed to their social group will be motivated to assert that groups' distinctiveness, resulting in intergroup differentiation. Such motives could be described as uncertainty reduction (e.g., Hogg & Mullin, 1999), and may apply particularly to the minimal social contexts that provide the empirical foundations of social identity theory. Ironically, the motives behind this behavior are group definition and meaning creation, rather than self-enhancement. It seems reasonable to argue that, when applied to real rather than minimal groups, this behavioral response might be more common in individualistic cultures where the centrality of social identities is more negotiable.

One final context of relevance to our debate occurs when highly committed group members experience threat at a personal level because they are not valued or accepted by other group members. Ellemers et al. (2002) argue that the likely response in such situations is to engage in behaviors which will increase acceptance by other members, one of which may well be ingroup bias and/or outgroup derogation. This example provides a third potential motivation for intergroup differentiation.

Current conceptualizations of social identity theory strongly suggest that the view that a single motivation (self-enhancement) leads to a single category of social behavior (intergroup differentiation) is over-simplistic. The original assumption may well have arisen precisely because of the minimal nature of the minimal group paradigm. Intragroup comparisons may be more important than intergroup comparisons in collectivistic cultures. In such cultures, the structure of intergroup relationships is relatively clear and stable, with people habitually defined according to their social groups, so categorization is not experienced as threatening, and group identification tends to be high. Consequently, identity needs may best be met through competition with other members of the group to be a "good group member", rather than through group-serving comparisons at the intergroup level. Measures of intergroup differentiation may well not be the best way of detecting such identity motives. As mentioned earlier, not all social categories are defined by a competitive relationship with an outgroup (Hinkle & Brown, 1990). Even for those social categories that include a competitive element (e.g., company affiliation), intragroup relations may be more personally relevant and important in collective cultures. Such motives are likely to be enacted through behaviors other than intergroup differentiation, such as collective effort, investment, or cooperativeness.

In individualistic cultures, identification with main social categories varies more widely, and it is more likely that individuals may experience categorization as threatening. Status relationships between social categories are perhaps more negotiable. Cultural emphasis is on personal achievements rather than affiliations, resulting in a more self-serving orientation towards social identities, especially where identification is not particularly high.

Yuki (2003) obtained some limited empirical support for these contrasts. Students in Japan and the USA reported their levels of identification and loyalty to a small group that was important to them and also their identification and loyalty to their nation. Among US respondents, but not among the Japanese, loyalty and identification were predicted by the perceived status and homogeneity of the ingroup. Yuki's prediction that Japanese identification and loyalty would be better predicted by a measure reflecting intragroup dynamics was supported, although this measure did also explain significant variance in the US responses.

In summary, intergroup differentiation is not the only way of maintaining or enhancing collective (or personal) self-esteem. Group membership serves other functions that in turn may vary in their importance to individuals, depending on their cultural background.

Culture and self-enhancement

Some cross-cultural researchers have also questioned the assumption that self-enhancement is universal, particularly in intergroup contexts. A prominent argument has been that self-enhancement processes are likely to benefit the individual self in individualistic cultures, but will more likely be manifest at the social level in collectivist cultures (Markus & Kitayama, 1991). Heine and Lehman (1997) questioned this argument, proposing that the concept of self-enhancement is simply not meaningful in cultures where the self is defined in relational terms (e.g., Japan). In support of their argument, Heine and Lehman pointed to the lack of evidence of self-enhancement effects in some Chinese and Japanese samples, in contrast to the abundance of evidence of such effects in North American samples. More recent studies support an alternative view. Where respondents are asked to rate themselves on traits that they consider important, Japanese have been found to rate themselves superior to others (Brown & Kobayashi, 2002), as have respondents from Singapore and Israel (Kurman & Sriram, 1997). Heine and his colleagues now suggest that self-enhancement, whether at individual or group level, is fostered more in individualistic cultures than it is in collectivistic cultures. Furthermore, the level of self-enhancement that is found is shown to be mediated by individualistic self-construal (Heine & Renshaw, 2002). In a similar way, Kurman and Sriram (2002) found that self-enhancement effects in Israeli kibbutzim and in Singapore are attributable to *low* vertical collectivism, mediated by beliefs in modesty. Thus the relative strength of self-enhancement motives across cultures may vary in ways that are determined not just by type of self-construal, but also in terms of how it is measured, and of the salience of other less-frequently studied social motives such as modesty and face. These findings indicate the need to broaden the focus of research to consider motives other than self or group enhancement.

Prospects for integration

In commencing this chapter, we noted the long running struggle between researchers' desire to achieve experimental control over the phenomena under study and the arguments in favor of maximizing external validity by taking account of environmental contingencies. In seeking to test the strength of the bridges between cross-cultural psychology and the work of social identity theorists, we have neglected to comment on the continuing contrast between the methods that the two groups of researchers mostly use. Social identity theorists like to manipulate experimentally the key measures in which they are interested, for instance identification. Cross-culturalists often start out by comparing mean scores from different samples, and more recently have been moving toward using correlations and regressions to determine whether their hypothesized explanatory variables can account for the mean differences observed. In consequence (and on a bad day), social identity theorists might consider cross-cultural research as primitive, while cross-culturalists might see work on social identity as unduly focused on effects that are transient and therefore probably unimportant.

Some of the recent studies that rely on experimental priming provide a test of whether this type of polarization can be transcended. Trafimow, Triandis, and Goto (1991) established that they could induce their US respondents to describe themselves in collectivist or individualist ways, simply by asking them to sit for five minutes and visualize either all their links with the family, or all the things that make them different from others. Over the past decade an increasing number of studies have been published that use a variety of experimental primes to test hypotheses relating to individualism and collectivism. Among North American bi-culturals, reference to ethnic identity, exposure to flags and other icons, and presentation of materials in different languages all achieve significant priming effects (Morris, Menon, & Ames, 2001; Oyserman, Sakamoto, & Lauffer, 1998; Ross, Xun, & Wilson, 2002). Protagonists of this approach see it as providing a way in which studies of cultural differences can be brought within the ambit of experimental method (Hong & Chiu, 2001; Hong, Morris, Chiu, & Benet Martinez, 2000). However, most results to date that use primes rest upon sampling of bi-culturals, among whom alternative cognitive frames can be presumed to be more readily present and accessible.

If increasing use of such methods were to show that the effects with which cross-culturalists concern themselves could *all* be reproduced experimentally within single-nation laboratory settings, then cross-culturalists could indeed take their seats within the domain of mainstream social psychology. It would be time to abandon debates as to the best ways of defining culture and to conclude that cultural differences are explicable in terms of the manner in which short-term life experiences are constantly priming us to act in culturally appropriate ways. Some examples have already come to light of how this might occur. For instance, E. S. Kashima and Y. Kashima (1998) showed that most languages spoken within collectivist nations permit the dropping of the personal pronoun "I", whereas those that are most spoken in individualist nations do not permit pronoun drop. By speaking in certain ways, we may be priming a particular cultural orientation.

However, before concluding that culture is just a matter of recurring primes, we would need much stronger evidence of the magnitude and durability of priming effects in a good range of different monocultural settings, preferably using more robust dependent variables than are provided by scenario studies. It seems more likely that primes could account for only some of the variance currently attributed to cultural effects. Even within the range of phenomena with which they have so far been shown to be influential, broader sampling is likely to show that primes have different effects in different locations. If this proves so, it will be time to explore what other aspects of cultural difference have not yet been captured by the popular but over simple contrast between individualism and collectivism. Even within the more delimited focus of social identity studies, the present chapter has touched on several candidates for such consideration. Thus the interplay of experimentation and field research will need to continue a while yet.

References

Abrams, D., Ando, K., & Hinkle, S. (1998). Psychological attachment to the group: Cross-cultural differences in organizational identification and subjective norms as predictors of workers' turnover intentions. *Personality and Social Psychology Bulletin*, 24, 1027–1039.

Brown, J. D., & Kobayashi, C. (2002). Self-enhancement in Japan and America. *Asian Journal of Social Psychology*, 5, 145–168.

Capozza, D., Voci, A., & Licciardello, O. (2000). Individualism, collectivism and social identity theory. In D. Capozza & R. Brown (Eds.), *Social identity processes: Trends in theory and research* (pp. 62–80). London: Sage.

Chen, Y. R., Brockner, J., & Chen, X. P. (2002). Individual–collective primacy and in-group favoritism: Enhancement and protection effects. *Journal of Experimental Social Psychology, 38*, 482–491.

Chen, Y. R., Brockner, J., & Katz, T. (1998). Toward an explanation of cultural differences in in-group favoritism: The role of individual versus collective primacy. *Journal of Personality and Social Psychology, 75*, 1490–1502.

Cinnirella, M. (1997). Towards a European identity? Interactions between the national and European social identities manifested by university students in Britain and Italy. *British Journal of Social Psychology, 36*, 19–31.

Derlega, V. J., Cukur, C. S., Kuang, J. C. Y., & Forsyth, D. R. (2002). Interdependent construal of self and the endorsement of conflict resolution strategies in interpersonal, intergroup and international disputes. *Journal of Cross Cultural Psychology, 33*, 610–625.

Ellemers, N., Spears, R., & Doosje, B. (1997). Sticking together or falling apart: In-group identification as a psychological determinant of group commitment versus individual mobility. *Journal of Personality and Social Psychology, 72*, 617–626.

Ellemers, N., Spears, R., & Doosje, B. (2002). Self and social identity. *Annual Review of Psychology, 53*, 161–186.

Graham, J. L., Mintu, A. T., & Rodgers, W. (1994). Exploration of negotiation behaviors in ten foreign cultures using a model developed in the United States. *Management Science, 40*, 72–95.

Heine, S. J., & Lehman, D. R. (1997). The cultural construction of self-enhancement: An examination of group-serving biases. *Journal of Personality and Social Psychology, 72*, 1268–1283.

Heine, S. J., & Renshaw, K. (2002). Interjudge agreement, self-enhancement, and liking: Cross-cultural divergences. *Personality and Social Psychology Bulletin, 28*, 578–587.

Hinkle, S., & Brown, R. (1990). Intergroup comparisons and social identity: Some links and lacunae. In D. Abrams & M. A. Hogg (Eds.), *Social identity theory: Constructive and critical advances* (pp. 48–70). London: Harvester Wheatsheaf.

Hofstede, G. (1980). *Culture's consequences: International differences in work-related values.* Beverly Hills, CA: Sage.

Hofstede, G. (2001). *Cultural consequences: Comparing values, behaviors, institutions and organizations across nations.* Thousand Oaks, CA: Sage.

Hogg, M. A. (2001). Social identity and the sovereignty of the group: A psychology of belonging. In C. Sedikides & M. B. Brewer (Eds.), *Individual self, relational self, collective self* (pp. 123–143). Philadelphia: Psychology Press.

Hogg, M. A., & Mullin, B.-A. (1999). Joining groups to reduce uncertainty: Subjective uncertainty reduction and group identification. In D. Abrams & M. A. Hogg (Eds.), *Social identity and social cognition* (pp. 249–279). Oxford, UK: Blackwell.

Hong, Y., & Chiu, C. (2001). Toward a paradigm shift: From cross-cultural differences in social cognition to social-cognitive mediation of cultural differences. *Social Cognition, 19*, 181–196.

Hong, Y., Morris, M. W., Chiu, C., & Benet Martinez, V. (2000). Multicultural minds: A dynamic constructivist approach to culture and cognition. *American Psychologist*, *55*, 709–720.

Hui, C. H., Triandis, H. C., & Yee, C. (1991). Cultural differences in reward allocation: Is collectivism the explanation? *British Journal of Social Psychology*, *30*, 145–157.

Jetten, J., Postmes, T., & McAuliffe, B. J. (2002). "We're all individuals": Group norms of individualism and collectivism, levels of identification, and identity threat. *European Journal of Social Psychology*, *32*, 189–207.

Kashima, E. S., & Kashima, Y. (1998). Culture and language: The case of cultural dimensions and personal pronoun use. *Journal of Cross Cultural Psychology*, *29*, 461–486.

Kashima, Y., Yamaguchi, S., Kim, U., Choi, S. C., Gelfand, M. J., & Yuki, M. (1995). Culture, gender, and self: A perspective from individualism–collectivism research. *Journal of Personality and Social Psychology*, *69*, 925–937.

Kurman, J., & Sriram, N. (1997). Self-enhancement, generality of self-evaluation, and affectivity in Israel and Singapore. *Journal of Cross Cultural Psychology*, *28*, 421–441.

Kurman, J., & Sriram, N. (2002). Interrelationships among vertical and horizontal collectivism, modesty, and self-enhancement. *Journal of Cross Cultural Psychology*, *33*, 71–86.

Leung, K., & Bond, M. H. (1984). The impact of cultural collectivism on reward allocation. *Journal of Personality and Social Psychology*, *47*, 793–804.

Lind, E. A., Tyler, T. R., & Huo, Y. J. (1997). Procedural context and culture: Variation in the antecedents of procedural justice judgments. *Journal of Personality and Social Psychology*, *73*, 767–780.

Markus, H. R., & Kitayama, S. (1991). Culture and the self: Implications for cognition, emotion, and motivation. *Psychological Review*, *98*, 224–253.

Mlicki, P. P., & Ellemers, N. (1996). Being different or being better? National stereotypes and identifications of Polish and Dutch students. *European Journal of Social Psychology*, *26*, 97–114.

Morris, M. W., Menon, T., & Ames, D. R. (2001). Culturally conferred conceptions of agency: A key to social perception of persons, groups, and other actors. *Personality and Social Psychology Review*, *5*, 169–182.

Mullen, B., Brown, R., & Smith, C. (1992). Ingroup bias as a function of salience, relevance, and status: An integration. *European Journal of Social Psychology*, *22*, 103–122.

Mummendey, A., Klink, A., & Brown, R. (2001). Nationalism and patriotism: National identification and out-group rejection. *British Journal of Social Psychology*, *40*, 159–172.

Oyserman, D., Sakamoto, I., & Lauffer, A. (1998). Cultural accommodation: Hybridity and the framing of social obligation. *Journal of Personality and Social Psychology*, *74*, 1606–1618.

Poppe, E., & Linssen, H. (1999). In-group favoritism and the reflection of realistic dimensions of difference between national states in Central and Eastern European nationality stereotypes. *British Journal of Social Psychology*, *38*, 85–103.

Ros, M., Huici, C., & Gomez, A. (2000). Comparative identity, category salience and intergroup relations. In D. Capozza & R. Brown (Eds.), *Social identity processes: Trends in theory and research* (pp. 81–95). London: Sage.

Ross, M., Xun, W. Q. E., & Wilson, A. E. (2002). Language and the bicultural self. *Personality and Social Psychology Bulletin, 28*, 1040–1050.

Rutland, A., & Cinnirella, M. (2000). Context effects on Scottish national and European self-categorization: The importance of category accessibility, fragility and relations. *British Journal of Social Psychology, 39*, 495–519.

Singelis, T. M. (1994). The measurement of independent and interdependent self-construals. *Personality and Social Psychology Bulletin, 20*, 580–591.

Singelis, T. M., Triandis, H. C., Bhawuk, D. P., & Gelfand, M. J. (1995). Horizontal and vertical dimensions of individualism and collectivism: A theoretical and measurement refinement. *Cross Cultural Research, 29*, 240–275.

Smith, P. B., & Schwartz, S. H. (1997). Values. In J. W. Berry, M. H. Segall, & Ç. Kagitçibasi (Eds.), *Handbook of cross-cultural psychology* (Vol. 3, pp. 77–118). Needham Heights, MA: Allyn & Bacon.

Spears, R., Doosje, B., & Ellemers, N. (1997). Self-stereotyping in the face of threats to group status and distinctiveness: The role of group identification. *Personality and Social Psychology Bulletin, 23*, 538–553.

Tajfel, H. (1972). Experiments in a vacuum. In H. Tajfel & J. Israel (Eds.), *The context of social psychology: A critical assessment*. Oxford, UK: Academic Press.

Tajfel, H. (1981). *Human groups and social categories*. Cambridge, UK: Cambridge University Press.

Tajfel, H., Billig, M. G., Bundy, R. P., & Flament, C. (1971). Social categorization and intergroup behaviour. *European Journal of Social Psychology, 1*, 149–178.

Tinsley, C. H., & Pillutla, M. M. (1998). Negotiating in the United States and Hong Kong. *Journal of International Business Studies, 29*, 711–727.

Torres, A. R. R., & Brown, R. (1996). Exploring group diversity: relationships between in-group identification and in-group bias. *International Journal of Psychology, 31*(3/4), 8.

Trafimow, D., Triandis, H. C., & Goto, S. G. (1991). Some tests of the distinction between the private self and the collective self. *Journal of Personality and Social Psychology, 60*, 649–655.

Triandis, H. C., McCusker, C., & Hui, C. H. (1990). Multimethod probes of individualism and collectivism. *Journal of Personality and Social Psychology, 59*, 1006–1020.

Uleman, J. S., Rhee, E., Bardoliwalla, N., Semin, G. R., & Toyama, M. (2000). The relational self: Closeness to ingroups depends on who they are, culture, and the type of closeness. *Asian Journal of Social Psychology, 3*, 1–17.

Verkuyten, M., & Nekuee, S. (1999). Ingroup bias: The effect of self-stereotyping, identification and group threat. *European Journal of Social Psychology, 29*, 411–418.

Wade-Benzoni, K. A., Okumura, T., Brett, J. M., Moore, D. A., Tenbrunsel, A. E., & Bazerman, M. H. (2002). Cognitions and behavior in asymmetric social dilemmas: A comparison of two cultures. *Journal of Applied Psychology, 87*, 87–95.

Wetherell, M. S. (1982). Cross-cultural studies of minimal groups: Implications for the social identity theory of intergroup relations. In H. Tajfel (Ed.), *Social identity and intergroup relations* (pp. 207–240). Cambridge, UK: Cambridge University Press.

Yuki, M. (2003). Intergroup comparison versus intragroup relationships: A cross-cultural examination of social identity theory in North American and East Asian cultural contexts. *Social Psychology Quarterly, 66,* 166–183.

Emotions in intergroup relations

Chapter 9

It's about time: Intergroup emotions as time-dependent phenomena

Eliot R. Smith and Diane M. Mackie

One of the most immediately obvious facts about intergroup relations is that they often involve emotions, particularly in terms of people's negative reactions to outgroups. People often feel angry, resentful, frustrated, disgusted, or afraid when they think about or encounter members of rival or challenging groups. Yet, as many of the chapters in this volume note, the role of emotions has received relatively little attention from researchers and theorists in this area until recently.

Specifically, there have been two major conceptual approaches to understanding stereotyping, prejudice, and intergroup behavior in general. One is based in the social cognition tradition, emphasizing the role of stereotypes, attitudes, and other mental representations of the perceiver's beliefs and evaluations concerning social groups. Research in this tradition has led to great advances in our understanding of how such beliefs are acquired, activated, applied, and (sometimes) altered. Yet in its focus on beliefs and evaluations, the approach has given relatively little attention to emotions. The same is true of the other major conceptual approach, based in the social identity theory/self-categorization theory tradition. This tradition has produced tremendous insights into the ways that group membership shapes perceptions and actions toward other people, but despite Tajfel's (1981) acknowledgement that ingroups have affective significance for their members, again emotions have received relatively little emphasis in the actual research literature.

In our own recent work we have developed a new theoretical model that puts emotions very much in the picture. In this chapter, we first briefly review this model and some recent evidence that supports it. We then turn to a question that we have not emphasized in our previous writings, the implications of our model for thinking about emotions and other intergroup phenomena as time-dependent phenomena – that is, as unfolding across time in a way that may differ from one moment to the next.

Intergroup emotions theory

Intergroup emotions theory (Mackie, Devos, & Smith, 2000; Smith, 1993, 1999) takes the notion of a socially extended self as its starting point, borrowing directly from the social identity approach. When a group membership is salient, people think of themselves as interchangeable members of the ingroup, rather than in terms of their unique personal identities. As group membership becomes part of the self in this way, it functions in all the ways that the psychological self does, as several studies have demonstrated (Smith & Henry, 1996). Importantly, this includes the regulation of emotional responses.

In our original conceptualization of intergroup emotions theory we adopted the assumptions of popular appraisal theories of emotions (later in this chapter we will discuss a newer model of emotion that makes somewhat different basic assumptions). We postulated that events, objects, and groups are appraised in terms of their implications for the ingroup (not just the individual self). Intergroup emotions theory holds that group-based emotions are generated by this appraisal process, just as individual emotions are generated by appraisals of objects or events that impinge on the individual self (Frijda, 1986; Roseman, 1984). For example, if people thinking of themselves as members of a group perceive that their ingroup is threatened by an outgroup's goals or actions, and believe that the ingroup is weak, they may experience group-based anxiety or fear. Among the consequences may be a desire or impulse to avoid or escape from the outgroup. Group-based emotions may be directed at the ingroup as well. For example, someone may feel collective pride if they believe that their group has produced some worthwhile accomplishment. Or feelings of collective guilt may result if someone appraises their group as having violated important moral principles (Doosje, Branscombe, Spears, & Manstead, 1998).

In summary, intergroup emotions theory postulates that when people identify with a group, they will appraise social objects or events in terms of their implications for the group. These appraisals produce group-based emotions and in turn collective action tendencies. The emotions are predicted to mediate the effects of the appraisals on the action tendencies, demonstrating their functional role in the overall process.

Evidence supporting intergroup emotions theory

Our research and that of others has already provided several types of evidence supporting the hypotheses of intergroup emotions theory. Space limitations do not allow a complete review of that evidence here, but fuller summaries are available elsewhere (Devos, Silver, Mackie, & Smith, 2002).

Studies by Yzerbyt, Dumont, Gordijn, and Wigboldus (2002) demonstrated the role of self-categorization in producing emotional reactions to events that affect ingroup members – even though they do not affect the perceiver personally. In these studies participants read about an action that negatively affected another person, who shared one group membership with the participants (i.e., psychology student) but differed in terms of another group membership (i.e., was a student at a rival university). The researchers subtly manipulated the salience of one or other of these group memberships, and asked about the participants' emotional reactions to the described event. Notably, although the event had absolutely no personal implications for the participants, when their common group membership with the victim was salient they had corresponding emotions (such as anger and unhappiness). This result suggests that the reaction was based on the collective self elicited by the currently salient ingroup membership.

Initial evidence also exists for the role of identification with the group in producing intergroup emotions. Shortly after the September 2001 attacks on the USA, for example, we (Mackie, Silver, Maitner, & Smith, 2002) measured UCSB students' identification with the group "Americans" and assessed the extent to which they felt a series of emotions in reaction to a hypothetical terrorist attack on their country (not the 9/11 events in particular, although we can be sure that these were most salient). The more strongly participants identified as Americans, the more anger and the more fear they reported about terrorist attacks on their country. As suggested by intergroup emotions theory, then, the more central the group membership to the self, the more intensely emotions are experienced on behalf of the group.

Other studies (Mackie et al., 2000) provided evidence for the nature and impact of intergroup appraisals, as well as the distinctiveness of specific intergroup emotions and their action tendency consequences. Once participants had identified themselves as members of one of two opposing groups, we manipulated the perception of ingroup or outgroup strength. We did so by exposing participants to a series of alleged newspaper headlines, which appeared to reflect popular and political support either for their own group or for the outgroup. We then assessed emotions felt toward the outgroup. Analyses of responses to these questions revealed clearly differentiated negative emotions. Factor analyses revealed that responses to items related to fear (fearful, anxious, worried, frightened) were closely related to one another but quite different from the closely related responses to items tapping anger (annoyed, irritated, angry, mad) or contempt (disgusted, contemptuous, repulsed). Those perceiving the ingroup to be strong reported considerable anger at the other group, whereas those in the weak condition reported little. Moreover, these emotions were associated with distinct action tendencies. Those who experienced anger reported increased desires to take action against the outgroup ("I want to confront/oppose/argue with/attack them"). Importantly, mediational analyses indicated that the relation between appraisals and action tendency was significantly mediated by the experienced emotion.

Time as a key parameter in intergroup emotions theory

Emotion episodes

In comparing intergroup emotions theory with other conceptions of intergroup relations, one fundamental difference emerges clearly. In traditional conceptions, both stereotypes and prejudice are typically viewed as highly stable over time. Indeed, entire literatures have arisen as researchers and theorists have attempted to explain this stability in the face of encounters with non-stereotypic group members, even when people desire to rid themselves of deep-seated prejudices (e.g., Devine, 1989).

In contrast, emotions are *episodic states*. That is, an emotion is an experience that occurs at a specific point in time, although its duration may vary (perhaps from less than a second up to moods lasting for hours or days). The proximal causes of emotions are occurrent events, whether actual events in the real world or recalled, imagined, or otherwise mentally constructed events (Russell, 2003; Weiss & Cropanzano, 1996).

For a specific description of the time course and nature of emotional episodes, we draw on a recent integrative theory of emotion by James Russell (2003). This model is related to appraisal theories, but alters some basic assumptions, as we will describe shortly. In this model, core affect states, which fit within a two-dimensional space whose axes are pleasantness and arousal, are fundamental components of all emotions (as well as moods). Core affect can change in response to many types of external stimuli, such as pleasant or unpleasant environmental states or positive or negative events, as well as internal physiological processes (such as ingestion of caffeine or diurnal rhythms). Core affect is assumed to be readily subjectively perceptible (leading to the sense of feeling good, bad, energized, tired, etc.).

A change of core affect that is consciously noted and attributed to some cause constitutes the beginning of an emotional episode. This attribution marks the transition between just feeling negatively aroused and feeling negatively aroused *because* of a threatening-looking stranger, or between feeling good and feeling good *about* America's military strength. Making an attribution is adaptively important, because it allows the person to direct attention and behavior appropriately with regard to the object that is responsible for the feeling. Of course, because the true causes of affective states are not always obvious, people may misattribute the emotion. Someone feeling unpleasantly aroused for irrelevant reasons (such as unpleasantly hot temperatures) may misattribute this affective state to another person's provocative behavior, experience anger, and potentially commit aggression (Berkowitz, 1998).

The next stage in the core affect model is that various factors, including the core affect and its perceived cause, as well as the situational context, one's overt behaviors, and bodily experiences (such as physiological changes), are input to a perceptual categorization process in which the person consciously decides that he or she is angry, sad, guilty, etc. The emotion is categorized and verbally labeled based on the extent of resemblance between these factors and a mental representation of a given emotion's prototype. Now the person could say that he or she feels *afraid* of the threatening stranger, or *proud* of America's strength. This labeling process produces what Russell (2003) terms "emotional meta-experience" or the conscious awareness of having an emotion.

The core affect model incorporates the essential predictions of appraisal theories, by postulating that appraisals (interpretations of various aspects of the situation) are among the inputs that lead to the categorization and self-perception of a specific emotion. That is, people are likely to conclude that they are feeling anger when they perceive themselves as having been harmed or attacked unjustly by another person or group, see themselves as strong and able to cope with the situation, etc. But the core affect model identifies these appraisals as contributing to the emotion-labeling process (the emotional "meta-experience") rather than to the changes in core affect that may kick off the attributional and interpretive process. In other words, the core affect model reverses the causal ordering assumed in appraisal theories of emotion. Appraisal theories hold that appraisals of some event cause a specific emotion (such as fear), which in turn has multiple observable effects including subjective feelings (being afraid), nonverbal expressions, autonomic changes, and instrumental actions. The problem with this view is that it predicts that feelings, expressions, autonomic changes, and actions, as multiple effects of a single internal event, should all strongly covary, which Russell (2003) argues is not empirically the case.

Applying the core affect model to intergroup emotions, we suggest the following. An event occurs, which people see as having implications for their group memberships. Or they recall such an event that has happened in the past. Consideration of the event may lead to core affect changes that are attributed to the event itself or might be misattributed, because there are other potential influences on core affect. Finally, the person may draw on his or her feelings and attributions to label the emotion, as an instance of feeling frustrated, angry, disgusted, proud, guilty, sympathetic, etc. These reactions to events are the fundamental starting point for intergroup emotions theory. Example group emotional events might include:

- Witnessing an African American mother using food stamps at the supermarket, and reflecting that the taxpayers help "those people" with their grocery costs, while "we" have to work hard to buy food for our families, resulting in feelings of anger and resentment.
- Seeing a sign for a store in a local shopping center in an Asian language, and feeling anxious that "they" are coming in and taking over more and more of "our" country.

- Learning of bombings or attacks carried out by Arab Muslims on Americans or on institutions associated with America, and feeling fearful.
- Encountering a non-native English speaker as a retail clerk, restaurant server, or telephone receptionist, and feeling annoyed that the person is hard to understand or does not readily understand a request.
- Hearing that inhabitants of a distant Third World country are victimized by civil war or natural disaster, and feeling distress and sympathy about their plight (intergroup emotions are not always negative).

These examples illustrate several important points. First, we suggest that the reaction is virtually immediately experienced as an emotional reaction to "them" – to an entire outgroup – rather than to a specific individual. This illustrates the idea, at the core of social identity theory (Tajfel, 1981) and self-categorization theory (Turner, Hogg, Oakes, Reicher, & Wetherell, 1987), that in intergroup situations the self and others are experienced as interchangeable members of groups rather than as unique individuals. The attribution process seems to identify the group rather than a specific individual as the cause of the emotional reaction.

Second, according to Frijda (1993), often emotional reactions are not to singular or unique events, but involve an ongoing, recurrent series of events with a single underlying theme. The same applies to emotional reactions to group-relevant events. The theme may be "undeserved government benefits" (in the food-stamp case), "invasion of our territory" (in the foreign-language store-sign case), etc. Indeed, a single event hardly constitutes an important or noteworthy threat to an ingroup, but a recurrent series of similarly themed events may rise to that level of threat. In addition, if several similar events occur, excitation transfer (Zillman, 1979) may intensify emotional reactions to the later events.

Third, a group stereotype (i.e., a set of attributes culturally associated with the group) frequently feeds into interpretations of the event. For example, a cultural stereotype of African Americans as lazy, or of immigrants as unwilling to assimilate to our culture, no doubt is an important contributing factor to the emotions experienced in some of the example episodes just described. Thus, stereotypes are far from irrelevant to emotional reactions to groups, in our view. However, the connection between stereotypes and emotions may be indirect. In particular, their valence may not match. A positive stereotype – for example, a view of a rival group as intelligent, hard-working, and ambitious – may make the rival group a stronger threat and therefore feed into negative emotions such as fear or resentment. Similarly, a negative stereotype of a group (e.g., as weak and incompetent) may lead to positive emotions of pity and sympathy, assuming the group is not seen as a competitor (Fiske, Cuddy, & Glick, 2002).

Fourth, at the time an emotion is aroused, it may produce an immediate action tendency. Feeling annoyed with the woman in the supermarket, the observer may want to lash out at her verbally. People may or may not carry out such actions, but the potential for specific emotion-driven behaviors to occur during the time course of an emotion episode is an important prediction. An individual may suppress the desire to make a negative remark at the woman using food stamps, but if he or she is still feeling frustrated and resentful, on the way out of the supermarket the person may be particularly willing to sign a petition for a political candidate promising a crackdown on welfare abuse.

Sources of over-time variability in emotional reactions

We emphasize the importance of time in the conceptualization of intergroup processes as involving emotion, for emotion is intrinsically a time-dependent state. This approach invites us to consider some of the reasons why emotional reactions, even to the same or similar events, may differ from one time to another.

One major reason is that appraisals are subjective interpretations, not objective perceptions of events as they exist in reality. Therefore the perceiver's own state including, crucially, the availability and accessibility of interpretive schemas (knowledge representations in memory), will affect them. In the realm of person perception it is well recognized that the same behavior, say sharing test answers with a classmate, may be interpreted in one way (as helpful) by one perceiver but in a different way (as dishonest) by another (Higgins, 1996). Similarly, an intergroup event (the woman using food stamps at the supermarket) may be interpreted as freeloading or irresponsible behavior by one perceiver, giving rise to irritation and anger. But another perceiver – or the same one at a different time, depending on knowledge accessibility – may see it as evidence of how the public generously helps people who are out of work so that their children do not suffer unduly, and may feel emotions of pity or sympathy for the person or even pride because of the generosity of the public.

Another major reason for variability in emotional reactions is that some (perhaps most) intergroup events are complex and afford appraisals that are linked to more than one emotion. When enemies of America attacked on September 11, 2001, those events gave rise to many emotions among Americans. Anger would be a natural reaction to being attacked. Fear would be reasonable because of the salient possibility of additional attacks. Sadness at the tragic loss of life is another potential reaction. Even positive emotions, such as feelings of collective pride at the heroism of rescue workers, could be felt. In fact, we found evidence for co-existing emotions in the study designed to measure emotional reactions to hypothetical acts of terrorism, run approximately two weeks after the September 11th attacks on the United States. When asked how they would feel if a terrorist group from another country attacked their country, participants reported high levels of both anger and fear as well as moderate levels of guilt. In citing reasons for their emotions, participants often referred to different aspects of the events as the antecedents of their different emotions.

A third reason for variability in emotional reactions is variability in group identification. People sometimes think of themselves as individuals, and at other times in terms of group membership (Turner et al., 1987). Further, they have many group memberships simultaneously, and first one and then another may be salient. For example, an American may read about an attack conducted by US troops in a foreign country such as Afghanistan or Iraq. The perceiver may identify as American and feel satisfaction if the attack's outcome is seen as positive (or guilt if it is negative). Or the person may identify as a Democrat and thereby dissociate him or herself from the action, choosing to identify it as the act of a Republican outgroup. As this example suggests, shifts in group identification may even be motivated by the resulting emotions, as when people downplay a group identification that would result in feeling collective guilt (Doosje et al., 1998).

A fourth reason for variability is that people are not limited to being passive observers of their emotions. Instead, they actively seek to regulate them. Emotion regulation is a complex story, but it is important to note that it is not driven simply by valence. That is, people do not simply try to reinforce positive emotions and damp down negative ones (Erber, 1996). People adopt emotions that are socially appropriate, for example feeling grief at a funeral (which may involve suppressing positive emotions such as laughter at a remembered funny incident involving the deceased). Importantly, they may try to feel or at least express emotions like anger when involved in a conflict, because anger is socially appropriate in that setting or because feeling anger makes one feel strong (which may be better than experiencing fear and feeling oneself to be weak). Whatever its underlying motives, emotion regulation contributes to emotional variability over time, as people seek to reinforce or suppress emotions depending on a variety of factors and with varying degrees of success.

Implications of emotional variability

Whatever the source of variability in emotions – shifting interpretations of events or appraisals, multiple appraisal possibilities linked to distinct emotions, shifting group identifications, emotion regulation processes – the result seems likely to be a subjective feeling that different emotions are being experienced somewhat simultaneously. It is not clear whether such emotions are perceived as rapidly changing from one to the next and perhaps back, or whether people feel that they hold multiple, perhaps even conflicting, emotions entirely simultaneously. Alternatively, emotions may be experienced as blending, such as a feeling of guilt tinged with sadness when one reflects on the tragic consequences of past wrongdoings of one's group. Future research effort might well be directed at disentangling these possibilities, or perhaps demonstrating that each kind of experience can exist and under what conditions.

Regardless of the exact nature of the emotions, the experience of multiple emotions itself has several possible implications for intergroup relations. First, feeling several different emotions, or a blend of emotions, especially if they conflict in valence, may reasonably be expected to produce feelings of uncertainty and confusion, with their attendant motivational and capacity consequences for the processing of social information. Such a state will likely also be characterized by conflicting approach and avoidance tendencies, as well as perhaps the specific desire to resolve the confusion. Second, rapidly changing or conflicting emotional reactions might also contribute to intergroup anxiety (Stephan & Stephan, 1985). Although most work on intergroup anxiety has focused on the awkwardness of interaction with unfamiliar groups, multiple emotions might be either a mediator of this effect (as interactions progress from moments of smooth coordination through awkward mismatching and then to positive resolution or negative dissolution), or an independent source of anxiety in interaction with outgroups (even familiar ones).

The recognition that intergroup events might trigger multiple emotions recalls the classic literature on ambivalent prejudice. Both an inability to form or report a clear evaluation, and the presence of both positive and negative components in group evaluations, have been usefully characterized as ambivalent. Katz and his colleagues (Katz, 1981; see also Kinder & Sears, 1981; Sears, 1988) focused on the presence of incompatibility among precursors to an ambivalent evaluation. For example, they suggested that adherence to some values (such as egalitarianism) gave White Americans positive reactions to stigmatized groups, while adherence to other values (such as belief in a meritocracy) simultaneously triggered negative reactions (Katz & Hass, 1988). In the intergroup emotions theory framework, positive emotional reactions are likely to be triggered by an event or some aspect of an event that activates appraisal precursors to pride, satisfaction, contentment, or gratitude, for example. Other aspects of the same event (perhaps because of changing value accessibility) may equally activate appraisal precursors of anger or fear. Imagine a White American reading about the high percentage of first generation Asian-American students accepted at the country's most prestigious universities. On the one hand, the event might confirm the belief that anyone can get ahead in a true democracy, an event that reflects well on the ingroup, making feelings of pride and contentment likely. At the same time, the event may lower the probability of White students being accepted at the same institutions, and thus constitutes a threat to the ingroup. Ambivalent prejudice may well be described as ambivalence of emotional reactions triggered simultaneously or in rapid succession by intergroup events. Pending research on the issue, we speculate that emotional ambivalence may be experienced if different emotions of the same valence (such as fear and anger) are combined, as well as when the emotions have opposite valences.

What might be the consequences of intergroup emotional ambivalence? Katz and Glass (1979) postulate response amplification as one outcome. Thus, under conditions of ambivalence, reactions to groups could be extremitized in either a positive or negative direction. That is, when the actions of a threatening outgroup produce both anger and fear, ambivalence may intensify negative reactions and produce excessive retaliation. Interestingly, then, generalization of the ambivalence-amplification hypothesis to the domain of intergroup emotion suggests the counter-intuitive hypothesis that anger-related action tendencies in the presence of anger and fear might be more extreme than anger-related action tendencies in the presence of anger alone.

Other potential consequences of intergroup emotional ambivalence can also be hypothesized on the basis of the attitude ambivalence literature. Ambivalent attitudes are reported more slowly and show greater instability. Objects about which people hold ambivalent attitudes are responded to more slowly (Bargh, Chaiken, Govender, & Pratto, 1992; Katz, 1981) and behavior toward them is not as clearly dictated by current attitudes (Erber, Hodges, & Wilson, 1995; Moore, 1980). Thus intergroup targets that elicit multiple or ambivalent emotions may elicit action tendencies more slowly than other targets, and the action tendencies they elicit may not be as closely associated to the currently triggered emotion as appraisal theories might postulate. The direction in which action tendencies might deviate is suggested by the fact that negative reactions might dominate positive ones, as avoidance tendencies typically produce stronger effects than approach tendencies (Cacioppo & Berntson, 1994). These possibilities await empirical assessment, but illustrate some of the potential benefits of considering the consequences of over-time variability in emotional reactions to outgroups.

Longer-term effects of emotion episodes

As we have described, a fundamental postulate of intergroup emotion theory is that emotional reactions are episodic, varying across time and occurring in response to specific events. Still, the theory does have implications for longer-term, more stable reactions to groups. Most obviously, if a specific emotion is experienced repeatedly over time in response to a particular group, this feeling will become associated with the mental representation of the group, through the process of classical conditioning. The emotion is then likely to be reactivated when group members are encountered or thought about, even in neutral contexts that do not involve any specific emotional events. Action tendencies may become chronically accessible in the same way, so that the perceiver may feel impulses to attack or harm the group every time he or she thinks about them. Our hypothetical perceiver may feel annoyance on seeing a Black person using food stamps, anger at reading about Black welfare recipients in the newspaper, and other similar negative responses many times over months and years. As a result, he or she may feel flooded with angry feelings when a Black candidate runs for mayor of the city, and decide to work or vote for an opposing candidate, even if the Black candidate has no specific connection to the original emotion-inspiring events. The idea that negative affect directed at specific groups is a powerful contributor to political attitudes and behaviors has been well developed and empirically tested by researchers in the "symbolic politics" tradition (Kinder & Sears, 1981; Sears, 1988).

Empirical evidence for the long-lasting effects of immediate emotional reactions comes from a study by Skitka, Bauman, and Mullen (2004) of reactions to the September 11th attacks. The researchers surveyed a national sample in the USA by telephone just days after the attack and asked to what extent they felt the emotions of fear and anger. A follow-up survey 3–4 months later asked a variety of questions regarding the American responses to the attacks, such as support for restrictions on civil liberties in the name of "fighting terrorism", and also asked about the respondent's own actions (such as flying the American flag, spending more time with family, trying to be nicer to people, etc.). The key finding is that many longer-term effects were strongly and directly predicted by the respondent's emotions immediately after the attack. Moreover, fear and anger predicted systematically different responses – for example, fear was more strongly related to value-affirming thoughts and behaviors, while anger was more related to outgroup derogation. This study shows, then, that distinct emotional reactions immediately after the attack were associated with meaningfully different reactions in the longer term, over several months.

Implications and conclusion

Thinking of intergroup relations as involving emotions, and particularly of their time-dependent nature, has implications for both methodology and theory in social psychology.

The most obvious methodological implication is that researchers should look at emotions over time, with multiple measurements, rather than assuming that prejudice (conceptualized as an attitude) is stable and independent of the time of measurement. Multiple waves of questionnaires, or experience-sampling methodology, suggest themselves as appropriate measurement techniques. The use of several measurement occasions obviously can contribute to reliability and validity, by allowing the researcher to average over unsystematic effects that vary over time. Equally important, it may allow examination of other parameters (such as the degree of variability of emotions toward a particular group, or the maximum emotion experienced rather than the average), to test the possibility that they may improve prediction and understanding of important aspects of intergroup behavior. But most important of all is the goal of relating emotions at specific points in time to their potential causes (events that occur or are thought about at those times) and effects (behaviors that are performed at those specific times). Ultimately over-time variation in emotion should not be just averaged across, but predicted.

One substantive implication of thinking about emotions as having an intrinsic time course is that they may have effects either during a specific emotion episode, or at a later time after many emotion episodes have occurred. During an episode (i.e., while an emotion is being experienced), many behaviors or judgments may be affected by the emotion. For example, Dovidio, Esses, Beach, and Gaertner (2002) have shown that willingness to interact with outgroup members is affected by emotional reactions to the outgroup, so such intergroup contact may be specifically affected during an emotion episode. Similarly, emotions have been shown to influence on-line processing, both by altering cognitive capacity and motivation, and also in more specific ways depending on the specific dimensions being considered or judged (Lerner & Keltner, 2000; Niedenthal, Halberstadt, & Innes-Ker, 1999; Tiedens & Linton, 2001). Incidental emotions have been shown to have these kinds of predictable effects on intergroup-relevant judgments (Bodenhausen, 1993; Mackie, Queller, Stroessner, & Hamilton, 1996). However, investigation of such effects from intergroup emotions specifically has not even begun.

In addition to immediate effects on on-line processing, emotional episodes should have further, and perhaps different, effects as they accumulate over time. As noted above, emotions felt repeatedly about a particular group or situation will become associated with the mental representation of the object and become able to be elicited by simple cues. Thus, the emotions will become part of the perceiver's intrinsic and perhaps automatic reaction to the object, and will be available to affect evaluations, judgments, or behaviors.

In summary, thinking of prejudice and intergroup behavior as involving emotions, following our intergroup emotion theory, leads to important new predictions and research questions based on the fundamental observation that emotions are time-dependent phenomena that unfold over seconds, minutes, and hours. We have described some ideas about the time course of individual emotion episodes, and speculated on potentially different short-term and long-term effects of experiencing intergroup emotions. By drawing on the attitudinal ambivalence literature, we also described some hypotheses regarding effects of conflicting or mixed emotions in intergroup contexts. Many of the ideas presented here have yet to be empirically tested. But our goal is not to advance them as firm conclusions, as much as to illustrate the conceptual and empirical advances that can stem from thinking about the role of emotion in intergroup behavior.

References

Bargh, J. A., Chaiken, S., Govender, R., & Pratto, F. (1992). The generality of the automatic attitude activation effect. *Journal of Personality and Social Psychology*, *62*, 893–912.

Berkowitz, L. (1998). Affective aggression: The role of stress, pain, and negative affect. In R. G. Geen & E. Donnerstein (Eds.), *Human aggression: Theories, research, and implications for social policy* (pp. 49–72). San Diego, CA: Academic Press.

Bodenhausen, G. V. (1993). Emotions, arousal and stereotypic judgments: A heuristic model of affect and stereotyping. In D. M. Mackie & D. L. Hamilton (Eds.), *Affect, cognition, and stereotyping: Interactive processes in group perception* (pp. 13–37). San Diego, CA: Academic Press.

Cacioppo, J. T., & Berntson, G. G. (1994). Relationship between attitudes and evaluative space: A critical review, with emphasis on the separability of positive and negative substrates. *Psychological Bulletin*, *115*, 401–423.

Devine, P. G. (1989). Stereotypes and prejudice: Their automatic and controlled components. *Journal of Personality and Social Psychology*, *56*, 5–18.

Devos, T., Silver, L. A., Mackie, D. M., & Smith, E. R. (2002). Experiencing intergroup emotions. In D. M. Mackie & E. R. Smith (Eds.), *From prejudice to intergroup emotions: Differentiated reactions to social groups* (pp. 111–134). New York: Psychology Press.

Doosje, B., Branscombe, N. R., Spears, R., & Manstead, A. S. R. (1998). Guilty by association: When one's group has a negative history. *Journal of Personality and Social Psychology*, *75*, 872–886.

Dovidio, J. F., Esses, V. M., Beach, K. R., & Gaertner, S. L. (2002). The role of affect in determining intergroup behavior: The case of willingness to engage in intergroup contact. In D. M. Mackie & E. R. Smith (Eds.), *From prejudice to intergroup emotion: Differentiated reactions to social groups* (pp. 153–171). New York: Psychology Press.

Erber, R. (1996). The self-regulation of moods. In L. L. Martin & A. Tesser (Eds.), *Striving and feeling: Interactions among goals, affect, and self-regulation* (pp. 251–275). Hillsdale, NJ: Lawrence Erlbaum Associates Inc.

Erber, R., Hodges, S. D., & Wilson, T. D. (1995). Attitude strength, attitude stability, and the effects of analyzing reasons. In R. E. Petty & J. A. Krosnick (Eds.), *Attitude strength: Antecedents and consequences* (pp. 433–454). Mahwah, NJ: Lawrence Erlbaum Associates Inc.

Fiske, S. T., Cuddy, A. J. C., & Glick, P. (2002). Emotions up and down: Intergroup emotions result from perceived status and competition. In D. M. Mackie & E. R. Smith (Eds.), *From prejudice to intergroup emotions: Differentiated reactions to social groups* (pp. 247–264). New York: Psychology Press.

Frijda, N. H. (1986). *The emotions*. Cambridge, UK: Cambridge University Press.

Frijda, N. H. (1993). Moods, emotion episodes and emotions. In M. Lewis & J. M. Haviland (Eds.), *Handbook of emotions* (pp. 381–403). New York: Guilford Press.

Higgins, E. T. (1996). Knowledge activation: Accessibility, applicability, and salience. In E. T. Higgins & A. W. Kruglanski (Eds.), *Social psychology: Handbook of basic principles* (pp. 133–168). New York: Guilford Press.

Katz, I. (1981). *Stigma: A social psychological analysis.* Hillsdale, NJ: Lawrence Erlbaum Associates Inc.

Katz, I., & Glass, D. C. (1979). An ambivalence-amplification theory of behavior toward the stigmatized. In W. G. Austin & S. Worchel (Eds.), *The social psychology of intergroup relations* (pp. 55–84). Monterey, CA: Brooks/Cole.

Katz, I., & Hass, R. G. (1988). Racial ambivalence and American value conflict: Correlational and priming studies of dual cognitive structures. *Journal of Personality and Social Psychology, 55,* 893–905.

Kinder, D. R., & Sears, D. O. (1981). Prejudice and politics: Symbolic racism versus racial threats to the good life. *Journal of Personality and Social Psychology, 40,* 414–431.

Lerner, J. S., & Keltner, D. (2000). Beyond valence: Toward a model of emotion-specific influences on judgement and choice. *Cognition and Emotion, 14,* 473–493.

Mackie, D. M., Devos, T., & Smith, E. R. (2000). Intergroup emotions: Explaining offensive action tendencies in an intergroup context. *Journal of Personality and Social Psychology, 79,* 602–616.

Mackie, D. M., Queller, S., Stroessner, S. J., & Hamilton, D. L. (1996). Making stereotypes better or worse: Multiple roles of positive affect in group impressions. In R. M. Sorrentino & E. T. Higgins (Eds.), *Handbook of motivation and cognition: The interpersonal context* (Vol. 3, pp. 371–396). New York: Guilford Press.

Mackie, D. M., Silver, L. A., Maitner, A. T., & Smith, E. R. (2002). *Intergroup emotions in response to and as a predictor of intergroup aggression.* Unpublished manuscript.

Moore, M. (1980). Validation of the Attitude Toward Any Practice Scale through the use of ambivalence as a moderator variable. *Educational and Psychological Measurement, 40,* 205–208.

Niedenthal, P. M., Halberstadt, J. B., & Innes-Ker, A. H. (1999). Emotional response categorization. *Psychological Review, 106,* 337–361.

Roseman, I. J. (1984). Cognitive determinants of emotion: A structural theory. In P. Sharver (Ed.), *Review of Personality and Social Psychology* (Vol. 5, pp. 11–36). Beverly Hills, CA: Sage.

Russell, J. A. (2003). Core affect and the psychological construction of emotion. *Psychological Review, 110,* 145–172.

Sears, D. O. (1988). Symbolic racism. In P. A. Katz & D. A. Taylor (Eds.), *Eliminating racism* (pp. 53–84). New York: Plenum Press.

Skitka, L. J., Bauman, C. W., & Mullen, E. (2004). Political tolerance and coming to psychological closure following the September 11, 2001 terrorist attacks: An integrative approach. *Personality and Social Psychology Bulletin, 30,* 743–756.

Smith, E. R. (1993). Social identity and social emotions: Toward new conceptualizations of prejudice. In D. M. Mackie & D. L. Hamilton (Eds.), *Affect, cognition, and stereotyping: Interactive processes in group perception* (pp. 297–315). San Diego, CA: Academic Press.

Smith, E. R. (1999). Affective and cognitive implications of a group becoming a part of the self: New models of prejudice and of the self-concept. In D. Abrams & M. A. Hogg (Eds.), *Social identity and social cognition* (pp. 183–196). Oxford, UK: Blackwell.

Smith, E. R., & Henry, S. (1996). An ingroup becomes part of the self: Response time evidence. *Personality and Social Psychology Bulletin, 22,* 635–642.

Stephan, W. G., & Stephan, C. W. (1985). Intergroup anxiety. *Journal of Social Issues, 41,* 157–175.

Tajfel, H. (1981). *Human groups and social categories.* Cambridge, UK: Cambridge University Press.

Tiedens, L. Z., & Linton, S. (2001). Judgment under emotional certainty and uncertainty: The effects of specific emotions on information processing. *Journal of Personality and Social Psychology, 81,* 973–988.

Turner, J. C., Hogg, M. A., Oakes, P. J., Reicher, S. D., & Wetherell, M. S. (1987). *Rediscovering the social group: A self-categorization theory.* Oxford, UK: Blackwell.

Weiss, H. M., & Cropanzano, R. (1996). Affective events theory: A theoretical discussion of the structure, causes and consequences of affective experiences at work. In B. M. Staw & L. L. Cummings (Eds.), *Research in organizational behavior: An annual series of analytical essays and critical reviews* (Vol. 18, pp. 1–74). Stamford, CT: JAI Press.

Yzerbyt, V. Y., Dumont, M., Gordijn, E. H., & Wigboldus, D. (2002). Intergroup emotions and self-categorization: The impact of perspective-taking on reactions to victims of harmful behavior. In D. M. Mackie & E. R. Smith (Eds.), *From prejudice to intergroup emotions: Differentiated reactions to social groups* (pp. 67–88). New York: Psychology Press.

Zillman, D. (1979). *Hostility and aggression.* Hillsdale, NJ: Lawrence Erlbaum Associates Inc.

Chapter 10

Connecting social identity theory and cognitive appraisal theory of emotions

Patricia Garcia-Prieto and Klaus R. Scherer

To account for intergroup phenomena, social identity theory has evoked the cognitive (i.e., social categorization) and motivational (i.e., self-enhancement) processes underlying social identity (Tajfel & Turner, 1986). However, the way in which these processes may interact and translate into specific emotional responses in intergroup settings remains to be clearly explained. Little is still known about why, how, and when groups display emotion toward each other, and adding an affective component remains one of the key challenges for future development in social identity theory (Brown, 2000). Cognitive appraisal theories of emotion have much to offer in this regard.

Cognitive appraisal theories of emotion suggest that emotions are determined by the cognitive evaluation or appraisal of an event that is personally relevant. The results of our appraisal of the causes and the potential consequences of an event determine the emotion we feel (Frijda, 1986; Lazarus, 1991b; Ortony, Clore, & Collins, 1988; Scherer, 2001a; C. A. Smith & Ellsworth, 1985). From this perspective, there are as many potential emotion responses to an event as there are ways of appraising it. This approach has significantly improved our understanding of emotion as a complex individual process consisting of multiple components, including cognition, physiological changes, motor expression, motivation, and subjective feelings (Frijda, 1986; Scherer, 2001a).

However, despite explicit acknowledgements from appraisal theorists that social context can influence the emotional process (e.g., see Lazarus, 1991a) and that emotions have important social functions (e.g., Frijda & Mesquita, 1994), few studies have directly examined social context effects (for exceptions see Jakobs, Fischer, & Manstead, 1997; Jakobs, Manstead, & Fischer, 1999; Kappas, 1996). Moreover, some authors maintain that current appraisal theories remain unsatisfactory in accounting for the effects of the social context and of ongoing interactions on the emotional process (see Manstead & Fischer, 2001; Parkinson, 2001; Parkinson & Manstead, 1993). For these authors, appraisal researchers have been primarily concerned with how appraisal of events relevant to us as individuals can determine *emotions we feel as individuals*, almost irrespective of the social context.

Notwithstanding, the appraisal approach to emotions provides a particularly useful framework for the study of social emotions because it conceptualizes emotion as a process in which subjective appraisal and personal meaning are fundamental, and allows for an unlimited range of emotional responses. In addition, several appraisal theories recognize the social context of appraisal and have suggested dimensions such as: (a) agency, which is used to evaluate the role of other(s) in causing an emotion-eliciting event; (b) coping potential, which is used to evaluate one's sense of control or power over the consequences of the event; and (c) legitimacy, value relevance, and compatibility with external standards, which are used to evaluate the compatibility of an event with the perceived normative standards of a social group (for a review of these dimensions, see Ellsworth & Scherer, 2003). Empirical research has confirmed the sensitivity of these specific appraisal dimensions to the influence of national culture (Mesquita, 2003; Scherer, 1997). However, appraisal theorists have paid little attention to the identification of the psychological mechanisms through which the social and cultural aspects of the context – particularly the functions that reference groups have for the individual – may systematically influence these specific dimensions of appraisal and the resulting emotions. In this chapter we argue that *social identity salience* is one of the most promising potential mechanisms.

There is abundant empirical evidence in the intergroup relations field suggesting that when social identity becomes salient it can influence cognitive focus, how information is perceived, as well as the affective and behavioral responses (for a review see Brown, 2000). More recently, researchers in the field of intergroup relations have become increasingly interested in the study of intergroup emotions and in applications of appraisal theories to intergroup settings (e.g., Dijker, 1987; Dijker, Koomen, van den Heuvel, & Frijda, 1996; Dumont, Yzerbyt, Wigboldus, & Gordijn, 2003; Mackie, Devos, & Smith, 2000; Mackie & Smith, 2002; E. R. Smith, 1993, 1999; E. R. Smith & Ho, 2002; Vanman & Miller, 1993; Yzerbyt, Dumont, Gordijn, & Wigboldus, 2002; Yzerbyt, Dumont, Wigboldus, & Gordijn, 2003). In contrast to appraisal researchers, intergroup relations researchers are interested in *emotions experienced by individuals as members of social groups* in intergroup settings.

However, up till now, research in the intergroup domain has concentrated on testing whether the effect of social identity on intergroup behavior (as suggested by measures of action tendencies) is mediated by specific emotions (e.g., anger, fear, guilt). Only a few researchers have tested the links between specific appraisal dimensions and specific emotions in intergroup contexts (for exceptions, see Dumont et al., 2003; Mackie et al., 2000). Moreover, little is known about the ways in which social identity salience might affect some of the standard appraisal dimensions proposed by the main appraisal theories. This chapter addresses precisely this last question. After briefly reviewing research on intergroup emotions, we will outline propositions about the influence of social identity salience on those specific appraisal dimensions (see Scherer's appraisal theory, 1984, 2001a) that have been identified as being particularly sensitive to the effects of the socio-cultural context.

Research on intergroup emotions

In his 1993 work, E. R. Smith borrowed from several appraisal theories (including Frijda, Kuipers, & ter Schure, 1989; Roseman, 1984; Scherer, 1988) to speculate about the types of appraisal-emotion-action tendency patterns that could be relevant to the study of emotion in intergroup relations. For E. R. Smith, the appraisal processes that generate social emotions are identical to the appraisal processes proposed by cognitive theories of emotion for individuals, with the difference that appraisal involves aspects of social identity instead of only aspects of personal identity. In 1999, E. R. Smith's position breaks away from one of the basic constructs of social identity theory, which is that intergroup behavior such as prejudice is primarily motivated by the maintenance of self-esteem. For E. R. Smith, the evaluation of self-esteem targets the self (personal or collective) and ranges from positive to negative. In contrast, he sees prejudice as a group-based emotional reaction to the appraisal of an outgroup that has some implication for the ingroup, and reactions may involve a whole range of emotions (e.g., fear, anger, resentment). To cite E. R. Smith (1999) ". . . appraisals refer to the position of the outgroup in relation to the ingroup, just as, in emotion theories, the appraisals that trigger emotion by definition refer to an object's or situation's implication for the self" (p. 187). The intergroup emotion theory afterwards proposed by E. R. Smith and his colleagues (Mackie et al., 2000; also see E. R. Smith & Mackie, Chapter 9, this volume) constitutes the first attempt to adapt appraisal theories to the area of intergroup relations.

From this perspective, individuals may experience emotions toward the outgroup as a whole just as they can experience emotional reactions toward individual outgroup members. Based on intergroup emotion theory one could argue that, if the outgroup is appraised as threatening the ingroup's interests or goals, and if the ingroup is appraised as more powerful than the outgroup, the resulting emotion may be anger accompanied by the tendency to move against the outgroup. In contrast, if the outgroup is appraised as more powerful than the ingroup, the response may be fear or anxiety accompanied by the tendency to move away from the outgroup. Research by Mackie et al. (2000) has confirmed that, in situations of intergroup conflict, appraisals of the ingroup as stronger (in terms of perceived support from the community to the ingroup) in comparison to the outgroup lead to an increase in anger toward the outgroup (but not associated with fear, nor with contempt), and to a tendency to want to move against the outgroup (arguing with, confronting, opposing, and attacking), but not away from it. Other researchers have demonstrated that one can experience malicious pleasure or "schadenfreude" at the suffering of an outgroup, and that this emotion is more common when the outgroup's misfortune occurs (a) in a domain of interest to the ingroup, (b) under increased threat to the status of the ingroup, and (c) when it is considered to be legitimate to enjoy the misfortune of the outgroup (Leach, Spears, Branscombe, & Doosje, 2003).

Moreover, individuals may also experience emotions toward the ingroup and toward individual ingroup members. For example, it has been found that individuals can experience guilt when they acknowledge that the ingroup is responsible for moral violations (Branscombe, Doosje, & McGarty, 2002), when they are presented with evidence that the ingroup has treated the outgroup unfairly in the past (Doosje, Branscombe, Spears, & Manstead, 1998), and when they hold the belief that the ingroup has an illegitimate or immoral advantage over the outgroup (Branscombe, 1998; Iyer, Leach, & Crosby, 2003). Other research has shown that emotional responses to prejudice against one's ingroup (including emotions such as sadness, failure, anger, irritation, etc.) are determined by how prejudice is perceived (e.g., in terms of attributions of causality, extent to which people felt personally threatened) and this effect is moderated by ingroup identification (McCoy & Major, 2003; Schmitt & Branscombe, 2002). Interestingly, McCoy and Major have shown that, when prejudice against the ingroup is salient, people with high ingroup identification appraise a threat against the ingroup as a threat to the self. In addition, these authors predicted and found that appraisal of threat to the self mediated the effect of ingroup identification on emotional response to prejudice.

Finally, even in situations when individuals are not "personally" involved in the event, they can experience emotions on behalf of other ingroup members (see Devos, Silver, Mackie, & Smith, 2002). For example, it has been demonstrated that when a victim of a harmful behavior is perceived to belong to the same group as the self, one is more likely to feel emotions (including fear and anger) and the corresponding action tendencies on behalf of the victim even in situations that do not directly confront the self (Dumont et al., 2003; Yzerbyt et al., 2002; Yzerbyt et al., 2003).

Exploring the influence of social identity salience on appraisal dimensions

In the 1980s four appraisal theories were developed that proposed rather similar appraisal dimensions (Frijda, 1986; Roseman, 1984; Scherer, 1984;

Table 10.1 Comparative overview of major appraisal dimensions

Frijda (1986)	Roseman (1984)	Scherer (2001a)	C. A. Smith/ Ellsworth (1985)
		Relevance detection	
Change		Novelty	Attentional
Familiarity		– suddenness	activity
		– familiarity	
		– predictability	
Valence		Intrinsic pleasantness	Pleasantness
		Implication assessment	
Focality	Appetitive/ aversive motives	Goal conduciveness and obstructiveness Discrepancy from prior expectations	Importance
Certainty	Certainty	Probability of alternative outcomes	Certainty
Intent/Self-other	Agency	Causal agency and responsibility	Human agency
		Coping potential determination Control Power Adaptability	
		Normative significance evaluation	
Value relevance		Compatibility with standards internal external	Legitimacy

Adapted from Ellsworth and Scherer, 2003.

C. A. Smith & Ellsworth, 1985). Ellsworth and Scherer (2003) have recently reviewed these appraisal dimensions (see Table 10.1 for a list of these dimensions).

Given the high degree of convergence between different appraisal theories we will focus on the appraisal dimensions suggested by the most recent version of Scherer's (2001a) appraisal theory. The first appraisal dimension, *relevance detection* involves the detection of novelty (in the sense of suddenness, familiarity, and predictability) and intrinsic pleasantness (as an innate or permanently acquired quality) of an object or event as well as a rudimentary assessment of its pertinence or importance for the individual's momentarily dominant goals/needs. The second dimension, *implication assessment*, determines the potential consequences of an event for the individual. It involves the attribution of causal agency and responsibility, the estimation of the discrepancy from prior expectations and of the probability of alternative outcomes, as well as, most importantly, the assessment of how conducive or obstructive the event is for the individual's needs, interests, goals, and immediate plans. On this basis the individual also needs to determine the urgency of action to change or adapt to the situation. The third dimension, *coping potential determination*, entails the determination of how much the event or its outcomes can be influenced or controlled by the individual, how much power the individual has to exert control or to recruit others to help, and how easily the individual can adjust, adapt to, or live with the consequences of the event after all possible means of intervention have been used. Finally, there is *normative significance evaluation* which consists of evaluating the extent to which an event falls short of or exceeds the individual's internal standards, such as personal self ideal (desirable attributes) or internalized moral code (obligatory conduct), or perceived external standards, such as norms or demands of a salient reference group in terms of both desirable and obligatory conduct. Relevance detection often operates unconsciously and automatically, and determines the level of attention devoted to the event. Implication assessment, coping potential determination, and normative significance evaluation may require more complex cognitive processing, due to more elaborated schema processing, conceptual reasoning, or comparison with internal and external standards.

The appraisal process is proposed (Scherer 1984, 2001a) to be constantly operative, with evaluations being continuously performed to update the individual's information on an event or situation, including information about the individual's current needs or goals and the possibility to act on these. This continuous operation can explain the sudden changes that can occur during emotion episodes and which are often based on re-appraisals of the event, of one's coping potential, or even of the importance of specific goals or values. The latter is particularly important for the topic under discussion because it is precisely in a situation in which a social identity may suddenly become salient (e.g., by a remark made on group membership), that a complete re-appraisal may take place, with changes in: (a) the importance of goals and values in the assessment of conduciveness; (b) the assessment of coping potential (adopting a group rather than an individual perspective); and, particularly, (c) salience of specific internal and external standards that may become suddenly pertinent to the appraisal of the eliciting event.

Since appraisal theories predict that the type and intensity of an emotion elicited by an event is essentially determined by the profile of appraisal results, such re-appraisals are expected to bring about important changes in the nature and intensity of the resulting emotion. This account underlines the dynamic nature of emotional episodes, which have to be considered as processes rather than steady states (Scherer, 2000). It also suggests that the number of distinct emotions is not just limited to a small set of basic

Table 10.2 Extension of Scherer's (2001a) appraisal dimensions to the
intergroup level

Appraisal dimension	Propositions for the interpersonal context	Propositions for the intergroup context
	Self vs. other	When a social identity is salient Ingroup vs. outgroup
Implication assessment		
Goal conduciveness/ obstructiveness	• Likely to be appraised in terms of personal goals	• Likely to be appraised in terms of salient ingroup goals
Causal agency and responsibility	• Likely to be appraised in terms of the self in relation to other(s) interpersonally	• Likely to be appraised in terms of the salient ingroup in relation to the target outgroup
Coping potential determination		
Control Power Adaptability	• Likely to be appraised in terms of personal control, power and adaptability in regards to the consequences of the event	• Likely to be appraised in terms of the salient ingroup's control, power and adaptability in regards to the consequences of the event
Normative significance evaluation		
External standards	• Likely to be appraised in terms of general social norms	• Likely to be appraised in terms of salient ingroup norms

emotions, or to a range of positive/negative states, or to the positioning of
an emotion in respect to valence (positive/negative) and arousal (high/low
intensity) dimensions, but actually comprises a much larger set of variants.
Scherer (1984) has suggested that there are as many different emotions as
there are recurrent and stable profiles of appraisal results, acknowledging
that some of the profiles occur much more frequently than others (Scherer,
1994).

What this postulate of a very high variability of emotion processes (due
to differences in the underlying appraisal profiles) entails for the current
topic is the possibility that appraisal processes that are highly affected by
salient social identity may systematically differ in quality from appraisal
processes in which individual needs and goals are predominant. In what
follows we will elaborate preliminary propositions that could serve as a
basis for more specific hypotheses on how social identity salience might
influence Scherer's (2001a) appraisal dimensions of implication assessment,
coping potential determination, and normative significance evaluation
(Table 10.2). These have been identified as being particularly sensitive to the
influence of contextual factors (Ellsworth & Scherer, 2003).

Before presenting these propositions, we should clarify what we mean by social identity salience. In social identity literature, distinctions have been drawn between the simple categorization into group memberships, the process of social identification whereby individuals internalize group memberships as a part of their self-concept, and the salience of these social identifications as a function of the situation (e.g., see McGarty, 2001). In social cognitive terms, Higgins (2000) proposes that salience "can be used to capture the notion that not all of the features of a stimulus receive equal attention at any point in time. The salient features of a stimulus event are those features that draw, grab, or hold attention relative to alternative features" (p. 16). In this chapter social identity salience refers to a situation where the features of the self-concept that "draw, grab, or hold" people's attention in defining "who they are" are derived from a particular group membership.

Social identity salience effects on appraisal of implications

Appraisal of goal conduciveness/obstructiveness

Proposition 1   (see Table 10.2) When a social identity becomes salient, the individual's appraisal of goal conduciveness/obstructiveness of an emotion-eliciting event is likely to be affected by the fact that ingroup goals will tend to become more important than personal goals; the latter having priority in interpersonal contexts.

Experimental research on social dilemmas has shown that ingroup salience can influence the perception of goals, so that the goals of the ingroup (i.e., collective) become more important than individual goals (e.g., Brewer & Kramer, 1986; Wit & Kerr, 2002). There is also evidence suggesting that, when people consider another person to represent an integral part of their identity, not only do they feel a sense of "ownership" over the target's outcomes (e.g., success or failure) but they can also have emotional reactions similar to those they would have experienced for their personal success or failure (McFarland, Buehler, & MacKay, 2001).

The influence of social identity salience on appraisal of goal conduciveness/obstructiveness could be particularly useful in explaining the phenomenon of empathy which has been somewhat neglected by appraisal theorists. The study of empathy has significant implications for improving intergroup relations (e.g., Stephan & Finlay, 1999). Indeed, empathy may be of major importance in situations in which a particular social identity becomes salient. Scherer (2001b) has suggested a mechanism whereby appraisal theory can be used to predict empathy or "commotion", based on our ability to infer the needs and goals of others and to share values and norms. Based on this framework, one can assume that the probability of empathic responding to the plight of another person should be greatly enhanced if that person belongs to the same social group, as there may be both a greater amount of sharing of relevant appraisal criteria and a greater ability to infer the underlying appraisal processes of the other. This is supported by the research of Yzerbyt and his associates on emotional reactions to victims of harmful behaviors (Dumont et al., 2003; Yzerbyt et al., 2002; Yzerbyt et al., 2003). Most importantly, there might be a much higher disposition to take an interest in a person belonging to our social group and to make his/her well-being part of our main goals.

Attribution of causal agency and responsibility

Proposition 2   (see Table 10.2) When a social identity becomes salient, individuals will appraise the causal agency/responsibility of an emotion-eliciting event more in terms of the ingroup in relation to the target outgroup, than interpersonally, namely in terms of the self in relation to other individuals.

In intergroup contexts attributions are influenced by person's salient social identity and stereotypes and existing knowledge attached to that identity in a given situation, which, in turn, depend on the history of intergroup relations and on how groups are structured in society (Deschamps & Beauvois, 1994). There is evidence that people are more likely to make negative internal attributions (i.e., dispositions) when explaining undesirable behaviors of outgroups than ingroups, and less positive internal attributions when explaining desirable behaviors of outgroups than ingroups (for a review on intergroup causal attribution, see Hewstone, 1990). In addition, intergroup biases in attribution processes have been demonstrated by the research on linguistic intergroup bias (Maass, Salvi, Arcuri, & Semin, 1989). This latter has shown that people tend to generate more abstract descriptions (i.e., implying a more stable disposition of the actor) when talking about positive ingroup and negative outgroup behaviors, than when talking about positive outgroup and negative ingroup behaviors (for a review, see Maass & Arcuri, 1992).

We argue that intergroup biases in attribution processes, which might occur when a social identity becomes salient, are particularly likely to affect intergroup emotions through appraisal of causal agency. It has been shown that attributions of causal agency (self, other, circumstance) are particularly useful in determining negative emotions including anger (other-agency), guilt (self-agency), and sorrow (circumstance-agency) (Ellsworth & Smith, 1988). In intergroup settings, attributions of causal agency (ingroup, outgroup) might prove particularly useful in determining between anger (outgroup-agency) and remorse (ingroup-agency) emotions felt in response to harmful actions toward ingroups. Vanman and Miller (1993) have suggested that findings showing a biased tendency to attribute positive actions to ingroups and negative actions to outgroups would mean that feelings of reproach and anger toward outgroup members should be more common.

Finally, attribution of intergroup causal agency might also determine either disgust (outgroup-agency) or guilt (ingroup-agency) emotions in response to harmful actions toward outgroups.

Social identity salience effects on appraisal of coping potentials

Appraisals of control, power and adaptability

Proposition 3   (see Table 10.2) When a social identity becomes salient, people's appraisals of power, control, and adaptability in regard to the consequences of an emotion-eliciting event are likely to be affected by the power, control, and adaptability of the ingroup in comparison to the target outgroup.

Mackie and her colleagues (2000) have demonstrated that the stronger the appraised strength of the ingroup (operationalized in terms of increased support by the community to the ingroup) the stronger the anger responses toward the outgroup, and the stronger the tendency to move against the outgroup. Schmitt, Branscombe, Kobrynowicz, and Owen (2002) have also shown that the objective status of the ingroup in comparison to the outgroup (in terms of being privileged or disadvantaged in a given social structure) can affect perceptions of prejudice and measures of psychological well-being, including self-evaluative emotions (i.e., positive affect and depression). When these authors compared men and women's perceptions of gender discrimination, only women's perceptions of discrimination were negatively related to measures of psychological well-being, and ingroup identification moderated this effect. McCoy and Major (2003) have also shown that perceived discrimination by disadvantaged groups (including women and Latino-Americans) affect self-evaluative emotions, and that ingroup identification moderates this effect.

Social identity salience effects on appraisal of normative significance

Appraisal of compatibility with external standards

Proposition 4   (see Table 10.2) When a social identity becomes salient, people will appraise compatibility of the emotion-inducing event with external standards or norms more in terms of the salient ingroup standards than in terms of general social standards or norms.

Much of appraisal is about comparing a current state with a criterion, standard, or expectation. And, as shown by research on social comparison theory (Festinger, 1954), many of our standards for comparison are socially constructed and may change with context, especially in ambiguous situations. This is obvious with respect to group standards that, due to their very nature, are socially constituted such as cultural values and group norms. But in many ways even comparison standards that generally seem mostly determined by individual preferences and learning histories may become subject to powerful social influences once group identification becomes salient. For example, Mikula, Scherer, and Athenstaedt (1998) showed that perceived injustice is one of the most powerful appraisal criteria, strongly increasing the intensity of many emotions, not just anger. As shown by the extensive literature on social justice (e.g., Lerner & Mikula, 1994), perception of injustice is based on perceived entitlement, which in turn may be strongly affected by social identity being salient at the time of appraisal. There is evidence that group norms affect perception of fairness when the person identifies with the ingroup (Terry & Hogg, 1996). In addition, it has been shown that a situation of higher gains for the self is perceived to be more fair when the other is an outgroup member (Hertel, Aarts, & Zeelenberg, 2002).

Another example is perceived immorality of certain actions. If the identity as a member of a church is salient, comparison standards may be quite different from the case in which the identity as a member of a business organization is salient. This is the obvious reason why companies, sports coaches, and military instructors place a premium on identity bolstering just before the staff, players, or soldiers engage in action, which may not always correspond to the highest moral maxims. Similarly, the assessment of the discrepancy between a current outcome and an expected outcome could be strongly affected by social identity salience. Since expected outcome is construed and is thus amenable to various influences, it may be strongly affected by what seems reasonable to expect as a member of a particular group. The consideration of how changing social identities can influence appraisals has the welcome effect of reminding appraisal theorists of the fact that comparison standards in the process are rarely stable and may vary considerably over different social contexts.

Individual differences

Not all people are affected equally by group memberships (e.g., Hinkle & Brown, 1990). Several researchers have highlighted the need to take into account individual differences in identification (which may become the most apparent when social identity is threatened) by comparing low and high identifiers when studying intergroup phenomena (e.g., see Branscombe & Wann, 1991; Ellemers, Spears, & Doosje, 1999). Indeed, appraisals and emotion responses of high identifiers might be more likely to be affected by social identity salience than those of low identifiers. However, as pointed out by Doosje and colleagues (1998), the general underlying hypothesis of stronger identification–stronger intensity of intergroup emotion should be qualified by the type of emotion, and the meaning that an emotion has in a specific intergroup situation. For example, high identifiers may be more likely to feel stronger happiness about an ingroup member's success during a sporting event (Branscombe & Wann, 1991), and stronger anger toward gender and ethnic prejudiced behavior by outgroups (McCoy & Major, 2003), but they may also feel less guilty about the past history of the ingroup if they are defensive about this past (Doosje et al., 1998). Similarly, in stable appraisal tendencies there are major individual propensities or biases, which may be the result of organic predispositions, cognitive styles, and personality traits (these factors are discussed in van Reekum & Scherer, 1997), that may to some extent affect the degree of influence of social identity salience on appraisals.

Implications and conclusion

The major implications of studying intergroup emotions for issues of prejudice and discrimination have been widely developed by researchers working on intergroup emotion theory and by several proponents of the social identity perspective (e.g., Brown, 2000; Crisp, Ensari, Hewstone, & Miller, 2002; Doosje et al., 1998; Iyer et al., 2003; Mackie et al., 2000; Yzerbyt et al., 2002). The integration of appraisal perspectives into this domain holds the promise to allow better differentiation of the conditions that lead to specific cognitive, emotional, and behavioral responses toward different outgroups and ingroups. For instance, research on emotions such as collective guilt experienced toward negative actions of ingroups (e.g., Branscombe et al., 2002; Doosje et al., 1998) has important implications for understanding under which conditions affirmative action programs are supported or rejected by individuals (e.g., Iyer et al., 2003). In addition, the study of intergroup emotions sheds some light on the cognitive and motivational processes underlying emotional responses felt toward victims of harmful behavior (empathy) or by the victims toward the aggressor (fear or anger; see, e.g., Yzerbyt et al., 2002). Concretely, better grasp of these processes could help explain when, why, and how empathy leads to approach toward the victim and when it leads to avoidance (Stephan & Finlay, 1999). It also seems important to clarify the role that intergroup emotions play in explaining the differences observed between members of advantaged and disadvantaged social groups in terms of perceptions of prejudice, and its effects on psychological well-being (McCoy & Major, 2003; Schmitt & Branscombe, 2002). In these ways, behavioral and emotional responses observed in real-life intergroup settings can be linked to specific appraisal patterns or viewpoints about life events. Finally, a longer-term benefit of studying intergroup emotions from an appraisal perspective is that of preparing the ground for new theories and models of prejudice and discrimination that can foster more effective prevention and intervention programs.

Given the inherent importance of motivation for the study of appraisal and emotion in general, future research into the different motivational determinants of social identity seems of primary importance for the study of intergroup emotions. Future research needs to clarify the role of motivation in the interaction between social identity, appraisal, emotion, and intergroup behavior. Indeed, motivation is one of the major components of emotion (e.g., Griner & Smith, 2000; C. A. Smith & Kirby, 2001; C. A. Smith & Pope, 1992). As shown by the research of C. A. Smith and his colleagues (C. A. Smith & Kirby, 2001) ". . . how motivationally relevant a given set of circumstances is likely to be appraised as (and thus how strongly one is likely to react to those circumstances) is a function not only of how relevant those circumstances are to particular goals or sets of goals but also to how invested, or committed, the individual is in regards to those goals" (p. 127). Lazarus (2001) has also underlined the important role played by different types of "ego involvements" as motivational components of emotion, including: self or social self-esteem, moral values, ego ideals, commitment to certain meanings and ideas, the well-being of other persons, and life goals. Unfortunately, empirical evidence linking specific types of motives to appraisals and emotions is still scarce (for exceptions, see Griner & Smith, 2000; C. A. Smith & Pope, 1992; Zurbriggen & Sturman, 2002).

Motivation is also a major component of social identity. Social identification and the salience of social identity are not just the result of social categorization processes. Identification is also the result of a basic motivation to enhance self-esteem and self-representation that can be attained by engaging in intergroup differentiations positively reflecting on the ingroup (Tajfel & Turner, 1986). Yet, more than twenty years of research have not provided unequivocal support for the centrality of self-esteem motive, and it has been argued that researchers should explore a wider range of motives (Brown, 2000; Rubin & Hewstone, 1998; Vignoles, Chryssochoou, & Breakwell, 2003). Social identity may also be affected by other motivations such as the need to reduce subjective uncertainty (see Hogg, 2000; Hogg & Abrams, 1993) and the conflicting need to feel "unique" (distinctiveness) and "similar" (inclusion) at the same time (as stated by optimal distinctiveness theory, see Brewer, 1991). Recent work comparing motivational theories of social identification suggests that these different motivations (self-esteem, uncertainty avoidance, and optimal distinctiveness) may in fact influence different features of social identification (i.e., awareness of belonging, self-stereotyping, evaluation, and emotional attachment to groups) (Capozza, Brown, Aharpour, & Falvo, 2001). More and more, researchers in this area agree that we may identify with groups for motivations other than self-esteem enhancement (see

Capozza et al., Chapter 3, this volume; Deaux, 2000; Vignoles et al., 2003). One important determinant of the different motivations could be the functions that memberships play in a particular social context (e.g., Deaux, 2000; Deaux, Reid, Mizrahi, & Cotting, 1999). Ellemers, Spears, and Doosje (2002) have also suggested that contextual features (e.g., the nature of the characteristics associated with groups) may shape the motivational implications of a social identity. Future research needs to consider in which way different motives underlying social identity could determine appraisal and emotional responses in intergroup contexts.

Another key challenge for scholars working on intergroup emotions will be the development of theoretical models that integrate knowledge about processes involved in appraisal and emotions *with* knowledge about processes involved in social identity, *while* taking into account the influence of individual differences, social context and time (e.g., see E. R. Smith & Mackie, Chapter 9, this volume). As discussed by Parkinson (2001), appraisal and emotion process as ongoing in a context has been best articulated in the models proposed by Scherer (e.g., 1984, 2001a) and Frijda (e.g., 1986). Indeed, Scherer's model proposes appraisal as a continuously updating sequence of checks that can adapt to the ongoing situation, and Frijda's model proposes that action tendencies can be modified to become specific responses as a function of information coming from the situation. We hope that the connections proposed between social identity and Scherer's (2001a) appraisal dimensions in this chapter will contribute to the ongoing dialogue between appraisal and intergroup relations researchers.

References

Branscombe, N. R. (1998). Thinking about one's gender group's privileges or disadvantages: Consequences for well-being in women and men. *British Journal of Social Psychology, 37*, 167–184.

Branscombe, N. R., Doosje, B., & McGarty, C. (2002). Antecedents and consequences of collective guilt. In D. M. Mackie & E. R. Smith (Eds.), *From prejudice to intergroup emotions: Differentiated reactions to social groups* (pp. 49–66). New York: Psychology Press.

Branscombe, N. R., & Wann, D. L. (1991). The positive social and self concept consequences of sport team identification. *Journal of Sport and Social Issues, 15*, 115–127.

Brewer, M. B. (1991). The social self: On being the same and different at the same time. *Personality and Social Psychology Bulletin, 17*, 475–482.

Brewer, M. B., & Kramer, R. M. (1986). Choice behavior in social dilemmas: Effects of social identity, group size, and decision framing. *Journal of Personality and Social Psychology, 50*, 543–549.

Brown, R. (2000). Social identity theory: Past achievements, current problems and future challenges. *European Journal of Social Psychology, 30*, 745–778.

Capozza, D., Brown, R., Aharpour, S., & Falvo, R. (2001, September). *A comparison of motivational theories of identification.* Paper presented at the Small Group Meeting of the European Association of Experimental Social Psychology, "Social Identity: Motivational, Emotional and Cultural Aspects", Villasimius, Cagliari, Italy.

Crisp, R. J., Ensari, N., Hewstone, M., & Miller, N. (2002). A dual-route model of crossed categorisation effects. In W. Stroebe & M. Hewstone (Eds.), *European review of social psychology* (Vol. 13, pp. 35–73). Chichester, UK: Wiley.

Deaux, K. (2000). Models, meaning and motivations. In D. Capozza & R. Brown (Eds.), *Social identity processes: Trends in theory and research* (pp. 1–14). London: Sage.

Deaux, K., Reid, A., Mizrahi, K., & Cotting, D. (1999). Connecting the person to the social: The functions of social identification. In T. R. Tyler, R. M. Kramer, & O. P. John (Eds.), *The psychology of the social self* (pp. 91–113). Mahwah, NJ: Lawrence Erlbaum Associates Inc.

Deschamps, J.-C., & Beauvois, J. L. (1994). Attributions intergroupes. In R. Y. Bourhis & J.-Ph. Leyens (Eds.), *Stéréotypes, discrimination et relations inter-groupes* (pp. 97–126). Liège, Belgium: Mardaga.

Devos, T., Silver, L. A., Mackie, D. M., & Smith, E. R. (2002). Experiencing intergroup emotions. In D. M. Mackie & E. R. Smith (Eds.), *From prejudice to intergroup emotions: Differentiated reactions to social groups* (pp. 111–134). New York: Psychology Press.

Dijker, A. J. (1987). Emotional reactions to ethnic minorities. *European Journal of Social Psychology, 17,* 305–325.

Dijker, A. J., Koomen, W., van den Heuvel, H., & Frijda, N. H. (1996). Perceived antecedents of emotional reactions in inter-ethnic relations. *British Journal of Social Psychology, 35,* 313–329.

Doosje, B., Branscombe, N. R., Spears, R., & Manstead, A. S. R. (1998). Guilty by association: When one's group has a negative history. *Journal of Personality and Social Psychology, 75,* 872–886.

Dumont, M., Yzerbyt, V. Y., Wigboldus, D., & Gordijn, E. H. (2003). Social categorization and fear reactions to the September 11th terrorist attacks. *Personality and Social Psychology Bulletin, 29,* 1509–1520.

Ellemers, N., Spears, R., & Doosje, B. (Eds.). (1999). *Social identity: Context, commitment, content.* Oxford, UK: Blackwell.

Ellemers, N., Spears, R., & Doosje, B. (2002). Self and social identity. *Annual Review of Psychology, 53,* 161–186.

Ellsworth, P. C., & Scherer, K. R. (2003). Appraisal processes in emotion. In R. J. Davidson, H. Goldsmith, & K. R. Scherer (Eds.), *Handbook of the affective sciences* (pp. 572–595). New York: Oxford University Press.

Ellsworth, P. C., & Smith, C. A. (1988). From appraisal to emotion: Differences among unpleasant feelings. *Motivation and Emotion, 12,* 271–302.

Festinger, L. (1954). A theory of social comparison. *Human Relations, 7,* 117–140.

Frijda, N. H. (1986). *The emotions.* Cambridge, UK: Cambridge University Press.

Frijda, N. H., Kuipers, P., & ter Schure, E. (1989). Relations among emotion, appraisal, and emotional action readiness. *Journal of Personality and Social Psychology, 57,* 212–228.

Frijda, N. H., & Mesquita, B. (1994). The social roles and functions of emotions. In S. Kitayama & H. R. Markus (Eds.), *Emotion and culture: Empirical studies of mutual influence* (pp. 51–87). Washington, DC: American Psychological Association.

Griner, L. A., & Smith, C. A. (2000). Contributions of motivational orientation to appraisal and emotion. *Personality and Social Psychology Bulletin, 26*, 727–740.

Hertel, G., Aarts, H., & Zeelenberg, M. (2002). What do you think is "fair"? Effects of ingroup norms and outcome control on fairness judgments. *European Journal of Social Psychology, 32*, 327–341.

Hewstone, M. (1990). The "ultimate attribution error"? A review of the literature on intergroup causal attribution. *European Journal of Social Psychology, 20*, 311–335.

Higgins, E. T. (2000). Social cognition: Learning about what matters in the social world. *European Journal of Social Psychology, 30*, 3–39.

Hinkle, S., & Brown, R. (1990). Intergroup comparisons and social identity: Some links and lacunae. In D. Abrams & M. A. Hogg (Eds.), *Social identity theory: Constructive and critical advances* (pp. 48–70). London: Harvester Wheatsheaf.

Hogg, M. A. (2000). Subjective uncertainty reduction through self-categorization: A motivational theory of social identity processes. In W. Stroebe & M. Hewstone (Eds.), *European review of social psychology* (Vol. 11, pp. 223–255). Chichester, UK: Wiley.

Hogg, M. A., & Abrams, D. (1993). Towards a single-process uncertainty-reduction model of social motivation in groups. In M. A. Hogg & D. Abrams (Eds.), *Group motivation: Social psychological perspectives* (pp. 173–190). London: Harvester Wheatsheaf.

Iyer, A., Leach, C. W., & Crosby, F. J. (2003). White guilt and racial compensation: The benefits and limits of self-focus. *Personality and Social Psychology Bulletin, 29*, 117–129.

Jakobs, E., Fischer, A. H., & Manstead, A. S. R. (1997). Emotional experience as a function of social context: The role of the other. *Journal of Nonverbal Behavior, 21*, 103–130.

Jakobs, E., Manstead, A. S. R., & Fischer, A. H. (1999). Social motives, emotional feelings, and smiling. *Cognition and Emotion, 13*, 321–345.

Kappas, A. (1996). The sociality of appraisals: Impact of social situations on the evaluation of emotion antecedent events and physiological and expressive reactions. In N. H. Frijda (Ed.), *Proceedings of the Ninth Conference of The International Society for Research on Emotions* (pp. 116–120). Toronto: International Society for Research on Emotions.

Lazarus, R. S. (1991a). *Emotion and adaptation.* Oxford, UK: Oxford University Press.

Lazarus, R. S. (1991b). Progress on a cognitive-motivational-relational theory of emotion. *American Psychologist, 46*, 819–834.

Lazarus, R. S. (2001). Relational meaning and discrete emotions. In K. R. Scherer, A. Schorr, & T. Johnstone (Eds.), *Appraisal processes in emotion: Theory, methods, research* (pp. 37–67). Oxford, UK: Oxford University Press.

Leach, C. W., Spears, R., Branscombe, N. R., & Doosje, B. (2003). Malicious pleasure: Schadenfreude at the suffering of another group. *Journal of Personality and Social Psychology, 84*, 932–943.

Lerner, M. J., & Mikula, G. (1994). *Entitlement and the affectional bond: Justice in close relationships.* New York: Plenum Press.

Maass, A., & Arcuri, L. (1992). The role of language in the persistence of stereo-types. In G. R. Semin & K. Fiedler (Eds.), *Language, interaction and social cognition* (pp. 129–143). London: Sage.

Maass, A., Salvi., D., Arcuri, L., & Semin, G. R. (1989). Language use in intergroup contexts: The linguistic intergroup bias. *Journal of Personality and Social Psychology*, *57*, 981–993.

Mackie, D. M., Devos, T., & Smith E. R. (2000). Intergroup emotions: Explaining offensive action tendencies in an intergroup context. *Journal of Personality and Social Psychology*, *79*, 602–616.

Mackie, D. M., & Smith, E. R. (Eds.). (2002). *From prejudice to intergroup emotions: Differentiated reactions to social groups*. New York: Psychology Press.

Manstead, A. S. R., & Fischer, A. H. (2001). Social appraisal: The social world as object of and influence on appraisal processes. In K. R. Scherer, A. Schorr, & T. Johnstone (Eds.), *Appraisal processes in emotion: Theory, methods, research* (pp. 221–232). Oxford, UK: Oxford University Press.

McCoy, S. K., & Major, B. (2003). Group identification moderates emotional responses to perceived prejudice. *Personality and Social Psychology Bulletin*, *29*, 1005–1017.

McFarland, C., Buehler, R., & MacKay, L. (2001). Affective responses to social comparisons with extremely close others. *Social Cognition*, *19*, 547–586.

McGarty, C. (2001). Social identity theory does not maintain that identification produce bias, and self-categorization theory does not maintain that salience is identification: Two comments on Mummendey, Klink and Brown. *British Journal of Social Psychology*, *40*, 173–176.

Mesquita, B. (2003). Emotions as dynamic cultural phenomena. In R. J. Davidson, H. Goldsmith, & K. R. Scherer (Eds.), *Handbook of the affective sciences* (pp. 871–890). New York: Oxford University Press.

Mikula, G., Scherer, K. R., & Athenstaedt, U. (1998). The role of injustice in the elicitation of differential emotional reactions. *Personality and Social Psychology Bulletin*, *24*, 769–783.

Ortony, A., Clore, G. L., & Collins, A. (1988). *The cognitive structure of emotions*. New York: Cambridge University Press.

Parkinson, B. (2001). Putting appraisal in context. In K. R. Scherer, A. Schorr, & T. Johnstone, (Eds.), *Appraisal processes in emotion: Theory, methods, research* (pp. 173–186). Oxford, UK: Oxford University Press.

Parkinson, B., & Manstead, A. S. R. (1993). Making sense of emotion in stories and social life. *Cognition and Emotion*, *7*, 295–323.

Roseman, I. J. (1984). Cognitive determinants of emotion: A structural theory. In P. Shaver (Ed.), *Review of personality and social psychology* (Vol. 5, pp. 11–36). Beverly Hills, CA: Sage.

Rubin, M., & Hewstone, M. (1998). Social identity theory's self-esteem hypothesis: A review and some suggestions for clarification. *Personality and Social Psychology Review*, *2*, 40–62.

Scherer, K. R. (1984). Emotion as a multicomponent process: A model and some cross-cultural data. In P. Shaver (Ed.), *Review of personality and social psychology* (Vol. 5, pp. 37–63). Beverly Hills, CA: Sage.

Scherer, K. R. (1988). Criteria for emotion-antecedent appraisal: A review. In

V. Hamilton, G. H. Bower, & N. H. Frijda (Eds.), *Cognitive perspectives on emotion and motivation* (Vol. 4, pp. 89–126). New York: Kluwer.

Scherer, K. R. (1994). Toward a concept of "modal emotions". In P. Ekman & R. J. Davidson (Eds.), *The nature of emotion: Fundamental questions* (pp. 25–31). Oxford, UK: Oxford University Press.

Scherer, K. R. (1997). The role of culture in emotion-antecedent appraisal. *Journal of Personality and Social Psychology, 7*, 902–922.

Scherer, K. R. (2000). Emotions as episodes of subsystem synchronization driven by nonlinear appraisal processes. In M. D. Lewis & I. Granic (Eds.), *Emotion, development, and self-organization: Dynamic systems approaches to emotional development* (pp. 70–99). New York: Cambridge University Press.

Scherer, K. R. (2001a). Appraisal considered as a process of multi-level sequential checking. In K. R. Scherer, A. Schorr, & T. Johnstone (Eds.), *Appraisal processes in emotion: Theory, methods, research* (pp. 92–120). Oxford, UK: Oxford University Press.

Scherer, K. R. (2001b). Emotional expression is subject to social and technological change: Extrapolating to the future. *Social Science Information, 40*, 125–151.

Schmitt, M. T., & Branscombe, N. R. (2002). The internal and external causal loci of attributions to prejudice. *Personality and Social Psychology Bulletin, 28*, 620–628.

Schmitt, M. T., Branscombe, N. R., Kobrynowicz, D., & Owen, S. (2002). Perceiving discrimination against one's gender group has different implications for well-being in women and men. *Personality and Social Psychology Bulletin, 28*, 197–210.

Smith, C. A., & Ellsworth, P. C. (1985). Patterns of cognitive appraisal in emotion. *Journal of Personality and Social Psychology, 48*, 813–838.

Smith, C. A., & Kirby, L. D. (2001). Toward delivering on the promise of appraisal theory. In K. R. Scherer, A. Schorr, & T. Johnstone (Eds.), *Appraisal processes in emotion: Theory, methods, research* (pp. 121–138). Oxford, UK: Oxford University Press.

Smith, C. A. & Pope, L. K. (1992). Appraisal and emotion: The interactional contribution of dispositional and situational factors. In M. S. Clark (Ed.), *Review of personality and social psychology* (Vol. 14., pp. 32–62). Thousand Oaks, CA: Sage.

Smith, E. R. (1993). Social identity and social emotions: Toward new conceptualization of prejudice. In D. M. Mackie & D. L. Hamilton (Eds.), *Affect, cognition, and stereotyping: Interactive processes in group perception* (pp. 297–315). San Diego, CA: Academic Press.

Smith, E. R. (1999). Affective and cognitive implications of a group becoming part of the self: New models of prejudice and of the self-concept. In D. Abrams & M. A. Hogg (Eds.), *Social identity and social cognition* (pp. 183–196). Oxford, UK: Blackwell.

Smith, E. R., & Ho, C. (2002). Prejudice as intergroup emotion: Integrating relative deprivation and social comparison explanations of prejudice. In I. Walker & H. Smith (Eds.), *Relative deprivation: Specification, development, and integration* (pp. 332–348). New York: Cambridge University Press.

Stephan, W. G., & Finlay, K. (1999). The role of empathy in improving intergroup relations. *Journal of Social Issues, 55*, 729–743.

Tajfel, H., & Turner, J. C. (1986). The social identity theory of intergroup behavior. In S. Worchel & W. G. Austin (Eds.), *Psychology of intergroup relations* (pp. 7–24). Chicago: Nelson-Hall.

Terry, D. J., & Hogg, M. A. (1996). Group norms and the attitude–behavior relationship: A role for group identification. *Personality and Social Psychology Bulletin, 22*, 776–793.

Vanman, E. J., & Miller, N. (1993). Applications of emotion theory and research to stereotyping and intergroup relations. In D. M. Mackie & D. L. Hamilton (Eds.), *Affect, cognition and stereotyping: Interactive processes in group perception* (pp. 213–238). San Diego, CA: Academic Press.

van Reekum, C. M., & Scherer, K. R. (1997). Levels of processing for emotion-antecedent appraisal. In G. Matthews (Ed.), *Cognitive science perspectives on personality and emotion* (pp. 259–300). Amsterdam: Elsevier Science.

Vignoles, V. L., Chryssochoou, X., & Breakwell, G. M. (2003). Evaluating models of identity motivation: Self-esteem is not the whole story. *Self and Identity, 1*, 201–218.

Wit, A. P. & Kerr, N. L. (2002). "Me versus just us versus us all" categorization and cooperation in nested social dilemmas. *Journal of Personality and Social Psychology, 83*, 616–637.

Yzerbyt, V. Y., Dumont, M., Gordijn, E. H., & Wigboldus, D. (2002). Intergroup emotions and self-categorization: The impact of perspective taking on reactions to victims of harmful behavior. In D. M. Mackie & E. R. Smith (Eds.), *From prejudice to intergroup emotions: Differentiated reactions to social groups* (pp. 67–88). New York: Psychology Press.

Yzerbyt, V. Y., Dumont, M., Wigboldus, D., & Gordijn, E. H. (2003). I feel for us: The impact of categorization and identification on emotions and action tendencies. *British Journal of Social Psychology, 42*, 533–549.

Zurbriggen, E. L., & Sturman, T. S. (2002). Linking motives and emotions: A test of McClelland's hypotheses. *Personality and Social Psychology Bulletin, 28*, 521–535.

Chapter 11

Intergroup contact and the promotion of intergroup harmony: The influence of intergroup emotions

Stefania Paolini, Miles Hewstone, Alberto Voci, Jake Harwood, and Ed Cairns

The British city of Bradford has a large Asian population that is educationally and residentially segregated from the white population. So deep is the division that the local education authority has started a "Linking project", bussing children from all-Asian schools to all-white schools, and vice versa. The hope is that barriers will be broken down, and contact made among children from different ethnic groups (Malik, 2003). A journalist asked an Asian child what it was like the first time he visited the all-white school. "I was *nervous*," the child replied. "Why?" "Because *I didn't know* what they'd be like. I'd never *met* them before." "You'd never met white children before?" "No." This brief exchange shows why intergroup contact is so important, and suggests why the interplay between increased knowledge and revised affect may be central to it. Knowledge, rather than affect, has been at the heart of research on the contact hypothesis. The causal sequence traditionally implied in most contact research is that lack of or biased (i.e. stereotyped) knowledge about the outgroup promotes prejudice, which in turn promotes discrimination (Mackie & Smith, 1998). From this premise, contact with outgroup members is meant to increase or rectify the knowledge about the outgroup and reverse this sequence of events (W. G. Stephan & Stephan, 2000). However, intergroup contact cannot be considered only in terms of its cognitive processes (Johnston & Hewstone, 1990; Pettigrew, 1998); a deeper understanding requires recognition of the role of affective processes.

Fortunately, recent advances in social psychology, particularly in the area of affect research, now allow researchers to view intergroup relations in general, and intergroup contact in particular, within a new framework which encompasses both cognition and affect (Fiske, Cuddy, Glick, & Xu, 2002; Mackie, Devos, & Smith, 2000). It is now recognized that affect plays a more significant role in the formation of intergroup judgments than was once believed (Esses & Dovidio, 2002). Our research on intergroup contact is part of and fosters this emerging interest in affect, and shows that affect plays an equally important role in *changing* intergroup judgments. We aim in this chapter to identify the qualities of this cultural climate in the literature on both intergroup relations and contact, and to point out the existence of a growing body of evidence about intergroup contact that is compatible with a new process of prejudice reduction, a process that we call "affect generalization". Hence, after providing a brief overview of the major contributions to the historical development of research on intergroup emotions, we discuss models and evidence that are consistent with this affect-driven process of prejudice reduction and we suggest new directions to explore more consistently the affective underpinnings of contact effects and intergroup relations.

The emerging interest in intergroup emotions

Affective conditioning (Rachman, 1980), the affective basis of memories (Cairns & Roe, 2003), and the close interdependence of thoughts and feelings (Forgas, 2002), all make affect a central player in intergroup interactions. Despite this, research on affect and intergroup relations has traditionally suffered from a focus on *incidental* affect (Bodenhausen, 1993; Greenland & Brown, 2000), the type of affect that is generated prior to, and independently of, the intergroup context and that carries over from other events (e.g., mood). Fortunately, this trend has recently changed in favor of research that focuses on *integral* affect, the type of affect that is generated by one's experience, or anticipation, of interactions with members of the outgroup. Evidence for integral affect can now be found both in early contributions of attitude research and in contemporary models of inter-group emotions.

Within a tripartite view of attitudes (Zanna & Rempel, 1988), the perceiver's emotional reactions toward outgroup members (i.e., integral affect) represent the affective component that makes up prejudiced attitudes, beside a cognitive component (the perceiver's beliefs about the outgroup members) and a behavioral component (the perceiver's behaviors related to the outgroup members). Although the relative weight of this affective component is likely to vary from individual to individual (Stangor, Sullivan, & Ford, 1991) and from intergroup context to intergroup context (Haddock, Zanna, & Esses, 1993), this research clearly suggests that people's emotions and feelings are important predictors of prejudiced responding (Islam & Jahjah, 2001) and powerful tools of persuasion (Edwards & von Hippel, 1995), often more powerful than thoughts and beliefs. This "prominence of affect" probably reflects a variety of factors. Affective responses are experienced as phenomenologically valid (Zajonc, 1998) and central to our internal and external reality (Forgas, 2002). They more often reflect first-hand, rather than second-hand, experience (Stangor et al., 1991) and, as a consequence, are more heavily self-referential and associated with heightened attitudinal conviction (Edwards & von Hippel, 1995). Lastly, affective responses may be more potent means of change because they are less vulnerable to subcategorization; that is, they may be more difficult to discount on the basis of the fact that they are non-representative of their class (Batson et al., 1997; Zajonc, 1998) or because prejudice itself is an affective state (Smith, 1993). We return to this final point later on in the chapter.

Smith (1993) also conceives intergroup emotions as part of a cognition-affect-behavior triad. Unlike models of attitude structure, however, his intergroup appraisal theory of emotions (and its interpersonal precursors, e.g., Frijda, 1986) clearly spells out the structural relationships between the triad elements. In Smith's perspective, specific intergroup emotions (e.g., fear, disgust) are triggered by specific cognitive appraisals of relevant features of the ingroup–outgroup relationship (e.g., differential power and status, goal incompatibility), and in turn trigger specific action tendencies towards outgroup members (e.g., tendencies to move against, or to move away from). Recently, work by Mackie et al. (2000) has provided some empirical support for Smith's triad of constructs and research into the content of stereotypes (e.g., Alexander, Brewer, & Hermann, 1999; Fiske et al., 2002) can be seen as further elaborating on this idea. For instance, in Fiske et al.'s research, distinct intergroup emotions have been found to be systematically associated with the four combinations yielded by crossing low–high outgroup warmth with low–high outgroup competence, dimensions which in turn reflect the appraisal of intergroup goal compatibility and power differential. Specifically, outgroups seen as high in competence and low in warmth (among others, the rich and Jews) elicit envy; outgroups low in competence and high in warmth (e.g., disabled, elderly) elicit pity; outgroups low in competence and low in warmth (e.g., poor, homeless) elicit contempt (and also pity). Admiration is reserved for the participants' referential groups (i.e., white, middle-class), which score high on both competence and warmth.

This recent work by Mackie, Brewer, and Fiske's research teams not only brings back the social context (and its cognitive internalizations) into the analysis of intergroup judgments (Sherif, 1966; Tajfel, 1981) but, by investigating *specific* intergroup emotions, also has the merit of introducing new layers of complexity into the study of integral affect. Their data confirm (Smith, 1993) that outgroups are not simply disliked. Instead, they are seen to be hostile, threatening, even dirty and disgusting.

There is a risk, however, in challenging the traditional global and unitary conceptualization and assessment of prejudice. By reframing specific intergroup emotions in terms of "envious prejudice" or "paternalistic prejudice" (Fiske et al., 2002) and, similarly, by reframing prejudice in terms of an affective state (Smith, 1993), there is a risk of theoretical and empirical circularity. Our work on intergroup contact reflects the deliberate effort to keep intergroup anxiety and other intergroup emotions conceptually and empirically separate from prejudice and other group judgments (Voci & Hewstone, 2003b). This approach is fruitful for three main reasons: it allows us to distinguish, to compare, and to connect. Specifically, by assessing various intergroup emotions (i.e., intergroup anxiety, empathy, etc.), we are able to distinguish between the diverse affective responses elicited by different outgroups and in different intergroup settings. By retaining prejudice (i.e., people's generalized liking and disliking for the outgroup) as our primary outcome variable, we can compare contact findings across settings and studies. Finally, by investigating the structural relationship between specific intergroup emotions and prejudice, we are ultimately able to identify the finely grained mechanism(s) responsible for contact effects, thus simultaneously achieving a differentiated and an integrated view of the process and of the outcome of intergroup contact.

Also, although contemporary models of intergroup emotions have clear implications for intergroup relations, none of them are models of contact, that is, they have not been developed and tested in the context of the "actual face-to-face interaction between members of clearly distinguishable and defined groups" (Pettigrew & Tropp, 2000, p. 95, emphasis removed). It is only when one considers intergroup relations *as they happen* during contact encounters and *for their long-term effects* on prejudiced responding that the relevance of the distinction between episodic and chronic integral affect becomes apparent. We discuss the articulation and the dynamics of this distinction before turning to the evidence of intergroup emotions and contact.

From episodic to chronic integral affect: The process of affect generalization

In its *chronic* form, integral affect involves enduring and stable affective reactions to social groups and their members. Stigmatized groups, for example, elicit negative affective reactions (e.g., contempt and anger) and admired or socially valued groups elicit positive affective reactions (e.g., admiration and sympathy; Fiske et al., 2002). The appreciation of relative intergroup differences in power and strength (Smith, 1993), pre-existing stereotypes (W. G. Stephan & Stephan, 1985), and affect-laden memories of prior intergroup encounters (Cairns & Roe, 2003) can all be catalysts for the emergence of this type of affect. *Episodic* integral affect, on the contrary, involves situationally created and transient affective states, which are experienced in a particular intergroup situation and with particular outgroup members. To this second category would belong, for example, the relief experienced during an unexpectedly lively conversation with an otherwise depressed neighbour or the anger at being injured by a rival player during the final round of a football tournament. Hence, episodic integral affect is produced by the specific configuration of factors that make up specific intergroup encounters.

Repeated experiences of episodic integral affect can crystallize and eventually develop into chronic integral affective responses. For instance, we may generally feel admiration or disgust for a group because a feeling of admiration or disgust has accompanied the previous times we heard about, saw, and met members of that group. This dynamic articulation between episodic and chronic affect was foreseen in Smith's early discussion of intergroup emotions:

> Suppose almost every encounter with a group member leads to similar emotions, and that the ingroup-outgroup distinction is so salient that the outgroup is viewed as quite homogeneous (. . .). Then the perceiver would end up reacting in the same way to just about any outgroup member.
>
> (Smith, 1993, p. 305)

Not all the encounters with group members, however, necessarily lead to similar emotions (Blascovich, Mendes, Hunter, Lickel, & Kowai-Bell, 2001; Bodenhausen, Mussweiler, Gabriel, & Moreno, 2001). Specific encounters with a group member may result in emotions that are different in degree and/or in quality from the emotions experienced most of the time or with most of the outgroup members, as the relief during the lively conversation with the depressed neighbour mentioned above clearly testifies. This dissociation implies that (a) transient and situationally created positive (or less negative) affect experienced during contact with specific outgroup members can occur against a background of pre-existing negative, enduring, and stable affect for the outgroup (Bodenhausen et al., 2001), and that (b) transient affect for specific group members can gradually change or even replace this pre-existing affect for the outgroup.

Hence, this potential dissociation between episodic and chronic integral affect gives room for a conceptually "new" type of beneficial contact effect. We say "new" because traditionally successful intergroup encounters have been those that allow for (positive) stereotype disconfirming *information* (Hewstone, 1989; Paolini, Hewstone, Rubin, & Pay, 2004) or for positive *evaluations* of specific outgroup members (Bodenhausen, Schwarz, Bless, & Wänke, 1995; Desforges et al., 1997) to generalize to the judgment of the outgroup as a whole (Paolini, 2001). In this chapter, we call the complex and dynamic chain of relationships that links contact to group judgments through episodic and chronic integral affect "affect generalization" and we expect it to be the affective underpinning of many contact effects reported in the literature (Pettigrew & Tropp, 2000).

Research has already shown that episodic emotional experiences can sometimes generate attitudinal judgments that are stable over time

(Abelson, Kinder, Peters, & Fiske, 1982). But it is our and our colleagues' (Devine, Evett, & Vasquez-Suson, 1996; Greenland & Brown, 2000; W. G. Stephan & Stephan, 2000) work on intergroup anxiety – the anxiety that people experience when anticipating or engaging in contact with outgroup members – that provides the most systematic support for the existence of affect generalization. Hence, our review of evidence will concentrate on this specific intergroup emotion and will attempt to demonstrate that improved intergroup judgments after contact are often achieved through this affective process. For simplicity, we will break down our review of evidence into manageable segments: the relationship between contact and intergroup anxiety; the relationship between intergroup anxiety and group judgments; and the mediational role of intergroup anxiety within the contact–group judgments link.

Intergroup emotions in contact: The centrality of intergroup anxiety

Intergroup anxiety as a consequence of contact

W. G. Stephan and Stephan (1985) expected various qualities of the contact experience (e.g., high ratio of outgroup to ingroup members, unstructured group activities) to produce intergroup anxiety by triggering negative expectations about ingroup–outgroup interactions. In their view, when approaching encounters with members of different social groups, people would fear embarrassment or frustration due to their own or others' incompetent or offensive behavior (Frable, Blackstone, & Scherbaum, 1990). People's concerns would include fear of rejection, discrimination, ridicule, or simply misunderstanding (W. G. Stephan & Stephan, 1985) or concerns over presenting a positive, nonprejudiced self-image (Devine et al., 1996). In general terms, intergroup anxiety would emerge any time that people see outgroup members as posing a threat to the ingroup (and to themselves as ingroup members) in terms of their goals, motives, or sensitivities (Smith, 1993). Borrowing from multifaceted models of generic anxiety (Lang, 1985) and emotions (Zajonc, 1998), Blascovich and colleagues (2001; Mendes, Blascovich, Lickel, & Hunter, 2002) have recently distinguished between three types of anxious or threat responses: physiological (i.e., responses of the autonomic system like sweating and increased heart rate), behavioral (i.e., depleted performance and contact avoidance), and subjective (i.e., self-reported anxiety responses). For obvious practical reasons, contact researchers using correlational designs have often preferred measures of subjective intergroup anxiety, whereas researchers using experimental designs have sometimes included measures of more than one type.

Extensive evidence now demonstrates that intergroup anxiety is central to and systematically associated with experiences of intergroup contact. The nature of such an association, however, is unclear and mixed in nature, sometimes reflecting a beneficial effect of contact (i.e., a decrease in anxiety with increases in contact) and sometimes reflecting a detrimental effect of contact (i.e., an increase in anxiety with increases in contact). Table 11.1 lists relevant studies.[1] From this table we gather that a positive link between contact and anxiety is common in investigations of the relationship between black and white people in North America (for a European exception, see Dijker, 1987), whereas an inverse or negative link has been found in different continents and in a variety of intergroup settings, including those based on race, religion, nationality, and physical ability.

Although this first look at Table 11.1 suggests the desirable possibility that the anxiety-provoking effects of contact may be limited to specific intergroup settings, we believe that the story is more complicated than this. Differences in the relationship between contact and anxiety may rather reflect differences in the type of intergroup anxiety captured by different research designs. Studies reporting a detrimental effect of contact are experimental studies that looked at either anticipated contact or contact while it was still in progress under controlled conditions and used either psychophysiological, behavioral measures of anxiety (e.g., Blascovich et al., 2001; Mendes et al., 2002) or measures of (subjective) state anxiety (e.g., Britt, Boniecki, Vescio, Biernat, & Brown, 1996; Plant & Devine, 2003). Studies reporting a beneficial effect of contact, on the other hand, are cross-sectional correlational studies that looked at contact retrospectively, and used adaptations of W. G. Stephan and Stephan's (1985) measure of intergroup anxiety.[2] Due to these differences in research design, we believe that the experimental studies likely detected episodic intergroup anxiety – that is, the anxiety-provoking effects of a specific, individual meeting with outgroup members – whilst the correlational studies more likely detected chronic forms of intergroup anxiety, thus gauging the cumulative anxiety-reducing effects of contact over time.

Indirect support for this interpretation comes from Blascovich et al.'s (2001) data. In their laboratory studies, participants who interacted with stigmatized individuals (e.g., a black individual) had higher physiological threat responses and depleted performance when compared with participants who interacted with non-stigmatized individuals (i.e., a white individual), thus exhibiting the positive relationship between contact and anxiety of other experimental studies. In their third study, however, the amount of contact participants had with black people prior to coming to the laboratory was found to moderate the size of these physiological threat responses. Threat responses were high among those who had limited prior contact with the outgroup, but were low among those who had substantial prior contact. This moderating pattern of evidence is in line with the negative relationship found between contact and anxiety in correlational studies.

Table 11.1 Studies testing the relationship between contact dimensions and intergroup anxiety

Study	Target group	Country	Contact dimension[a] (predictors and moderators)	Contact–anxiety relationship
Blascovich, Mendes, Hunter, Lickel, & Kowai-Bell (2001)[b,c]	People with facial birthmarks, Whites and Blacks, socio-economically advantaged and disadvantaged	United States	Presence of contact At low quantity of prior contact At high quantity of prior contact	Positive positive less positive
Britt, Boniecki, Vescio, Biernat, & Brown (1996)[b,c]	Whites and Blacks	United States	Expected contact	Positive
Brown, Maras, Masser, Vivian, & Hewstone (2001)	British and French	British Channel	Quantity of contact Quality of contact	Null Negative
Dijker (1987)[c]	Dutch, Surinamers, Turks, Moroccans	The Netherlands	Quantity of contact	Positive
Greenland & Brown (1999, Study 1)[d]	Japanese and British	United Kingdom	Interpersonal contact Category salience Superordinate contact	Negative Positive Null
Greenland & Brown (1999, Study 2)[b]	Japanese and British	United Kingdom	Quality of contact Intergroup contact	Null Null
Greenland, Masser, & Prentice (2001)	Teachers and HIV-infected children	United Kingdom	Quantity of contact	Negative
Harwood, Hewstone, Paolini, & Voci (2005, Study 2)[d]	Youngsters and elderly	United Kingdom	Quality and quantity of contact At low category salience At high category salience	Negative null negative
Islam & Hewstone (1993)[d]	Hindus and Muslims	Bangladesh	Quantity Quality of prior contact Category salience	Negative Negative Positive

Study	Groups	Location	Contact measure	Result
Levin, van Laar, & Sidanius (2003)[c]	Whites, Asians, Latinos, African Americans	United States	Direct cross-group friendship	Negative
Mendes, Blascovich, Lickel, & Hunter (2002)[b,c]	Whites and Blacks	United States	Presence of contact	Positive
Paolini, Hewstone, Cairns, & Voci (2004)[d]	Catholics and Protestants	Northern Ireland	Direct cross-group friendship	Negative
			Indirect cross-group friendship	Negative
Plant & Devine (2003, Study 1)[c,d]	Whites and Blacks	United States	Quantity of contact	Null
			Quality of contact	Negative
C. W. Stephan & Stephan (1992)[b]	Americans and Moroccans	Morocco	Quantity of contact	
			At low quality of contact	Positive
			At high quality of contact	Negative
C. W. Stephan, Stephan, Demitrakis, Yamada, & Clason (2000)[d]	Men and Women	United States	Quality of contact	Null
W. G. Stephan et al. (2002)[d]	Whites and Blacks	United States	Quality of contact	Negative
W. G. Stephan, Diaz-Loving, & Duran (2000)[d]	Americans and Mexicans	United States	Quantity of contact	Null
			Quality of contact	Negative
W. G. Stephan & Stephan (1985)	Hispanics and Anglo-Saxons	United States	Quantity of contact	Negative
W. G. Stephan & Stephan (1989)	Whites, Asians, Hispanics	United States	Quantity and quality of contact	Negative
Voci & Hewstone (2003b, Studies 1 & 2)[d]	Italians and North African immigrants	Italy	Quantity and quality of contact	Negative
			At low category salience	null-less negative
			At high category salience	negative

continued overleaf

Table 11.1 (Continued)

Study	Target group	Country	Contact dimension[a] (predictors and moderators)	Contact–anxiety relationship
Voci & Hewstone (2003b, Study 1)[d]	Italians and non-EU immigrants	Italy	Quantity and quality of contact	
			At low category salience	Negative
			At high category salience	null
				negative
Vorauer & Kumhyr (2001)[b,c]	White Canadians and Aboriginal Canadians	Canada	Presence of contact	
			At low partner's prejudice	null
			At high partner's prejudice	positive
Young (1985)[c]	Whites and Blacks	United States	Contact proximity	Positive

[a] Variables listed in the indented lines were tested as moderators of the contact dimension–anxiety relationship. [b] Indicates a longitudinal or experimental study. [c] Indicates a study that did not use an adaptation of W. G. Stephan and Stephan's (1984) intergroup anxiety scale. [d] Indicates a study that investigated the relationship between contact and intergroup anxiety in the context of testing the mediational role of intergroup anxiety in the relationship between contact and group judgments.

Altogether, Blascovich et al.'s (2001) findings and the mixed nature of the other contact findings are consistent with our hypothesis of affect generalization. They confirm that over time contact with specific outgroup members and the episodic anxiety experienced with them may act to reduce chronic and relatively context-free feelings of anxiety experienced toward the outgroup (or unknown outgroup members). This effect is similar to the effect detected in clinical settings when repeated exposure to fearful stimuli eventually reduces anxiety by inducing either habituation to the fearful stimulus (Lader & Wing, 1966), extinction of anxiety responses (Martin & Levey, 1985), or the appraisal of differences between episodic and chronic anxiety (Foa & Kozak, 1986). In contact settings, the link between episodic and chronic anxiety would eventually result in more benign group judgments (unfortunately Blascovich et al. do not test for this last segment of the process).

Other factors, beyond the distinction between episodic and chronic intergroup anxiety, may contribute to the mixed relationship reported in the literature between contact and anxiety; the most obvious is the quality – pleasant versus unpleasant – of the contact experience itself (Allport, 1954; C. W. Stephan & Stephan, 1992). As far as levels of intergroup anxiety are concerned, however, it is possible that the moderating effect of contact quality may not be long lasting and may matter more at the early, rather than late, stages of group acquaintance. The literature on the mere exposure effect is consistent with such a claim. It indicates that increased stimulus liking after repeated stimulus exposure occurs *even when* the stimulus is (initially) disliked or is associated with an aversive reaction (Zajonc, 1998). Similarly, clinical evidence shows that continuous exposure to anxiety-producing stimuli eventually leads to a reduction in anxiety responses *despite the fact* that the individual stimuli are aversive and that individuals do exhibit anxiety responses in their presence (Barlow, 1988). The policy implications of this evidence are significant, especially for traditionally segregated societies (e.g., Northern Ireland, South Africa). If the quality of contact really matters only at the early stages of group acquaintance, then working towards increasing people's opportunities for (any) intergroup contact may be more efficient than creating the conditions for positive and carefully structured contact experiences. Longitudinal research that combines measures of episodic intergroup anxiety with measures of (change in) chronic intergroup anxiety (Britt et al., 1996; Plant & Devine, 2003, Study 2) will be in a better position to ascertain whether *repeated* encounters with outgroup members can indeed, and almost paradoxically, override the potentially aversive effects of *individual* encounters with them. Moreover, such research will be in a better position to capture the finely grained nature of affect generalization as it unfolds over time.

More controversial is the relationship between category salience during contact and intergroup anxiety (Greenland & Brown, 2000; cf. Harwood,

Hewstone, Paolini, & Voci, 2005). In our research we have progressively moved away from conceiving category salience as a simple determinant of intergroup anxiety (Greenland & Brown, 1999; Islam & Hewstone, 1993) and rather preferred to investigate its moderating role (Harwood et al., 2005; Voci & Hewstone, 2003b) in a way that is more compatible with the role of category salience within contemporary models of contact (Ensari & Miller, 2002; Hewstone & Brown, 1986).

Our work suggests that, although increased intergroup salience may be generally associated with increased intergroup anxiety (Islam & Hewstone, 1993; W. G. Stephan & Stephan, 1985; Vivian, Hewstone, & Brown, 1997), it also systematically affects the size of the contact–anxiety relationship, as suggested by the earlier quotation from Smith (1993). More specifically, in our data participants who were relatively more aware of their group memberships during contact were those most likely to benefit from the anxiety-reduction effects of individual (Harwood et al., 2005, Study 2) or repeated (Voci & Hewstone, 2003a, 2003b) contact experiences; whereas those who were relatively less aware exhibited either poor (Harwood et al., 2005, Study 2; Voci & Hewstone, 2003b, Study 1) or null (Voci & Hewstone, 2003b, Study 2; Voci & Hewstone, 2003a, Study 1) anxiety reduction after contact. These moderation findings were found in notably different intergroup settings (for cursory and generic contact or extensive and work-related contact between Northern Italians and non-EU immigrants, see Voci & Hewstone, 2003a, 2003b; for intimate and extensive contact within British and North American families between grandchildren and their grandparents, see Harwood et al., 2005).[3]

We need to point out an important and somehow disconcerting implication of this novel moderating evidence. If episodic affect for specific outgroup members is more likely to generalize into chronic affect towards the group when the salience of categorization is high, but not (or less) when category salience is low, then the process of affect generalization resembles rather than departs from well-known and more *cognitive* processes of member-to-group generalization (for similar moderating evidence within these cognitive processes, see Desforges et al., 1997; Hewstone, 1994; Vivian et al., 1997; for an overview, see Paolini, 2001). It has been argued that affect-based forms of prejudice reduction (i.e., empathy) should be more powerful generalization devices than cognitive-based forms because they are less prone to subcategorization (Batson et al., 1997). Our data introduce a note of caution. They suggest the undesired possibility that affect generalization (with the associated reduction in prejudiced responding) may also occur *only* when social categories are salient or when outgroup members and situations are perceived to be typical of their classes (Ensari & Miller, 2002).

That subcategorization can limit affect generalization is evident in clinical settings. In these contexts, temporary reductions in anxiety achieved after controlled exposure to the anxiety-provoking stimulus (for an overview, see Barlow, 1988) often fail to generalize into stable reductions of anxiety and outside the therapeutic setting because a host of limiting factors encourage the subcategorization of the therapeutic experience (Foa & Kozak, 1986; Rachman, 1980). Direct tests of the robustness of affect generalization against subcategorization are now needed in a controlled intergroup environment.

If our understanding of *when* contact is associated with anxiety is fast growing, our understanding of *why* contact leads to (increased or reduced) anxiety is still at an early stage. Promising, though, is the explanatory power of a biopsychosocial model of challenge and threat (Blascovich et al., 2001). According to this model, threat and anxiety responses are associated with perceived lack of control. Thus, anxiety would occur when individuals perceive the demands of the situation they are in (e.g., contact) outweighing the resources they have available. This idea is consistent with most popular explanations of the anxiety-provoking effects of contact, which indeed invoke either factors increasing situational demands or factors reducing individuals' resources. For example, among the first type of factors, there is people's appraisal of increased effort made in interactions with stigmatized others to initiate conversations and to ensure smooth interactions (Frable et al., 1990), and to suppress negative feelings (Devine et al., 1996) or stereotypes (Macrae, Bodenhausen, Milne, & Wheeler, 1996) in order to appear non-prejudiced. Among the second type of factors, there is people's perception of reduced external support as cued by expectations of intergroup dissimilarities and limited mutual knowledge (Greenberg, Solomon, & Pyszczynski, 1997; W. G. Stephan & Stephan, 1985, 2000). Hence, this biopsychosocial model helps us to overcome an otherwise scattered view of the relationship between intergroup anxiety and its diverse correlates (Greenland & Brown, 2000; W. G. Stephan & Stephan, 2000).

Once Blascovich et al.'s (2001) idea that intergroup anxiety reflects lack of control is adopted, new ways to reduce prejudice also become conceivable. In clinical psychology, perceived (lack of) control and self-efficacy have traditionally been associated with the onset of anxiety and simple phobias (Lang, 1985). More interestingly for our discussion, increased perceived control and self-efficacy have been found to be potent predictors of successful interventions to reduce anxiety (e.g., C. Lee, 1984; Williams, Dooseman, & Kleifield, 1984). Beside Blascovich et al.'s model, these clinical data suggest the exciting possibility that behavioral or cognitive treatments (for individuals or groups) that focus on increasing individuals' sense of control and predictability during contact may, one day, be used to achieve sizeable reductions in intergroup anxiety and, as a result, in intergroup prejudice. Recent correlational data reported by Plant and Devine (2003, Study 1) give us hope. In this study, the relationship between more positive interracial contact and reduced intergroup anxiety in white college students was found to be mediated at least partly by a reduction in the perceived uncertainty (i.e., lack of control) about the outcome of future interracial contact. Importantly, more outcome certainty was part of the broader relationship linking more positive contact to reduced outgroup hostility.[4]

However, before even attempting the ambitious enterprise of adapting clinical tools into tools for *social* interventions, a more systematic assessment of the similarities and the differences between generic anxiety, social anxiety, and intergroup anxiety is needed. A null finding by Plant and Devine (2003) already speaks in favor of a substantial overlap between intergroup anxiety and other types of social (i.e., interpersonal) anxiety. In their second study, when white college students anticipated an imminent social interaction with another individual, the perceived uncertainty of the interaction outcome predicted pre-interaction anxiety (and contact avoidance a week after). Importantly, these findings were not qualified by the race (black versus white) of the expected partner, suggesting that some of the effects of intergroup anxiety reported in the literature may reflect generic interpersonal anxiety, rather than intergroup anxiety per se. Only research that includes measures of conceptually related forms of anxiety within the same design will be able to clarify whether there is any potential for "carrying over effects" between anxiety types, so that the reduction in one type of anxiety is fruitfully used to achieve a reduction in other types of anxiety (including intergroup anxiety).

To add more complexity to the picture, we must point out that the relationship between contact and intergroup anxiety is hardly uni-directional (see Gray, 1982, for mutual relationships between avoidance behavior and generic anxiety). Unfortunately, as much as contact leads to reduced intergroup anxiety, intergroup anxiety is likely to lead to increased contact avoidance (Henderson-King & Nisbett, 1996). For instance, in a longitudinal study by Levin, van Laar, and Sidanius (2003), the amount of cross-group friendship reported by over 2000 American students from various ethnic backgrounds during their second and third year of college predicted reduced intergroup anxiety at the end of college. Consistent with the suggested bi-directionality, however, the degree of intergroup anxiety reported at the end of the first year of college predicted *reduced* amount of cross-group friendship (i.e., contact avoidance) at the end of college. The main implication of a mutual relationship between contact and anxiety is that if people can potentially benefit from the anxiety-reducing effects of contact, such positive effects may be undermined or even missed altogether because of the contact avoidance effects of intergroup anxiety. This bi-directionality is not a good enough reason to abandon hope though. Over and above the bi-directionality of the contact–prejudice link, Pettigrew (1997) found the effects of *being* in contact on prejudice to be larger than the effects of prejudice on *avoiding* contact. In a similar vein, Mohr and Sedlacek (2000) found that about 40% of their American college respondents reported a desire to have homosexual friends despite anticipating discomfort and anxiety when interacting with them. Clinical psychologists have called this approaching of feared situations, despite physiological arousal and the subjective experience of fear, "bravery" or "courage" (Rachman, 1978).

People's bravery or courage when faced with opportunities for intergroup encounters may be less irrational and more adjusted than one may initially suspect. At least there is room for bravery (and for encouraging bravery) in Wright, Aron, and Tropp's (2002) model of self-expansion. According to Wright and colleagues, people are intrinsically and ultimately driven to seek out intergroup encounters (and to "avoid contact avoidance") in order to achieve a desirable expansion of their self-concept. Put differently, people's tendency to seek out intergroup contact should prevail over their tendency to avoid contact because contact allows their self-expansion, whereas contact avoidance prevents it. If this is really the case, then we can be more confident that the negative spiral of anxiety leading to contact avoidance can be circumvented or at least remain weaker than the desirable spin of contact leading to reduced anxiety.

Intergroup anxiety as a predictor of intergroup judgments

Most of the consequences of intergroup anxiety originally contemplated by W. G. Stephan and Stephan's (1985) model of intergroup anxiety have now received empirical support. These include contact avoidance and suspicion (Henderson-King & Nisbett, 1996), simplified information processing and reduced attention to disconfirming information (Wilder & Shapiro, 1989), increased concerns for the self (Vorauer & Kumhyr, 2001), negative emotional reactions (Crandall & Eshleman, 2003), and increased dominant responses toward the outgroup (Islam & Hewstone, 1993). Table 11.2 lists studies that investigated specifically the relationship between intergroup anxiety and outgroup judgments. This body of evidence demonstrates persuasively that intergroup anxiety does indeed affect intergroup judgments in the direction of worsening people's reactions to groups.

Much has been suggested (Greenland & Brown, 2000; Wilder & Simon, 2001), but little is actually known about how exactly states of intergroup anxiety are incorporated into the process of judgment formation. The most classic accounts (Islam & Hewstone, 1993; Wilder, 1993) invoke the effects of heightened arousal and equate intergroup anxiety with cognitive busyness (Greenland & Brown, 2000). More specifically, the heightened arousal associated with intergroup anxiety is either seen to be responsible for increasing attendance to threat-relevant information (Gray, 1982) or for narrowing the span of attention (Easterbrook, 1959). These two latter effects could both explain depleted performance, increased heuristic processing, poor attendance to expectancy incongruent information, and ultimately augmented dominant responses (Barlow, 1988).

Table 11.2 Studies testing the relationship between intergroup anxiety and group judgments

Study	Target group	Country	Anxiety–group judgment relationship[a]	Type of group judgment
Bizman & Yinon (2001)	Israelis and Russian immigrants	Israelis	Bias increase	Outgroup prejudice
Dijker (1987)	Dutch, Surinamers, Turks, Moroccans	The Netherlands	Bias increase	Attitudes toward the outgroup
Duran & Stephan (1999)	Majority and Affirmative Action Beneficiaries	United States	Bias increase	Attitudes toward outgroup
Greenland & Brown (1999, Study 1)[b]	Japanese and British	United Kingdom	Bias increase Bias increase	Ingroup bias Negative affect toward the outgroup
Greenland, Masser, & Prentice (2001)	Teachers and HIV-infected children	United Kingdom	Bias increase	Willingness to engage in contact
Harwood, Hewstone, Paolini, & Voci (2005)[b]	Youngsters and Elderly	United Kingdom	Bias increase	Attitudes toward the outgroup
Islam & Hewstone (1993)[b]	Hindus and Muslims	Bangladesh	Bias increase	Outgroup attitudes Perceived outgroup variability
Paolini, Hewstone, Cairns, & Voci (2004)[b]	Catholics and Protestants	Northern Ireland	Bias increase	Outgroup prejudice Perceived outgroup variability
Plant & Devine (2003, Study 1)[b]	Whites and Blacks	United States	Bias increase	Perceived hostility towards the outgroup
C. W. Stephan, Stephan, Demitrakis, Yamada, & Clason (2000)[b]	Men and Women	United States	Bias increase	Attitudes toward outgroup

Study	Groups	Country	Result	Dependent measure
W. G. Stephan, Diaz-Loving, & Duran (2000)[b]	Americans and Mexicans	United States	Bias increase	Attitudes toward outgroup
W. G. Stephan & Stephan (1985)	Hispanics and Anglo-Saxons	United States	Bias increase	Outgroup stereotypicality
W. G. Stephan et al. (2002)[b]	Whites and Blacks	United States	Bias increase	Outgroup prejudice
W. G. Stephan, Ybarra, & Bachman (1999)	Whites, Mexicans, Asians, Cubans	United States	Bias increase	Outgroup prejudice
W. G. Stephan, Ybarra, Martinez, Schwarzwald, & Tur-Kaspa (1998)	Spanish and Moroccans	Spain	Bias increase	Attitudes toward outgroup
Voci & Hewstone (2003b, Study 1)[b]	Italians and non-EU immigrants	Italy	Bias increase Bias increase Null	Attitude toward outgroup Outgroup subtle prejudice Perceived outgroup variability
Voci & Hewstone (2003b, Study 2)[b]	Italians and non-EU immigrants	Italy	Bias increase (indirect) Bias increase (indirect) Bias increase	Attitude toward immediate outgroup Attitude toward distal outgroup Rights for immigrants
Voci & Hewstone (2003a, Study 1)	Italians and non-EU immigrants	Italy	Bias increase Bias increase	Attitude toward outgroup Subtle outgroup prejudice

[a] Bias increase indicates cases of detrimental effects of anxiety. [b] Indicates a study that investigated the relationship between intergroup anxiety and group judgments while testing the mediational role of intergroup anxiety in the relationship between contact and group judgments.

Alternatively, intergroup anxiety may mimic the behavior of more incidental and transient forms of affect and lead to negative reactions towards the outgroup by means of an affect congruence effect (Forgas, 2002). This means that intergroup anxiety may be used as one among other pieces of judgment-relevant information that is immediately accessible at the time of making an intergroup judgment (see the affect-as-information model, Schwarz & Clore, 1988). Under these circumstances, intergroup anxiety would increase outgroup prejudice because of the established association between the outgroup and the aversive quality of heightened anxiety (see also Crandall & Eshleman, 2003). Another possibility is that the affect congruence effects of intergroup anxiety are memory driven (Bower & Forgas, 2001; however, see results of Ciarrochi & Forgas, 1999). That is, intergroup anxiety may affect intergroup judgments by activating a variety of valence-congruent (i.e., negative) information in memory at the time of making the prejudiced judgment. Under this second set of circumstances, intergroup anxiety would increase prejudice because it triggers the recall of negative contents from memory (for clinical evidence supporting selective memory for anxiety-related material, see e.g., McNally, Foa, Donnell, 1989; cf. Foa, McNally, & Murdoch, 1989).

Direct tests of these distinct (but not necessarily mutually exclusive) accounts of the detrimental effects of intergroup anxiety are now needed in contact settings. Future research should also embark on a more systematic investigation of moderators of the relationship between intergroup anxiety and group judgments. Although this relationship is unlikely to be unconditional in nature, direct tests are still scarce and unsystematic (for some preliminary attempts, see Bizman & Yinon, 2001; Harwood et al., 2005). Forgas' (2002) affect infusion model provides an interesting set of moderating hypotheses, however it remains untested in intergroup settings.

Intergroup anxiety as a mediator of the link between contact and intergroup judgments

Allport (1954) and contact researchers after him have long failed to specify the psychological processes responsible for the beneficial effects of contact (Pettigrew & Tropp, 2000). Pettigrew (1998) has recently identified four key processes: (a) learning about the outgroup, (b) changed behaviors toward the outgroup, (c) ingroup reappraisal, and (d) affective ties between the ingroup and the outgroup. These four processes are clearly not mutually exclusive nor do they provide an exhaustive explanation of the underpinnings of contact effects. In effect, the process of affect generalization that we have hypothesized at the beginning of this chapter, although close to Pettigrew's fourth type, does not clearly fit in any of his categories. However, growing evidence demonstrates that it plays a pivotal role in contact settings.

Work carried out independently by our research team, by W. G. Stephan and Stephan (2000), and by Greenland and Brown (2000) shows that experiences of both generic and optimal contact often improve intergroup judgments at least partly because they reduce the anxiety produced by the anticipation of encounters with outgroup members. Tables 11.1 and 11.2 report relevant evidence that we now discuss (superscripts for studies cited in the tables identify research that assessed the contact–anxiety and the anxiety–judgments links while testing the mediational role of intergroup anxiety).

Affect generalization in generic contact

In W. G. Stephan and Stephan's (1985) original model, intergroup anxiety was given the status of a central mechanism of contact effects. Our early work on the intergroup relations between Hindus and Muslims in Bangladesh provided evidence for this central role (Islam & Hewstone, 1993). Consistent with the Stephans' claim, intergroup anxiety partly mediated the positive relationship between both contact quality and contact quantity as predictors, and outgroup attitudes and perceived outgroup variability, as outcomes. Moreover, it fully mediated the negative relationship between category salience and both outcomes.

After Islam and Hewstone (1993), a quite impressive body of evidence gathered by the Stephans' research team and by Greenland and colleagues has confirmed that a mechanism of anxiety reduction is indeed partly responsible for the improvement of group judgments after experiences of generic contact (see Tables 11.1 and 11.2). This seems to be true for a variety of intergroup settings (based on ethnicity, nationality, gender, and physical wellbeing) and for a variety of participant types (college students, adults from the general population, and specific professionals). As a result, intergroup anxiety has maintained a central role in W. G. Stephan and Stephan's (2000) more recent integrated threat theory. In this model intergroup anxiety is one among four sources of perceived threat to the ingroup, beside realistic and symbolic threat and negative stereotypes, expected to mediate the effects of generic contact on intergroup judgments. Not all four sources are believed to operate in all intergroup settings (W. G. Stephan & Stephan, 2000), nonetheless intergroup anxiety has been found to be the most robust mediator (W. G. Stephan et al., 2002), once again confirming the pervasive role of this intergroup emotion in intergroup contact.

Affect generalization in optimal contact

If affect generalization has to contribute to achieve sizeable improvements in intergroup relations, it must be involved in those circumstances that are most propitious for achieving more harmonious intergroup relations.

Optimal contact occurs between individuals of equal status, with common goals, who are engaged in cooperative activities and receive institutional support (Allport, 1954). Although meta-analytic evidence now indicates that optimal contact is not essential for the beneficial effects of contact to occur (Pettigrew & Tropp, 2000), the same evidence demonstrates that it still produces the largest effect sizes. Our most recent research has therefore turned to investigate intergroup anxiety under conditions that implement, in one way or another, Allport's conditions for optimal contact.

The idea that friendships across group boundaries may be particularly powerful vehicles of intergroup change (Pettigrew, 1998) has been validated directly by recent tests of the direct cross-group friendship hypothesis (e.g., Pettigrew, 1997, 1998; Phinney, Ferguson, & Tate, 1997), and indirectly by evidence suggesting that simply knowing of cross-group friendships (i.e., indirect friendship) is sufficient to obtain a reduction in outgroup prejudice (Wright, Aron, McLaughlin-Volpe, & Ropp, 1997). In two surveys carried out in Northern Ireland (Paolini, Hewstone, Cairns, & Voci, 2004), we tested whether an anxiety-reduction mechanism explained the relationships between both direct and indirect cross-group friendships between Catholics and Protestants and our outcome variables (outgroup prejudice and perceived outgroup variability). We found that reductions in intergroup anxiety significantly mediated (sometimes fully and other times only partly) all the relationships between both direct and indirect cross-group friendships and both outgroup prejudice and perceived outgroup variability. This was true both in a convenience sample of university students from three geographically distant Northern Irish campuses and in a representative sample of Catholic and Protestant adults drawn from the general population. Figure 11.1 reports the estimated model with latent variables for the student sample.

These studies (Paolini, Hewstone, Cairns, & Voci, 2004a) clearly show that in contexts characterized by a long history of intergroup conflict, the beneficial effects of direct and indirect cross-group friendship result from a reduced feeling of anxiety (see also Hewstone et al., 2005), anxiety often stemming from the expectation that future intergroup encounters will be characterized by mutual embarrassment, misunderstanding, and discrimination. There may, however, be less room for this type of affect generalization in less virulent and affect-based intergroup settings. To test this possibility, in another of our studies (Paolini et al., 2003) we first used an open-ended measure of attitude structure (Esses & Dovidio, 2002) to assess the degree to which emotions (rather than cognitions) were involved in the reactions of Australian students to various salient outgroups. This pilot work allowed us to then test the direct and indirect cross-friendship hypotheses in intergroup settings that spanned significantly along an ideal continuum, ranging from predominantly affect-based settings to predominantly cognition-based intergroup settings. This study revealed the *un*conditional nature of our

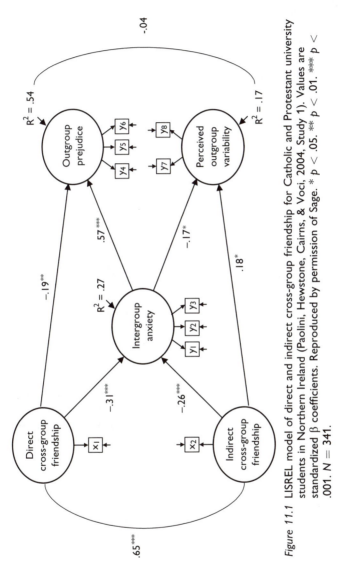

Figure 11.1 LISREL model of direct and indirect cross-group friendship for Catholic and Protestant university students in Northern Ireland (Paolini, Hewstone, Cairns, & Voci, 2004, Study 1). Values are standardized β coefficients. Reproduced by permission of Sage. * $p < .05.$ ** $p < .01.$ *** $p < .001.$ $N = 341.$

anxiety-reduction mechanism. Specifically, intergroup anxiety was found to be a significant mediator of cross-group friendship effects *across* affect-based and cognitive-based intergroup settings (i.e., this effect was *not* qualified), thus suggesting that the process of affect generalization is not limited to those intergroup relations that elicit frequent and intense intergroup emotions.

In our research, we have tested another way in which the effects of this anxiety-reduction mechanism can generalize; that is, in the proximal–distal nature of the target of attitudes (see also Pettigrew, 1997). In this study (Voci & Hewstone, 2003b, Study 2), optimal contact was operationalized by creating a single index of frequent *and* positive contact (Brown, Maras, Masser, Vivian, & Hewstone, 2001). We found that, among Italian hospital workers, intergroup anxiety partly mediated the beneficial impact that optimal contact with non-EU co-workers (i.e., immigrants) had on attitudes towards non-EU co-workers. However, this effect did not extend directly to a more distal target group (i.e., non-EU immigrants in general), as measured by items tapping attitude and endorsement of pro-immigrant policies. But it did so only indirectly through their attitudes towards non-EU co-workers. This evidence for a relatively narrow generalization across attitude targets is new in the literature on the process of affect generalization, but not in the literature on more cognitive mechanisms of member-to-group generalization (e.g., Quattrone & Jones, 1980; Wilder, Simon, & Faith, 1996).

The process of affect generalization is not limited to intergroup anxiety. In one of the studies looking at contact between Northern Italian adults and non-EU immigrants (Voci & Hewstone, 2003a, Study 1), we extended our assessment of integral affect to a positive intergroup emotion, empathy (Batson et al., 1997). Results showed that intergroup anxiety and empathy *simultaneously* explained the negative relationship between optimal contact (once again the product of frequent and positive contact) and both blatant and subtle prejudice. Moreover, we found that both mediation effects were significantly moderated by category salience. Hence, reductions of intergroup anxiety and increases in empathy after contact (partly) explained improved outgroup judgments among those who were aware of their group memberships during contact, but not among those who were not (or were less) aware.

These data confirm that, rather than reflecting complete immunity from subcategorization, the special prejudice-reducing powers of outgroup friendships and optimal contact may stem from the concurrent activation of various mechanisms that operate in parallel. In one of our studies assessing the intergenerational relationships between grandchildren and grandparents (Harwood et al., 2005, Study 2), we tested the mediating potential of three classes of psychological constructs. Affective constructs were intergroup anxiety and perspective taking; the cognitive construct was individuation; and communicative constructs were self-disclosure and accommodation.

This time, optimal contact was assessed by looking at the quality of contact that young American students had with their most frequently visited grandparents. Within this intergenerational relationship, we found that intergroup anxiety, perspective taking, and communication accommodation all mediated the association between contact and attitudes towards the elderly (with perspective taking being the most robust mediator); while individuation and self-disclosure – but not intergroup anxiety – mediated the effects of contact on perceived outgroup variability (individuation was this time the most robust mediator). Altogether, these results (see also Paolini et al., 2003) suggest that a more powerful explanation of this and other intergroup phenomena may be achieved by drawing knowledge from traditionally separate areas of social psychology, such as interpersonal and communication research (for other examples of this successful practice, see Galinsky & Moskowitz, 2000; Wright et al., 2002).

Concluding remarks

As a result of this chapter, intergroup anxiety in particular and intergroup emotions in general will hopefully regain the role they deserve in the theoretical and empirical investigation of contact between groups. We started by arguing for the existence of a new underlying process of contact effects, a process that we called "affect generalization", whereby intergroup contact leads to more benevolent group judgments by allowing for positive (or less negative) and transient affective states experienced with specific outgroup members to generalize into positive (or less negative) chronic affective reactions to the group as whole. We then reviewed extensive evidence that is consistent with this process and that demonstrates that a specific type of intergroup emotion, intergroup anxiety, is indeed central to many contact effects. As much as augmented intergroup anxiety contributes to the development of prejudiced responding, so an anxiety-reduction mechanism seems actively and pervasively involved in the prejudice-reduction effects of intergroup contact across intergroup settings and category systems.

It is evident that we now know more about intergroup emotions than at the time in which Bodenhausen (1993) rightly complained of the limited research on integral affect. There is, however, much more we need to know before we can make good use of these findings and achieve sizeable reductions of prejudice in settings of intergroup contact via affect generalization. Longitudinal and experimental research is scarce in the contact literature in general (Pettigrew & Tropp, 2000) and in the intergroup anxiety literature in particular (for exceptions, see Greenland & Brown, 1999; Levin et al., 2003). We need more of this research to clarify many of the issues of reciprocal relationships and causal order discussed earlier in the context of the contact – intergroup emotions – group judgments sequence, and to detect the process of affect generalization as it unfolds temporally.

Notes

1 Two search procedures were used to aggregate the studies reported in Tables 11.1 and 11.2: a computer-based search of abstracts contained in psychological research periodicals and reporting the key word "intergroup anxiety" (Ovid Technologies: PsycInfo 1872–2003) and a review of the reference lists from relevant theoretical and empirical papers in the area. The search was ended in December 2003.

2 The measures of intergroup anxiety designed by W. G. Stephan and Stephan (1985), by Britt and colleagues (1996), and by Plant and Devine (2003, Study 2) all measure Blascovich et al.'s (2001) third type of anxiety responses (i.e., subjective threat responses). However, they are differently bound to a specific contact situation and outgroup member. In Plant and Devine, for instance, after being told about an *imminent* interaction with an outgroup member and having inspected this individual's identification card, participants are asked to indicate how they feel about the upcoming interaction on scales anchored with anxiety-related adjectives. In studies using Stephan and Stephan's scale, on the other hand, no expectation of real contact exists. Participants are first asked to imagine that they are the only person from their own social category within a group of people from the other social category. They are then asked to rate their antici-pated feelings to this *hypothetical* intergroup scenario on a series of scales anchored with anxiety-related adjectives, while using as a standard of comparison their anticipated feelings for a situation in which they are in a group of people from their own social category only.

3 Interestingly, in one of the studies investigating contact between youngsters and their grandparents (Harwood et al., 2005, Study 1), we discovered that category salience was not acting as a *trait* facilitating the generalization of various contact experiences. It was rather the salience and the optimal contact with a *specific* target that, once combined, produced prejudice reduction. In both Harwood et al. (2005) and Voci and Hewstone (2003a, 2003b), category salience also moderated the relationship between contact and prejudice, of which the contact–anxiety link was part. However, this more general moderation effect was driven by a significant moderating effect of category salience at the level of the relationship between contact and anxiety, but not of the level of the relationship between anxiety and prejudice.

4 The uncertainty-reducing properties of familiar stimuli have also been invoked (A. Y. Lee, 2001) to explain why increased liking (or reduced disliking) for a stimulus occurs after repeated exposure to it ("the mere exposure effect", Zajonc, 1998). The commonalities existing between the evidence regarding increased perceived control in the mere exposure effects, in the clinical treatment of social and non-social anxiety, and in the contact effects suggest that the link between contact and anxiety at least partly reflects a basic, fundamental, and *not* necessarily *social* link between repeated exposure to a stimulus and increased liking.

References

Abelson, R. P., Kinder, D. R., Peters, M. D., & Fiske, S. T. (1982). Affective and semantic components in political person perception. *Journal of Personality and Social Psychology, 42*, 619–630.
Alexander, M. G., Brewer, M. B., & Hermann, R. K. (1999). Images and affect: A

functional analysis of out-group stereotypes. *Journal of Personality and Social Psychology, 77*, 78–93.

Allport, G. W. (1954). *The nature of prejudice.* New York: Addison-Wesley.

Barlow, D. H. (1988). *Anxiety and its disorders: The nature and treatment of anxiety and panic.* New York: Guilford Press.

Batson, C. D., Polycarpou, M. P., Harmon-Jones, E., Imhoff, H. J., Mitchener, E. C., Bednar, L. L., et al. (1997). Empathy and attitudes: Can feeling for a member of a stigmatized group improve feelings toward the group? *Journal of Personality and Social Psychology, 72*, 105–118.

Bizman, A., & Yinon, Y. (2001). Intergroup and interpersonal threats as determinants of prejudice: The moderating role of in-group identification. *Basic and Applied Social Psychology, 23*, 191–196.

Blascovich, J., Mendes, W. B., Hunter, S., Lickel, B., & Kowai-Bell, N. (2001). Perceiver threat in social interactions with stigmatized others. *Journal of Personality and Social Psychology, 80*, 253–267.

Bodenhausen, G. V. (1993). Emotions, arousal, and stereotypic judgments: A heuristic model of affect and stereotyping. In D. M. Mackie & D. L. Hamilton (Eds.), *Affect, cognition, and stereotyping: Interactive processes in group perception* (pp. 13–37). San Diego, CA: Academic Press.

Bodenhausen, G. V., Mussweiler, T., Gabriel, S., & Moreno, K. N. (2001). Affective influences on stereotyping and intergroup relations. In J. P. Forgas (Ed.), *Handbook of affect and social cognition* (pp. 319–343). Mahwah, NJ: Lawrence Erlbaum Associates Inc.

Bodenhausen, G. V., Schwarz, N., Bless, H., & Wänke, M. (1995). Effects of atypical exemplars on racial beliefs: Enlightened racism or generalized appraisal? *Journal of Experimental Social Psychology, 31*, 48–63.

Bower, G. H., & Forgas, J. P. (2001). Mood and social memory. In J. P. Forgas (Ed.). *Handbook of affect and social cognition* (pp. 95–120). Mahwah, NJ: Lawrence Erlbaum Associates Inc.

Britt, T. W., Boniecki, K. A., Vescio, T. K., Biernat, M., & Brown, L. M. (1996). Intergroup anxiety: A person * situation approach. *Personality and Social Psychology Bulletin, 22*, 1177–1188.

Brown, R., Maras, P., Masser, B., Vivian, J., & Hewstone, M. (2001). Life on the ocean wave: Testing some intergroup hypotheses in a naturalistic setting. *Group Processes and Intergroup Relations, 4*, 81–97.

Cairns, E., & Roe, M. D. (Eds.). (2003). *The role of memory in ethnic conflict.* Basingstoke, UK: Palgrave Macmillan.

Ciarrochi, J. V., & Forgas, J. P. (1999). On being tense yet tolerant: The paradoxical effects of trait anxiety and aversive mood on intergroup judgments. *Group Dynamics, 3*, 227–238.

Crandall, C. S., & Eshleman, A. (2003). A justification-suppression of the expression and experience of prejudice. *Psychological Bulletin, 129*, 414–446.

Desforges, D. M., Lord, C. G., Pugh, M. A., Sia, T. L., Scarberry, N. C., & Ratcliff, C. D. (1997). Role of group representativeness in the generalization part of the contact hypothesis. *Basic and Applied Social Psychology, 19*, 183–204.

Devine, P. G., Evett, S. R., & Vasquez-Suson, K. A. (1996). Exploring the interpersonal dynamics of intergroup contact. In R. M. Sorrentino & E. T. Higgins

(Eds.), *Handbook of motivation and cognition: The interpersonal context* (Vol. 3, pp. 423–464). New York: Guilford Press.

Dijker, A. J. (1987). Emotional reactions to ethnic minorities. *European Journal of Social Psychology, 17*, 305–325.

Duran, A., & Stephan, W. G. (1999). *The role of threats in attitudes toward affirmative action and its beneficiaries.* Unpublished manuscript, New Mexico State University, Las Cruces.

Easterbrook, J. A. (1959). The effect of emotion on cue utilization and the organization of behavior. *Psychological Review, 66*, 183–201.

Edwards, K. & von Hippel, W. (1995). Hearts and minds: The priority of affective versus cognitive factors in person perception. *Personality and Social Psychology Bulletin, 21*, 996–1011.

Ensari, N., & Miller, N. (2002). The out-group must not be so bad after all: The effects of disclosure, typicality, and salience on intergroup bias. *Journal of Personality and Social Psychology, 83*, 313–329.

Esses, V. M., & Dovidio, J. F. (2002). The role of emotions in determining willingness to engage in intergroup contact. *Personality and Social Psychology Bulletin, 28*, 1202–1214.

Fiske, S. T., Cuddy, A. J. C., Glick, P., & Xu, J. (2002). A model of (often mixed) stereotype content: Competence and warmth respectively follow from perceived status and competition. *Journal of Personality and Social Psychology, 82*, 878–902.

Foa, E. B., & Kozak, M. J. (1986). Emotional processing of fear: Exposure to corrective information. *Psychological Bulletin, 99*, 20–35.

Foa, E. B., McNally, R. J., & Murdoch, T. B. (1989). Anxious mood and memory. *Behaviour Research and Therapy, 27*, 141–147.

Forgas, J. P. (2002). Feeling and doing: Affective influences on interpersonal behavior. *Psychological Inquiry, 13*, 1–28.

Frable, D. E., Blackstone, T., & Scherbaum, C. (1990). Marginal and mindful: Deviant in social interactions. *Journal of Personality and Social Psychology, 59*, 140–149.

Frijda, N. H. (1986). *The emotions.* Cambridge, UK: Cambridge University Press.

Galinsky, A. D., & Moskowitz, G. B. (2000). Perspective-taking: Decreasing stereotype expression, stereotype accessibility, and in-group favoritism. *Journal of Personality and Social Psychology, 78*, 708–724.

Gray, J. A. (1982). *The neuropsychology of anxiety: An enquiry into the functions of the septo-hippocampal system.* Oxford, UK: Oxford University Press.

Greenberg, J., Solomon, S., & Pyszczynski, T. (1997). Terror management theory of self-esteem and cultural worldviews: Empirical assessments and conceptual refinements. In M. P. Zanna (Ed.), *Advances in experimental social psychology* (Vol. 29, pp. 61–139). San Diego, CA: Academic Press.

Greenland, K., & Brown, R. (1999). Categorization and intergroup anxiety in contact between British and Japanese nationals. *European Journal of Social Psychology, 29*, 503–521.

Greenland, K., & Brown, R. (2000). Categorization and intergroup anxiety in intergroup contact. In D. Capozza & R. Brown (Eds.), *Social identity processes: Trends in theory and research* (pp. 167–183). London: Sage.

Greenland, K., Masser, B., & Prentice, T. (2001). "They're scared of it": Intergroup determinants of attitudes toward children with HIV. *Journal of Applied Social Psychology, 31,* 2127–2148.

Haddock, G., Zanna, M. P., & Esses, V. M. (1993). Assessing the structure of prejudicial attitudes: The case of attitudes towards homosexuals. *Journal of Personality and Social Psychology, 65,* 1105–1118.

Harwood, J., Hewstone, M., Paolini, S., & Voci, A. (2005) Grandparent–grandchild contact and attitudes towards older adults: Moderator and mediator effects. *Personality and Social Psychology Bulletin, 31,* 393–406.

Henderson-King, E. I., & Nisbett, R. E. (1996). Anti-black prejudice as a function of exposure to the negative behaviour of a single black person. *Journal of Personality and Social Psychology, 71,* 654–664.

Hewstone, M. (1989). Changing stereotypes with disconfirming information. In D. Bar-Tal, C. F. Graumann, A. W. Kruglansky, & W. Stroebe (Eds.), *Stereotyping and prejudice: Changing conceptions* (pp. 207–223). New York: Springer-Verlag.

Hewstone, M. (1994). Revision and change of stereotypic beliefs: In search of the elusive subtyping model. In W. Strobe & M. Hewstone (Eds.), *European review of social psychology* (Vol. 5, pp. 69–109). Chichester, UK: Wiley.

Hewstone, M., & Brown, R. (1986). Contact is not enough: An intergroup perspective on the contact hypothesis. In M. Hewstone & R. Brown (Eds.), *Contact and conflict in intergroup encounters* (pp. 1–44). Oxford, UK: Blackwell.

Hewstone, M., Cairns, E., Voci, A., Paolini, S., McLernon, F., Crisp, R. J., et al. (2005). Intergroup contact in a divided society: Challenging segregation in Northern Ireland. In D. Abrams, M. A. Hogg, & J. Marques (Eds.), *Social psychology of inclusion and exclusion* (pp. 265–292). Philadelphia: Psychology Press.

Islam, M. R., & Hewstone, M. (1993). Dimensions of contact as predictors of intergroup anxiety, perceived out-group variability, and out-group attitude: An integrative model. *Personality and Social Psychology Bulletin, 19,* 700–710.

Islam, M. R., & Jahjah, M. (2001). Predictors of young Australians' attitudes toward Aboriginals, Asians and Arabs. *Social Behavior and Personality, 29,* 569–579.

Johnston, L., & Hewstone, M. (1990). Intergroup contact: Social identity and social cognition. In D. Abrams & M. Hogg (Eds.), *Social identity theory: Constructive and critical advances* (pp. 185–210). London: Harvester Wheatsheaf.

Lader, M. H., & Wing, L. (1966). *Physiological measures, sedative drugs, and morbid anxiety.* London: Oxford University Press.

Lang, P. J. (1985). The cognitive psychophysiology of emotion: Fear and anxiety. In A. H. Tuma & J. D. Maser (Eds.), *Anxiety and the anxiety disorders.* Hillsdale, NJ: Lawrence Erlbaum Associates Inc.

Lee, A. Y. (2001). The mere exposure effect: An uncertainty reduction explanation revisited. *Personality and Social Psychology Bulletin, 27,* 1255–1266.

Lee, C. (1984). Efficacy expectations and outcome expectations as predictors of performance in a snake-handling task. *Cognitive Therapy and Research, 8,* 37–48.

Levin, S., van Laar, C., & Sidanius, J. (2003). The effects of ingroup and outgroup friendship on ethnic attitudes in college: A longitudinal study. *Group Processes and Intergroup Relations, 6,* 76–92.

Mackie, D. M., Devos, T., & Smith, E. R. (2000). Intergroup emotions: Explaining offensive action tendencies in an intergroup context. *Journal of Personality and Social Psychology*, *79*, 602–616.

Mackie, D. M., & Smith, E. R. (1998). Intergroup relations: Insights from a theoretically integrative approach. *Psychological Review*, *105*, 499–529.

Macrae, C. N., Bodenhausen, G. V., Milne, A. B., & Wheeler, V. (1996). On resisting the temptation for simplification: Counterintentional effects of stereotype suppression on social memory. *Social Cognition*, *14*, 1–20.

Malik, K. (2003, October 29). The dirty D-word. *The Guardian*.

Martin, I., & Levey, A. B. (1985). Conditioning, evaluations and cognitions: An axis of integration. *Behaviour Research and Therapy*, *23*, 167–175.

McNally, R. J., Foa, E. B., & Donnell, C. D. (1989). Memory bias for anxiety information in patients with panic disorders. *Cognition and Emotion*, *3*, 27–44.

Mendes, W. B., Blascovich, J., Lickel, B., & Hunter, S. (2002). Challenge and threat during social interactions with white and black men. *Personality and Social Psychology Bulletin*, *28*, 939–952.

Mohr, J. J., & Sedlacek, W. E. (2000). Perceived barriers to friendship with lesbians and gay men among university students. *Journal of College Student Development*, *41*, 70–80.

Paolini, S. (2001). *Member-to-group generalization: Moderators, mediators, and social consequences*. Unpublished doctoral dissertation, Cardiff University, UK.

Paolini, S., Hewstone, M., Cairns, E., & Voci, A. (2004). Effects of direct and indirect cross-group friendships on judgments of Catholics and Protestants in Northern Ireland: The mediating role of an anxiety-reduction mechanism. *Personality and Social Psychology Bulletin*, *30*, 770–786.

Paolini, S., Hewstone, M., Rubin, M., & Pay, H. (2004). Increased group dispersion after exposure to one deviant group member: Testing Hamburger's model of member-to-group generalization. *Journal of Experimental Social Psychology*, *40*, 569–585.

Paolini, S., Lawson, E., Spencer, M., Stevens, S., Turner, Z., & Waller, A. (2003). *Exploring direct and indirect cross-group friendship effects across intergroup contexts: The moderating and mediating effects of affect and cognition*. Unpublished manuscript, University of Newcastle, Australia.

Pettigrew, T. F. (1997). Generalized intergroup contact effects on prejudice. *Personality and Social Psychology Bulletin*, *23*, 173–185.

Pettigrew, T. F. (1998). Intergroup contact theory. *Annual Review of Psychology*, *49*, 65–85.

Pettigrew, T. F., & Tropp, L. R. (2000). Does intergroup contact reduce prejudice? Recent meta-analytic findings. In S. Oskamp (Ed.), *Reducing prejudice and discrimination* (pp. 93–114). Mahwah, NJ: Lawrence Erlbaum Associates Inc.

Phinney, J. S., Ferguson, D. L., & Tate, J. D. (1997). Intergroup attitudes among ethnic minority adolescents: A causal model. *Child Development*, *68*, 955–969.

Plant, E. A., & Devine, P. G. (2003). The antecedents and implications of interracial anxiety. *Personality and Social Psychology Bulletin*, *29*, 790–801.

Quattrone, G. A., & Jones, E. E. (1980). The perception of variability within in-groups and out-groups: Implications for the law of small numbers. *Journal of Personality and Social Psychology*, *38*, 141–152.

Rachman, S. J. (1978). *Fear and courage*. San Francisco, CA: Freeman.

Rachman, S. J. (1980). Emotional processing. *Behaviour Research and Therapy, 18,* 51–60.

Schwarz, N., & Clore, G. L. (1988). How do I feel about it? Informative functions of affective states. In K. Fiedler & J. P. Forgas (Eds.), *Affect, cognition, and social behavior* (pp. 44–62). Toronto, Ontario: Hogrefe.

Sherif, M. (1966). *Group conflict and cooperation: Their social psychology.* London: Routledge.

Smith, E. R. (1993). Social identity and social emotions: Toward new conceptualizations of prejudice. In D. M. Mackie & D. L. Hamilton (Eds.), *Affect, cognition, and stereotyping: Interactive processes in group perception* (pp. 297–315). San Diego, CA: Academic Press.

Stangor, C., Sullivan, L. A., & Ford, T. E. (1991). Affective and cognitive determinants of prejudice. *Social Cognition, 9,* 359–380.

Stephan, C. W., & Stephan, W. G. (1992). Reducing intercultural anxiety through intercultural contact. *International Journal of Intercultural Relations, 16,* 89–106.

Stephan, C. W., Stephan, W. G., Demitrakis, K. M., Yamada, A. M., & Clason, D. L. (2000). Women's attitudes toward men: An integrated threat theory analysis. *Psychology of Women Quarterly, 24,* 63–73.

Stephan, W. G., Boniecki, K. A., Ybarra, O., Bettencourt, B. A., Ervin, K. S., Jackson, L. A., et al. (2002). The role of threats in the racial attitudes of Blacks and Whites. *Personality and Social Psychology Bulletin, 28,* 1242–1254.

Stephan, W. G., Diaz-Loving, R., & Duran, A. (2000). Integrated threat theory and intercultural attitudes: Mexico and the United States. *Journal of Cross Cultural Psychology, 31,* 240–249.

Stephan, W. G., & Stephan, C. W. (1984). The role of ignorance in intergroup relations. In N. Miller & M. B. Brewer (Eds.), *Groups in contact: The psychology of desegregation* (pp. 229–255). New York: Academic Press.

Stephan, W. G., & Stephan, C. W. (1985). Intergroup anxiety. *Journal of Social Issues, 41,* 157–175.

Stephan, W. G., & Stephan, C. W. (1989). Antecedents of intergroup anxiety in Asian-Americans and Hispanic-Americans. *International Journal of Intercultural Relations, 13,* 203–219.

Stephan, W. G., & Stephan, C. W. (2000). An integrated threat theory of prejudice. In S. Oskamp (Ed.), *Reducing prejudice and discrimination* (pp. 23–45). Mahwah, NJ: Lawrence Erlbaum Associates Inc.

Stephan, W. G., Ybarra, O., & Bachman, G. (1999). Prejudice towards immigrants: An integrated threat theory. *Journal of Applied Social Psychology, 29,* 2221–2237.

Stephan, W. G., Ybarra, O., Martinez, C. M., Schwarzwald, J., & Tur-Kaspa, M. (1998). Prejudice toward immigrants to Spain and Israel: An integrated threat theory analysis. *Journal of Cross Cultural Psychology, 29,* 559–576.

Tajfel, H. (1981). *Human groups and social categories.* Cambridge, UK: Cambridge University Press.

Vivian, J., Hewstone, M., & Brown, R. (1997). Intergroup contact: Theoretical and empirical developments. In R. Ben-Ari & Y. Rich (Eds.), *Enhancing education in heterogeneous schools: Theory and application* (pp. 13–46). Ramat-Gun, Israel: Bar-Ilan University Press.

Voci, A., & Hewstone, M. (2003a, October). *Contact and prejudice reduction in the*

Italian context: The impact of empathy, perspective taking, and group salience. Paper presented at the SESP Conference, Boston, MA, USA.

Voci, A., & Hewstone, M. (2003b). Intergroup contact and prejudice toward immigrants in Italy: The mediational role of anxiety and the moderational role of group salience. *Group Processes and Intergroup Relations, 6*, 37–54.

Vorauer, J., & Kumhyr, S. M. (2001). Is this about you or me? Self- versus other-directed judgments and feelings in response to intergroup interaction. *Personality and Social Psychology Bulletin, 27*, 706–719.

Wilder, D. A. (1993). Freezing intergroup evaluations: Anxiety fosters resistance to counterstereotypic information. In M. A. Hogg & D. Abrams (Eds.), *Group motivation: Social psychological perspectives* (pp. 68–86). London: Harvester Wheatsheaf.

Wilder, D. A., & Shapiro, P. N. (1989). Effects of anxiety on impression formation in a group context: An anxiety-assimilation hypothesis. *Journal of Experimental Social Psychology, 25*, 481–499.

Wilder, D. A., & Simon, A. F. (2001). Affect as a cause of intergroup bias. In R. Brown & S. L. Gaertner (Eds.), *Blackwell handbook of social psychology: Intergroup processes* (pp. 153–72). Oxford, UK: Blackwell.

Wilder, D. A., Simon, A. F., & Faith, M. (1996). Enhancing the impact of counterstereotypic information: Dispositional attributions for deviance. *Journal of Personality and Social Psychology, 71*, 276–287.

Williams, S. L., Dooseman, G., & Kleifield, E. (1984). Comparative effectiveness of guided mastery and exposure treatments for intractable phobias. *Journal of Consulting and Clinical Psychology, 52*, 505–518.

Wright, S. C., Aron, A., McLaughlin-Volpe, T., & Ropp, S. A. (1997). The extended contact effect: Knowledge of cross-group friendships and prejudice. *Journal of Personality and Social Psychology, 73*, 73–90.

Wright, S. C., Aron, A., & Tropp, L. R. (2002). Including others (and groups) in the self: Self-expansion and intergroup relations. In J. P. Forgas & K. D. Williams (Eds.), *The social self: Cognitive, interpersonal and intergroup perspectives* (pp. 343–363). Philadelphia: Psychology Press.

Young, R. L. (1985). Perceptions of crime, racial attitudes, and firearms ownership. *Social Forces, 64*, 473–486.

Zajonc, R. B. (1998). Emotions. In D. T. Gilbert, S. T. Fiske, & G. Lindzey (Eds.), *The handbook of social psychology* (Vol. 1, 4th ed., pp. 591–632). New York: McGraw-Hill.

Zanna, M. P., & Rempel, J. K. (1988). Attitudes: A new look at an old concept. In D. Bar-Tal & A. W. Kruglanski (Eds.), *The social psychology of knowledge* (pp. 315–334). Cambridge, UK: Cambridge University Press.

Chapter 12

Emotional antecedents and consequences of common ingroup identity

Kelly M. Johnson, Samuel L. Gaertner, John F. Dovidio, Missy A. Houlette, Blake M. Riek, and Eric W. Mania

Research in intergroup relations and conflict has relied heavily on the role of social cognitive processes to understand the causes and consequences of intergroup bias (Brewer, 1979; Brown & Turner, 1981; Tajfel & Turner, 1979). Social cognition concerns how people process, store, and retrieve information, and the effects of these processes on how people perceive and interact with others (Hogg & Abrams, 1999). In addition, social cognitive processes, such as social categorization, have also been emphasized in developing strategies to reduce bias (e.g., Gaertner & Dovidio, 2000). Nevertheless, emotions also play an important, although much less researched, role (Mackie & Smith, 2002). The present chapter examines cognitive and affective processes relating to both the creation and the elimination of bias from the perspective of the common ingroup identity model (Gaertner & Dovidio, 2000; Gaertner, Dovidio, Anastasio, Bachman, & Rust, 1993).

We begin the chapter by presenting an overview of research on the effects of social categorization, which forms the basis of the common ingroup identity model. We then consider the potential role of affect within this framework, distinguishing between the moderating role of antecedent affect and the mediating role of consequent affect. After that, we examine the potential impact of positive and negative emotions on psychological processes generally, as well as with respect to how antecedent affect can influence the development of group representations within the model. Next, we explore how the affective consequences of social categorization and group representations contribute to intergroup attitudes and relations. We conclude by considering the conceptual and practical implications of affective processes on social cognition generally, and in the context of the common ingroup identity model specifically.

Social categorization and the common ingroup identity model

Social categorization into discrete groups begins a process whereby people benefit ingroup members relative to outgroup members in several ways. The mere categorization of people into ingroups and outgroups is sufficient to initiate, typically spontaneously (Otten & Moskowitz, 2000), an overall evaluative bias in which people categorized as ingroup members are evaluated more favorably than outgroup members (Brewer, 1979; Tajfel, 1970). Upon categorization, ingroup members are favored in reward allocation (Tajfel, Billig, Bundy, & Flament, 1971), qualitative recall of their behaviors (Howard & Rothbart, 1980), and evaluation of their work products (Ferguson & Kelley, 1964). These biases occur even when group membership is random (Billig & Tajfel, 1973) or created based on socially irrelevant criteria, such as whether one is an "overestimator" or "underestimator" (Howard & Rothbart, 1980). Perceptually, when people or objects are categorized into groups, actual differences between members of the same category tend to be minimized (Tajfel, 1969) and often ignored in making decisions or forming impressions, while between-group differences tend to become exaggerated (Abrams, 1985; Turner, 1985).

In addition, social categorization of people as ingroup and outgroup members has immediate affective consequences. Not only does social categorization make accessible specific group-associated traits, but it also elicits differently-valenced evaluative and affective reactions (Dovidio & Gaertner, 1993). At the most basic level is a more positive emotional response to ingroup members. As Brewer (1999) explained, "many forms of discrimination and bias may develop not because outgroups are hated, but because positive emotions such as admiration, sympathy, and trust are reserved for the ingroup and withheld from outgroups" (p. 438). However, unique emotional reactions (e.g., fear, disgust; see Mackie & Smith, 2002) may also be elicited through social categorization of people as members of meaningful and consequential outgroups. Also, people tend to attribute the capacity for different emotions to ingroup members than to outgroup members. Ingroup members are attributed higher-order, uniquely human emotions (or *sentiments*), such as love, hope, contempt, resentment, whereas outgroup members are attributed more basic, non-uniquely human emotions, such as joy, surprise, fear, and anger (Paladino et al., 2002).

Importantly, social categorization processes are not completely uncontrollable or unalterable, nor are they completely independent of emotion. Categories are hierarchically organized, and higher-level categories (e.g., animals) are more inclusive of lower-level ones (e.g., cats and dogs). By modifying a perceiver's goals, motives, past experiences, expectations, as well as factors within the perceptual field and the situational context more broadly, there is opportunity to alter the level of category inclusiveness that will be primary in a given situation. According to the common ingroup identity model, cognitive restructuring of how intergroup boundaries are conceived in terms of their level of inclusiveness alters how ingroup and outgroup members are perceived. Affect is relevant in two ways in this process. Antecedent affect can either facilitate or inhibit the development of a common ingroup identity. In addition, once group representations are developed, how people are socially categorized influences affective feelings toward them.

Specifically, perceptions that ingroup and outgroup members are one group, subgroups within a larger group, separate groups, or separate individuals, relate to intergroup affective reactions. For example, we have found converging evidence from laboratory experiments and field studies that stronger "one-group" and weaker "different-groups" representations lead to more positive affective reactions and behaviors toward the initial outgroup members (Gaertner & Dovidio, 2000). The evidence for the benefits of the "subgroups within a larger group" and the "separate individuals" representations is more mixed, however, and our current research is directed toward understanding when and why these representations lead to more positive or more negative intergroup outcomes.

These ideas about recategorization have also provided an explanation for how the apparently loosely-connected diverse features specified by Allport's (1954; see also Williams, 1947) contact hypothesis (i.e., equal status, cooperation, self-revealing interactions between the members, and supportive norms by authorities) may operate psychologically to reduce bias. Our model proposes that these features facilitate the benefits of contact because they transform members' cognitive representations of the memberships from "us" and "them" to a more inclusive "we" (Gaertner & Dovidio, 2000).

Although the emphasis of the common ingroup identity model has been on social categorization processes and cognitive representations of groups, affective processes have also been implicated. Indeed, bias resulting from social categorization produces emotionally-laden consequences from basic, emotion-free cognitive processes. In the next section, we review ways that affect can influence the types of processes hypothesized in the common ingroup identity model.

Affect and the common ingroup identity model

There are two basic qualities of affect that are important for understanding the role of emotions in the common ingroup identity model. First, within the common ingroup identity model (see Figure 12.1), affect can either precede cognitive representations and moderate or mediate the influence of structural factors, such as cooperation or competition, on the development of group representations, or it can be a consequence of the development of different cognitive representations, reflecting an outcome in its own right or acting as a mediator to other consequences, such as attitudes and actions. The second dimension is the valence of the emotion; that is, whether it represents positive or negative affect. Although we recognize the role that

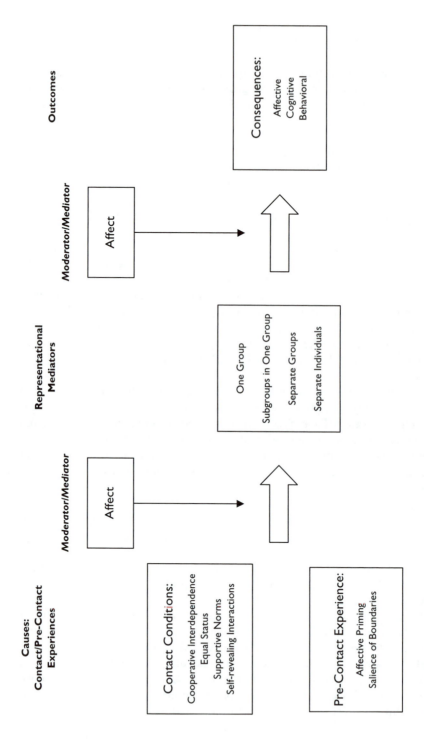

Figure 12.1 Affect and the common ingroup identity model.

differentiated emotions have in intergroup relations (Mackie & Smith, 2002), we focus in this chapter on the general influence that positive and negative affect can have in the context of the model. In the next section we explore how antecedent affect can influence key processes in intergroup relations hypothesized in the common ingroup identity model.

The role of antecedent affect

Within the common ingroup identity model, antecedent affect can significantly influence the social categorization process, and ultimately facilitate or inhibit recategorization processes. This affect may occur incidentally, generated by a seemingly-irrelevant source within the intergroup context, or it may be integral to the nature of the intergroup context (Bodenhausen, 1993). For example, incidental affect may result from a serendipitous event, such as receiving an unexpected gift of candy, before intergroup interaction. In contrast, integral affect (e.g., disgust) may be aroused directly from anticipated interaction with a member of a hated group. Although incidental and integral affect may differ in their attributional implications, they may also have similar influences on basic processes.

Emotions energize and organize thoughts and behavior (Izard, 1991). Not only do people experience emotions because of an event, but those emotions consequently influence how people interpret and respond to others, thereby having implications for intergroup encounters and impressions. Affect can cause selective attention to, and recall of, information that is congruent with one's mood (Bower, 1981). For example, happy, relative to sad, individuals form more favorable impressions and recall more positive information about others (Forgas & Bower, 1987).

Affect can also differentially influence the use of heuristics (i.e., mental shortcuts) in social judgments, which is associated with stereotyping (e.g., Bodenhausen, Kramer, & Süsser, 1994; Bodenhausen, Sheppard, & Kramer, 1994). In some circumstances, such as those that are cognitively demanding, affect may generally facilitate heuristic processing (Mackie & Worth, 1989). Under these conditions, the physiological arousal associated with affect, whether positive or negative, may further tax the person's limited processing capacity, leading to increased reliance on stereotypes and to salient cues in the context (for review, see Bodenhausen, 1993; cf. Bohner & Weinerth, 2000).

Under different circumstances, positive and negative affect can both produce *decreased* reliance on heuristics in cognitive processing. Isen (1987) has argued that positive affect influences the organization of cognitive material by encouraging elaborative processing. According to Isen, positive affect increases the accessibility of diverse ideas and produces a more complex associative context than normally occurs (Isen, Johnson, Mertz, & Robinson, 1985). In other situations, though, positive affect can reduce the *motivation* to engage in elaborative thinking because it signals the safety of the current situation (e.g., Schwarz, 1990; Schwarz & Clore, 1983). Negative emotions, such as fear and guilt, can decrease heuristic responses and produce more elaborated thinking because these emotions signal a need to respond carefully to the environment (Bohner & Weinerth, 2000). Thus, the effects of emotion are complex, moderated by contextual cues, cognitive demand, and the valence and nature of the affect involved.

Within the common ingroup identity model, because of its significant emphasis on cognitive processing and hence social categorization, antecedent affect, both positive and negative, can substantially influence the nature of intergroup interaction. In the next section we illustrate how antecedent positive and negative affect can influence central processes within the common ingroup identity model.

Positive affect

Our work on positive affect has focused primarily on how it can moderate categorization, particularly social categorization (see Figure 12.1; see also Dovidio, Gaertner, & Loux, 2000). In particular, Dovidio, Gaertner, Isen, and Lowrance (1995) hypothesized that in nonthreatening and less cognitively demanding contexts, such as those involving arbitrarily assigned laboratory groups, positive affect could produce more inclusive social categorization with a positively-valenced category, the ingroup, facilitating the recategorization of outgroup members as ingroup members.

Using nonsocial stimuli, Isen and Daubman (1984) found that incidental positive affect induced with humorous tapes or gifts of candy or cookies caused more flexible thinking and broader category inclusion among participants asked to categorize various objects. Specifically, when asked to rate how well certain objects (e.g., belt) fit into various categories (e.g., clothing), participants experiencing positive affect rated non-typical, but plausible, objects as more highly characteristic of the category relative to those experiencing neutral affect. Extending these findings to social stimuli, Isen, Niedenthal, and Cantor (1992) found that positive affect increased the inclusion of non-typical exemplars (e.g., a bartender) into categories, particularly socially desirable categories (e.g., nurturant people), as well.

We further examined the hypothesis that antecedent positive affect can moderate social categorization (see Figure 12.1) in an experiment in which university students participated in a "group problem-solving" activity (Dovidio et al., 1995). Participants first formed a group by working together on a problem-solving task. Next, the *affective-priming* manipulation was introduced. After the small group interaction, participants in the condition designed to produce positive affect were given a gift of candy (Isen & Daubman, 1984); in the control condition, no mention of candy was made. Then participants were informed that they would be interacting with another group on a different problem-solving task. After viewing a brief videotape of the other group, supposedly to provide baseline measures, participants were asked their impressions about whether the groups would interact as different entities or as one group, and to evaluate each of the members of the other group and their own group.

Supporting the hypothesis that positive affect increases cognitive flexibility and ingroup inclusiveness, participants who experienced positive affect, relative to those in the control condition, had stronger perceptions of a common ingroup identity, more favorable evaluations of outgroup members and, consequently, lower levels of bias. Furthermore, the relation between priming positive affect and intergroup bias was mediated by participants' inclusive group representations. Bias was lower when participants saw the people more as one group and less as two groups. Thus, in the absence of strong contextual cues or well-defined intergroup relations, positive affect produced more favorable intergroup relations through the processes hypothesized in the common ingroup identity model. As illustrated in Figure 12.1, affective priming prior to contact influences cognitive representation and ultimately intergroup attitudes.

The manner in which affect influences cognitive processes may also vary as a function of the context of decision making (Isen, 1993). That is, if, as Isen (1987, 1993) suggests, positive affect facilitates elaborative processing, then the nature of information available can moderate the influence of positive affect on attitudes and behavior. If the intergroup context is one that promotes more inclusive group representations and favorable interactions, such as exists during cooperative activities (Gaertner et al., 1993), positive affect could facilitate more positive intergroup attitudes. In contrast, if the situation is one that reinforces separate group identities and negative interactions, such as occurs with competitive tasks, positive affect may produce greater levels of intergroup bias compared to neutral affect. Thus, the effects we obtained by manipulating affect in the previous experiment may not necessarily generalize to situations involving explicit competitive relations between groups or to group with histories of competition, conflict, and biases that have produced strong and meaningful intergroup boundaries.

To explore this possibility, in a subsequent study of the moderating effects of antecedent positive affect we manipulated whether participants experienced positive or neutral affect (induced via humorous or informational videotapes) and whether they expected an upcoming intergroup interaction to be cooperative or competitive (Dovidio et al., 2000, Study 2). As predicted, under cooperative conditions, participants induced to have positive affect had more favorable impressions of outgroup members relative to those in the neutral condition; when competition was anticipated, however, positive-affect participants had less positive attitudes toward outgroup members than did neutral-affect participants. Further analyses across conditions revealed that, as hypothesized, when participants expected cooperation, greater positive affect was associated with significantly stronger perceptions of a common ingroup identity ($r = .36$). In contrast, when participants anticipated competition, greater positive affect tended to be related to weaker perceptions of a common ingroup identity ($r = -.11$). These results generally support the hypothesis that positive affect, in this case incidental affect, can moderate the impact of contextual features of the intergroup contact situation (see Figure 12.1) and influence common ingroup perceptions and consequent intergroup attitudes.

Not only does affect interact with intergroup context to influence cognitive representation and outgroup evaluations, but affect can also interact with manipulations of cognitive representations to shape outgroup evaluations (Dovidio, Gaertner, Isen, Rust, & Guerra, 1998). For example, in a study using groups with meaningful boundaries (e.g., liberals and conservatives), Dovidio et al. manipulated incidental affect (positive or neutral) by offering some participants candy just before the manipulation of the type of social categorization that was emphasized (i.e., two separate groups vs. subgroups within a group – a dual identity). Salience of categorization was manipulated by the manner in which participants were instructed to refer to their own and the other group throughout the experiment. In the different-groups condition, participants referred to one another solely by their subgroup identities (i.e., "Liberals" and "Conservatives"). In the dual-identity condition, they used both their common superordinate, Colgate university identity and their political subgroup identities (i.e., "Colgate Liberals" and "Colgate Conservatives").

The results indicated that, in the different-groups context, participants in the positive affect condition exhibited more negative evaluations of outgroup members and higher bias relative to neutral affect participants. In the dual-identity condition, however, positive affect participants reported more positive evaluations for outgroup members and lower bias relative to those with neutral affect. Also, as expected, path analyses for the dual-identity condition indicated that manipulation of positive affect created higher levels of self-reported positive affect which predicted more inclusive group representations, which then predicted lower levels of bias. Although in this particular study positive or neutral affect was introduced prior to manipulating members' separate groups or dual-identity representations, we believe that reversing the order by first manipulating cognitive representations and then affect would have similar interactive effects on intergroup bias. Hence, in Figure 12.1, affect is positioned as a potential moderator both before and after cognitive representations.

Crisp and Hewstone (2000) have similarly found that under conditions of crossed categorization, when a person shared category membership on one dimension but not the other, participants in a positive affect condition showed lower levels of discrimination than did those in a neutral mood condition. These findings converge to illustrate the way that positive affect can interact with manipulations of group identities to produce more positive outgroup evaluations and lower levels of intergroup bias.

In the next section we review the consequences of *negative* affect, in particular intergroup anxiety, on the development of a common ingroup identity and intergroup bias.

Negative affect

Intergroup anxiety and fear are integral emotions that commonly characterize intergroup interaction (Schopler & Insko, 1992; Stephan & Stephan, 1985). As depicted in Figure 12.1, antecedent negative affect can moderate or mediate the processes identified in the common ingroup identity model, and the reduction of negative affect as a consequence of recategorization can mediate reductions in bias.

Negative affect can moderate the processes implicated in the common ingroup identity model by reducing the likelihood that people will engage in behaviors, such as intergroup contact, that can reduce intergroup bias, at least in part because of cognitive representations. For example, we found that intergroup anxiety was significantly associated with lower levels of intergroup contact for both Whites ($r = -.38$) and minorities ($r = -.27$) on a college campus (Dovidio & Gaertner, 2003). The avoidance of outgroups caused by intergroup anxiety and fear (Plant & Devine, 2003) precludes improving intergroup relations through positive intergroup contact experiences.

Alternatively, negative affect can influence the effectiveness of interventions, such as those involving contact. That is, even when contact occurs, anxiety and fear may exacerbate instead of reduce bias (see Pettigrew & Tropp, 2000; Voci & Hewstone, 2003) through processes identified in the common ingroup identity model. Both anxiety and fear increase selective attention to threatening stimuli and produce negative interpretations of ambiguous information (Mathews & MacLeod, 1994). As a consequence, flexibility in cognitive processes is decreased for attributes directly associated with potential threat (Beck & Clark, 1997). Higher levels of intergroup anxiety and perceived threat therefore tend to strengthen original ingroup–outgroup boundaries, increasing category-based thinking (Wilder, 1993) and reducing the opportunity for recategorization to occur. In one study (Dovidio & Gaertner, 2003), we found that negative affective reactions (e.g., feeling uneasy) of Whites to Blacks predicted weaker one-group representations for Whites ($r = -.23$), and these affective reactions of Blacks to Whites predicted stronger different-groups representations for Blacks ($r = .36$).

Affective reactions, however, can also mediate the relation between conditions of contact and cognitive representations. In one study guided by the common ingroup identity model, Bachman (1993) examined retrospective reports of banking executives who experienced a corporate merger. Using path analysis (LISREL) to test the assumed causal chain proposed by our model between contact conditions, intergroup threat, and cognitive representations, in addition to other variables not directly relevant to this chapter (see Figure 12.1), Bachman (see Gaertner, Bachman, Dovidio, & Banker, 2001) found that more positive perceptions of the conditions of contact predicted decreased intergroup threat ($\beta = -.28$), which in turn predicted decreased employees' representations of the merged organization as two separate groups ($\beta = .30$). These results support the idea that the relationship between intergroup contact and cognitive representations can be mediated by affective experience. Nevertheless, because this survey study is cross-sectional, support for the proposed causal order between affect and cognitive representations is somewhat equivocal.

Greenland and Brown's (1999, Study 2) longitudinal study (over 12 months) of Japanese college students in the United Kingdom allowed a more powerful causal examination of the potential effect of negative affect on group representations. Consistent with our proposed direction of causality, Greenland and Brown's analyses revealed that students who reported higher levels of intergroup anxiety early in the program more strongly maintained their representation of the Japanese and English students as two different groups later in the program. Thus, Greenland and Brown's longitudinal analyses indicate that intergroup anxiety can *precede* and influence cognitive representation of intergroup boundaries.

The overall pattern of findings across studies offers some support for the proposed mediating effects of emotions (illustrated in Figure 12.1) between conditions of intergroup contact and members' cognitive representations (as one group or two groups). That is, contact conditions can influence threat and anxiety (Bachman, see Gaertner et al., 2001), which in turn alter perceptions of the intergroup boundary (Greenland & Brown, 1999).

As we noted earlier, both positive and negative affect can be either incidental or integral. For example, in terms of integral affect, intergroup interdependence can yield successful or unsuccessful outcomes. Successful outcomes, which produce positive affective reactions, are likely to facilitate more inclusive group representations and thereby reduce intergroup bias more effectively. In contrast, failure in intergroup endeavors is likely to elicit negative affect, which would increase the salience of the different group boundaries and consequently increase bias. Although the processes hypothesized in the common ingroup identity model have not been fully explored under these conditions, the predicted outcomes have been obtained. Intergroup contact that yields success reduces bias more effectively than intergroup contact that does not result in success, and intergroup interdependence associated with failure exacerbates bias (Blanchard, Adelman, & Cook, 1975; Worchel, 1978).

Taken together these results illustrate, as depicted in Figure 12.1, the significant but complex moderating and mediating roles of positive and negative affect on group representations and intergroup relations. Thus far we have discussed how affect (a) can directly influence cognitive representations, (b) can interact with whether contact is cooperative or competitive to influence cognitive representations, (c) can interact with manipulations of cognitive representation as separate groups and subgroups within a superordinate boundary (i.e., a dual identity), and (d) can mediate the relation between conditions of contact and perceptions of intergroup boundaries. We have argued that it is the interplay between affect and cognitive representations that can influence attitudes toward outgroup members. In the next section we discuss evidence suggesting that cognitive representation can have affective consequences, which in turn influence overall attitudinal favorability toward outgroup members.

Affective consequences of social categorization

As reviewed earlier, categorizing a person as an ingroup member results in more positive affect, beliefs, and behavior toward that person. For example, Otten and Moskowitz (2000) found that simply classifying individuals as members of the same group spontaneously increased their positive affective regard for one another. Additional research related to the common ingroup identity model (see Gaertner & Dovidio, 2000) consistently suggests that recategorization of people from separate groups to a common superordinate identity that is inclusive of ingroup and former outgroup members engages those same cognitive and motivational processes that produce favorable reactions to ingroup members. For example, we found that inducing a common identity among the members of two formerly separate groups increases perceptions of trust, honesty, valuableness, and likeableness of the initial outgroup members (Gaertner, Mann, Dovidio, Murrell, & Pomare, 1990), increases self-disclosure of personally revealing information across group boundaries, and also increases pro-social behavior (Dovidio et al., 1997).

We have found, among a variety of laboratory experiments and field studies involving diverse populations (ranging from elementary school children to corporate executives and stepfathers), that inducing a common ingroup identity between groups increases positive feelings, beliefs, and behaviors toward people who were initially categorized as outgroup members. One was a field study in a multicultural high school (Gaertner, Rust, Dovidio, Bachman, & Anastasio, 1994) involving many different groups including sizable numbers of White, Black, Japanese, Vietnamese, and Korean students. Our survey included students' perceptions of the quality of the contact conditions, their representations of the student body as one group, different groups on the same team, or separate groups, their affective reactions toward ingroup and outgroup members (e.g., frequency that a particular race/ethnicity made the participant feel good, bad, uneasy, or respectful), and a measure of their overall attitudinal favorability toward their ingroup and each of the outgroups.

The results of this study supported the proposed mediating role of reducing consequent negative affect on the reduction of bias (see Figure 12.1). Supportive of our expectations, students' responses indicated that the more favorably they perceived the conditions of contact between the different student groups at school, the lower their bias in affective reactions toward ingroups and outgroups as well as their bias in overall favorability toward these groups. Similarly, favorable conditions of contact predicted stronger one-group and two-subgroup representations, as well as weaker perceptions of the student body as separate groups. Mediation analysis revealed that the relation between conditions of contact and bias in affective feelings was mediated partly by students' conceptual representations of the student body. Thus, the stronger their common identity representations (one group and two subgroups), the lower their bias in affective reactions to outgroup members. In addition, supportive of the earlier work of Stangor, Sullivan, and Ford (1991) that revealed the importance of affect for determining overall attitudinal favorability, we found that bias in students' affective feelings toward the different groups, as well as their different group representations, mediated the relationship between the favorableness of the conditions of contact and overall attitudinal favorability. In other words, these analyses suggested a particular path of effects; specifically, that contact led to changes in cognitive representation, which led to changes in affective reaction, which then, together with their cognitive representation of the student body, led to perceptions of overall outgroup favorability. Importantly, these paths of effects revealed by mediation analyses suggest that both cognitive representation and affect can independently, and in concert, influence overall favorability of intergroup attitudes.

Evidence also shows that a common ingroup identity can increase positive affect for outgroup members, reflected by increased likelihood to select outgroup members as friends. That is, choosing an outgroup member as a friend is an indirect indication of positive affect experienced toward that outgroup member, and potentially toward the outgroup as a whole. For example, Levin, van Laar, and Sidanius (2003), in a four-year, longitudinal study of college students, found that a stronger common ingroup identity as students during their first year at college increased students' likelihood of having outgroup friends. Specifically, the more students perceived the student body as one group rather than separate groups (in terms of racial makeup) at the end of their first year, the more outgroup friendships they had in their second and third college years. Thus, positive affective consequences resulting from the broadening of ingroup boundaries increase the likelihood of embracing outgroup members as friends.

In a recent study (Houlette et al., 2004), we attempted to evaluate these principles further in the context of an elementary school intervention program, Green Circle, designed to combat a range of biases (based on weight and sex, as well as race and ethnicity) with young children. The guiding assumption of the Green Circle Program, which is practically and theoretically compatible with the common ingroup identity model, is that helping children to bring people from different groups conceptually into their own circle of caring and sharing fosters appreciation of their common humanity as well as respect for their differences. In particular, facilitators who visit each class for about forty minutes per session four times over a four-week period engage children in a variety of exercises designed to expand their circle of inclusion. During the sessions, children are shown a small green circle on a felt board and told, "Whenever you see the green circle, you should think about your world of people; the people who you care about and the people who care about you." A stick figure is added to the circle and the students are told that the figure represents themselves. The facilitator explains that each person has "a big job of deciding who is going to be in your circle, how to treat people, and how big your circle will grow". At this point, the facilitator shows additional stick figures placed outside the circle. Then, after removing the smaller green circle, the facilitator replaces it with a larger circle, one large enough to include the other figures. Using different contexts, the facilitator repeats this procedure several times. Eventually, the facilitator points out that "All of us belong to one family – the human family."

Paralleling the common ingroup identity model, Green Circle assumes that an appreciation of common humanity will increase children's positive attitudes toward people who would otherwise remain outside their circle of inclusion. First- and second-graders either participated in the Green Circle Program or were in a control group of classes that did not yet have the program.

In terms of outcomes, the Green Circle intervention motivated the children to be more inclusive in their most preferred playmate. Specifically, compared to control children, those who were part of Green Circle showed significantly greater change in willingness to select other children (from a series of specially commissioned drawings) who were different from themselves in race and in sex as a child that they would "most want to play with." This finding suggests that the children exposed to the program increased their positive evaluations of children who were different from themselves because they broadened their circle of inclusion. These changes in the most preferred playmate involve a child's greater willingness to cross group boundaries in making friends – a factor that is one of the most potent influences in producing more positive attitudes toward the outgroup as a whole (Pettigrew, 1998). In addition, these intergroup friendships can have cascading effects by reducing bias among peers. Making people aware that their friends have friends from another group also reduces prejudice toward the group as a whole (Wright, Aron, McLaughlin-Volpe, & Ropp, 1997).

Conclusion

Although social cognition has played a central role in the study of prejudice and discrimination generally and in the development and tests of the common ingroup identity model, affect is also fundamentally important. Prejudice, discrimination, and racism are words that evoke images suffused with emotions, and history is rife with examples of clashing group interests accompanied by intense emotional reactions. Even in the absence of prior contact, anticipating contact with a particular group (Stephan & Stephan, 1985) or the mere knowledge that it exists can generate strong emotional responses (Sherif, Harvey, White, Hood, & Sherif, 1961). Also, as exemplified by the Sherif et al.'s classic summer camp studies, the functional relation between groups during intergroup interaction determines the nature of the members' emotional reactions to one another. When two groups of summer campers competed in a series of athletic events, they expressed anger, intense dislike, and aggressive behaviors toward each other. When the groups interacted cooperatively to achieve goals desired by each group, members of both groups were cheerful, expressed outgroup friendship preferences, and behaved generously and compassionately toward each other.

Recent approaches that examine the role of emotion and social cognition on intergroup behavior consider how cognitive and affective systems interact and influence each other in a dynamic, integrative framework (see Bless & Forgas, 2000; Mackie & Hamilton, 1993). In the current chapter we described research related to the common ingroup identity model (Gaertner & Dovidio, 2000; Gaertner et al., 1993) in which cognitive and affective factors are assumed to play an important but complicated role. The work related to the common ingroup identity model described in this chapter identifies the critical influence of affect in two general aspects of the framework, both as an antecedent moderating factor for social categorization and as an important consequence of social categorization (see Figure 12.1). As an *antecedent* factor, affect influences how intergroup boundaries are cognitively represented directly or as a moderating influence for structural factors, such as the nature of intergroup interdependence, or for interventions aimed at altering group representations (e.g., dual-identity or crossed categorization interventions).

Affect as a *consequence* of social cognitive processes within the common ingroup identity model is a significant outcome in itself, but it also can further mediate intergroup attitudes and behaviors as well (Stangor et al., 1991). With respect to behavior, an emotional reaction toward an outgroup increases the tendency to enact behaviors such as moving against or away from the group (Mackie, Devos, & Smith, 2000; Smith, 1993). For example, anger toward an outgroup increases the desire to confront, oppose, or argue (Mackie et al., 2000). Thus, both antecedent and consequent affect represent potential routes to be used separately, or in unison, to improve intergroup relations.

Moreover, antecedent and consequent affect may be iterative and reinforcing. As we described earlier, positive affect can lead people to focus on the favorable qualities of others, emphasize similarities more than differences, be more inclusive in positively-valenced categories (such as the ingroup), and think beyond stereotypes in more elaborated and differentiated ways (Isen, 1987). Thus, as stereotypes are undermined and others are seen in more individuated ways, intergroup contact is more likely to occur and to occur in more personalized ways (Pettigrew, 1998). Favorable personalized interaction is then likely to produce more positive outcomes and affect, which will continue to erode original group boundaries and facilitate recategorization. Analogously, increasing the salience of different group boundaries can elicit both negative affective reactions and stereotypic associations, which further emphasize difference and potential threat. Thus, affect that is the consequence of social categorization processes (see Figure 12.1) can, in operating as antecedent affect in subsequent situations, further influence social cognitive and social categorization processes.

As a consequence of the potentially iterative influence of antecedent and consequent affect, altering the two in combination may improve intergroup outcomes to a greater extent than simply relying on one over the other. For example, inducing positive affect among executives in a newly-merged corporation using rewards, while simultaneously emphasizing common ingroup membership in the new organization, would be expected to improve relations among the two groups to a greater extent than merely increasing positive affect or common ingroup perceptions separately. Nevertheless, it must be kept in mind that contextual factors such as presence of cooperative or competitive interdependence may moderate the effects of either variable. Therefore to fully utilize the strengths of affective or cognitive representation manipulations in intergroup contexts, one must simultaneously consider other important intergroup variables such as those described in the current chapter. Nonetheless, influencing affect and increasing a common ingroup identity generally offer two promising avenues for more harmonious intergroup relations.

Acknowledgement

Preparation of this chapter was supported by NIMH Grant MH 48721 to the second and third authors.

References

Abrams, D. (1985). Focus of attention in minimal intergroup discrimination. *British Journal of Social Psychology, 24*, 65–74.

Allport, G. W. (1954). *The nature of prejudice.* New York: Addison-Wesley.

Bachman, B. A. (1993). *An intergroup model of organizational mergers.* Unpublished doctoral dissertation, University of Delaware, Newark.

Beck, A. T., & Clark, D. A., (1997). An information processing model of anxiety: Automatic and strategic processes. *Behaviour Research and Therapy, 35*, 49–58.

Billig, M. G., & Tajfel, H. (1973). Social categorization and similarity in intergroup behaviour. *European Journal of Social Psychology, 3*, 27–52.

Blanchard, F. A., Adelman, L., & Cook, S. W. (1975). Effect of group success and failure upon interpersonal attraction in cooperating interracial groups. *Journal of Personality and Social Psychology, 31*, 1020–1030.

Bless, H., & Forgas, J. P. (Eds.). (2000). *The message within: The role of subjective experience in social cognition and behavior.* Philadelphia: Psychology Press.

Bodenhausen, G. V. (1993). Emotions, arousal, and stereotypic judgments: A heuristic model of affect and stereotyping. In D. M. Mackie & D. L. Hamilton (Eds.), *Affect, cognition, and stereotyping: Interactive processes in group perception* (pp. 13–37). San Diego, CA: Academic Press.

Bodenhausen, G. V., Kramer, G. P., & Süsser, K. (1994). Happiness and stereotypic thinking in social judgment. *Journal of Personality and Social Psychology, 66*, 621–632.

Bodenhausen, G. V., Sheppard, L. A., & Kramer, G. P. (1994). Negative affect and social perception: The differential impact of anger and sadness. *European Journal of Social Psychology, 24*, 45–62.

Bohner, G., & Weinerth, T. (2000). Negative affect and persuasion: The role of affect interpretation. In H. Bless & J. P. Forgas (Eds.), *The message within: The role of subjective experience in social cognition and behavior* (pp. 216–239). Philadelphia: Psychology Press.

Bower, G. H. (1981). Mood and memory. *American Psychologist, 36*, 129–148.

Brewer, M. B. (1979). Ingroup bias in the minimal intergroup situation: A cognitive-motivational analysis. *Psychological Bulletin, 86*, 307–324.

Brewer, M. B. (1999). The psychology of prejudice: Ingroup love or outgroup hate? *Journal of Social Issues, 55*, 429–444.

Brown, R., & Turner, J. C. (1981). Interpersonal and intergroup behaviour. In J. C. Turner & H. Giles (Eds.), *Intergroup behaviour* (pp. 33–65). Oxford, UK: Blackwell.

Crisp, R. J., & Hewstone, M. (2000). Crossed categorization and intergroup bias: The moderating roles of intergroup and affective context. *Journal of Experimental Social Psychology, 36*, 357–383.

Dovidio, J. F., & Gaertner, S. L. (1993). Stereotypes and evaluative intergroup bias. In D. M. Mackie & D. L. Hamilton (Eds.), *Affect, cognition, and stereotyping: Interactive processes in group perception* (pp. 167–193). San Diego, CA: Academic Press.

Dovidio, J. F., & Gaertner, S. L. (2003). [*Unpublished raw data*]. Colgate University, Hamilton, New York.

Dovidio, J. F., Gaertner, S. L., Isen, A. M., & Lowrance, R. (1995). Group representations and intergroup bias: Positive affect, similarity, and group size. *Personality and Social Psychology Bulletin, 21*, 856–865.

Dovidio, J. F., Gaertner, S. L., Isen, A. M., Rust, M. C., & Guerra, P. (1998). Positive affect, cognition, and the reduction of intergroup bias. In C. Sedikides, J. Schopler, & C. A. Insko (Eds.), *Intergroup cognition and intergroup behavior* (pp. 337–366). Mahwah, NJ: Lawrence Erlbaum Associates Inc.

Dovidio, J. F., Gaertner, S. L., & Loux, S. (2000). Subjective experiences and intergroup relations: The role of positive affect. In H. Bless & J. P. Forgas (Eds.), *The message within: The role of subjective experience in social cognition and behavior* (pp. 340–371). Philadelphia: Psychology Press.

Dovidio, J. F., Gaertner, S. L., Validzic, A., Matoka, K., Johnson, B., & Frazier, S. (1997). Extending the benefits of recategorization: Evaluations, self-disclosure, and helping. *Journal of Experimental Social Psychology, 33*, 401–420.

Ferguson, C. K., & Kelley, H. H. (1964). Significant factors in over evaluations of own-groups' product. *Journal of Abnormal and Social Psychology, 69*, 223–228.

Forgas, J. P., & Bower, G. H. (1987). Mood effects on person-perception judgments. *Journal of Personality and Social Psychology, 53*, 53–60.

Gaertner, S. L., Bachman, B. A., Dovidio, J. F., & Banker, B. S. (2001). Corporate mergers and stepfamily marriages: Identity, harmony, and commitment. In M. A. Hogg & D. J. Terry (Eds.), *Social identity processes in organizational contexts* (pp. 265–282). Ann Arbor, MI: Sheridan Books.

Gaertner, S. L., & Dovidio, J. F. (2000). *Reducing intergroup bias: The common ingroup identity model.* Philadelphia: Psychology Press.

Gaertner, S. L., Dovidio, J. F., Anastasio, P. A., Bachman, B. A., & Rust, M. C. (1993). The common ingroup identity model: Recategorization and the reduction of intergroup bias. In W. Stroebe & M. Hewstone (Eds.), *European review of social psychology* (Vol. 4, pp. 1–26). Chichester, UK: Wiley.

Gaertner, S. L., Mann, J. A., Dovidio, J. F., Murrell, A. J., & Pomare, M. (1990). How does cooperation reduce intergroup bias? *Journal of Personality and Social Psychology, 59*, 692–704.

Gaertner, S. L., Rust, M. C., Dovidio, J. F., Bachman, B. A., & Anastasio, P. A. (1994). The contact hypothesis: The role of a common ingroup identity on reducing intergroup bias. *Small Group Research, 25*, 224–249.

Greenland, K., & Brown, R. (1999). Categorization and intergroup anxiety in contact between British and Japanese nationals. *European Journal of Social Psychology, 29*, 503–521.

Hogg, M. A., & Abrams, D. (1999). Social identity and social cognition: Historical background and current trends. In D. Abrams & M. A. Hogg (Eds.), *Social identity and social cognition* (pp. 1–25). Oxford, UK: Blackwell.

Houlette, M. A., Gaertner, S. L., Johnson, K. M., Banker, B. S., Riek, B. M., & Dovidio, J. F. (2004). Developing a more inclusive social identity: An elementary school intervention. *Journal of Social Issues, 60*, 35–55.

Howard, J. W., & Rothbart, M. (1980). Social categorization and memory for in-group and out-group behavior. *Journal of Personality and Social Psychology, 38*, 301–310.

Isen, A. M. (1987). Positive affect, cognitive processes, and social behavior. In L. Berkowitz (Ed.), *Advances in experimental social psychology* (Vol. 20, pp. 203–253). San Diego, CA: Academic Press.

Isen, A. M. (1993). Positive affect and decision making. In M. Lewis & J. M. Haviland (Eds.) *Handbook of emotions* (pp. 261–277). New York: Guilford Press.

Isen, A. M., & Daubman, K. A. (1984). The influence of affect on categorization. *Journal of Personality and Social Psychology, 47*, 1206–1217.

Isen, A. M., Johnson, M. M., Mertz, E., & Robinson, G. F. (1985). The influence of positive affect on the unusualness of word associations. *Journal of Personality and Social Psychology, 48*, 1413–1426.

Isen, A. M., Niedenthal, P. M., & Cantor, N. (1992). An influence of positive affect on social categorization. *Motivation and Emotion, 16*, 65–78.

Izard, C. E. (1991). *The psychology of emotions.* New York: Plenum Press.

Levin, S., van Laar, C., & Sidanius, J. (2003). The effects of ingroup and outgroup friendships on ethnic attitudes in college: A longitudinal study. *Group Processes and Intergroup Relations, 6*, 76–92.

Mackie, D. M., Devos, T., & Smith, E. R. (2000). Intergroup emotions: Explaining offensive action tendencies in an intergroup context. *Journal of Personality and Social Psychology, 79*, 602–616.

Mackie, D. M., & Hamilton, D. L. (Eds.). (1993). *Affect, cognition, and stereotyping: Interactive processes in group perception.* San Diego, CA: Academic Press.

Mackie, D. M., & Smith, E. R. (Eds.). (2002). *From prejudice to intergroup emotions: Differentiated reactions to social groups.* New York: Psychology Press.

Mackie, D. M., & Worth, L. T. (1989). Processing deficits and the mediation of positive affect in persuasion. *Journal of Personality and Social Psychology, 57*, 27–40.

Mathews, A., & MacLeod, C. (1994). Cognitive approaches to emotion and emotional disorders. *Annual Review of Psychology, 45*, 25–50.

Otten, S., & Moskowitz, G. B. (2000). Evidence for implicit evaluative in-group bias: Affect-based spontaneous trait inference in a minimal group paradigm. *Journal of Experimental Social Psychology, 36*, 77–89.

Paladino, M. P., Leyens, J.-Ph., Rodriguez, R., Rodriguez, A., Gaunt, R., & Demoulin, S. (2002). Differential association of uniquely and non uniquely human emotions with the ingroup and the outgroups. *Group Processes and Intergroup Relations, 5*, 105–117.

Pettigrew, T. F. (1998). Intergroup contact theory. *Annual Review of Psychology, 49*, 65–85.

Pettigrew, T. F., & Tropp, L. R. (2000). Does intergroup contact reduce prejudice? Recent meta-analytic findings. In S. Oskamp (Ed.), *Reducing prejudice and discrimination* (pp. 93–114). Mahwah, NJ: Lawrence Erlbaum Associates Inc.

Plant, E. A., & Devine, P. G. (2003). The antecedents and implications of interracial anxiety. *Personality and Social Psychology Bulletin, 29*, 790–801.

Schopler, J., & Insko, C. A. (1992). The discontinuity effect in interpersonal and intergroup relations: Generality and mediation. In W. Stroebe & M. Hewstone (Eds.), *European review of social psychology* (Vol. 3, pp. 121–151). Chichester, UK: Wiley.

Schwarz, N. (1990). Feelings as information: Informational and motivational functions of affective states. In E. T. Higgins & R. M. Sorrentino (Eds.), *Handbook of motivation and cognition: Foundations of social behavior* (Vol. 2, pp. 527–561). New York: Guilford Press.

Schwarz, N., & Clore, G. L. (1983). Mood, misattribution, and judgments of well-being: Informative and directive functions of affective states. *Journal of Personality and Social Psychology, 45,* 513–523.

Sherif, M., Harvey, L. J., White, B. J., Hood, W. R., & Sherif, C. W. (1961). *Intergroup cooperation and competition: The Robber's Cave experiment.* Norman, OK: University Book Exchange.

Smith, E. R. (1993). Social identity and social emotions: Toward new conceptualizations of prejudice. In D. M. Mackie & D. L. Hamilton (Eds.), *Affect, cognition, and stereotyping: Interactive processes in group perception* (pp. 297–315). San Diego, CA: Academic Press.

Stangor, C., Sullivan, L. A., & Ford, T. E. (1991). Affective and cognitive determinants of prejudice. *Social Cognition, 9,* 359–380.

Stephan, W. G., & Stephan C. W. (1985). Intergroup anxiety. *Journal of Social Issues, 41,* 157–175.

Tajfel, H. (1969). Cognitive aspects of prejudice. *Journal of Social Issues, 25,* 79–97.

Tajfel, H. (1970). Experiments in intergroup discrimination. *Scientific American, 223,* 96–102.

Tajfel, H., Billig, M. G., Bundy, R. P., & Flament, C. (1971). Social categorization and intergroup behaviour. *European Journal of Social Psychology, 1,* 149–178.

Tajfel, H., & Turner, J. C. (1979). An integrative theory of intergroup conflict. In W. G. Austin & S. Worchel (Eds.), *The social psychology of intergroup relations* (pp. 33–47). Monterey, CA: Brooks/Cole.

Turner, J. C. (1985). Social categorization and the self-concept: A social cognitive theory of group behavior. In E. J. Lawler (Ed.), *Advances in group processes: Theory and research* (Vol. 2, pp. 77–122). Greenwich, CT: JAI Press.

Voci, A., & Hewstone, M. (2003). Intergroup contact and prejudice toward immigrants in Italy: The mediational role of anxiety and the moderational role of group salience. *Group Processes and Intergroup Relations, 6,* 37–54.

Wilder, D. A. (1993). The role of anxiety in facilitating stereotypic judgments of outgroup behavior. In D. M. Mackie & D. L. Hamilton (Eds.), *Affect, cognition, and stereotyping: Interactive processes in group perception* (pp. 87–109). San Diego, CA: Academic Press.

Williams, R. M. Jr. (1947). *The reduction of intergroup tensions.* New York: Social Science Research Council.

Worchel, S. (1978). Determinants of the effect of intergroup cooperation on intergroup attraction. *Journal of Conflict Resolution, 22,* 393–410.

Wright, S. C., Aron, A., McLaughlin-Volpe, T., & Ropp, S. A. (1997). The extended contact effect: Knowledge of cross-group friendships and prejudice. *Journal of Personality and Social Psychology, 73,* 73–90.

Chapter 13

Intergroup contact and levels of categorization: Effects on intergroup emotions

Roberto González and Rupert Brown

Undoubtedly, one of the cultural changes we inherited from the last century is the so-called trend of "globalization" and "interconnection" between global systems (at the economical, political, racial, and even religious level). Modernization has transformed social life in several aspects, drawing people everywhere into larger and more complicated networks of exchange. As a result, "contact" among different people in modern times is increasing, with both positive and negative consequences. The positive ones (e.g., getting to know each other, learning from other experiences, etc.) may result from cooperative contact and optimization of scarce resources. The dramatic effects that recent ethnic conflicts have produced in people's lives in the former Yugoslavia, Nigeria, and Indonesia, as well as the impact of international terrorism (e.g., the attacks in Spain, Thailand and the US in recent years), are clear examples of the negative ones.

Undoubtedly, many of these conflicts have their roots in historic, economic, and territorial disputes. Some are based on incompatible religious belief systems. However, there are reasons to assume that these conflicts are also related to group identity. People belong to groups which are relevant for them and toward which they *feel* attached and committed. Any form of identity threat (e.g., as experienced by minority groups when at risk of disappearing or being absorbed by the dominant majority) is likely to be associated with the activation of negative feelings toward the outgroup. If there is something we have learned from the conflicts mentioned above, it is the role that emotions might play in underlying discrimination, prejudice, and in the more extreme cases, retaliation and aggression toward outgroup members that are perceived as the enemy.

This chapter aims to contribute to this field by discussing the central benefits and limitations of the contact hypothesis and its related theories for promoting positive intergroup attitudes, particularly regarding affective outcomes. New research evidence will be presented which supports the central role that group salience plays in moderating the generalization of attitude change at the emotional level (positive affect toward outgroup members and feelings of intergroup anxiety).

The contact hypothesis and modern socio-psychological perspectives

Gordon Allport, one of the most remarkable social psychologists of the last century, had a deep impact on the study of both prejudice and intergroup relations. In 1954 he published *The Nature of Prejudice*, in which the contact hypothesis occupied an important position, specifying the critical situational conditions that promote the development of positive intergroup attitudes and the reduction of prejudice. He identified many factors (nearly thirty in all) that he supposed would improve intergroup relations and decrease prejudice. At the core of his thinking was the hypothesis that prejudice may be reduced by sustained equal-status contact between majority and minority groups in the pursuit of common goals. The effect should be greatly enhanced if the contact is sanctioned by institutional support.

In the fifty years since its publication, the main assumptions of the contact hypothesis have been well tested in a wide diversity of settings: in school desegregation programs (Cohen, 1984; Cook, 1985; Gerard, 1983, Schwarzwald & Amir, 1984; Stephan, 1986; Wade & Wilson, 1971; Webster, 1961); desegregated housing projects (Amir, 1976; Deutsch & Collins, 1951; Jackman & Crane, 1986; Wilner, Walkley, & Cook, 1955); and in organizational settings (Harding & Hogrefe, 1952), including the military (Brophy, 1946; Roberts, 1953). Although research has often found that contact per se may not be enough to reduce prejudice between groups, a recent meta-analysis conducted by Pettigrew and Tropp (2000), involving over 90,000 participants of various nationalities, did find that contact in itself may produce some positive attitude change and reduction of prejudice. However, Pettigrew and Tropp found that this effect was substantially stronger in those contexts which Allport's facilitating conditions applied (equal status, cooperation, institutional support). Moreover, and relevant for the present discussion, the effect of contact on affect was usually stronger in comparison to other dependent measures (e.g., beliefs, social distance, and sociometric respectively). The affect measures included significant effects for strong emotions, favorability, and evaluative dimension of semantic differential scale, where the stronger the affect measure, the larger the mean effect. These results revealed that beyond beliefs (the emphasis of the contact hypothesis), emotional outcomes of contact have started to be considered important aspects to explore (Pettigrew, 1998).

The original optimism of the contact hypothesis was rapidly tempered by an acknowledgement of the complexity of the business of prejudice reduction (Hewstone & Brown, 1986; Pettigrew, 1998). Two issues in particular are relevant to the current chapter. One concerns a predominance of research investigating the effects of changing the majority group's attitudes toward minorities rather than vice versa (Cohen & Roper, 1972; Sigelman

& Welch, 1993). Whilst understandable, this bias in research focus may be obscuring potentially important moderating effects of group size and status on contact outcomes. In some of the studies to be reported here, we will address the issue of generalization in intergroup contexts in which groups of unequal size and status cooperate with each other under different conditions of category salience. The second topic concerns the difficulty of achieving generalization of attitude change induced by the positive contact experience from the individual group members encountered to the outgroup as a whole (Cook, 1978; Hewstone & Brown, 1986). We predict that intergroup contact should be moderated by additional variables under which contact will successfully reduce prejudice and increase the level of positive affects toward outgroup members. One of these is the hypothesized role of *categorization* which lies at the heart of the three most promising modern theoretical approaches of intergroup contact: Brewer and Miller's (1984) decategorization model, Gaertner and Dovidio's (2000) common ingroup identity model, and Hewstone and Brown's (1986) mutual intergroup differentiation model.

Although all these models have their origins in social identity theory (Tajfel & Turner, 1986) and recognize the important effect of social identification on both individuals' self-definitions and on intergroup relations, they make different and, in some cases, opposite predictions concerning the reduction of bias. Importantly, however, they diverge when specifying how to generalize positive intergroup attitudes beyond the cooperative contact setting itself. In this chapter we aim to provide a critical assessment of these developments, focusing mainly on the third one which provided the point of departure for several research programs on contact over the past fifteen years. It is noteworthy, however, that these theoretical approaches have mainly studied the effect of contact on cognitive dimensions (e.g., change in stereotypes or ingroup bias built on evaluative ratings or reward allocation measures) and have rather neglected its impact on affective outcomes, such as liking, trust, admiration, anger, and hate (but see González, Saiz, et al., 2003; Pettigrew, 1998; Smith, 1993; Stephan & Stephan, 1985).

The decategorization contact model

Brewer and Miller (1984) assume that the mere categorization of people into distinct groups is sufficient to elicit intergroup discrimination (Brewer, 1979; Tajfel, Billig, Bundy, & Flament, 1971). Since category-based interaction is often associated with the perception of ingroup and outgroup members in homogeneous or stereotypical terms (Brown & Turner, 1981), they infer that the "personalization" of the contact situation should lead to a more individuated mode of information processing and, thereby, enhance the potential for group stereotype disconfirmation (Brewer & Miller, 1984, 1996; Miller & Brewer, 1986; Miller, Brewer, & Edwards, 1985). Therefore, intergroup contact should be structured so as to reduce the salience of category distinctions and to promote opportunities to get to know outgroup members as persons.

This perspective has received support in crossed categorization studies (e.g., Hewstone, Islam, & Judd, 1993; Marcus-Newhall, Miller, Holtz, & Brewer, 1993), studies of friendship (Hamberger & Hewstone, 1997; Pettigrew, 1998; Pettigrew & Tropp, 2000) and, more directly, in experimental manipulations aimed at increasing personal (vs. task-oriented) contact. The latter have proved to be successful in reducing ingroup favoritism, not just toward the members of the outgroup actually encountered but also generalized to other outgroup members not yet met (Bettencourt, Brewer, Croak, & Miller, 1992; Bettencourt, Miller, & Hume, 1999; Brewer, Weber, & Carini, 1995).

However, there are some limitations with this approach. First, despite the above-mentioned evidence on successful generalization,[1] there is an inherent difficulty in trying to promote generalization when there is no psychological means of connecting the individuals in the contact situation with their many other fellow outgroup members outside it (Brown & Turner, 1981; Ensari & Miller, 2002; Rothbart & John, 1985; Vivian, Hewstone, & Brown, 1997). Second, the model has been conceived to induce attitude change at the cognitive level, principally by reducing ingroup bias by promoting group stereotype disconfirmation. Thus, bias reduction has usually been observed on cognitive measures like evaluative ratings or reward allocations but not on affective ones (liking, trust, love, anger, etc.). Third, people might infer that positive interpersonal interactions with particular outgroup members simply represent "exceptions to the rule", and hence they may classify them as unrepresentative of the outgroup as a whole, rendering generalization more difficult to achieve (Weber & Crocker, 1983). Finally, complete decategorization would presumably be problematic for contexts that involve real-life groups which may be unable or unwilling to relinquish their identities so easily (Simon & Klandermans, 2001; van Oudenhoven, Prins, & Buunk, 1998). All things considered, there are reasons to believe that the decategorization approach, if pursued exclusively or to extremes, might not offer an optimal strategy for promoting positive intergroup attitudes beyond the contact setting in itself.

The common ingroup identity model

The second perspective is the common ingroup identity model, first proposed by Gaertner, Mann, Murrell, and Dovidio (1989) and recently updated by Gaertner and Dovidio (2000). In order to promote positive intergroup attitudes toward outgroup members, this model proposes that contact strategies should be oriented to re-categorize the intergroup situation so that ingroup and outgroup members can be subsumed into an inclusive common identity. The rationale behind this approach is to alter members' perceptions of group borders so as to allow some of the cognitive and motivational processes that may have contributed initially to ingroup bias to be redirected toward the development of more positive intergroup relationships. Several experimental and field studies have provided support for this model (see Gaertner & Dovidio, 2000, for full review).

In spite of its extensive empirical support, however, this model also has some limitations. First, a large number of the studies providing support for the common ingroup identity model have been restricted to observing a reduction in intergroup bias in the contact setting itself and and have mainly used cognitive measures of bias (Dovidio, Gaertner, Isen, & Lowrance, 1995; Gaertner et al., 1999; Gaertner et al., 1989). Indeed, only a few of them have successfully proved the power of the common ingroup identity model to promote generalization of attitude beyond the particular contact situation (Dovidio et al., 1997; Gaertner, Rust, Dovidio, Bachman, & Anastasio, 1994). Second, the creation of a common ingroup identity may not be politically or psychologically practicable, especially in real intergroup settings, because it involves the abandonment of what may be important group identities (Ensari & Miller, 2002; Gaertner, Dovidio, Anastasio, Bachman, & Rust, 1993). In order to overcome this limitation, Gaertner and colleagues postulated the development of a dual identity as a strategy for promoting generalization of attitude change beyond the contact setting. Indeed, there is already evidence that it may offer advantages over the "pure" common ingroup identity approach, particularly in minority–majority settings (Dovidio, Gaertner, & Validzic, 1998; González & Brown, in press; Hornsey & Hogg, 2000a, 2000b, 2002).

The mutual intergroup differentiation model

The third perspective – the mutual intergroup differentiation model – proposed by Hewstone and Brown (1986) and subsequently reformulated by Vivian et al. (1997) was conceived to identify the conditions which will allow the generalization of attitudes and behavior change beyond the specific context in which the contact occurs. This model asserts that equal-status interaction may ameliorate intergroup bias because the original group identities remain to some extent salient and are not threatened by contact. Groups need to maintain some salience for their members primarily because this facilitates generalization, since the respective ingroup and outgroup members are more likely to be seen as representative or typical of their group. Thus, the contact situation should be perceived by participants as a process in which groups can be distinguished by the experience and expertise that they bring to the situation (Brown & Wade, 1987; Hewstone & Brown, 1986; Vivian et al., 1997). Taking into account the fact that a convergence of group boundaries may activate negative feelings (threat to the distinctiveness of the groups), this model recognizes the importance of maintaining group division on dimensions that are perceived to be equally important to group members (Brown & Wade, 1987; Deschamps & Brown, 1983). An important feature of this model is that it recognizes the value of diversity rather than assimilation, rendering it as a more pluralistic approach to managing intergroup relations, particularly for contexts that involve groups of different size and status.

The mutual intergroup differentiation model has received support, especially regarding generalization of positive attitude from cooperative contact situations that emphasized group membership enhancement in several research settings. For instance, by systematically varying both the typicality of outgroup members and the nature of intergroup contact (pleasant or unpleasant), Wilder (1984) demonstrated that the reduction of intergroup bias was particularly evident in participants who interacted with the typical-pleasant member of the outgroup. Participants evaluated the outgroup as a whole (generalization) more favorably when they interacted with the typical-pleasant member of the outgroup (see a similar pattern in Brown, Vivian, & Hewstone, 1999). Van Oudenhoven, Groenewoud, and Hewstone (1996) were the first ones to provide direct evidence in support of the mutual intergroup differentiation model by manipulating group salience in the context of cooperative intergroup contact. Increasing ethnic salience during a cooperative learning experience led participants to a generalized positive attitude toward the ethnic outgroup in question (see also Brown, Maras, Masser, Vivian, & Hewstone, 2001; Brown et al., 1999; Maras & Brown, 1996).

As can be seen, most of the studies reported so far have been conceived to compare the effectiveness of individualized or decategorized contact and the group salience strategy for promoting positive intergroup attitudes. In that sense, they could be regarded as competitive tests of the Brewer–Miller and Hewstone–Brown models. Recent work has been interested in comparing these two accounts with the Gaertner–Dovidio model. It will be recalled that the latter have suggested a dual-identity approach might be a particularly useful strategy for promoting generalization attitude change after positive contact. Indeed, the latter represents a rapprochement of the Gaertner–Dovidio and Hewstone–Brown models, since the subgroup identities remain salient within the more inclusive common category.

González and Brown (2003, in press) conducted three studies aimed to contribute to the understanding of the effectiveness of the above models for promoting bias reduction both *during* and *beyond* the contact situation (generalization). In the first one, artificial groups of four participants – of equal size and status – were randomly divided into two separate groups with distinctive labels and names to complete a short problem-solving task. They then met to perform a cooperative task under one of four conditions:

"separate-individuals", "two-groups", "one-group", and "dual-identity". Overall, and consistent with the original contact hypothesis (Allport, 1954), all categorization strategies were effective in not activating intergroup bias during the cooperative interaction itself (Brewer & Miller, 1984; Dovidio et al., 1998; Gaertner et al., 1989; Pettigrew, 1998). However, on the generalized measures (of the videotaped participants) more bias was shown in the "separate-individuals" and "two-group" conditions than in the "one-group" and "dual-identity" conditions. The latter two both seemed to be effective in reducing bias to zero and could not be distinguished from one another. In two follow-up studies (using the same paradigm but dropping the "two-groups" condition), group status and size were manipulated (González & Brown, in press). Once again, ingroup bias within the contact setting did not vary as a function of the cognitive strategies (decategorization model, common ingroup identity model, and dual identity); all three conditions equally reduced bias to almost zero. But again, only the dual-identity and superordinate category conditions were shown to be optimal to promote generalized positive intergroup attitudes. The relative benefits of these two strategies, however, varied as a function of group size and status. For minority groups, whether of low or high status, only the "dual" condition was optimal for reducing bias; for majority groups, on the other hand, none of the three categorization conditions differed from the others. Group status was the unique determining factor for predicting bias: high-status groups were more biased than low-status groups (González & Brown, in press).

Mutual intergroup differentiation model predicting intergroup emotions

The experimental work already reported has sought to investigate whether group salience, as experienced and reported by participants, both moderates the effects of contact on various indicators of intergroup bias and promotes generalization of positive attitude from individual contacted to the outgroup as a whole. Based on participant's evaluative ratings (e.g., how intelligent, sociable, hard-working ingroup and outgroup members are) or symbolic reward allocation measures, the majority of these studies have used various non-affective ingroup bias indices as the central criterion variables for representing intergroup attitude both during and beyond contact (generalization). However, does Hewstone–Brown model produce a similar pattern of outcomes regarding emotional reactions toward outgroup members as a whole? The research evidence to be reported in the following section hopes to contribute to that goal by illustrating the significant impact of group salience on emotions (e.g., positive affect and intergroup anxiety). We include studies conducted in various real intergroup contact settings in

European and Latin-American countries, involving nationalities, political groups, indigenous peoples, religions, elderly people, immigrants, and people with disabilities as target groups.

As a follow-up of Brown et al.'s (1999) study, González and Brown (2001) conducted an inter-nation attitude study in Europe aimed to clarify role of national and European identity in predicting intergroup bias, and two intergroup emotions, positive affect toward various outgroup members in the EU and intergroup anxiety. The effect of the traditional contact-related criteria (amount and quality of contact) in interaction with nationality membership salience during contact was also addressed. Finally, the study also assessed how the degree of nationality salience reported by respondents in their interaction with a member of the several outgroup targets may moderate the effect of their evaluative ratings on generalized attitudes toward the outgroup as a whole.

To answer these questions, González and Brown (2001) asked university student respondents ($N = 570$) from four European countries (England, Italy, the Netherlands, and Portugal) to rate contact and salience of nationality membership they experienced with someone they knew from each of four outgroup countries (held constant for all respondents, Germans, Belgians, Spanish, and Greeks). Salience was computed by a combination of perceived typicality of the outgroup person(s) with respect to their group and a report of how frequently participants make reference to their nationality during contact with the target person(s). Participants rated those contact persons on several positive and negative evaluative rating traits (e.g., hard working, intelligent, arrogant, unfriendly, etc.). Then, after being primed with information regarding the size and the status of each of the four target countries independently,[2] they rated the target countries as a whole using the same evaluative ratings measures used to describe the contact person and assessed the extent to which participants liked, admired, and trusted the target groups as a whole (positive affect). Participants had not received information regarding their own country size and relative status by the time they judged the target groups.

Several social psychological predictions were made concerning the role of national and European identifications in determining intergroup attitudes. First, it was hypothesized from social identity theory that there would be a negative correlation between national identification and positive affect toward the outgroup as a whole (the mean of liking, trust, and admiration); the more people identify with their own country, the less they like, admire, and trust the outgroup. On the other hand, following the common ingroup identity model principles, the more respondents identify with Europe, the higher the level of positive affect toward outgroups. However, this latter effect was predicted to be qualified by the level of national identification. The more people were identified with their own country and with Europe simultaneously (dual-identity prediction), the greater positive affect toward outgroup members compared to people who identified only with their own country or mainly with Europe. Second, because the threat of losing group distinctiveness and social identity is especially acute for groups whose small size makes them vulnerable to being "swallowed up" by the larger or dominant group, it was predicted that a dual-identity approach would facilitate the generalization of positive intergroup attitudes particularly for *minority* groups. Maintaining subgroup salience within a superordinate category offered a measure of protection against such a threat. In order to test the predictions concerning the relative size of the countries, several hierarchical regression analyses were conducted separately in the minority and majority countries.

Consistent with social identity theory prediction, analyses revealed that the national identity measure accounted for a significant amount of variation of positive affect toward outgroup targets as a whole in both the minority and the majority samples. The more people identified with their country, the less positive affect they exhibited toward outgroups. In contrast, and consistent with Gaertner and Dovidio's (2000) common ingroup identity model, in both the minority and majority samples, the more people identified with Europe, the more positive the affect they expressed toward outgroups. However, the interaction between national and European identity had an independent effect on the emotional measure over and above the effects of the European and national identity predictors, but this time in the *minority* sample only (Dutch and Portuguese participants). At low levels of national identification, European identity did not correlate with positive affect toward the outgroups. At high levels of national identification, on the other hand, there was a reliable and significant positive correlation between levels of European identification and affect. The more people identified with both their own country and Europe (dual-identity prediction), the more they liked, admired, and trusted the total outgroup targets as a whole (the mean of positive emotions across all targets was computed).

The analyses also revealed a multiplicative effect of national and European identification measures in predicting negative emotions – that is, the levels of intergroup anxiety that respondents reported when experiencing contact with foreigners. Once again, the pattern of results involving the minority and majority countries varied. In the minority countries (the Dutch and the Portuguese), neither the national nor the European identification measure predicted intergroup anxiety independently, but they did interact following the same pattern of the positive affect measure reported above. Looking at the majority sample (the British and Italian participants), on the other hand, the results showed only the effect of national and European identification predicting intergroup anxiety independently but in opposed directions. The more participants of the majority identified with their own country, the higher the levels of intergroup anxiety; the more they identified with Europe, the lower the levels of intergroup anxiety (thus supporting the common ingroup identity model).

Consistent with the contact hypothesis and Hewstone and Brown's (1986) model, the quality of contact and the salience of the membership measures significantly predicted affect toward the outgroup targets. That is, the better the quality of the contact situation and the higher the salience of the membership during the encounter, the more positive the affect toward the outgroup targets. Although the amount of contact predicted in the same direction, its contribution to the explained variance of affect was very limited. However, the correlation between quality of contact and affect toward the outgroups also varied as a function of the salience of the nationality membership. Consistent with mutual intergroup differentiation model prediction, and exactly mirroring the pattern observed by Brown et al. (1999), for those participants who reported a high degree of nationality salience in their interaction with members of the outgroup targets there was a significant correlation between quality of contact and affect toward the outgroup as a whole. In contrast, for those reporting a lower degree of nationality salience, the correlation between the quality of contact and affect toward the outgroup as a whole was not reliable (see also Voci & Hewstone, 2003b).

The power of nationality salience to facilitate generalization from the individual to the group as a whole was then tested in several regression analyses. In three of the four target groups, results confirmed the interactive effects of nationality salience and evaluative rating of the contacted person for predicting evaluative ratings of the outgroup in general. To describe these interactions, respondents were then dichotomized into high- and low-salience groups and the correlations between the ratings of individual foreigners and of their countries of provenance were computed for each group (this provides a measure of stimulus generalization). Reliable, positive, and larger correlations were observed in the high- compared to the low-nationality-salience group between evaluative ratings of the person with whom they reported to have had contact and the general evaluative rating of the outgroup targets as a whole. Thus, the impression of the outgroup person was more likely to be associated with a favorable attitude (positive evaluative ratings) toward the outgroups as a whole if the degree of nationality salience was kept relatively high in their interactions. This is the first time that this generalization process has been clearly demonstrated in real intergroup settings.

Current research is extending the investigation of salience moderation effects to other less commonly studied intergroup contexts. González, Saiz, et al. (2003) asked male and female Chilean secondary and high-school students ($N = 1965$ from 63 schools of different economic backgrounds) for their attitudes toward several minority groups: the Mapuche (local aborigine group), elderly people, disabled people, evangelicals, and Peruvians. Reliable measures of group salience and intergroup contact were used to predict prejudice and intergroup emotions (positive affect) toward the various target groups independently.

Consistent with the contact hypothesis, quality of contact was one of the strongest predictors of prejudice (negative correlation), followed by the amount of contact. Group salience, on the other hand, was also negatively correlated with prejudice except for the disabled people group. In addition, the greater the amount of contact and the better its quality, the more the students exhibited positive affect toward members of the target groups (see similar results in Pettigrew & Tropp, 2000). Using structural equation modelling, the results revealed that contact significantly predicted attitude toward the outgroup contacted person in three of the five groups. In turn, this variable was strongly associated with evaluative ratings and positive affect toward the outgroup as a whole. However, the latter relationship was again moderated by group salience in two of the target groups (Mapuche and elderly people). Consistent with the results obtained by Voci and Hewstone (2002, 2003b), significant, positive, and stronger correlations were observed in the high- compared to the low-salience group between evaluative ratings of the person with whom they reported to have had contact (e.g., Mapuche person) and the general evaluative rating and positive affect of the outgroup targets as a whole. In addition, making salient group membership during contact was also an optimal way of increasing the positive impact of direct contact on affect toward the minorities. This moderating effect of salience was detected in three of the five target groups (Peruvians, elderly people, and evangelicals). Contact affected significantly the level of liking, trust, and admiration (positive emotions) toward the outgroup as a whole in the high-salience condition only.

In a rather different intergroup setting, González, Manzi, et al. (2003) conducted another survey in Chile that studied the relationship between political identity, intergroup contact, and intergroup attitudes (including evaluative rating and intergroup emotions) toward five different political target groups belonging to two political coalitions with a history of conflict that has still not been completely resolved (because of the coup of 1973 and subsequent violations of human rights). Relevant for the present discussion, the study also examined the role of political group membership salience in moderating the overall effect of contact on positive affect toward the outgroup as a whole and the generalization of those feelings from individual contacted to the outgroup in general.

Following the same procedure of González and Brown (2001), they asked university student respondents ($N = 1416$) from 14 different universities to report, among several other issues, their political party and coalition preferences and identity, amount of contact, and salience of political party membership they experienced with someone they met from each of five political targets (including their ingroup). Salience was again computed by a combination of perceived typicality of the outgroup person with respect to their political party and frequency of reference to their political membership during contact with the target person. Participants assessed those contacted persons on several positive and negative evaluative rating traits (e.g., loyal, organized, ambitious, disciplined, honest, corrupt, authoritarian, intelligent, etc.) and affect (trust, admiration, and liking). Then they rated the target party as a whole with the same evaluative ratings and affective measures.

Overall, and consistent with the contact hypothesis and Hewstone and Brown's (1986) model, the quality of contact and salience of the political membership significantly predicted affect toward the outgroup targets. That is, the better the quality of the contact situation and the higher the salience of the membership during the encounter, the more positive the affect toward the political outgroup as a whole. However, group salience also moderated the impact of quality of contact on affect toward the political parties as a whole in three of five political groups. Quality of contact with outgroup political party members had a bigger positive impact on attitude toward the outgroup in general under high-salience conditions than in low-salience conditions.

Mirroring González and Brown's (2001) European Union study, results strongly confirmed that the degree of political group membership salience reported by respondents in their interaction with a member of several political party targets also moderated the effect of their positive emotions (expressed toward the outgroup contact person) on generalized affect toward the political parties as a whole (interaction terms were significant for all political target groups). Again, generalization of positive affect from the individual to the group level was greater under high compared to low political salience conditions.

These moderating effects of salience on intergroup emotions are by no means restricted to university samples or to internation contexts. Brown et al. (2001) found a similar, if weaker, interaction between salience and contact in a study conducted on a cross-channel ferry with an opportunity sample of British adults ($N = 352$). Maras and Brown (1996) conducted a study to assess young children's liking toward their peers with severe disabilities in the context of an exchange program between a primary school and a special school for children with profound learning and physical disabilities. Using a quasi-experimental longitudinal design, half the children were randomly selected to take part in weekly visits to the special school, the remainder constituted the control group. Children who took part in the exchange program increased their liking for disabled strangers while the controls did not. Similar results have been reported recently in several studies involving contact and attitude toward immigrants in a sample of Italian hospital workers, and toward elderly people by their grandchildren (Harwood, Hewstone, Paolini, & Voci, 2005; Voci & Hewstone, 2003a, 2003b).

However, this model is not without its problems. First, the enhancement of group membership salience for effective intergroup contact produces something of a dilemma. On the one hand, if the contact situation fosters the development of positive experiences with outgroup members that disconfirm negative stereotypes about them, then it is possible that generalization of positive attitudes to the outgroup as a whole will occur. However, if contact provides *negative* experiences, they too are likely to be generalized which increases the risk of perpetuating stereotypes and prejudices about the outgroup. Evidence of this problem has already been unearthed by Brown et al. (1999) and Wilder (1984). This suggests that careful attention needs to be paid to Allport's (1954) basic conditions for successful intergroup contact any time that group membership is made salient (Brewer & Miller, 1996).

Second, the reformulated version of the Hewstone and Brown model (Vivian et al., 1997) incorporates an important mediator of the impact of the various forms of intergroup contact: intergroup anxiety, an anticipation of negative consequences of contact (Greenland & Brown, 1999). Evidence for the mediational role of intergroup anxiety among the contact hypothesis conditions and positive intergroup attitudes has begun to be addressed in several studies (Greenland & Brown, 1999; Islam & Hewstone, 1993; Paolini, Hewstone, Cairns, & Voci, 2004; Voci & Hewstone 2003a, 2003b). However, there is still some uncertainty regarding the exact causal relationship between salience and intergroup anxiety. Islam and Hewstone found that increased intergroup salience was associated with intergroup anxiety, suggesting that some balance between group salience and a more personalized form of contact might be desirable. However, Greenland and Brown provided evidence that the causal direction was from anxiety to intergroup categorization rather than the other way around. Finally, Voci and Hewstone have observed that group salience seems to moderate the effects of contact on anxiety in a positive fashion, contrary to Islam and Hewstone's conclusion. That is, those experiencing contact under high-salience conditions showed a stronger positive relation between contact and anxiety than those for whom group salience was lower. Clearly, the precise link between contact, salience, and anxiety will repay further investigation.

Conclusion

Looking at the several studies providing evidence in favor of the contact models presented here, it is clear that the contact hypothesis has become a central theoretical approach to understand what the optimal conditions for promoting positive intergroup attitudes and emotions toward outgroup members are. All the models (Brewer–Miller, Gaertner–Dovidio, and Hewstone–Brown) have tested their main predictions in both experimental and field studies, the results being consistent with what they expected, particularly regarding attitude change in the contact situation. However, the more challenging question – namely the power of the models for promoting generalization of attitude change (at the cognitive and emotional level) from the contact to the outgroup as a whole – remains less clear when comparing the models. The evidence presented here seems to demonstrate that the Hewstone and Brown model has a particular advantage for promoting such an effect. In several studies, conducted in a wide range of different intergroup and cultural contexts (ethnic, racial, religious, political, sexual, generational, social, and other intergroup settings in Europe and South America), group salience has consistently been found to moderate the relationship between contact and intergroup emotions. Participants who reported they were more aware of category memberships in their intergroup encounters with outgroup members, and who perceived those people as more typical of their group, showed stronger relationships between contact and positive intergroup emotions (e.g., liking, trust, and admiration) than those who did not.

However, the role of friendships, a more interpersonal base contact outcome, has also demonstrated to be a significant mediator of attitude change. Moreover, the benefit of building a common ingroup identity or making group membership within a superordinate category (dual-identity strategy) simultaneously salient has also been shown to be particularly beneficial for minorities. Thus, it seems theoretically plausible that intergroup and interpersonal approaches are orthogonal and not opposed strategies for promoting positive intergroup attitudes. Thinking along these lines, Hewstone (1996), Brewer and Miller (1996), and later Pettigrew (1998) suggested articulating these strategies in order to take the advantages that each of them provides for the contact to succeed. Particularly relevant is the model presented by Pettigrew which, assuming a temporal perspective, predicts that group members with a history of conflict would benefit if interpersonal, group, and superordinate strategies are promoted sequentially during contact. However, it is noteworthy that Pettigrew's approach seems to assume that interpersonal contact is opposed to intergroup contact. So, research particularly testing this model may contribute to this discussion, ideally in both experimental and field settings (Eller & Abrams, 2003).

Certainly, more research has to be done regarding the expected effects of these models, either by themselves or integrated with more negative and enduring emotions such as hate, anger, or distrust – emotions that unfortunately shape many real intergroup situations nowadays. Particularly relevant is the need to conduct research involving other emotions, such as collective shame, collective guilt, sympathy, and remorse, to better understand the emotional bases for promoting reparation, intergroup forgiveness, apology, and other forms of restorative justice and compensation in intergroup settings that have a history of conflict and mutually negative intergroup attitudes.

Notes

1 In fact, it is likely that in the Bettencourt et al. (1992) and subsequent paradigms, some vestige of group salience remained in the "generalization" phase of the experiment.
2 Based on the information regarding population size and economic position in the European Union (gross domestic product), four target countries were assessed: Minority high status (Belgium); Minority low status (Greece); Majority high status (Germany); and Majority low status (Spain).

References

Allport, G. W. (1954). *The nature of prejudice.* New York: Addison-Wesley.

Amir, Y. (1976). The role of intergroup contact in change of prejudice and race relations. In P. A. Katz (Ed.), *Towards the elimination of racism* (pp. 245–308). New York: Pergamon Press.

Bettencourt, B. A., Brewer, M. B., Croak, M. R., & Miller, N. (1992). Cooperation and the reduction of intergroup bias: The role of reward structure and social orientation. *Journal of Experimental Social Psychology, 28,* 301–319.

Bettencourt, B. A., Miller, N., & Hume, D. L. (1999). Effects of numerical representation within cooperative settings: Examining the role of salience in in-group favoritism. *British Journal of Social Psychology, 38,* 265–287.

Brewer, M. B. (1979). In-group bias in the minimal intergroup situation: A cognitive-motivational analysis. *Psychological Bulletin, 86,* 307–324.

Brewer, M. B., & Miller, N. (1984). Beyond the contact hypothesis: Theoretical perspectives on desegregation. In N. Miller & M. B. Brewer (Eds.), *Groups in contact: The psychology of desegregation* (pp. 281–302). New York: Academic Press.

Brewer, M. B., & Miller, N. (1996). *Intergroup relations.* Buckingham, UK: Open University Press.

Brewer, M. B., Weber, J. G., & Carini, B. (1995). Person memory in intergroup contexts: Categorization versus individuation. *Journal of Personality and Social Psychology, 69,* 29–40.

Brophy, I. N. (1946). The luxury of anti-Negro prejudice. *Public Opinion Quarterly, 9,* 456–466.

Brown, R., Maras, P., Masser, B., Vivian, J., & Hewstone, M. (2001). Life on the ocean wave: Testing some intergroup hypotheses in a naturalistic setting. *Group Processes and Intergroup Relations, 4,* 81–97.

Brown, R., & Turner, J. C. (1981). Interpersonal and intergroup behaviour. In J. C. Turner & H. Giles (Eds.), *Intergroup behaviour* (pp. 33–65) Oxford, UK: Blackwell.

Brown, R., Vivian, J., & Hewstone, M. (1999). Changing attitudes through intergroup contact: The effects of group membership salience. *European Journal of Social Psychology, 29,* 741–764.

Brown, R., & Wade, G. (1987). Superordinate goals and intergroup behaviour: The effect of role ambiguity and status on intergroup attitudes and task performance. *European Journal of Social Psychology, 17,* 131–142.

Cohen, E. G. (1984). The desegregate school: Problems in status power and interethnic climate. In N. Miller & M. B. Brewer (Eds.), *Groups in contact: The psychology of desegregation* (pp. 77–96). New York: Academic Press.

Cohen, E. G., & Roper, S. S. (1972). Modification of interracial interaction disability: An application of status characteristics theory. *American Sociological Review, 37,* 643–657.

Cook, S. W. (1978). Interpersonal and attitudinal outcomes in cooperating interracial groups. *Journal of Research and Development in Education, 12,* 97–113.

Cook, S. W. (1985). Experimenting on social issues: The case of school desegregation. *American Psychologist, 40,* 452–460.

Deschamps, J.-C., & Brown, R. (1983). Superordinate goals and intergroup conflict. *British Journal of Social Psychology, 22,* 189–195.

Deutsch, M., & Collins, M. (1951). *Interracial housing: A psychological evaluation of a social experiment.* Minneapolis, MN: University of Minnesota Press.

Dovidio, J. F., Gaertner, S. L., Isen, A. M., & Lowrance, R. (1995). Group representations and intergroup bias: Positive affect, similarity, and group size. *Personality and Social Psychology Bulletin, 21,* 856–865.

Dovidio, J. F., Gaertner, S. L., & Validzic, A. (1998). Intergroup bias: Status, differentiation, and a common in-group identity. *Journal of Personality and Social Psychology, 75,* 109–120.

Dovidio, J. F., Gaertner, S. L., Validzic, A., Matoka, K., Johnson, B., & Frazier, S. (1997). Extending the benefits of recategorization: Evaluations, self-disclosure, and helping. *Journal of Experimental Social Psychology, 33,* 401–420.

Eller, A., & Abrams, D. (2003). "Gringos" in Mexico: Cross-sectional and longitudinal effects of language school-promoted contact on intergroup bias. *Group Processes and Intergroup Relations, 6,* 55–75.

Ensari, N., & Miller, N. (2002). The out-group must not be so bad after all: The effects of disclosure, typicality, and salience on intergroup bias. *Journal of Personality and Social Psychology, 83,* 313–329.

Gaertner, S. L., & Dovidio, J. F. (2000). *Reducing intergroup bias: The common ingroup identity model.* Philadelphia: Psychology Press.

Gaertner, S. L., Dovidio, J. F., Anastasio, P. A., Bachman, B. A., & Rust, M. C. (1993). The common ingroup identity model: Recategorization and the reduction of intergroup bias. In W. Stroebe & M. Hewstone (Eds.), *European review of social psychology* (Vol. 4, pp. 1–26). Chichester, UK: Wiley.

Gaertner, S. L., Dovidio, J. F., Rust, M. C., Nier, J., Banker, B., Ward, C. M., et al. (1999). Reducing intergroup bias: Elements of intergroup cooperation. *Journal of Personality and Social Psychology, 76,* 388–402.

Gaertner, S. L., Mann, J. A., Murrell, A., & Dovidio, J. F. (1989). Reducing intergroup bias: The benefits of recategorization. *Journal of Personality and Social Psychology, 57,* 239–249.

Gaertner, S. L., Rust, M. C., Dovidio, J. F., Bachman, B. A., & Anastasio, P. A. (1994). The contact hypothesis: The role of a common ingroup identity on reducing intergroup bias. *Small Group Research, 25,* 224–249.

Gerard, H. B. (1983). School desegregation: The social science role. *American Psychologist, 38,* 869–877.

González, R., & Brown, R. (2001, September). *The contact hypothesis and levels of categorization: Predicting inter-nation attitudes in the European Union.* Paper presented at the Small Group Meeting of the European Association of

Experimental Social Psychology, "Social Identity: Motivational, Emotional and Cultural Aspects", Villasimius, Cagliari, Italy.

González, R., & Brown, R. (2003). Generalization of positive attitude as a function of subgroup and superordinate group identifications in intergroup contact. *European Journal of Social Psychology, 33*, 195–214.

González, R., & Brown, R. (in press). Dual identities in intergroup contact: Group status and size moderating the generalization of positive attitude change. *Journal of Experimental Social Psychology.*

González, R., Manzi, J. M., Saiz, J. L., Brewer, M. B., De Tezanos, P., Torres, D., et al. (2003, July). *Political parties and coalitions in Chile: intergroup political attitudes and positive affects as a function of political identity and intergroup contact.* Paper presented at International Society of Political Psychology 26th Annual Scientific Meeting: Political leadership in divided societies and a dangerous world, Boston, MA, USA.

González, R., Saiz, J. L., Manzi, J. M., Ordóñes, G., Millar, A., Sirlopú, D., et al. (2003b, June). *Intergroup contact, social norms and group salience: Predicting prejudice and positive affect towards minority groups in secondary and high school student in Chile.* Paper presented at: Anti-bias education: Practice, research and theory, Evanston, IL, USA.

Greenland, K., & Brown, R. (1999). Categorization and intergroup anxiety in contact between British and Japanese nationals. *European Journal of Social Psychology, 29*, 503–521.

Hamberger, J., & Hewstone, M. (1997). Inter-ethnic contact as a predictor of blatant and subtle prejudice: Tests of a model in four west European nations. *British Journal of Social Psychology, 36*, 173–190.

Harding, J., & Hogrefe, R. (1952). Attitudes of white department store employees toward Negro co-workers. *Journal of Social Issues, 8*, 18–28.

Harwood, J., Hewstone, M., Paolini, S., & Voci, A. (2005) Grandparent–grandchild contact and attitudes towards older adults: Moderator and mediator effects. *Personality and Social Psychology Bulletin, 31*, 393–406.

Hewstone, M. (1996). Contact and categorization: Social psychological interventions to change intergroup relations. In C. N. Macrae, C. Stangor, & M. Hewstone (Eds.), *Stereotypes and stereotyping* (pp. 323–368). New York: Guilford Press.

Hewstone, M., & Brown, R. (1986). Contact is not enough: An intergroup perspective on the contact hypothesis. In M. Hewstone & R. Brown (Eds.), *Contact and conflict in intergroup encounters* (pp. 1–44). Oxford, UK: Blackwell.

Hewstone, M., Islam, M. R., & Judd, C. M. (1993). Models of crossed categorization and intergroup relations. *Journal of Personality and Social Psychology, 64*, 779–793.

Hornsey, M. J., & Hogg, M. A. (2000a). Assimilation and diversity: An integrative model of subgroup relations. *Personality and Social Psychology Review, 4*, 143–156.

Hornsey, M. J., & Hogg, M. A. (2000b). Subgroup relations: A comparison of mutual intergroup differentiation and common ingroup identity models of prejudice reduction. *Personality and Social Psychology Bulletin, 26*, 242–256.

Hornsey, M. J., & Hogg, M. A. (2002). The effects of status on subgroup relations. *British Journal of Social Psychology, 41*, 203–218.

Islam, M. R., & Hewstone, M. (1993). Dimensions of contact as predictors of intergroup anxiety, perceived outgroup variability, and outgroup attitude: An integrative model. *Personality and Social Psychology Bulletin, 19,* 700–710.

Jackman, M. R., & Crane, M. (1986). "Some of my best friends are Black . . .": Interracial friendship and Whites' racial attitudes. *Public Opinion Quarterly, 50,* 459–486.

Maras, P., & Brown, R. (1996). Effects of contact on children's attitudes toward disability: A longitudinal study. *Journal of Applied Social Psychology, 26,* 2113–2134.

Marcus-Newhall, A., Miller, N., Holtz, R., & Brewer, M. B. (1993). Cross-cutting category membership with role assignment: A means of reducing intergroup bias. *British Journal of Social Psychology, 32,* 125–146.

Miller, N., & Brewer, M. B. (1986). Categorization effects on ingroup and outgroup perception. In S. L. Gaertner & J. F. Dovidio (Eds.), *Prejudice, discrimination and racism* (pp. 209–230). San Diego, CA: Academic Press.

Miller, N., Brewer, M. B., & Edwards, K. (1985). Cooperative interaction in desegregated settings: A laboratory analogue. *Journal of Social Issues, 41,* 63–79.

Paolini, S., Hewstone, M., Cairns, E., & Voci, A. (2004). Effects of direct and indirect cross-group friendships on judgments of Catholics and Protestants in Northern Ireland: The mediating role of an anxiety-reduction mechanism. *Personality and Social Psychology Bulletin, 30,* 770–786.

Pettigrew, T. F. (1998). Intergroup contact theory. *Annual Review of Psychology, 49,* 65–85.

Pettigrew, T. F., & Tropp, L. R. (2000). Does intergroup contact reduce prejudice? Recent meta-analytic findings. In S. Oskamp (Ed.), *Reducing prejudice and discrimination* (pp. 93–114). Mahwah, NJ: Lawrence Erlbaum Associates Inc.

Roberts, H. W. (1953). The impact of military service upon the racial attitudes of Negro servicemen in World War II. *Social Problems, 1,* 65–69.

Rothbart, M., & John, O. P. (1985). Social categorization and behavioral episodes: A cognitive analysis of the effects of intergroup contact. *Journal of Social Issues, 41,* 81–104.

Schwarzwald, J., & Amir, Y. (1984). Interethnic relations and education: An Israeli perspective. In N. Miller & M. B. Brewer (Eds.), *Groups in contact: The psychology of desegregation* (pp. 53–76). New York: Academic Press.

Sigelman, L., & Welch, S. (1993). The contact hypothesis revisited: Black–White interaction and positive racial attitudes. *Social Forces, 71,* 781–795.

Simon, B., & Klandermans, B. (2001). Politicized collective identity: A social psychological analysis. *American Psychologist, 56,* 319–331.

Smith, E. R. (1993). Social identity and social emotions: Toward new conceptualizations of prejudice. In D. M. Mackie & D. L. Hamilton (Eds.), *Affect, cognition, and stereotyping: Interactive processes in group perception* (pp. 297–315). San Diego, CA: Academic Press.

Stephan, W. G. (1986). Effects of schools desegregation: An evaluation 30 years after Brown. In M. Saks & L. Saxe (Eds.), *Advances in applied social psychology* (Vol. 3, 181–206). New York: Lawrence Erlbaum Associates Inc.

Stephan, W. G., & Stephan, C. W. (1985). Intergroup anxiety. *Journal of Social Issues, 41,* 157–175.

Tajfel, H., Billig, M. G., Bundy, R. P., & Flament, C. (1971). Social categorization and intergroup behaviour. *European Journal of Social Psychology*, *1*, 149–178.

Tajfel, H., & Turner, J. C. (1986). The social identity theory of intergroup behavior. In S. Worchel & W. G. Austin (Eds.), *Psychology of intergroup relations* (pp. 7–24). Chicago: Nelson-Hall.

Van Oudenhoven, J. P., Groenewoud, J. T., & Hewstone, M. (1996). Cooperation, ethnic salience and generalization of interethnic attitudes. *European Journal of Social Psychology*, *26*, 649–661.

Van Oudenhoven, J. P., Prins, K. S., & Buunk, B. P. (1998). Attitudes of minority and majority members towards adaptation of immigrants. *European Journal of Social Psychology*, *28*, 995–1013.

Vivian, J., Hewstone, M., & Brown, R. (1997). Intergroup contact: Theoretical and empirical developments. In R. Ben-Ari & Y. Rich (Eds.), *Enhancing education in heterogeneous schools: Theory and application* (pp. 13–46). Ramat-Gan, Israel: Bar-Ilan University Press.

Voci, A., & Hewstone, M. (2002). Contatto intergruppi in ambito lavorativo e riduzione del pregiudizio: Effetti di mediazione e moderazione [Intergroup contact at work and prejudice reduction: Mediational and moderational effects]. *Testing Psicometria Metodologia*, *9*, 5–15.

Voci, A., & Hewstone, M. (2003a, October). *Contact and prejudice reduction in the Italian context: The impact of empathy, perspective taking, and group salience.* Paper presented at the SESP Conference, Boston, MA, USA.

Voci, A., & Hewstone, M. (2003b). Intergroup contact and prejudice toward immigrants in Italy: The mediational role of anxiety and the moderational role of group salience. *Group Processes and Intergroup Relations*, *6*, 37–54.

Wade, K., & Wilson, W. (1971). Relatively low prejudice in a racially isolated group. *Psychological Reports*, *28*, 871–877.

Weber, R., & Crocker, J. (1983). Cognitive processes in the revision of stereotypic beliefs. *Journal of Personality and Social Psychology*, *45*, 961–967.

Webster, S. W. (1961). The influence of interracial contact on social acceptance in a newly integrated school. *Journal of Educational Psychology*, *52*, 292–296.

Wilder, D. A. (1984). Intergroup contact: The typical member and the exception to the rule. *Journal of Experimental Social Psychology*, *20*, 177–194.

Wilner, D. M., Walkley, R. P., & Cook, S. W. (1955). *Human relations in interracial housing: A study of the contact hypothesis.* Minneapolis, MN: University of Minnesota Press.

Author index

Subject index